MODERN
AMERICAN
HISTORY ★ A
Garland
Series

Edited by
 FRANK FREIDEL
 Harvard University

GOVERNOR
ALFRED E. SMITH ★ The Politician
as Reformer

Paula Eldot

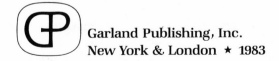 Garland Publishing, Inc.
New York & London ★ 1983

Library of Congress Cataloging in Publication Data

Eldot, Paula, 1927–
  Governor Alfred E. Smith : the politician as reformer.

  (Modern American history)
  Originally presented as the author's thesis (doctoral—Yale)
  Bibliography: p.
  Includes index.
  1. Smith, Alfred Emanuel, 1873–1944.   2. New York
(State)—Politics and government—1865–1950.   I. Title.
II. Series.
E748.S63E46   1983   974.7'04'0924   80-8469
ISBN 0-8240-4855-5

All volumes in this series are printed on acid-free,
250-year-life paper.
Printed in the United States of America

CONTENTS

If Alfred E. Smith is remembered beyond the groves of academe, it is as a politician in the pejorative sense of the word, the first Roman Catholic to be a serious contender for the presidency, and an outspoken foe of Prohibition. One can recognize the features of Al Smith in an image that does injustice to a talented executive and a creative reformer who deserves recognition for his attainments before the dramatic defeat of 1928. His record persuaded the voters of New York four times to elect him governor; his prominence as chief executive of the Empire State induced the Democratic party to nominate him for the presidency. Smith's governorship requires study, not only as the chapter in his biography that led to the presidential designation and as a time in the history of New York when it set governmental precedents to be followed for nearly half a century, but also as a component of a reform tradition that extends from progressivism to the New Deal.

Seen from the vantage point of Albany's executive chamber during the 1920s, reform aimed to make government at once more responsive and responsible. Reconstruction strengthened the hand of the executive, and centralization enabled Smith and his liberal successors to meet urgent needs. To Governor Smith, efficiency and economy meant better service, not lower expenditures, as he demonstrated in public finance. Under his administration, the state's contribution to education rose sharply, and its debt reached unprecedented proportions in order to fund parks, hospitals, prisons, and grade crossing elimination. Political reality required compromise of a Democratic executive facing a Republican legislature, and Smith often got only half a loaf. The lawmakers repulsed his initiatives for public authorities to finance low-cost housing and hydroelectric development, but he did gain legislative recognition of responsibility for housing and did manage to block private exploitation of water resources in the public domain. If Smith had to settle for less than he desired in labor and welfare legislation also, his regime enacted measures to expand workmen's compensation coverage, reduce the working hours of women and children, extend mothers' pensions, and establish rural health centers. Although Smith was not radical, he courageously defended the rights of radicals during the Red Scare. Governor Smith made his mark in administrative reform, intimations on the welfare state, and civil liberties.

In recent decades, the reform trend, which began with progressivism, persisted under Governor Smith, and culminated in the New Deal, has increasingly come under scholarly reconsideration and political denunciation. The former is sometimes misleading; the latter, often misguided. The Left criticizes the reformers for adopting palliatives inadequate to solve the problems inherent in American society; the Right condemns the same men and measures for making a drastic departure from the American Way. Nevertheless, reform in the earlier years of this century represented a humane tradition and improved the quality of life for a significant number of Americans. Now that the reformers' programs are being widely repudiated, it is appropriate to reexamine them. This book reviews their policies in the limited context of the career of Governor Alfred E. Smith, a politician who practiced as a reformer.

Because this book has been so long in the making, I have incurred many more debts than I can feasibly acknowledge in a brief preface. My work on Governor Smith began as a doctoral dissertation at Yale University under the late David Morris Potter who encouraged me to think of it as a book, once I had taken my degree. A graduate student could desire no better adviser. The late Helene Zahler was a source of inspiration and sage counsel at all stages from the thesis on. My former colleague, Joan Hoff Wilson, gave me the benefit of her criticism of several chapters and the stimulation that comes from agreeing

to disagree on certain assumptions. Donn Neal was exceedingly
generous in sharing bibliographic leads that he uncovered in
the course of his own research on Smith in the context of
national politics and in reviewing part of the manuscript.
Marion Koenen Perri alerted me to manuscript collections known
better to lawyers than historians who visited the New York State
Library where she was working in the legislative reference division. Timothy M. Taylor took time out from his legal practice
to assist me in understanding the intricacies of the rent control laws in New York. Roberto Cambria gave editorial help that
saved me from many infelicities of style. Gladys Kornweibel
did far more than type the text of the volume. A graduate
student, Vivian B. Kemps, aided in readying the book for publication. Marcia Meindl prepared the index. All of these people
have contributed to whatever excellence my work exhibits, but I
alone am responsible for its inevitable shortcomings.

My parents, Bertha W. Eldot and the late Herman Eldot,
offered moral and material support without which I could never
have written the book. They made real sacrifices to assure me
an education for the scholarly profession at a time when many
did not consider it an appropriate career for a woman.

Several institutions provided financial aid at different
stages of the work. Yale University supported the first year
of research on the Ph.D. dissertation with a graduate fellowship.
From the American Association of University Women, I received
an AAUW National Fellowship for the preparation of the thesis
and the postdoctoral Alice Freeman Palmer Fellowship for
research on the additional subjects necessary to complete the
book. California State University, Sacramento, where I have
been teaching since 1968, awarded me a grant from its Faculty
Writing Fund.

CHAPTER 1

A HOMECOMING

The time is noon, January 1, 1919. The place is the
assembly chamber in the New York State Capitol at Albany. The
main character is Alfred Emanuel Smith, amateur actor and professional politician, about to be inaugurated as governor. This
is the first of four performances.

The assembly chamber was draped with flags and decked with
evergreens. Two thousand people crowded into the room with a
capacity of fifteen hundred, while outside, soldiers turned
away many more, including a number of state senators. Even
Walter Smith, aged nine, nearly missed his father's inauguration.
The usual quota of politicians who frequent such affairs was
augmented by throngs of disinterested citizens who had journeyed
to Albany to see the man who stirred their imagination by
rising "Up from the City Streets" to the position of governor.
Several reporters spent their day off traveling to the capital
to attend—not cover—the inauguration. Probably none among the
multitudes was so affected as the new governor's family, seated
on the platform to the right of the Speaker's rostrum. The
solemnities that moved his white-haired mother almost to tears
brought smiles to the faces of the chief executive's wife and
five children. After administering the oath of office, the
secretary of state presented to the governor's mother the bible
on which he had sworn, and to his wife, the pen used to sign the
oath of office.[1]

Then Alfred E. Smith delivered his first inaugural address.
In it he alluded to the problems of postwar reconstruction.
Pointing to the need of "more stringent and more universal laws
. . . for the protection of the health, comfort, welfare and
efficiency of all our people," he unconsciously anticipated the
issues of his four administrations. When he observed, "I am
happy in the knowledge that I enjoy intimate personal friendship with the leaders and a great many members of both branches

1

of the Legislature," he referred to the fruits of an already
notable career in state politics. It was appropriate that he
should consider his arrival in Albany "somewhat like a home-
coming."[2]

Smith had travelled a long road from his birthplace on
South Street on Manhattan's Lower East Side before he came home
to the Executive Mansion on Albany's Eagle Street. Yet he was
better prepared to "faithfully discharge the duties of the
office of Governor" than the stereotypes of his origins imply.
Frances Perkins, who as a lobbyist became acquainted with the
maturing assemblyman, has helped to revise our understanding of
Smith's background.[3]

Although he dropped out of the eighth grade of Saint James
School at the time of his father's death, Smith was not an un-
educated man. He, himself, nurtured the misconception by
matching his F.F.M. (Fulton Fish Market) experience against the
Cornell and Yale degrees of his legislative colleagues and by
speaking in the accents of New York City. His presidential
campaign reinforced the image of an unintellectual, if not anti-
intellectual, political hack. But those who listened to what he
said rather than how he was saying it, detected the mark of
education in the mastery of language and in the analytic clarity
of his discourse. Such qualities impressed Miss Perkins who
reminds us that limited schooling was the rule rather than the
exception in the 1880s and that the Christian Brothers conducted
their schools with an academic rigor that distinguished them
from contemporary educational institutions.

Church and family combined to rear Smith with an identity
as a devout Irish Catholic. He was ignorant of his own
genealogy which included Italian, German, and English as well as
Irish forebears. Consequently, he played and symbolized the
Irish-American role in political life.

The Irish were the first in a succession of ethnic minorities to capture municipal government and manipulate it in their
own interest. They therefore antagonized WASP reformers who

held up the ideal of politics as disinterested public service.
In contrast, the Irish made a virtue of partisanship and entered
public life in quest of power and pelf. Patronage opened a road
for upward mobility to professional politicians. In this regard, Al Smith was a typical son of Erin. He served his apprenticeship in New York City's ward politics. As a young man, he
labored in Tom Foley's Democratic club in the Fourth Ward of
Manhattan's Second Assembly District and was rewarded with the
kind of job that characteristically supported the party faithful. From 1895 until his first term in the assembly in 1904,
he earned his living as a process server. If he began his
career as a representative of the Irish style in city politics,
he distinguished himself from the ward heelers by an understanding of the issues and an integrity that enabled him to
attain eminence, first in the state, and then in the nation.[4]

His presidential prospects signified, to an editor in
Kansas, the tilt in American life from the backwoods to the back
alley, from agriculture to industry, from a rural to an urban
democracy whose political instrument was the city boss and his
machine—in Smith's case, Charles Francis Murphy and Tammany
Hall. The New York County Democratic organization has suffered
from negative stereotypes even more than its favorite son. Reformers damned it for its corruption, without discerning any
saving grace. But the muckraker who exposed "Al Smith's Tammany
Hall" as a "Political Vampire" feeding on the poor conceded
that others duplicated its misdeeds more frequently than its
social services. A contemporary social scientist who analyzed
the political clubs in all their complexity, not only as the
dispensers of charity and graft, but also as agencies for
sociability and election, came closer to seeing what they meant
in the life of Smith. Recent scholarship has revised the picture of Murphy by taking into account the chief's personal
honesty and humanitarianism as well as the able candidates and
progressive welfare measures sponsored by his organization.
With officeholders like Smith, Tammany rose above its parochial
origins to become a force in state and national politics. It

built its initial success on the votes of the working-class Irish
who benefited in the distribution of the spoils at the expense
of the newer immigrants. Not until the 1920s, did the latter
comprise part of the state's Democratic constituency, which
anticipated the New Deal coalition in its ethnic, class, and
urban characteristics.[5]

Meanwhile, the party performed effectively in electing
Smith to the assembly for twelve successive terms beginning in
1904, by such wide margins that he usually received more than
twice as many votes as his closest rival.[6] In the legislature,
he displayed the vices and virtues of New York City machine
politics.

Smith's legislative career coincided with the progressive
era. His relationship with progressivism was ambivalent: he
promoted those reforms beneficial to his working-class constituency and frustrated those detrimental to his party's organization.[7] To lose sight of the progressive in the machine politician is to miss the significance of Smith's experience in the
assembly as well as to overlook the complexity of progressivism.

In New York, progressivism manifested itself first in the
ranks of the Republicans. It consisted of a series of adapta-
tions that enabled the party to retain power in the face of the
challenges arising from the acceleration of the pace of industrialization and urbanization. To avert defeat, the leadership
changed tactics. The intense partisan loyalties of the nineteenth century yielded to the pressures of independents; minimal
government, to regulation of business; and discreet favors to
corporate contributors, to the broker state with something for
everyone—at least for substantial interest groups. The party
leadership coopted the independents when it elected Theodore
Roosevelt and Charles Evans Hughes as governor. Hughes had
served as counsel to the legislative committees that exposed the
antisocial activities of utilities and insurance companies and
recommended government regulation out of fairness to the consumer. As chief executive, Hughes put honesty and efficiency
in administration above partisan considerations. Although he

emphasized the regulatory, rather than the distributive, functions of the state, his terms in office did witness the advent
of social legislation in New York.[8]

As a member of the assembly, Smith was ambivalent toward
the Republican progressivism that Hughes represented. The
Democrat balanced the interests of his constituents against the
claims of his party. He served on the insurance investigating
committee and voted for its regulatory bills, which would have
the effect of reducing the rates and affording better protection
to New Yorkers. But he sometimes declined to cooperate with
Governor Hughes, as in the case of a proposed reorganization of
the Public Service Commission which would not only strengthen
its authority, but also lessen political patronage. He numbered
among those who promoted a notorious franchise for the New York
Central Railroad and among those who frustrated the governor's
drive for a direct primary. During the Hughes administration,
Smith belonged to an unholy coalition of regular democrats and
old guard Republicans, which often stood in the way of progressive reforms. As majority leader, Smith sponsored both an
election law to minimize the effectiveness of independents and
a city charter to strengthen Tammany's control of New York.
He was not receptive to progressivism when it threatened the
political machine. In case of conflict between the two, loyalty
to the party stood higher in his scale of values.[9]

Because Smith often deviated from the progressive ideal of
good government, the Citizens' Union more than once urged the
voters to retire him from the assembly. Its committee on
legislation observed that he "made one of the worst records of
the session," "worked against public interest," "never gained
any reputation for independence," "continued his opposition to
progressive reforms," and "executed orders of the machine.
Opposed primary and election reform."[10] In his position, Smith
could hardly join a typical, nonpartisan, progressive civic
organization in its enthusiasm for independence and its outcry
against the machine. His record in this regard was not unlike
that of United States Senator Robert Wagner, then Democratic

leader in the New York State Senate. Professionals in both
major parties resisted those progressive reforms that challenged
their organization. Legislators with the most solid record of
achievement usually worked with—not against—their party.

The party regularity that antagonized the Citizens' Union
marked Smith's entire career in the assembly. It was apparent
in his behavior toward the progressives in his own party in two
spectacular political squabbles.

From 1906 to 1917, a progressive faction, in which Franklin
Delano Roosevelt was prominent, challenged Charles F. Murphy and
Tammany Hall for control of the Democratic party in New York
State. In 1911 the insurgents, under the leadership of State
Senator Roosevelt, prevented the legislature from naming
William F. Sheehan to the United States Senate. Although they
blocked Murphy's original nominee, they failed to elect their
own candidate and eventually compromised on a man more acceptable to the Tammany than to the progressive forces. As
assembly majority leader, Smith was one of those who marshaled
the regulars. Despite the assemblyman's fidelity to the organization, the insurgent senator gained from the incident "the
definite knowledge that Smith would play square with friend and
foe alike."[11]

Smith again went along with Tammany in 1913 when Boss
Murphy decreed the impeachment of a recalcitrant Democratic
governor. It ill became William F. Sulzer, who owed his position to the organization, to proclaim his independence and pose
as a progressive. The governor defied Tammany on patronage,
with a direct primary proposal, and by an investigation of
corruption. The party retaliated with a legislative inquiry
that uncovered irregularities in Sulzer's campaign funds and
recommended his impeachment. Although Smith may have advised
against revenge, as Speaker, he was instrumental in the proceedings; for his activity, the governor's supporters even
threatened him with prosecution. Any evaluation of the
assembly leader's part in this performance depends ultimately
upon the merits of the case against Sulzer. The standard mono-

graph on the subject balances the equivocal motivation of the
accusers against Sulzer's guilt and denies that the chief
executive was framed. From the debacle, the author derived the
moral, "no man can afford to pit himself against a powerful
political organization unless his own record is above reproach,"
and drew the conclusion that, "One may admit the worst about
Tammany, yet retain little sympathy for Sulzer."[12]

Tammany's progressive credentials were at least as authen-
tic as Sulzer's, as demonstrated most notably by the scholarship of J. Joseph Huthmacher. Like the GOP leadership before
him, Murphy embraced progressivism in self-defense; in time,
the Democrats assumed direction of the movement in New York.
Within the party, regulars produced more reform than insurgents.
Smith and Wagner, men unquestionably loyal to the organization
while sensitive to urban needs and exposed to the reformers'
solutions, prodded the machine into progressivism. New York
moved to the forefront in reform and labor legislation from 1911
to 1914 during a period of Democratic strength in the legislature, Tammany dominance in the party, and Smith's leadership in
the assembly. Reform in New York requires a revision of the
concept of progressivism to include the professional politicians
who sponsored welfare legislation as well as the middle class
professionals who identified progressivism with clean government and expert administration impervious to special interests.
The laws that made neighboring Massachusetts a model of progressive reform passed at a time when its government too, was
in the control of Irish Catholic machine politicians.[13]

A tragic fire at the Triangle Shirtwaist Company added impetus to the reform movement in New York, involved Smith directly in its programs, and brought him into intimate contact with
its leaders. In 1911 after the smoke had cleared, a temporary
state commission, with Wagner as chairman and Smith as vice-
chairman, was appointed to "inquire into the conditions under
which manufacturing is carried on in the cities of the first
and second class of the State." This Factory Investigating
Commission was responsible for regulations regarding fire pro-

tection, safety precautions, sanitary conditions in factories
and mercantile establishments, for curtailment of sweatshop production, and for teeth in this new industrial code. The study
prompted the passage of an effective workmen's compensation law.
It favored legislation extending the limitations on the hours of
labor for women and further restricting child labor. The commission even recommended a minimum wage law. The experience
with labor conditions, gained by service on this commission,
stood Smith in good stead during his subsequent political
career. In the assembly he introduced many of the bills to
implement the commission's reports.[14]

The assemblyman who in 1904, by his own admission, "did
not at any time during the session really know what was going
on," had risen by 1911 to a position of leadership recognized by
Democratic colleagues and Republican opponents alike. He made
the most of his innate ability and educated himself. James
Wadsworth, GOP assembly Speaker and later United States senator
and congressman, recalled that Smith "buckled down to the job of
learning from the ground up. . . . Al was attracting attention
not only because of his wit and his natural ability at making
friends, but because he talked sense." The nonpartisan
Citizens' Union was beginning to recognize him as "very much
above the average in intelligence, force, usefulness." Even
when it castigated Smith for subservience to the machine, it
acknowledged that he had "developed considerable ability in
floor leadership and real capacity for public service."[15] His
party chose Smith as majority leader and chairman of the Ways
and Means Committee in 1911, and Speaker of the assembly in
1913. When Republicans controlled the lower house in 1912,
1914, and 1915, Smith served as minority leader.

The qualities of mind and character that accounted for
Smith's advance in the legislature made him an outstanding
delegate to New York's 1915 constitutional convention. In a
company that included Elihu Root, Henry L. Stimson, and the
president of Cornell University, the man who had quit his
parish school before finishing the eighth grade, functioned

effectively because of his familiarity with the government and
laws of the state and because of his mastery of parliamentary
procedure. From the first day, when he joked, "and I think I
will go over and confer with him [Senator Edgar T. Brackett] how
to get a good seat," until the last day when, "Understanding the
question to be the final passage of the Constitution . . ." he
complained, "it is rather difficult for a man from New York to
support it," Smith spoke forcefully and intelligently on the
major issues before the convention.[16]

Smith voted no on the proposed constitution on the ground
that its apportionment and home rule provisions were unfair to
New York City. He ridiculed the convention's political principle "that the rule of the majority is all right, except when
that majority is in Greater New York." After adjournment, he
expostulated on the "ironclad nerve" and "galvanized gall" of
the Republicans who so blatantly discriminated against the city.
Antipathy to the constitution in New York City contributed to
its defeat in a referendum.[17]

So persistent was Smith's defense of his native city that
it provoked comment. Senator Brackett anticipated at his en-
trance to heaven the following scene: ". . . I expect as I am
making my plea to St. Peter to permit me to come in to hear
wheezing up the hill behind me the gentleman from New York with
his complaint that there are more Republicans getting in than
Democrats; and I am very sure that he will find that the reason
for it is that there is some inequity somewhere in the Constitution . . . that girds . . . too tight the city of New York in
its relation to the great Empire State."[18] It was as natural
for Smith at the 1915 constitutional convention to champion the
interests of New York City as it had been for him in the
assembly to uphold the prerogatives of Tammany. The two were
not unrelated. On city-state relations, partisan considerations
were uppermost, dividing Democrats from Republicans as each
group sought its own advantage.

There were policies on which the cleavage cut across
party lines and widened the rift between progressive and con-

servative Republicans. As governor, Smith would inherit the
progressive programs of the constitutional convention. He salvaged articles V and VI of the proposed constitution, providing
for an executive budget and administrative reorganization. On
the floor of the convention, he had debated extensively on both
proposals. There, too, he had enunciated his subsequent policies
on public development of water power and minimum wage legislation. There was no doubt where Smith stood on labor when he
opposed the Barnes amendment, which conservatives had devised
to "enact Herbert Spencer's Social Statics" by depriving the
legislature of the power to pass labor and welfare laws. To
attack this amendment was to defend the reforms of the factory
commission and the urban progressives. George Wickersham, who
had yielded the floor for the assemblyman's remarks, concurred
in his objections to the amendment and observed that "Mr. Smith
has expressed in measured terms a feeling which I find difficult to express in measured terms."[19]

Smith boosters often used such encomiums from prominent
Republicans in order to promote his presidential candidacy.
For example, campaign biographers liked to cite Elihu Root to
the effect that Smith was the most valuable delegate in attendance. Root, himself, believed that they were exaggerating
somewhat because of the "novelty in having a Republican say
something commendatory about a Tammany Hall man." Yet,
another participant recalled a conversation in which the onetime secretary of state had remarked "that Al Smith knows more
about the real needs of the State than do most of us," and "is
more disinterested" than usually credited. Men of the stature
of Henry L. Stimson derived from the convention a favorable
impression of Smith, which would stand him in good stead during
his governorship.[20]

The Republicans who admired him were more active in
national than state politics. Most of them were identified
with the progressive element in their party; many were veterans
of the Bull Moose revolt. On the important issues of the convention such as government reform and welfare legislation,

Smith was aligned with these progressive Republicans against
the upstate officeholders in their own party.[21] The continued
cooperation of the men whose respect he had earned in 1915 would
enable Smith to further progressivism in the state—after a
brief interlude in city government.

On September 1, he yielded the floor—to hear of his
nomination for the post of sheriff of New York County. After
one term, he went on in 1918 to preside over the New York City
Board of Aldermen, to the satisfaction of even the fastidious
Citizens' Union. He had barely settled into his office at City
Hall when he received a visit from James A. Farley, a neophyte
in his own job as Democratic chairman in Rockland County, who
urged Smith to run for governor.[22]

His experience in the assembly and at the constitutional
convention prepared Smith to grace the office of governor.
Good politician that he was, he would win it four times.

In his autobiography Smith told the story of his first
gubernatorial nomination. Boss Murphy, he recounted, "was
anxious that the upstate leaders should select a man . . . best
equipped to win in the upstate sections." They formed a committee which met in Syracuse but "could not agree on any candidate from the upper part of the state," and, in consultation
with the city machine, determined that "a Tammany Hall man would
be acceptable, provided upstate would declare in his favor
first." The committee compiled a list of potential nominees,
"and by a process of elimination my name was the last one left
on it." In deference to the Syracuse conference, the unofficial (unofficial, because state law required nomination by
direct primary) Democratic state convention in Saratoga subsequently made Smith its candidate for governor. Still, he
remembered, "I was not unopposed in the primary," in which he
easily defeated William Church Osborn.[23]

Smith's narrative is remarkable for what it omits—the
role of William Randolph Hearst. The leaders who gathered in
Syracuse were determined to keep the publisher off the ballot

and suspicious that Murphy might make a deal with him. They
preferred Osborn, but Tammany blackballed him. The chief could
act secure in the knowledge of substantial support for Smith
outside the inner circle of the wigwam.[24] Murphy prevailed
when the convention at Saratoga in July designated Smith for
governor. But Hearst and Osborn each announced his intention to
contest the nomination in the primary. The former eventually
withdrew, but the latter remained in order to frustrate any
plot to have Smith step aside in favor of the hated newspaperman. Contrary to the implications of Smith's memoir, Osborn's
candidacy did not materialize out of thin air, but expressed
the concerted opposition of independent Democrats to William
Randolph Hearst. Smith, nevertheless, won the September primary
by a landslide.[25]

In the fight for the Democratic nomination for governor
in 1918, the role of Franklin Delano Roosevelt, assistant
secretary of the navy, is enigmatic. Although he later intimated that such disparate figures as Woodrow Wilson and Charles
F. Murphy had encouraged him to run, he is more likely to have
enjoyed the support of the president than of the boss. During
the spring, FDR's name was mentioned in conjunction with the
New York election. Contrary to his own reminiscences however,
he did not initiate and promote Smith's candidacy. With his
penchant for upstate and insurgent elements in the Democratic
party, Roosevelt nominally endorsed Osborn. Faced with the
prospect of his defeat in the primary, Roosevelt hedged. Between primary and election day, he gave Smith the customary
blessing.[26]

Al Smith's nomination evoked mixed feelings in his own
party. President Wilson was unenthusiastic; his secretary of
the treasury congratulated the victor and wished him success.
Back in New York, Osborn hesitated to come out for his erst-
while rival. George Foster Peabody voiced the ambivalence of
the state's independent Democrats, desirous of a victory, but
distrustful of Tammany, when he praised Smith as "a capable
man who would make a real Governor . . . standing on his own

feet," and explained, "I do not mean that he should be disloyal
to Tammany, but that he should be completely independent of
their domination. . . ." A less sanguine Democrat perceived
Smith as little more than Murphy's satellite. Peabody speculated on a rumor that the boss would betray the statewide
ticket in exchange for Republican acquiescence in his control
of the city.[27]

The candidate, himself, evidently did not question the
commitment of the machine to his endeavor to unseat the Republican incumbent. Charles Seymour Whitman had achieved fame
and political fortune as a crusading district attorney whose
meteoric rise to the position of a state executive with presidential aspirations rested on his sensational prosecution of
a murder case which, according to a recent study, constituted a
flagrant miscarriage of justice. He was nevertheless, a hard
man to beat. In his quest for victory, Smith supplemented the
efforts of the regular organization with an independent
citizens' committee chaired by Abram I. Elkus, counsel to the
factory commission. Consequently, the campaign cemented a
relationship between Smith and progressives, of whom some had
been anti-Tammany Democrats; others, insurgent Republicans; and
still others, unaffiliated. He attracted professionals who
were not professional politicians: Belle Lindner Moskowitz,
Joseph M. Proskauer, and Robert Moses. For Smith's campaign,
the social worker provided "clever publicity"; the lawyer
wrote "witty speeches"; and the political scientist did
"intelligent research"; after it was over, all three would
contribute to the success of the governor's administration.[28]

The postwar influenza epidemic, which curtailed the usual
oratory, handicapped Smith who was less familiar to the upstate
voters than Governor Whitman after two terms in office. What
was said in the hustings placed the Republican to the right of
his challenger with regard to labor and public ownership of
utilities. Furthermore, on the burning—or quenching—question
of the day, Whitman was drier than Smith. The war effort and
Wilson's appeal for a Democratic Congress overshadowed state

issues. The governor laid a few more stripes on that convenient
whipping boy, Tammany Hall. At the Union League Club, he
quipped, "I cannot see how we can contribute toward making the
world safe for Democracy . . . by installing Tammany Hall at
Albany. . . ." Then Whitman complained that Smith "never undertook an official act that was not dictated by Tammany Hall."
About a week earlier, Whitman had identified the only question
before New York's voters, "Shall Albany be run from Fourteenth
Street?" Smith retaliated in kind: "Everybody in Albany from
a page boy to the highest salaried Commissioner, knows that
Whitman knows nothing about the finances of the State."[29]

Enough people believed Smith to elect him over Whitman by
a vote of 1,009,936 to 995,094. Smith carried into office with
him a Democratic lieutenant governor, but Republicans won the
other five statewide offices. Republicans retained control of
both houses of the legislature by sizeable majorities. Here
appeared a recurrent phenomenon in New York State politics, a
Democratic executive and a Republican legislature; this discrepancy arose partly from the apportionment provisions in New
York's constitution, favoring predominantly Republican, rural
areas over metropolitan centers. It is fair to attribute
Smith's predicament in 1918 less to the system than to an exceedingly close election. So close was the vote that Smith took
precautions to prevent tampering with ballots upstate. Whitman
spent a month in futile litigation to obtain a recount and to
prevent Smith from taking office. Disgusted with these tactics,
in an unusually sarcastic editorial on December 13, the *New York
Times* jibed: "Governor Whitman has thrown in the sponge at last.
With rare magnanimity he 'concedes the election of Mr. Smith.'"[30]

With the experience of the legislature and the constitutional convention to guide him, Governor Smith faced crises
fomented by World War I. During his first term, he took the
initial steps toward reconstructing state government along the
lines of the abortive constitution; toward labor, he showed the
sympathy already apparent in his opposition to the Barnes amendment. A willingness to depart from economic orthodoxy per-

mitted him to approve rent control in order to alleviate the
postwar housing shortage and made him receptive to more creative
solutions to the problem. Since the latter exposed him to
charges of radicalism, it is hardly surprising that Smith
objected to the repressive tactics of the Red Scare.

To challenge the Democratic governor in the conservative
climate of 1920, the GOP chose Nathan L. Miller, a veteran of
the bench and a corporation lawyer. Elkus, who had managed
Smith's campaign in 1918, now suggested that he capitalize on
the conflict of interest between Miller's business connections
and his official duties. If Smith refrained from this ad
hominem argument, he concentrated on the needs of New York State
for reform of its government, labor legislation, and public
power. His opponent addressed many audiences on the League of
Nations, foreign policy, the proposed St. Lawrence seaway, and
Prohibition. Each accused the other of evading the appropriate
issues. Smith pointed to his record in office and affirmed,
". . . I did make good, for if I did not Judge Miller would not
be talking about the St. Lawrence River. . . . He would not be
talking about Article X. I would be the article. I would be
the whole covenant."[31]

Lillian D. Wald, founder of the Henry Street Settlement,
concurred in this evaluation of Smith's record and declared, "I
hope that Governor Smith will be re-elected." In contrast,
William Randolph Hearst opined, ". . . I don't care whether
Smith is elected or not." The publisher eyed the governor
jealously as a threat to his own political ambitions. Hearst
had originally favored the Farmer-Labor candidate on account of
his progressivism but, at the last minute, switched to Smith as
a lesser evil than a corporation lawyer. On the eve of the
election Hearst's *New York Journal* admonished, "YOU WILL VOTE
TO RE-ELECT AL SMITH."[32]

The voters paid no more attention than usual to this advice. Miller defeated Smith by about seventy-five thousand; on
the other hand, Smith polled almost five hundred thousand more
votes than the Democratic presidential candidate. There was

consolation in the message, "Even in defeat you came nearer to
swimming up Niagara Falls than any man. . . ." Will Rogers
summed up the returns in this way: "Then come the election
when the People were sore at Wilson because he was right, so
they took it out on Smith."[33]

Not only was Smith ousted from office, but his policies on
such vital matters as administrative reform, labor legislation,
and public power were reversed by Governor Miller, a man once
characterized as having "the habits of mind and social approach
of an appeal judge of the McKinley era."[34] During the two-year
interregnum, Smith entered business as a director of several
corporations. He returned to politics in 1922 to fight another
and this time victorious campaign against Miller, but not until
he had first overcome that maverick Democrat, William Randolph
Hearst.

Hardly had the New Year been ushered in, when Hearst's
supporters began booming him as a Democratic candidate for
governor or senator on the 1922 ticket with Smith in the other
spot. Samuel Seabury for the opposition, in an open letter,
called upon Smith to save his party from the disaster of another
Hearst candidacy. The inevitable conference of upstate leaders
in July resolved that the party should designate "only Democrats
of proven standing for the high offices of Governor and Senator."
This was a blow to Hearst who had bolted on occasion. The conference favored Smith. Widespread applause greeted a letter
from the invalid, FDR, when he called for the renomination of
the former governor.[35]

Smith thanked Roosevelt for the boost. Roosevelt assured
Smith, "I realize full well the extremely difficult position you
are in and I was very careful in my letter to the Syracuse Conference not to call upon you for any kind of statement." Coming
to the heart of the matter, he continued, ". . . I am frankly a
little worried about the Hearst drive." A well publicized correspondence followed this private exchange. To Roosevelt fell
the task of formally soliciting Smith's candidacy. In an open
letter on August 13, Roosevelt pointed to rumors that Smith

would decline and asked him to state "now, not later, that if
nominated for governor you will accept." After alluding to the
financial sacrifice involved in exchanging a business for a
political career, Smith acknowledged that "during the past
twenty years I have been so honored by my party that even the
members of my family would be dissatisfied if I did not answer
the call." Consequently, he conceded: "If a majority . . .
desire me to accept the nomination for governor and lead the
party in this state to . . . certain victory, I am entirely
willing to accept this honor from their hands. . . ." At the
time Roosevelt felt he had "punctured the Hearst boom"; later he
confided to James M. Cox, Democratic presidential candidate of
1920, that this correspondence "brought forward Al Smith's
candidacy and eventually killed off Hearst's nomination."[36]

It was not that simple. Shortly before the convention
Hearst's *New York Journal* printed a letter from Mayor John Hylan
of New York City with the peroration: "The Democratic party
should nominate William Randolph Hearst for Governor . . . so
that government for the people may supplant government for the
corporations." Money, time, and newspaper space were all expendable in the effort to procure the nomination for Hearst. For
all that, Hearst delegates failed to win in the Albany and Erie
County primaries on September 19.[37] As the Syracuse convention
date drew near, the conflict between Smith and Hearst would not
down.

Attention focused on Charles F. Murphy, for it was evident
"Neither a Gubernatorial nor a Senatorial candidate can be named
without his sanction." To the question, "Who is going to be
nominated?" Murphy, leaving for Syracuse, responded evasively,
"You never can tell." His enigmatic attitude has given rise to
speculation about Murphy's motives. Contemporaries in both
camps, for example, James Farley, and the Hearst editor, Charles
Michelson, believed that Murphy was willing, if not obligated,
to place Hearst on the ticket. More than one biographer was
convinced that the sachem was committed to the nomination of
Hearst. It was the quid pro quo for the publisher's support,

which Murphy deemed indispensable for Democratic success.
Against this point of view, Bronx County Democratic leader,
Edward Flynn, has argued that the Tammany chieftain genuinely
desired the elimination of Hearst. Flynn agreed that Murphy's
pose of neutrality was deceptive, but it concealed his opposition—not his commitment—to Hearst. While maintaining the
appearance of being benevolently disposed toward the publisher,
Murphy gladly shifted to Smith, possibly in collusion with him,
the onus of stopping Hearst. If this interpretation seems farfetched, the evidence is ambiguous. Pointing to Flynn's conclusion is Murphy's complacency toward Farley's admission that
he was in Smith's corner. On the other hand, Murphy's behavior
before and during the convention raised the journalist's hopes.[38]

Whatever his intentions, Murphy needed to accommodate competing interests. The Democratic state chairman advised the New
York County leader to take advantage of the opportunity to
scuttle two troublemakers. But Smith was a proven votegetter,
and Hearst backers insisted on the popularity of their candidate.
If the party slighted the newspaperman, Mayor John Hylan
threatened Tammany with, not only loss of support in two journals
with a large circulation, but also withdrawal of patronage in
New York City. The Hearst men proposed a compromise: Smith for
governor, Hearst for senator. The boss apparently assented.[39]

A melodrama, played behind the scenes of the Syracuse convention, produced a different slate. Murphy secluded himself in
one room of the Onondaga Hotel; the hero, Smith, in another; the
villain, Hearst, commanded his forces at a distance. Smith refused to give in. With their counsel of expediency rejected,
Murphy's emissaries on behalf of compromise were sent packing.
Farley informed Smith that he had the votes to stop Hearst.
The publisher was more expendable than the politician. From
Smith's room came word of his resolution: he would not run for
senator in order to make way for Hearst as governor; he would
not run for governor on the same ticket as Hearst. Back in May,
Smith's friends had leaked this decision to the press, and now
it was patent that he loved Hearst no more in September than he

had in May. Smith would not forgive and could not forget the
publisher's vicious attacks upon him. Many New York City politicians pressed Smith for accommodation, but Tom Foley opened
the door of the hotel room and said, "Stick." Smith stuck it
out. Hearst capitulated. On September 29 he telegraphed his
campaign manager to withdraw his name. In the evening, amid
cheers for Smith and jeers for Hearst, the convention nominated
Smith for governor and Royal S. Copeland for senator.[40]

For Hearst, the events in Syracuse meant unconditional
surrender and the dashing of his political ambitions. He did
not even carry out his threat to bolt. Instead, he instructed
his editors to support Smith because the Democrats were "essentially more progressive" than the GOP. His *New York American*
subsequently praised Smith as "a man admittedly unsurpassed in
the knowledge of the mechanism of State administration."[41]

Following his triumph at the convention, Smith received
numerous congratulatory messages, but none gratified him more
than one from Henry L. Stimson. The statesman, who would serve
in the cabinet of Republican and Democratic presidents, expressed his admiration of Smith's behavior at Syracuse and
observed, "There are some things which are so fundamental that
they cannot be disregarded, even in the general easy-going good
fellowship of politics, and you have shown that you had a good
grasp on those things."[42] Smith appreciated this commendation
because he shared its sentiments. Despite the tremendous difference in background between the aristocratic, intellectual,
Protestant leader of the bar and the Roman Catholic, self-made
politician from the Lower East Side, both upheld the Christian
ethic in public and private life. In their eyes, the conflict
with Hearst was a moral as well as a political struggle.

After the rigors of the convention, the campaign for election was an anticlimax. Accepting the renomination at Cooper
Union, Miller contrasted the extravagance of Smith's administration with the thrift of his own; in Watertown, he accused Smith
of proposing reconstruction of the government in order to cover
up his inefficient and prodigal operation under existing forms.

In Albany, Smith retorted that to economize, it would be necessary to reform the state government; in Ogdensburg, he disputed
Miller's claims of frugality; in New York, he implied that
Miller's economies were achieved at the expense of labor. Miller
in Poughkeepsie charged Smith with subservience to labor interests; Smith in Syracuse rejoined with allegations of Miller's
favoritism to public utility corporations.[43] Alluding to Prohibition, Miller observed, "Mr. Smith can, therefore, do much
more . . . for beer and wine in the trucking business than he
can as Governor of New York." Smith's comeback was a classic:
"It is true . . . that I could in private life continue to advocate these reforms, but I intend to do so at the head of the
State Government, in which position I can be of greater service
to the people of this State than I possibly can be in the
trucking business. Governor Miller might better serve the State
. . . by returning directly to the practice of law, in the interest of the great corporations that he has always represented."[44]

        Both Smith and Roosevelt predicted the Smith victory. FDR
perceived Smith as a progressive, "essentially human, for it is
human to want to better conditions and seek new things," and
Miller as a standpatter, "an obstruction to navigation," as he
encouraged his fellow Democrat with a nautical metaphor, "It is
time to clear the channel." So decisive was the popular preference for the progressive over the conservative candidate that
the squire of Hyde Park could label election day as "a magnificent Tuesday." On it, the voters returned Smith to Albany by a
majority of nearly four hundred thousand and elected the entire
statewide Democratic ticket. By a margin of one, the Democrats
captured control of the senate. The assembly, as throughout
Smith's four administrations, remained Republican, but by a
narrowed margin. Elsewhere in the nation, progressives fared
well in the election of 1922. The Conference for Progressive
Political Action rejoiced in the success of many of its candidates, among them, Governor Smith.[45]

        Even his mother, reluctant to see him reenter public life,
was moved by the magnitude of Smith's victory. Proudly she

accompanied her son to Albany for his second inauguration. In
a violent snowstorm, the capital's citizenry thronged the
streets to welcome Smith home. The governor's grave demeanor
contrasted sharply with the boisterous demonstrations at the
inauguration ceremony, as if in reflection of Nathan Miller's
words, "I am laying down and you are taking up, sir, responsibilities, the burden of which no one who has not borne them can
understand."[46]

The Democrat shouldered the responsibilities of his second
term by reversing the direction in which the Republican governor
had been leading the state. Smith revived the plans for reform
of the government, recognized the interests of labor, and
checked the private exploitation of hydroelectric resources.
Although he had not intended to tamper with the status quo on
Prohibition, forces beyond his control identified his administration with repeal of the enforcement legislation adopted
under his predecessor.

To Smith, the liquor issue was a distraction that signified less about his gubernatorial performance than his presidential prospects, but in 1924 he was running both for national
and state office. After failing to be nominated for president
at a convention polarized by the Prohibition question, Smith
had to make the race for governor again. Whatever his personal
inclinations, he yielded to political realities. In order to
be a serious contender in 1928, he found it necessary to remain
in public service. Furthermore, there was unfinished business
on the state agenda, for he genuinely wished to achieve the
consummation of the programs that he had initiated. Finally,
the Democratic standard-bearer, John W. Davis, hoped to ride
on Smith's coattails in the Empire State.[47]

In 1924, New Yorkers witnessed a three-way contest for
governor among the Democratic Smith, the Republican Theodore
Roosevelt, Jr., and the Socialist Norman Thomas. The last,
who did not take the GOP candidate seriously, quipped, "he
is best known as the son of his father." Not quite fair,
for Roosevelt had served briefly as a member of the assembly

from Nassau County, conspicuously as an officer in World War I,
and embarrassingly as assistant secretary of the navy in the
Harding cabinet where his activities earned him a reputation
for being one of the "personally honest members of this Administration whose stupidity made possible the crookedness" of the
Teapot Dome and Elk Hills scandals. Campaigning upstate against
Cousin Theodore, Eleanor Roosevelt and Louis Howe mounted a
facsimile of a teapot on top of the automobile that they were
driving. Smith, meanwhile, reminded an audience on Staten Island that "the Republican party delivered the oil reserves that
were assigned to the Navy . . . to private oil interests, and
the Republican candidate for Governor, according to his own
sworn testimony acted as the important messenger in the delivery." Roosevelt was handicapped, not only by the debacle in
Washington, but also by the conservatism of the GOP in New
York. Smith was able to expose the Republican's ignorance of
state affairs. The governor's record deprived Thomas of much
of his natural constituency in Progressive, liberal, and labor
circles. For all practical purposes, the canvass turned into a
struggle between the major parties.[48]

At the time of the Republican convention, the candidate's
sister, the redoubtable Alice Longworth, apprised him, "They
have certainly handed you a fight." Norman Thomas appraised
that fight somewhat whimsically: "I 'also ran' rather anony-
mously, Roosevelt ran rather badly and Mr. Smith ran trium-
phantly." It was a personal triumph for Smith, since all of his
running mates for statewide office went down to defeat. The
Republicans regained control of the senate and increased their
majority in the assembly. At their annual frolic, the news-
papermen of the Inner Circle parodied the governor's predicament with a scene entitled "The Hermit on the Hill," showing
Smith playing solitaire and singing, "All alone in Albany."[49]

At his third inauguration, Smith sat in the chair
occupied on a similar occasion a century earlier by DeWitt
Clinton;[50] only one intervening governor had thrice held the
office. Many of Smith's previous efforts came to fruition in

his third, and most productive, term. The people amended the
constitution to implement the plans for restructuring the state
government. The executive and legislature compromised in order
to proceed with the extension of state parks and the construction of low cost housing. Bonds were approved for the elimination of grade crossings and the expansion of the state's
physical plant.

The bonds were so controversial that it is scant exaggera-
tion to suggest that the campaign of 1926 was really fought in
1925. In that year, Congressman Ogden Livingston Mills led a
concerted Republican challenge to Smith's fiscal policy. The
governor advocated and the GOP objected to a constitutional
amendment to permit the issuance of $100 million worth of bonds
for permanent public improvements. The voters ratified the
amendment by a small margin on election day in 1925.[51]

No wonder that Mills, having lost the preliminary, viewed
with less than boundless enthusiasm the Republican nomination
for governor in 1926. As a candidate, he repeated his earlier
criticism of Smith for extravagance and financial irresponsibility. The governor asserted that GOP budget cutting was
illusory and obtainable only at the expense of vital services.
The campaign soon turned from facts and figures and economic
theory to a more sensational, if less relevant, issue, New York
City's milk supply. Corruption at City Hall permitted the distribution of impure milk to consumers in the metropolis, charged
Mills, who insisted that Smith investigate. The chief executive
reminded his opponent, "The administration of the New York City
Health Department does not come under the Governor any more than
the oil scandals could be attributed to Congressman Mills because he happened to be a member of the national legislature."
Mills used Tammany as a scapegoat for the milk scandals and a
symbol of all government deficiencies. If the scheduled reorganization of the state government took place under a Democrat,
he declared, Tammany would run and ruin the state. "And back
of every issue is the overshadowing issue of whether the swollen
and irresponsible power of Tammany Hall . . . the abuse of

which power is well illustrated by this present milk scandal
. . . is to stretch out until it includes every bit of the great
Empire State." Smith summed up his opponent's attitude on
questions of state policy with these words, "His answer is
either milk or Tammany Hall."[52]

Making fun of the campaign at their stunt dinners, New York
journalists portrayed the state's last Republican, carrying a
banner, "milk-white with a broad streak of yellow," and Mills,
learning that the Milky Way was not the road to Albany. Smith
enjoyed a much wider margin of victory over Mills than over
Roosevelt two years earlier, and carried into office with him
all of his running mates except the Democratic aspirant for
attorney general. Republican majorities in both houses of the
legislature declined.[53]

After the election, Mayor Thatcher of Albany welcomed "the
next President of the United States, and our fellow Albanian,
Alfred E. Smith." A congratulatory message read, "I hope to be
very much in evidence at your next inauguration which will be in
Washington." By this time such allusions were no longer a
novelty. They had reached a crescendo following the victory
over Hearst in 1922. After Smith's election that year, Elkus
had wired, "Albany for two years with a magnificent record.
Then on to Washington!" On November 5, 1924, Will Rogers
escorted Smith to the stage at the Follies and introduced him
as the next Democratic President—"if there ever is one."
Rogers told the governor, "You have a trucking outfit, you know
and you . . . could move from Albany to Washington cheaper than
anyone else." When the humorist asked if he were contemplating
a move, the governor retorted, "if you came along as my
secretary." Mills's campaign manager astutely observed that in
1926, as in 1924, Smith was running, not only for governor of
New York, but also for president of the United States. In his
fourth inaugural address, Governor Smith alluded to the subject
on everyone's mind when he admitted, "No man could stand before
this intelligent gathering and say that he was not receptive
. . ." to the honor of the presidency. Despite the lure of

advancement, he pledged "that I will do nothing to achieve it
except to give to the people of the State the . . . service
that will make me deserve it."[54]

   As soon as he became governor, Smith was a candidate for
president. National conventions revealed his availability: as
New York's favorite son in 1920, Roosevelt's Happy Warrior who
fought McAdoo to a deadlock through 102 ballots in 1924, and
finally his party's nominee in 1928. Presidential aspirations
come naturally to a governor of the Empire State, whose office
has been labelled a "vestibule to the White House."[55] Through
that lobby, Smith's successor entered the classic abode.
   Roosevelt had seconded Smith's nomination in 1920 and
twice thereafter placed him in nomination for the presidency.
FDR emerges from the definitive biography as an opportunist who
manipulated his contact with Smith to advance his own political
career. The older man, too, endeavored to exploit their relationship.[56] Just as Davis had appealed to Smith to help him
carry New York State in 1924, the governor induced Roosevelt
to balance the ticket in 1928. In each year, the Democrat won
the governorship while his running mate lost, not only the
presidency, but also his home state.
   At his inauguration on January 1, 1929, Governor Roosevelt
could nevertheless declare, "This day is notable not so much for
the inauguration of a new Governor as that it marks the close
of the term of a Governor who has been our Chief Executive for
eight years." The new governor considered himself chosen to
carry on the tradition of his predecessor; once in office,
Roosevelt continued Smith's policies in Albany—and Washington.
FDR publicly expressed an admiration for Smith to which the
president's intimates bore witness.[57] The discovery of sources
of the New Deal in the Smith administration constitutes one
reason for the interest in it.
   Another is the intrinsic significance of his governorship.
The gubernatorial years comprise the focal chapter in Smith
biography, for they made him the leading Democrat in the nation

and a presidental hopeful. In the history of New York State,
his administration was crucial, establishing patterns in public
affairs that persist to this day. Three decades later, a
journalist reported that "politicians of both parties still run
on his record"; the chroniclers of the Rockefeller years evaluated their man as "the most important governor since Alfred E.
Smith."[58] Until the long incumbency of Nelson Rockefeller, the
state government remained essentially as Smith had reconstructed
it. He brought New York to the forefront in assuming responsibility for the quality of life in urban, industrial America.
At the same time that he increased the power of the state, he
defended the liberty of the individual by resisting the excesses
of the Red Scare. He could well afford to invite scrutiny of
his record.

The governorship of Alfred E. Smith provides an example
to substantiate the hypothesis that "the progressive movement
in the . . . states was far from dead in the 1920's." Smith had
absorbed the progressivism in the political atmosphere of the
assembly and the constitutional convention. It colored his outlook and influenced his actions as chief executive. As his
tenure was drawing to a close, the editor of *The Nation* termed
his policies "unquestionably progressive" and designated Smith
as the presidential candidate who "gives the fairest promise of
progessive leadership along social and humanitarian lines."[59]
Smith belonged to that modern American reform tradition, however
variegated and internally inconsistent, which reaches from progressivism to the New Deal. The following pages will demonstrate that Al Smith, the politican who ran for president,
deserves recognition as Governor Alfred E. Smith, the reformer
who bucked the conservatism of the age of normalcy.

CHAPTER 2
THE CITIZEN AND HIS GOVERNMENT

After his defeat in 1928, Alfred E. Smith reflected upon his years in office, not only in an autobiography, but also in *The Citizen and His Government*, a volume that drew primarily on his experience in reconstructing the government of New York State. Progressivism furnished the inspiration for his reforms and for his writings about them.[1]

Progressives who concentrated on increasing the control of the citizen over his government channeled their efforts into two distinct, but not unrelated, movements: one for direct democracy; another for efficiency and economy.[2] Both schools of reformers aimed to eliminate from government the influence of vested interests, whether of corporate business or political machine. The progressive rhetoric insisted on the transfer of authority from the special interests that had captured it to the disinterested citizenry in whose name it operated. If the two progressive programs shared a common ideal and a common enemy, they diverged when it came to the specifics of government reform.

Direct democracy consisted of a variety of devices to enable the governed more effectively to control their government. As we have seen, Assemblyman Smith sabotaged the direct primary, which would deprive his party's conventions of jurisdiction over nominations; Delegate Smith championed home rule, which would liberate his city from the domination of upstate legislators. By 1918, Candidate Smith accepted woman suffrage, and on several occasions, Governor Smith utilized the referendum with great success. He treated direct democracy as a means rather than an end and therefore distinguished among its components those that would serve his ends from those that would not.

Not his opportunistic approach to direct democracy, but his unwavering commitment to efficiency and economy, placed Governor Smith in the ranks of the progressive reformers of government. They assumed that efficient and economical opera-

27

tion required the concentration of power in a strong executive
with control over administration, divorced from politics and
conducted in a nonpartisan spirit. Perceiving governmental
functions as essentially technical, they exaggerated the role of
administration and underestimated that of politics. The efficiency economy theory, which applied primarily to administration,
drew sustenance from both the economic world of the corporation
and the academic world of the social sciences. The former contributed a model to be imitated and the vogue of scientific
management; the latter, the discipline of public administration,
professional training for public service, and research in public
affairs. Organizations such as the Bureau of Municipal Research,
which employed professionals and carried on investigations, promoted a series of interrelated reforms: the short ballot,
longer terms of office, administrative reorganization, the
cabinet, and the executive budget. They added up to a vision
of government that was at once hierarchical and functional with
the chief executive at the apex, his appointees at the summit
of their respective departments, and subordinates everywhere
chosen by the merit system. The model combined supervision with
specialization. With the initiative in personnel and budget,
the chief incurred the responsibility for governing efficiently
and economically.

Recent scholarship has raised the question of whether the
progressive drives for direct democracy, on the one hand, and
efficiency and economy, on the other, were complementary or contradictory, one bringing government closer to the people, the
other making it more remote. In other words, was the efficiency
economy movement essentially antidemocratic? An affirmative
answer would rest on the explicit centralization and implicit
elitism of a reform "to let the people rule through a program
in which the bulk of the people, most of the time, ruled hardly
at all." A contemporary student of *The Progressive Movement*
anticipated this charge when he argued that "more democracy
means the election of fewer officials; . . . the election of
fewer officials means more democracy, provided those few

officials can be effectively controlled." If the fewer officials exercised sufficient power to be held accountable for
the performance of the administration, the voter would be presented with truly meaningful alternatives, and government would
be more—not less—sensitive to the will of the people, in other
words, democratic. In publicizing their reforms, proponents
used, not only the slogan of efficiency and economy and the
model of the corporation, but also the language of responsible
and responsive government and the example of parliament, the
latter more suggestive of democracy than the former.[3]

Whether we probe for the degree of democracy in the political theory or the political practice of the efficiency economy
movement, the result is complex and equivocal. Jane S. Dahlberg
found a dedication to democracy in the crucial New York Bureau
of Municipal Research. When Martin J. Schiesl surveyed municipal reform around the turn of the century, he uncovered divergent implications: less lower class involvement in government,
middle class preemption of public employment, improved city
services to benefit variously the middle class or the entire
spectrum of the population, and finally, some political machines
that implemented the efficiency economy plan without losing the
common touch. To the extent that the political organizations
provided the poor with entree to power and social services,
nonpartisan reform was, at best, a mixed blessing to the
multitudes of the city. John D. Buenker consequently perceived structural reform as patrician and generally contrary
to the interest of the new stock machine politicians who generated urban liberalism in the progressive era, but he noted many
exceptions, for example in the New York of Boss Murphy and Al
Smith.[4]

Structural reform, which climaxed in the state in the
Smith administration, began under Republican auspices. Governor
Hughes injected the efficiency economy issue into state politics,
and Stimson assumed leadership of the movement after he lost the
election to succeed Hughes in 1910. Both men argued that the
changes that they were proposing, far from being inconsistent

with democracy, would reinforce popular rule. After the Bull
Moose revolt of 1912, Stimson and his cohorts viewed structural
reform as a plank on which to reunite their party and broaden
its appeal. They welcomed the prospect of a constitutional convention to put into execution their plans for the state government.[5]

At the constitutional convention of 1915, where Smith
represented his urban district, the progressive Republicans
gained a Pyrrhic victory with their blueprint for reconstructing
the government. It was good progressive practice to base reform
on research, and the social scientists at the New York Bureau of
Municipal Research, under the direction of Charles A. Beard and
Frederick A. Cleveland, prepared a survey and an evaluation of
the state government for the use of the delegates. The assumptions underlying the studies were those of the efficiency
economy theory. Meanwhile, its proponents moved to dominate
the convention by capturing control of its GOP majority. They
succeeded in committing the party to structural reform and
placing their adherents in positions of leadership. The convention chose Elihu Root as its president, and he appointed
Henry L. Stimson, Frederick C. Tanner, and George W. Wickersham
to chair the crucial committees. As a result, the document
that the convention produced included two amendments embodying
the efficiency economy principles: one for a short ballot and
administrative reorganization, and another for an executive
budget. The proposed constitution generated a test of strength
between the "federal crowd" and the upstate Republican bosses
who stood to lose the ability to control the government through
their influence over the legislative majority. They opposed
the reforms as undemocratic because of their tendency to degrade
the legislature and elevate the executive. Although the bosses
made little impression upon the convention, they prevailed in
the referendum that followed.[6]

As a machine politician and a legislator, Smith shared
their concerns in a way that goes far to explain his ambivalence
on the amendments. For this reason, he found it necessary to

begin a talk on reorganization by assuring his listeners of his
"intention of perfecting the bill" and to end by explaining that
his criticism "was made in the interests of the bill itself."
He protested too much the constructive nature of his intervening critical remarks. To imply, as he did, the existing mis-
government to be exaggerated, the legislature to be unjustly
accused of mismanagement attributable to the governor, and the
confidence in a strong executive to overcome the ills to be
misplaced, was to question the very premises on which the reformers operated. As an assemblyman, he resented the move to
deprive the lawmakers of the power to change the administrative
structure by requiring a constitutional amendment for this purpose. His expressed preference for the election rather than the
appointment of a superintendent of public works contravened the
principles of the short ballot which, on another occasion, he
termed "that iniquity known as the short-ballot bill." With
reference to the particular official, the main consideration
was patronage as Smith cheerfully acknowledged to the amused
convention when he said, "Give me that department . . . , and
the county that don't bring its delegates to me, I will send
after them."[7] In later years, his opponents would express the
same reservations about the program for efficiency and economy
that he entertained at the constitutional convention and use
them as arguments against the reform.

Despite his negative attitude on certain aspects of reorganization and the executive budget, Smith voted for both
amendments and, in debate, contributed to the understanding and
the improvement of their provisions. His suggestions, to
eliminate two proposed departments, to substitute a single
official for the commission in charge of the departments of
labor and taxation, and to make the civil service commissioner
dependent on the governor in place of an independent commission,
carried the principles of consolidation to their logical conclusion. The draft incorporated his recommendation to allow
gubernatorial appointment without senatorial confirmation in a
number of instances. To make the executive budget truly effec-

tive, he insisted, it would be necessary to include within it,
not only administrative expenses, but also outlays for local
construction. He pointed to these projects as a basic cause of
governmental extravagance when he derided the pork barrel bills
coming up with such regularity "that you do not have to introduce them any more; you can leave them up in the back of the
chamber and they will find their way into the bill-box themselves." In his remarks, Smith was upholding the principle of
the executive budget which the amendment's authors had compromised in order to induce politicians, who might otherwise kill
the reform, to support it.[8]

Having made the necessary concessions, the convention adjourned confident in the expectation of the ratification of
the constitution. But its leaders had reckoned without the
political realities that doomed it. It succumbed to a combination of strange bedfellows: Democrats, like Smith, whose constituency in organized labor and New York City felt short-
changed; old guard Republicans and Progressive party members
alike, who were jockeying for power within the GOP by discrediting the moderate leadership of the convention.[9] The
reformers, however, made a lasting impression on Smith, who as
governor would effect the changes they had initiated and secure
the adoption of amendments for administrative consolidation
and an executive budget. Only three years separated the poll
that defeated the 1915 constitution from the election that
elevated Smith to the executive chamber. The referendum meant
that initially he would preside over an unreconstructed administration.

In the proceedings of the convention, one finds, not only
the program for reform, but also a description of existing
institutions as they appeared to the reformers. The people
elected seven statewide officers, ranging from the governor to
the state engineer and surveyor (one person). They were
supposed to manage an administration comprised of more than one
hundred and fifty agencies, some accountable to various elective officials, others to the legislature, and still others

apparently to no one. Little provision and less power existed
for coordinating the activities of the different bodies. The
governor was not master in his own house, for he lacked the
ability to hire and fire most of his nominal subordinates. The
legislature was jealous of its prerogatives in the naming of
personnel and tampered frequently with the administrative
structure, largely for purposes of patronage. Legislative
budgetmaking offered a classic example of the evils of logrolling and the pork barrel. Although item veto enabled the
governor to blue pencil the worst extravagances, he could not
control the level of expenditures. The legislature, which
dominated this financial process, consisted of a lower house
serving for one year and an upper house for two years, the same
term as the executives chosen by the voters, and not long enough
for any of the officials to demonstrate their capacity, according to the reformers.[10] As chief executive, Smith experienced
all the difficulties outlined at the convention and championed
with greater enthusiasm the progressive plan for their rectifi-
cation.

The Reconstruction Commission took up the reforms which
the constitutional convention had been unable to bring about.
After working for Smith in the campaign of 1918, Belle Moskowitz
suggested the idea of such a task force. Frances Perkins has
reminisced about a dinner meeting to explore the subject to
which the governor-elect, "the soul of propriety," had invited
his wife and mother because "there were to be ladies present"
among the conferees.[11]

Following the conference, Governor Smith incorporated
the proposal in his 1919 annual message in which he announced
to the legislature his intention to appoint a commission to
deal with the problems of postwar reconstruction. To him,
reconstruction meant two things: temporarily aiding veterans
and their families in the transition from war to peace; and
permanently attaining "a full realization of democracy at
home, the ideal for which they fought so valiantly." Toward

the end of January, he named the members of the commission and
charged them with studying both aspects of the subject. His
commission had a broad base, for it included politicians of
both major parties as well as an avowed socialist, businessmen
and labor leaders, professionals and reformers, and even a
number of women. The members made Smith's campaign manager,
Abram I. Elkus, their chairman, and Belle Moskowitz their
secretary.[12] In composition and procedure, the group exemplified the progressive ideal of unpaid public service by well-
qualified, disinterested citizens.

With a competing interest in asserting its authority
against that of the executive, the legislature resented his
initiative in establishing the commission and refused to fund
it as he requested. Republican lawmakers denounced it as a
superlegislature, derided it as theoretical, and maintained
that construction afforded a more practical road to reconstruction by offering employment to veterans. When the GOP legislators voted against appropriating a small sum to defray the
commission's expenses, Smith denounced their partisanship.
His appointees solicited from private benefactors the money
with which to carry on their work.[13]

Their efforts culminated during Smith's first term in an
epochal series of studies that laid the groundwork for his
policies throughout his four administrations, not only on governmental reform, but also on housing, labor relations, and
public health. The commission was able to make a significant
contribution because Smith eschewed a narrow definition of
reconstruction in favor of one that included the resolution of
longstanding problems that beset the inhabitants of the state.
At the outset of his executive career in true progressive
fashion, he consulted experts and encouraged research in order
to acquire the information on which to formulate policy. For
example, the governor opened the deliberations of the Reconstruction Commission by admonishing its members, "First,
gather the facts and the evidence. . . ." Their reports were
a model of expertise in public affairs, for they divided into

committees that consulted specialists, conducted public
hearings, and did research in the field and in the literature
of the various problems. Smith's Reconstruction Commission made
a great impact on New York because of the nature of its mandate,
the method of its investigations, and the quality of its reports.[14]

The *Report of Reconstruction Commission to Governor
Alfred E. Smith on Retrenchment and Reorganization in the State
Government* established a continuity between the constitutional
convention and the new administration.[15] To head the staff
that prepared the report, Belle Moskowitz selected Robert Moses,
a rather unpopular employee of the New York Bureau of Municipal
Research, where he had worked on the 1915 studies. If the
bureau's scholars "made recommendations," then "Mrs. Moskowitz
made laws," for she injected a note of political realism which
required the social scientists to deviate enough from their
theories to accommodate the politicians whose votes they needed
to translate ideas into action. Governor Smith frequented the
commission's headquarters to support its efforts and to consult
Moskowitz.[16]

Compounding her savoir faire with the assumptions of the
efficiency economy movement, the report publicized reorganization as a way to retrenchment. On the need for economizing, a
figurative passage reversed the metaphorical description of
finances in pre-Revolutionary France where tax monies were
carried to the king in a leaky sieve: "The more spigots there
are in the barrel the more difficult it is to keep a watch on
them. There are too many streams and rivulets running out of
New York's treasury."[17] The study attributed the waste to the
legislature because of its inability to determine rational
priorities and its vulnerability to pork barrel projects.
Legislative financial initiative only encouraged insubordination and extravagance in an administration where members could
go over the head of a superior to a lawmaker in a quest for
funds. No administration that consisted of one hundred and
eighty-seven agencies without either proper coordination or

effective supervision could operate economically and efficiently. Criticism of the status quo had a familiar progressive ring.

Like earlier reformers, members of the Reconstruction Commission proposed to remedy the situation by strengthening the executive through constitutional amendments for a longer term of office, a shorter ballot, reorganization, and an executive budget. The report contained an outline for the consolidation of the various agencies into nineteen departments, most of them headed by a single official accountable to the governor and responsible for his own deputies. In addition to the functional departments, organized in conformity with the rules of the science of public administration, the commission suggested the innovation of an Executive Department to support the governor in his managerial capacity. The report reflected Smith's position at the constitutional convention by eliminating certain departments, substituting a commissioner for a commission in one instance, and dispensing with senatorial confirmation of at least a few appointments. Under the terms of the executive budget, the governor was authorized to propose and supervise expenditures; the legislature, to trim, but not to pad, his budget. For any increase, the lawmakers must pass a separate bill, subject to scrutiny—and veto. The commission insisted on constitutional rather than statutory provisions for the executive budget and reorganization, in order to insulate the reforms from the kinds of legislative abuse that they were designed to correct. The entire plan manifested the inclination of the efficiency economy movement to enhance the executive at the expense of the legislature.

In its report, the Reconstruction Commission anticipated and denied the charge that the concentration of so much power in the executive was undemocratic. Anything that enabled the voters to locate responsibility and judge intelligently was conducive to genuine democracy. In the words of the report:

> A Governor with a Cabinet of reasonable size, responsible for proposing a program in the annual budget and for administering the program as modified by the

Legislature may be brought daily under public scrutiny,
held accountable to the Legislature and public opinion,
and be turned out of office if he fails to measure up
to public requirements. If this is not democracy then
it is difficult to imagine what it is.

In an introductory statement, Smith made a similar observation:
"The people must give the Governor authority if they want to
hold him responsible."[18]

Governor Smith, therefore, asked the 1920 legislature to
accept the commission's recommendations for constitutional
amendments to institute reorganization, an executive budget,
and a four-year term. He transmitted the report on retrenchment and reorganization along with a message which echoed the
sentiments of the efficiency economy movement. Stimson welcomed the report as a renewal of the drive that he had led at
the 1915 convention for reorganization and an executive budget,
but he worried that administrative reform would encounter
"political opposition, as it involves an immediate and great
reduction of political patronage."[19]

The lawmakers who stood to lose patronage displayed less
enthusiasm for the reforms than the attorney or the governor.
Although Republicans introduced his proposed amendments in both
houses, they never got out of committee, for the majority party
was unsympathetic. The GOP decided to scrap the executive
budget and the longer term and to substitute a plan of its own
for consolidation. For this purpose, the legislature approved
the three alternative resolutions of Senator Henry M. Sage, in
a maneuver to leave the choice of the text to the next session.
(The amendment process involved passage in two successive
legislatures before submission to a referendum.) In the
original draft, the Sage amendments made a travesty on reform,
by preserving patronage and allowing the legislature to create
new departments. The worst features were eliminated during
their legislative progress. Shortly after adjournment, Robert
Moses reported to the governor that one of the Sage amendments
was acceptable.[20]

Smith had been eager to keep partisanship from defeating the reforms, and Moses, from his post with the Reconstruction Commission, had sought the cooperation of his fellow Republicans. A Citizens' Committee on Reorganization in the State Government, with Hughes, Stimson, and Wickersham among its members, functioned during the session of 1920.[21]

If they lent their prestige, the governor took to the lecture circuit to fight for his program. Between his receipt of the Reconstruction Commission's report in October and the introduction of its amendments in February, he solicited support in New York City from civic groups like the City Club, which Hughes addressed on the same occasion, and business organizations like the Brooklyn Chamber of Commerce.[22] When the measures bogged down in the legislature, Smith resumed his speechmaking upstate in resort to a tactic, in which he would ultimately excel, of appealing to the people to exert pressure on their representatives. At the Syracuse Chamber of Commerce, where Martin Saxe, another GOP reformer, commended the governor for adopting Republican proposals, Smith retorted, "If I had come in here and met Senator Saxe for the first time I would have said, 'There is a Tammany man I had never met before.'" On April 14 Smith emphasized the bipartisan character of the program to the Women's Civic League of Albany, charged, "The only influence opposed to it is that of placeholders who fear for the future safety of their positions," and challenged the legislature to bring the amendments out of committee.[23]

When the lawmakers considered the Sage substitutes instead, Belle Moskowitz, undoubtedly speaking for Smith, accused the GOP majority of making a "political football out of the Governor's reconstruction program" with the intent "to throw dust in the eyes of the people." At the same time that he urged his fellow democrats to stand behind the commission's recommendations, Smith threatened to call a special session in the event of their defeat.[24]

After adjournment, pressure for a special session mounted. The regular session of 1920 had been particularly devoid of

constructive legislation because of the distractions of the Red
Scare. Consequently, not only the Citizens' Committee on Reorganization in the State Government, but also the Citizens'
Union and the City Club appealed to Smith for a supplementary
meeting at which to complete the agenda of government reform
with the budget and four-year term amendments, which would
otherwise be deferred at least until 1923. The secretaries of
all three groups expressed confidence that the spotlight of an
extraordinary session would compel the lawmakers to reverse
themselves and adopt the desired resolutions. If Stimson was
more realistic in assessing the strength of the opposition, he
was nevertheless "inclined to think that Governor Smith would
do well to force the issue by calling an extra session which
would make it a clear issue for the coming campaign."[25]

On the call for a special session, Smith was indecisive.
At first he postponed his decision until the end of the thirty-
day bill period (the interval after adjournment for executive
action on bills passed at the close of the session). As that
time approached, he put the matter off until the conclusion of
the Democratic National Convention (July 5). Meanwhile, Robert
Moses prepared for the governor's use a statement that ended
with the words, "it is not necessary for me to make a definite
and final announcement at this time." Belle Moskowitz forwarded the statement to Smith, but there is no indication that
it was released.[26]

A special session was held in September because of a
housing shortage, but Smith did not then place the amendments
before the legislature. One can only speculate on his reasons.
Did he despair of success? Did he fear that injecting the
issue of government reform would hinder the solution of the
problem that the session was summoned to consider? Did he
think that he had a better campaign issue in the existing impasse between executive and legislature?

The platform on which he ran in 1920 endorsed the Reconstruction Commission's amendments and went on to "denounce the

Republican Legislature for its complete disregard of the commission's recommendations." Throughout the campaign, Smith contrasted his support with GOP sabotage of the reform. At
Ogdensberg he ridiculed an outmoded government in which,
"Inspectors and agents of all kinds are traveling constantly,
meeting each other on the road, all engaged in different lines
of business, overlapping of functions, duplication of effort.
A good many of them are going north in the Summer when the
Adirondacks are blooming and . . . south in the Winter when the
white light district is attractive." Indeed the state government was the best customer of the New York Central Railroad.
As Smith put it, he stood for 1920 government; his Republican
opponent, Nathan Miller, for 1890.[27]

        The GOP candidate anticipated little saving and much
danger from an increase of executive power; his platform found
it un-American. Henry L. Stimson, who was disgruntled with the
negative attitude of his party, tried to persuade its standard-
bearer to back the proposals of the Reconstruction Commission.
Shortly after his nomination, he promised "more careful study"
of the *Report on Retrenchment and Reorganization*. After further
investigation, in language almost identical with his subsequent
campaign addresses, he explained to Stimson that the reforms
"will not solve the problem of the growth in State expenditures." Stimson, who regarded government reform as the pre-
eminent issue, resolved to "treat Judge Miller's candidacy in
a way corresponding to his treatment of the Executive Budget
and the general program of State Government reconstruction."
When asked to endorse his party's nominee, he replied, "If
Judge Miller comes out for them I will be glad to come out for
him; if he comes out against them I will support Smith. So
long as he keeps in a neutral position I think I will keep
quiet. . . ."[28]

        After his election, Miller's conduct in office was
hardly reassuring to Stimson. The governor's first annual
message discounted the structural inadequacies of the state
government and expressed a preference for statutory, over con-

stitutional, reform in order to retain flexibility and legislative initiative. Some measure of statutory reorganization did
take place during his term, but he was responsible for the
failure of a consolidation amendment to receive approval a
second time. Although he acknowledged the need for greater
coordination in public finance, he emphasized the legislative
role in the budgetary process. On his recommendation, the
legislature revived the Board of Estimate and Control of the
progressive era, an agency consisting, not only of the governor
and comptroller, but also significantly of the chairmen of the
Senate Finance and Assembly Ways and Means Committees. To this
group, the law entrusted the preparation of the estimates and
the segregation of lump sum appropriations. Thus Miller frustrated the drive for a stronger executive and for constitutional
amendments.[29]

Whereas Miller used his office to thwart the movement for
efficiency and economy, Smith continued to work for reform as a
private citizen. He testified in favor of the constitutional
amendments at a legislative hearing and addressed a Town Hall
rally sponsored by the New York State Association, an organization formed by a merger of the Citizens' Committee on Reorganization in the State Government and other groups "to press for
progress toward responsive, responsible, efficient and democratic government." In addition to speaking on behalf of reform, he contributed an article to the *National Municipal Review* in which he asked, "How long would any great corporation
live if the man directing its affairs was compelled to spend
75 per cent of his time doing . . . work . . . that might well
be directed to a competent subordinate?"[30] Smith's activities
during this interlude in private life presaged his return to
politics.

In the election of 1922, Smith and Miller resumed their
fight over government reform. "Instead of the Executive and
the Legislature making faces at each other . . ." Miller
boasted that they worked harmoniously in his administration.
He claimed to have achieved the ends of efficiency and economy

by statute rather than by the more cumbersome mode of constitutional amendment. Smith accused the governor of giving the
word which defeated the amendments in the legislature and of
offering in their stead inadequate substitutes as a diversionary
tactic, which would preserve patronage by "legislating Democrats
out of office and Republicans in." Smith alleged that Miller's
legislation was a smoke screen to cover the Republican governor's defection from the reformers. Miller retorted that
Smith's program provided an excuse for his inefficient administration and compared him to a batter who blamed his bat for
striking out. One of Miller's supporters coined the name,
"Alibi Al." "I claim to have demonstrated that it is possible
to make the existing machinery work," Miller proclaimed to the
voters. Smith remarked that Miller had run, not the machinery,
but the machine. Smith pointed to his own militant advocacy of
the Reconstruction Commission's recommendations for better
government. Having been chided on the influence of special
interests in his administration, he inquired, "What group forced
Governor Miller to undo this work? The groups that came to see
me came to the Capitol in broad daylight, actuated by no selfish
purpose and moved only by desire for the common good."[31]

     Smith returned to office in 1923 with a determination to
carry on their fight for reform. Robert Moses, now secretary
of the recently formed New York State Association, plied the
governor-elect with information on administrative reform. He
began his second term by urging the legislature "to pass these
resolutions in the form in which they were originally presented"
by the Reconstruction Commission: for consolidation, an executive budget, and a four-year term.[32]
     Since the Republican leadership objected, the assembly
declined to act. By February 20, all three amendments had received favorable consideration in the Democratic senate where
many Republicans went along with the majority. On March 20,
a caucus of Republican assemblymen opposed the executive budget
and four-year term amendments and insisted on changes that

would substantially weaken reorganization. H. Edmund Machold,
the Speaker, denounced the whole program as "ill-advised and
ill considered," and the executive budget as "revolutionary and
dangerous." He defended the two-year term on the grounds that
"if the Governor is satisfactory to the people he will be re-
elected and if not he can be gotten rid of at the end of two
years." Smith retorted, "According to that . . . neither
Governor Miller nor myself was any good." In view of his mis-
representation of the executive budget, the governor guessed
"that the Speaker has never read the bill." At the same time
Smith renewed his demands for the reforms. The assembly accepted the adverse report of its Judiciary Committee on the executive budget and the four-year term. Smith and his adversaries
had reached an impasse.[33]

     At this point Machold proposed a conference between the
chief executive and the assembly leaders. Smith acceded but
announced, "I want progress for my legislation not conferences."
A *Times* editorial voiced doubts that a conference "can prevent
the Governor's reconstruction proposals from being 'knocked into
the middle of next week.'" However, the urban element in the
party exerted pressure on Machold for a compromise, in order to
avert a speaking tour by Smith with deleterious effects on the
GOP. A four-hour meeting of Smith, Moses, and the Republican
leadership of the lower house resulted in a compromise in which
the governor believed he had "won all the points that mean anything in the reorganization program."[34]

     Stimson complimented the chief executive on his progress
toward reconstructing the state government and wished him
"further successs in the more important conferences that are
coming over the Executive budget." On this subject, the
assembly leaders were adamant and a second conference futile.
The secretary of the Citizens' Union advised the governor to
veto the appropriation bill in a move to "attract state-wide,
if not nation-wide, attention to the fight you are waging for
an executive budget."[35]

Smith preferred other means of winning public support. At the beginning of the session, he had discussed the entire plan for reconstruction in an address to the League of Women Voters in Albany where he showed the need of a short ballot by bidding his audience, "Go down to the corner of State and Pearl streets . . . and stop the first one hundred people . . . and ask them who the State engineer is." In an amusing scenario, he dramatized the duplication that the amendment was designed to correct: "The Commission of Prisons visits Sing Sing to see that it is there . . . and after they have had dinner with the warden on their way out they meet the Board of Parole coming in. The Board of Parole waits for supper. And the next day the superintendent visits the prison." When his rationale for reform failed to convince the assembly, the governor turned for help to the Chamber of Commerce with talks before a number of upstate clubs.[36] In Syracuse he alleged that patronage and pork barrel explained the opposition to consolidation and to the executive budget respectively. When Speaker Machold tried to embarrass him by pointing out inconsistencies between his current stand and that of 1915, Smith rejoined, "A man who doesn't learn anything in eight years is a bonehead. The fact that I may have opposed some of these things in the past is no argument that I am not right now." To an audience in Schenectady, he affirmed that he had learned by experience—as governor.[37]

Smith stirred his listeners more than the legislature. It adopted the compromise on reorganization on which the first conference had agreed, but the assembly balked at the amendments for the four-year term and the executive budget. After adjournment, Smith castigated the assembly for flouting the will of the people as expressed in the 1922 gubernatorial election, which he interpreted as a mandate to reform the state government.[38]

In view of this conflict, the governor worked vigorously for the election of a Democratic assembly in 1923. The GOP campaigned on the premise that his proposals for the government would deliver the state into the clutches of Tammany Hall.

Speaking upstate, he ridiculed this "annual volley of bunk" and
threatened that "The Republican Party will look the way a piece
of rhubarb pie tastes to me when I get through with it." In
New York City where Congressman Mills advised Smith to "devote
more time to giving efficient government and less time to
talking about it," he disclaimed responsibility for the actions
of officials over whom he lacked control. Despite his participation in the contest, the Republicans increased their membership in the 150 man assembly from 81 in 1923 to 87 in 1924.[39]

When the legislature met in January, Smith resumed the
struggle under circumstances less favorable than in the session
immediately following his reelection. The impasse between the
two houses paralleled that of the year before—with one exception. The reorganization amendment would not be due for reconsideration until 1925 after the seating of a new senate.

In his annual message of 1924, Smith again urged the
legislature to adopt the executive budget and four-year term
amendments which would then become eligible for second approval
at the same time as reorganization. When he failed to convince
the Republicans at a meeting with the legislative leaders, he
suggested a second conference on reconstruction to include,
among others, Stimson, Root, and Wickersham. The GOP legislators, who declined to let the governor manipulate them in this
way through distinguished members of their own party, rebuked
him with the self-righteous assertion that it was not legitimate
for them "to meet behind closed doors and determine legislation."
Denying that he had proposed anything behind closed doors, Smith
quipped, "I would just as soon have it on the stage of Carnegie
Hall. . . .   The Speaker is the one talking about closed
doors. I guess he has closed doors on his mind. . . ." The
leap year did not render the governor's proposals any more
acceptable to the assembly, which by February 29 had done
nothing on the amendments already passed by the senate.[40]

This year Smith took his case to the people through the
press instead of personal appearances. "All I am asking the
Republican Assembly to do," he told a gathering of upstate

editors on March 26, "is to submit these questions to the people of the state." This was a reference to the referendum, which must follow favorable action by two legislatures. Smith implied that the newspapers might mold public opinion to force the hand of the lower house. That had been his purpose in inviting the journalists to Albany. "Governor, we are with you," was the response of many, roused to enthusiasm by Smith's discourse. Editorials soon reflected the conviction his remarks had carried.[41]

The assembly was not particularly sensitive to newspaper comment. As adjournment neared, Smith anticipated defeat, and the *New York Times* editorialized, "There is still time for the Republicans of the Assembly to make a deathbed repentance." A motion to bring the executive budget and four-year term amendments to the floor of the chamber failed on April 8.[42]

"This means the end of reconstruction—I doubt whether it will ever be heard of again," Machold asserted complacently. He condemned the governor for refusing to compromise on a statutory executive budget and accused him of desiring to usurp legislative prerogatives. In reply Smith patiently explained that such a law was futile, for in the future as in the past the legislature could throw into the wastebasket the executive's budget and a few key legislators could continue their concealed control of the administration through the appropriations bill. Stimson assured the governor of his sustained support in the battle for an executive budget and discussed the matter with Root who derided Republican legislators for "acting like damn fools" in resisting it.[43]

Smith echoed these sentiments in the 1924 election contest against Theodore Roosevelt, Jr. The governor opened his campaign upstate and closed it in New York City with addresses devoted to an analysis of the program for reconstruction of the state government. Almost everywhere he spoke, he defended the reforms.[44] The independent Democrat, George Foster Peabody, had encouraged Smith to run for reelection in 1924 lest, "if you do decline another nomination, the reorganization of the State government must fall by the way." In accepting the nomination Smith had acknowledged, ". . . I am moved by a desire to continue this work that I may . . . point to something that I did for a State that did so much for me."[45]

The Republican platform and the Republican candidate were both committed to oppose the budget amendment that, in Smith's eyes, complemented consolidation. Roosevelt promised a Rochester audience to introduce in Albany the budget system successfully operated by Republicans in Washington and warned that Smith's alternative would produce executive tyranny and Tammany domination. "Ted made a bad misstep in his speech on the budget," a disenchanted Stimson informed one of the candidate's campaign advisers.[46]

As the reform that attracted most attention in the 1924 election, the executive budget dominated the deliberations of the 1925 session and further exposed the rift between progressive and conservative Republicans. The right wing predominated both in public office and in official party positions in the state and controlled the GOP majority in the legislature. When it convened, the old guard published a manifesto voicing its continued antagonism to budgetary reform by constitutional amendment and proposing instead a statute like the one that passed the Republican assembly and failed in the Democratic senate of Smith's second administration. A constitutional amendment, on the other hand, brought all of the clichés on tyranny to the tongues of these Republicans who engaged in public debate with the governor. The New York City Bar Association listened to Senator John Knight invoke visions of a czar; at the sedate Women's City Club, hisses fell upon Lieutenant Governor Seymour Lowman who conjured up pictures of an unidentifiable king from whom sturdy English yeomen on the field of battle wrested the power of the purse strings. In the assembly, majority leader Simon Adler defended, with not exactly his last breath, this dearly won right. When the rhetorical flourishes faded, the orators' victory emerged in the defeat of the amendment and the passage of the bill in the three days from March 17 to 19.[47]

With these measures pending in the legislature, the progressive Republicans tried to avert the defeat of the executive budget principle. Henry L. Stimson conferred with Smith on the shortcomings of the Hewitt bill and soon thereafter obtained a memorandum on the subject, which had been drafted for the governor's information. The attorney sought this briefing in preparation for a conclave of distinguished Republicans associated with the movement for efficiency and economy. It was the sense of this meeting that the Root amendment, which had been accepted by the constitutional convention, was best, that the Walker resolution, which the Democrats were currently sponsoring, was inferior, and that the Hewitt bill was worthless because no statute could prevent the legislature from ignoring the governor's budget and resuming its usual practices. Those in attendance carried out the wishes of the meeting when Root testified at a legislative hearing and Stimson approached key figures in the state organization to persuade them of the virtues of the budget amendment. Smith was privy to these moves of the Republican reformers.[48]

In his annual message, he had delivered his usual plea for the executive budget amendment. He found "nothing new or revolutionary" in making the chief executive responsible for estimating the expenses of the departments under his administration, and nothing unreasonable in barring the legislature from incurring additional expenditures until it had provided for the maintenance of the government. He compared public finance to the practice of "the wise and prudent housewife who puts aside the money for rent, light, heat, the butcher, and the baker, before she contracts for a new piano, a victrola or a radio." The amendment would subject to the beneficial glare of publicity legislative decisions to spend more than the head of the administrative household advised. To secure these benefits, Smith asked the lawmakers, at the opening of their session, to approve the budget amendment.[49]

At their hearing he affirmed his faith in the Root amendment. He explained that the Walker resolution had deviated

from the earlier proposal in a spirit of compromise in order to
overcome Republican opposition. "If they will take up the
Root Plan . . . why God bless us, I will be down there on Monday night to sit down with them and agree on it right away,"
he expostulated in the course of a debate with the lieutenant
governor. Catcalls greeted Lowman's accusation that Smith
appropriated the ideas of others, until the governor himself
began to applaud. He laid no claim to originality but rather
took pride in the bipartisan nature of the movement for efficiency and economy.[50]

Smith acknowledged his indebtedness to the Republicans
of the constitutional convention in the memorandum accompanying
his veto of the Hewitt budget bill. The bill was not an acceptable substitute for the convention's proposals or his own, but
rather a fraud. "Aside from creating an additional $25,000 in
patronage, the proposed budget bill is about as useful to the
State as an extra tail would be to a white bull dog." The
governor weighed the consequences of his veto: "I am quite
sure that my disapproval . . . will insure action along the
right lines at the next session of the Legislature."[51]

The amendment for a four-year term with off-year elections
fared no better than the executive budget at the 1925 session.
Smith advocated both in his annual message and jousted against
Republican spokesmen in a tournament of speeches and statements.
Knight favored the existing two-year term; Lowman conceded the
advantages of longer tenure, if elections coincided with those
of the president. This version of the four-year term was
attractive to the lieutenant governor because "usually we could
elect a Republican Governor to the everlasting good of the
common people." The speech provoked Smith to retort that "the
audience went home and prayed that nothing would happen to me—
at least for two years." When the oratorical dust settled, the
legislature took no action on the four-year term.[52]

In contrast, the reorganization amendment passed easily,
after a brief flurry of Republican pronouncements seemed to
place it in jeopardy. It will be recalled that Smith's re-

election in 1924 was accompanied by the defeat of his running
mates. Had the reorganization amendment with its concentration
of appointive power in the hands of the chief executive been in
effect, it would have deprived his Republican subordinates of
patronage enjoyed under the status quo. Ruminating on this unpleasant hypothetical state of affairs, George K. Morris, the
Republican state chairman, proclaimed, "There will be no 'short
ballot' legislation at the coming session with my consent." The
Times took him to task editorially for impeding a program "devised by Republicans who preferred the permanent good of the
State to the loaves and fishes of partisanship." The president
of the New York State Association, who described himself as "a
black Republican from a section of the state so black that you
have to use a lantern to find a Democrat," joined in the condemnation of Morris and praise of Smith.[53]

When the legislature convened in January, 1925, it was
apparent that the progressive Republicans had triumphed over
their conservative brethren in one respect, for the GOP organization accepted the consolidation amendment as party policy.
Consequently, the legislature adopted it without even waiting
for the preadjournment rush. Shortly after its passage, in a
speech on government reform, Smith remarked, "It is just as
ridiculous to try to run a government with old-fashioned ideas
. . . as it would be for me to try to get into my first
communion suit." He called upon his listeners to vote for the
amendment in the fall referendum.[54]

The action of the 1925 session meant that the reorganization amendment would appear on the ballot on election day in
November. Support by both parties seemed to guarantee success
at the polls. Distinguished Republicans formed the vanguard of
the government reform movement. The 1924 GOP platform contained
a plank favoring the amendment. There was a Republican majority
in one house of the legislature in 1923 and in both houses in
1925 when the amendment passed.

Yet the Republican position was equivocal. With Republican legislative support assured in February, 1925, the lieutenant governor, who had done his best to obstruct passage, implied that his party would fulfill its duty by submitting the amendment to the people and intimated the desirability of its defeat at their hands. Ironically, Lowman here depended upon the same logic used by Smith in urging the Republican majority to pass the other two amendments to which it was opposed, in order to let the people decide the issue. Negative publicity from organization headquarters circulated widely in rural Republican strongholds. The attempts to sabotage the reform distressed its Republican proponents, among them Elihu Root and Nicholas Murray Butler. The progressives and their allies exerted enough pressure on the party to drive the opposition underground, if not to suppress it.[55]

Unlike the Republicans, Smith did not have to cope with a split in his ranks and, therefore, could direct his undivided attention to the electorate. He prodded his own organization to get out the vote and endorsed a good deal of campaign literature. Well before election day, he was confident but not complacent. He stumped vigorously for the amendment. If he was welcome in such hotbeds of the efficiency economy movement as the City Club with his discourse on government reform, he was also able to fill to overflowing large meeting halls, despite the fact that referenda typically exert less popular appeal than candidates. Limping with an injured foot, he prefaced his remarks on one occasion with the observation that his physician did not object to his tour—provided he did not speak with his feet. There on Staten Island, he alluded to the undercover GOP activities against the reorganization measure; elsewhere in the city, he termed it "the most progressive step taken in this State in half a century."[56]

The results of the referendum justified him. On November 3, 1925, 1,048,087 people voted yes and 775,768 voted no on question 3. It was defeated upstate but carried handily by the large New York City majority. Walter Lippman assured Smith

that with the triumph of this and other amendments he had scored
"one of the great achievements in modern American politics."
With a delightfully mixed metaphor, a reporter for the *Times*
exulted, "A new feather adorns Governor Smith's far-famed
brown derby."[57]

The acclaim was premature, for the 1925 amendment was not
self-executing. It required the 1926 session to legislate the
administrative structure into conformity with the revised constitution. The situation tempted Smith's opponents to undermine reform in the very process of ostensibly implementing it.
They were prevented from sabotaging reorganization and the
executive budget by the Hughes commission which climaxed the
efficiency economy drive begun by the constitutional convention
and continued by the Reconstruction Commission.

Smith, who was far from naive, anticipated the legislative pitfalls and took whatever steps he could to avoid them.
After legislative approval of the reorganization amendment and
in expectation of its success at the polls, the governor asked
the lawmakers to cooperate with him in appointing a commission
as distinguished as the 1915 delegation for the purpose of designing the necessary legislation. After the regular session
declined to act, the secretary of the Citizens' Union counseled
him to repeat his proposal to the special session scheduled for
June 22 to reconsider a controversial measure on state parks.[58]

Before Smith could follow the advice of the Citizens'
Union or his own inclination to appoint a group from the nominees of the New York State Association, he was presented with
a fait accompli in the form of a commission that boded ill for
the ultimate success of the reform. Getting wind of the governor's intentions, John Knight, president pro tempore of the senate, and Joseph McGinnies, Speaker of the assembly, preempted the
field by releasing to the press on June 20 the names of 64
people whom they were inviting to serve on a commission. While
Smith expressed satisfaction in public with this indication of
GOP support of the amendment, in private he maneuvered to assure

a committee more sympathetic to reform by proposing additional
members. In this way, the State Reorganization Commission expanded to include veterans of the Reconstruction Commission
such as Abram I. Elkus and Norman Mack, civic leaders such as
Walter T. Arndt of the Citizens' Union and Richard S. Childs of
the New York State Association, and Republicans prominent in
government reform such as Addison Colvin and Martin Saxe. The
Hughes commission included most of the distinguished New Yorkers
who were identified with the efficiency economy movement, with
the notable exceptions of Elihu Root who declined, and of Belle
Moskowitz, Robert Moses, and Raymond V. Ingersoll, secretary of
the City Club, all three nominated by Smith but rejected by the
legislative leaders. Not until the end of July, did they formally extend invitations to those whose appointment they had
announced so precipitately; in August Smith was still pressing
for consideration of his candidates.[59]

        The leadership as well as the membership of the commission
was a source of anxiety to the governor. Knight and McGinnies
had suggested to their appointees the name of H. Edmund Machold
for chairman, but he was suspect to the progressives on two
counts. Not only had he long been an outspoken foe of reorganization, but he was also closely identified with the electric
power companies whose interests he would be sure to protect in
any design of the administrative structure. Smith, who championed public power, objected to the former Speaker on both
grounds. The chief executive preferred to have Charles Evans
Hughes preside over the implementation of the reform that the
former governor had initiated. Smith had gone so far as to
contact the office of the secretary of state and had been
planning to call upon him when the legislative leaders loosed
their bombshell. After that, Smith worked behind the scenes
with Childs, who lobbied his fellow members of the commission
to secure its chairmanship for Hughes. With demand for the ex-
governor mounting, Machold withdrew, under pressure from the
progressive element of the GOP. When the commission met for
the first time on November 15, 1925, it unanimously selected

Hughes as chairman.[60]

With Hughes in control, the prospects for meaningful reform brightened. His leadership determined that the commission
would produce a report that reformers could approve. His prestige guaranteed its legislative success, for the Republican
majority was in no position to repudiate the work of its onetime presidential candidate. The achievements of the State
Reorganization Commission in New York signified the temporary
triumph of the progressives over the old guard within the GOP
and the collaboration of the former with receptive Democrats
like Smith and Wagner. As chairman, Hughes chose Henry L.
Stimson to head the subcommittee on the Executive and State
Departments, a position which Felix Frankfurther correctly perceived as dominant in the work of the commission.[61]

The cooperation between Smith and the progressive Republicans, which had proved so effective up to this point, continued
in the daily operations of the Hughes commission and of its subcommittee dealing with the role of the governor and with budgetary procedures. Stimson involved Smith intimately in the
deliberations of his group. A common goal, which was now within
reach, and a mutual respect, both dating to the constitutional
convention, enabled the two men to work together fruitfully.
Stimson consulted the governor regularly on the Executive Department and on the executive budget, which emerged as a proba-
bility in the process of outlining the financial responsibilities of the department.

The subcommittee on the Executive and State Departments
held its first meeting on Saturday, November 28; on Monday, its
chairman turned to the governor for his views. On Wednesday,
Smith, with one of his sons and a few associates, called upon
Stimson, and the two conferred for several hours. Smith insisted upon reverting to the 1915 variation of the executive
budget and protested that "he would stick to the so-called
Root budget and would take nothing less." To Stimson, he explained that he had been misled into supporting the Walker
resolution by the prospect of legislative approval for a weaker

version. The chief executive vehemently dismissed any budget
legislation as worse than useless. It was imperative to amend
the constitution in order to restrain the lawmakers in their
disposition of the budget. Stimson pointed out the problem of
legislative antipathy to an amendment. Whereupon Smith told
him "that the plan which we [the commission] recommended would
go through . . . and they [the legislators] could not dare
afford not to pass the plan which we recommended; that he proposed to keep them in special sessions all summer if necessary
until a proper program was adopted."[62]

Smith had misgivings about the interpretation that might
be placed on their conversation and adjured Stimson to refrain
from showing his memorandum on it to anyone but Hughes. The
governor was not spoiling for a fight. Stimson reassured him
that Hughes had taken the comments in the way they were
meant.[63]

To his old friend, Robert F. Wagner, who was serving on
Stimson's committee, the governor amplified the objections that
he had voiced to the chairman regarding a statutory executive
budget. Smith was apprehensive lest budget legislation relieve
the pressure for the indispensable constitutional amendment.
Because of its significance, "I think I should really talk to
you about this matter," for "I can tell it to you so much
better than I can write it. . . ." With that, the governor extended to Wagner an invitation to "Come when you feel like it,
stay as long as you like; there's a warm welcome for you."[64]

The two Democrats were limited in what they could do to
promote a budget amendment unless Stimson found a way to overcome Republican opposition. For this purpose, he conferred in-
tensively with Machold, now chairman of the committee on fiscal
departments. While engaged in these negotiations, Stimson kept
in touch with Smith. He agreed to maintain silence on the
issue in order to remove any obstacle to the parlays. Meanwhile, Stimson admonished him to round up support among his
fellow Democrats on the commission.[65]

The end of December and the beginning of January were spent
in effecting a compromise on the budget amendment. So strongly
were Hughes and Stimson committed to it that they were prepared,
in the event of adverse action, to subscribe to a minority
report. "If we do that, I don't think the majority will get
much out of it," Hughes wryly noted. Matters did not come to
such a pass. It was Hughes who found a way out. Machold represented Republican legislative opinion, unwilling to surrender
the power of making additions to the executive's budget.
Hughes realized that the spirit of the executive budget could
be preserved so long as such additions were rigidly segregated
and subject to veto. Stimson drafted an amendment with provisions to this effect. He composed it carefully to preclude the
danger of legislative tampering with administrative expenses by
striking from the governor's budget entire items, only to replace them with larger ones that he could not veto without
cutting out the activity for which he had requested a more
moderate sum. Stimson and Machold concurred in their intention
to compel the legislature to make each increase a separate item
which the chief executive could disallow. In time the compromise gained acceptance in the crucial circles. One by one the
Republican stalwarts came round: Machold, McGinnies, and
Knight. On January 14 Stimson and Machold embodied their compromise in a report, which the executive committee of the State
Reorganization Commission duly accepted.[66]

Stimson assured his colleagues on the subcommittee that
the alterations did not weaken the Root amendment. To its
author, Stimson explained, "The change permitting new items to
be added to the budget is so protected by the Governor's veto
that I don't think it can be abused. At the same time I think
the original budget is sufficiently preserved so that it will
not be torn up and a legislative budget substituted in its
place."[67]

Stimson and Smith had thus both reversed the positions
held during the 1925 session. The new compromise was essentially the Democrats' concurrent resolution of the year before.

Earlier, in order to induce legislative action, Smith had acceded to changes in the Root plan, while the progressive Republicans had adhered firmly to their 1915 position. Now it was
Stimson who yielded for the same reasons.

Robert Moses and Richard S. Childs both advised Smith to
reject Stimson's compromise as inconsistent with the Root amendment. They condemned the committee's budget formula as "absolutely worthless" and one which "far from improving the present
procedure would leave us worse off than we are now." Under its
terms, Childs warned the governor, "the Legislature might strike
out the entire budget or parts of it and then add an entirely
new budget of its own." This is exactly what Stimson had gone
to great pains to prevent. Childs also objected to the provision for the attendance of the legislative fiscal chairmen at
the executive's hearing as incompatible with the separation of
powers.[68]

Smith gave serious consideration to the reservations of
these men, but, as a politician, he was more inclined to promote
reform by compromise than to obstruct it by intransigence.
When the governor raised with Stimson the issues that they had
called to his attention, he was satisfied with the chairman's
explanations. It appeared to Smith that his opponents had
made the greater concessions; he told his advisers that he was
unwilling "to stand on any technicalities." In the subcommittee's proposal, he believed, "We are getting everything
that we fought for in principle."[69]

In its report, the Hughes commission maintained the
essence of the executive budget when it concluded that "constitutional amendment is the only way to preserve the State
from partisan and often ill-advised and hasty attempts to vary
the fundamental methods of fiscal procedure." The commission
drafted an amendment that deviated from the Root plan primarily
by incorporating the concessions that Stimson had made to secure acceptance. In accordance with its provisions, the
governor would revise the estimates, which the various agencies
submitted, and taking into account both revenues and outlays,

would formulate a coherent budget. The legislature retained the
power to make deletions and reductions and, in contrast to the
1915 arrangement, additions and increases, prior to enactment
of the governor's budget, but only in separate bills, each subject to veto. There was another innovation in the presence of
the chairmen of the Senate Finance and Assembly Ways and Means
Committees at the chief executive's budgetary conferences. The
Hughes commission, nevertheless, intended to enable the governor
to propose and the legislature to dispose of the budget, in a
reversal of the current procedure where the latter determined
the level of expenditures over which the former exercised only
whatever control the veto afforded. To complement the executive
budget amendment, the commission recommended the establishment
of a division of the budget within the Executive Department.[70]

When he called upon Stimson, Smith advocated, not only the
executive budget, but also the four-year term, both within the
purview of the subcommittee. The Hughes commission's report
favored the longer term, but without any specification on the
timing of elections.[71]

The recommendations on the budget and the term of office
were tangential to the commission's basic task of reorganizing
the state government. On this subject Smith expressed himself
very emphatically during his conference with Stimson.

> He said we would get nowhere if we simply trans-
> ferred existing offices to the twenty departments; that
> would simply leave the old expensive system of govern-
> ment operating under a new name or form. His idea was
> to describe the functions which each department should
> have, to impose upon the heads of the department the
> duty of carrying out these functions, and to give them
> lump sum appropriations and power to create the neces-
> sary agencies and subordinates with which to do it.

Such an arrangement would carry to their logical conclusion the
principles of executive responsibility. The conservative Republicans also preferred to have the Hughes commission draw up
only outlines—to be filled in by the legislature. If the
legislators should regain the initiative, the amendment would
fail to realize its goal of an efficient administration at
once free from the proclivities to insubordination and from

the extravagances of patronage. The conflict between the executive and the legislature over which would specify the organization and functions of the various departments was pregnant with
implications for the integrity of the reform. To carry out the
reformers' intentions, the Hughes commission filled in the details itself, even to the extent of supervising the drafting
of appropriate legislation.[72]

In its Reorganization of Government Report, the commission
drew the specifications for a hierarchical administration consisting of eighteen departments. The new structure bore the
impress of the theory of public administration, for in general
it provided for the governor to appoint and dismiss an individual as head of each department and vested in the commissioner
similar authority with reference to the divisions within his
department. To this pattern, the report made a number of inevitable exceptions as in the case of the Departments of Agriculture and Markets, Education, and Civil Service. In its outline of the Conservation Department, the Hughes commission re-
designed the agencies dealing with water power, removed prominent legislators from membership in them, and required the
approval of the governor for all hydroelectric projects. The
ideal of a strong executive, which would enable Smith, an advocate of public power, to frustrate the predilection of the Republican legislature for private development, was apparent also
in the proposal for an Executive Department unprecedented in
either federal or state administrative experience. With the
new department, the report placed the capstone of executive
supervision and coordination on the structure of the state
bureaucracy.[73]

Although the commission did not agree with Smith on all
the details of reorganization, it found his advice valuable.
It acceded to his wishes as made known to Stimson in a number
of its recommendations: for example, to make the governor the
head of the Executive Department, and to provide for charities,
corrections, and mental hygiene in separate units. On the
other hand, the report disregarded Smith's preference for

establishing a department rather than a division of architecture
and for dispensing entirely with the commissioners of the land
office. Nor did the governor's influence prevail against the
status quo in the Department of Agriculture and Markets whose
leadership, in deference to rural interests, was chosen by a
sympathetic legislature. Since his first year in office, Smith
had been complaining of mismanagement in this agency, which was
immune to proper oversight. Whatever the differences between
the governor and the Hughes commission, they worked together
for the common goal of more rational, responsible, and responsive government in New York. Clearly, to anyone familiar with
the inside story of their cooperation, Republicans who counted
on Smith to condemn the report were indulging in wishful
thinking.[74]

Even those Republicans who were unsympathetic to the
efficiency economy movement would find it awkward to reject a
work hallowed by the name of Charles Evans Hughes. The GOP
caucus affirmed its confidence in the State Reorganization
Commission and anticipated that "we will be in accord with their
recommendations when submitted." By making fine distinctions
among the different versions of the executive budget, the organization prepared to reverse itself. On February 26, 1926, the
Hughes commission issued its official report; on March 1, in a
concurrent resolution, the legislature expressed a gratitude
that some of its members undoubtedly did not feel. Meanwhile,
informed sources described Smith as "pleased with the report in
general, even though the recommendations did not in every respect meet his views." Senator Knight lauded the "monument to
the able men and women . . . on the commission"; less archi-
tectural in mood, Assemblyman McGinnies predicted that "the
Assembly will adopt the report."[75]

Smith suggested that this could best be done in a special
session called to deal exclusively with the reorganization
statutes. Stimson was noncommittal, and the legislative
leaders turned down the governor's proposal. Instead, contrary to the wishes of their Democratic minorities, both houses

voted to refer all bills pending on April 1 to their respective
Rules Committees and thereafter to concentrate on the government reform measures. Procedure no longer mattered.[76]

Appropriate legislation to enforce the reorganization
article was drafted under the direction of the Hughes commission.
It was introduced in due course and passed with utmost facility
in the month between March 24 and April 25, 1926. Governor
Smith undoubtedly experienced profound satisfaction when he
signed these measures. The nineteen statutes which reorganized
the government are known collectively as the State Departments
Law. This body of law conforms exactly to the ideas of the
Hughes commission, for both executive and legislature were
committed to the faithful implementation of its report.[77]

Few and futile were the attempts to tamper with the
commission's proposals. When the governor's staff called attention to the insertion in one of the bills of a provision to hand
over added patronage to a Republican official until the expiration of his term, the measure was peremptorily restored to its
pristine form. If politics-as-usual explains the bill-drafting
mystery, professional considerations motivated the distinguished individuals who pressed Smith for other modifications
in the reorganization scheme. Psychiatrists urged him to veto
provisions that made the tenure of the commissioner of mental
hygiene dependent on the will of the governor; State Architect
Sullivan Jones eventually resigned over the failure of architecture to attain departmental status, despite Smith's original
sympathy with his position.[78] Now however, the governor was
determined not to upset the tacit understanding on the enactment of the recommendations of the Hughes commission. Any other
course might spell disaster for reform. Once the door were
opened to change, what would inhibit the legislature from
making more extensive revisions and reconstructing the state
government by a patchwork of laws designed to yield perqui-
sites and patronage rather than efficiency and economy?

The drive for efficiency and economy in the government of
New York, which had begun in the progressive era, culminated in

the constitutional amendment of 1925 and in the State Departments Law of 1926. So closely did the resulting structure conform to the paradigm of public administration that a contemporary
scholar informed the readers of the *American Political Science
Review* of "one of the very few illustrations of a state government being rebuilt according to a definite plan," and concluded
that "The Governor today has both power and responsibility."
The *Reports and Studies*, which did for the constitutional convention of 1938 what the work of the Bureau of Municipal Research had done for that of 1915, credited the reforms of
Smith's administration with going far "to make the Governor of
New York its chief executive in fact as well as in theory."[79]
At the end of three terms, Smith could derive satisfaction from
his role in translating progressive theory into legislative
fact.

Whether or not the reorganized government could meet progressive expectations would depend in part upon the officials
in power when the State Departments Law took effect. The
Hughes commission recommended quite reasonably that this coincide with the advent of a new administration on January 1, 1927.
Smith attributed this decision to the partisanship of Republicans who expected a victory at the polls to place them in charge
of reorganization. As if to confirm the governor's suspicions,
Senator Knight had greeted the commission's report with strictures on "the necessity of the election of a Republican Governor."[80]

Republican hopes centered on the commission's chairman as
the candidate with the best chance to beat Smith. But Charles
Evans Hughes had no ambition to reoccupy the office in which
he had met frustration at the hands of his own party in the
legislature. Unlike a prospect for higher office, who did not
"choose to run," Hughes was not at all enigmatic about his refusal. Months before the 1926 convention he had announced,
". . . I should not be willing in any circumstances to become
a candidate for the office of Governor. Even if I were nomina-

ted I should decline."[81]

In his speech accepting the nomination, which Hughes disdained, Ogden L. Mills associated reorganization under Smith with domination of the state by Tammany Hall. As October wore on, Mills painted the wigwam in lurid colors for the voters to see. Of his opponent he forecast, "If he reorganizes the State of New York he will reorganize it in the interests of Tammany Hall."[82]

Hughes came to Mills's aid with an address in Rochester suggesting a new broom for the most effective reorganization. While giving credit to Smith for his efforts in behalf of the reform, Hughes informed his audience that ". . . it owes its birth and its final adoption to Republicans."[83]

A few days later from a Brooklyn platform, the governor reminded Hughes that reorganization nearly owed its death to the Republicans too. On the campaign trail, Smith questioned the qualifications of the GOP to preside over a reform that it had long resisted. In accepting renomination, the governor laid claim to the job of carrying out reorganization: "I am confident that the people will entrust that task and that responsibility to a demonstrated, devoted friend of this reform and not to a political machine which has viewed it always and only from the point of view of the patronage it might bring." In congratulating Smith upon his electoral victory, Stimson found it "fitting that one who has done so much to secure the reorganization of the State government should have the chief hand in carrying out that great reform."[84]

As he began his administration of the reformed government, Smith instituted a cabinet. Whenever during the long battle for reform he had let his imagination wander to the reconstructed state, he envisioned a cabinet where the leaders met for consultation and coordination of their efforts. To him, as to the progressives who had instructed him on efficiency and economy, the cabinet represented both a symbol and an instrument of reform. Therefore, he introduced one in New York despite the fact that it was prescribed, neither by the

constitutional amendment, nor by the State Departments Law.
Doubtless he shared the sentiments of the contributor to the
National Municipal Review who expected the new group to initi-
ate policy and to integrate the administration.[85]

The governor's cabinet consisted originally of sixteen
members, most of whom headed the newly consolidated departments.
Commissioners of regulatory and quasi-judicial agencies were
excluded; officials of lesser rank, but involved in policy formulation or administrative coordination, for example the director of the budget, were included. Smith intended to assemble
the group fortnightly. It convened at least seven times —
possibly more, for the record is fragmentary. Sometimes the
members received formal agenda in advance. The chief executive
appointed committees of the cabinet to study and report on particular problems. From the verbatim minutes, which survive for
six of the meetings, it is possible to derive a clear impression
of the proceedings. Smith conducted them with dispatch and
acuity apparent in his incisive questions and extensive comments.
Second only to the governor in the deliberations was Robert
Moses, the architect of reconstruction whom Smith persisted in
naming secretary of state despite the enmity that the political
scientist had incurred among politicians of both parties.[86]

At the first meeting on February 9, 1927, Smith talked at
length about the position of the cabinet in the reorganized
government. He viewed the administration as a hierarchy with
those in attendance serving as the liaison between himself and
the lower echelons. He emphasized the role of the cabinet in
synchronizing the activities of the various agencies and eliminating waste. On one occasion, when an exchange of views
brought to light an instance of duplication in the efforts of
two departments, he exulted, "Here is the first example of the
benefit we can get from all the department heads meeting around
the table. . . ."[87] The cabinet reviewed many state functions
such as public works and devoted a number of sessions to reorganization and the executive budget.

If consolidation secured the position of the governor at the apex of a hierarchy, the executive budget would enable him to control it and to demonstrate his qualities of leadership. Since governmental activities require funds, financial power provides a key to political power. The executive budget minimized insubordination in the New York bureaucracy, for officials who depended upon the chief executive for access to funds were in no position to defy him in collaboration with legislators— a common practice in the federal administration. Since the allocation of funds determines goals, the budget endowed the governor with legislative initiative as well.[88] The Hughes commission recognized the interrelationship between reorganization and fiscal reform in establishing executive leadership. Given the sacrosanct status of its recommendations, its report assured the enactment of a budget amendment.

In view of the violent partisanship that the amendment had engendered, its ultimate adoption was strangly anticlimactic. The Republicans engaged in doublethink on the subject. Upon release of the Reorganization of Government Report, they established a new party line, which they officially promulgated in their platform for the 1926 contest: "We commend the Legislature for rejecting the budget proposals of Governor Smith and for adopting a constitutional executive budget measure recommended by the Hughes commission." Smith did not let them get away with that. In one campaign address he explained, "The fact of the matter is that there is practically no difference between the constitutional budget recommended by the Hughes Commission and the one recommended by me."[89]

With both parties claiming credit for the executive budget, its legislative path was clear. The session that enacted the State Departments Law also complied with the recommendations of the Hughes commission on statutory and constitutional provisions for the executive budget. The budget amendment secured legislative approval for the first time in 1926. While it was under consideration, the secretary of the

Citizens' Union complained indignantly to Stimson of an attempt
by the chairman of the Senate Finance Committee to insert in
the amendment a provision for additional compensation for the
legislative fiscal chairmen. Arndt considered this magnifica-
tion of the legislators' role a travesty on the executive budget and had effectively quashed it. Smith, too, had protested
to Stimson. He made light of the matter and even conceded some
justification for the abortive addition. As for the constitutional amendment, Arndt anticipated "little difficulty next
year in obtaining a second approval."[90]

The budget amendment passed in due course on March 24,
1927—or so it seemed. Four days later, Robert Moses startled
observers of the New York scene with his announcement that "this
amendment did not pass at this session." In his capacity as
secretary of state, he had not received the resolution for inclusion on the November ballot. A technicality had apparently
invalidated legislative action on the budget. The intention
of having the senate concur in the assembly resolution was
frustrated when, through an oversight, identically worded, but
separately sponsored, measures were adopted in each house, in
a deviation from customary procedure. Republican legislative
leaders expressed regret for the mixup, but in view of their
history of opposition to the amendment, they were under suspicion of sabotaging it. Moses urged the governor to summon the
legislature into extraordinary session to remedy the defect and
to expedite the executive budget in order to avoid a delay of
two more years.[91]

Smith was unwilling to let the reform, which meant so
much to him, go by default. He did not, however, panic; he
turned instead for advice to leaders of the bar, Louis Marshall
and Henry L. Stimson. A close rereading of the state constitution convinced both of these attorneys that the amendment had
indeed passed, despite the procedural variation. Even the
Republican attorney general concurred when he delivered his
official opinion on the question. Smith construed it as a
directive to the clerks of the legislature to certify and trans-

mit the resolution to Moses, for an attorney general's decision
was legally binding on state officials. It authorized the
secretary of state to hold the referendum and relieved the
governor of any need to call a special session.[92]

Democratic politicians at their state convention heard
Smith instruct them to work diligently for the success of the
executive budget at the polls. He mused on the irony of current
Republican enthusiasm for a reform that the GOP had so long
stymied. That party, in its 1927 platform, credited Root,
Hughes, and Republican legislatures with advancing the executive
budget and urged its ratification. Bipartisan support facilitated the favorable outcome of the election. Out of a total of
1,738,097 votes cast on the question, the amendment received
1,291,990. Upstate as well as in the city, the majority was
for it.[93]

Although the amendment would become operative only in the
administration of the next governor, Smith was determined to
handle his 1928 budget as if the constitutional change were
already in effect. Towards the end of 1927, he devoted the
better part of two cabinet meetings to the executive budget because he was "exceedingly anxious that this be a success from
the beginning."[94] On the first occasion, the budget director
explained the revised fiscal process; when he was hospitalized,
the governor himself dominated a second session on public
finance.

To his cabinet, Smith conveyed his own perception of the
relationship between efficiency and economy, between the reconstructed administrative hierarchy and the elimination of waste.
On the requests for appropriations, he planned to consult only
his department heads to whom he delegated supervision over the
lower echelons. Smith placed on the commissioners the responsibility of preventing each specialist from overestimating the
amounts needed. "Don't let him put a lot of stuff in that he
don't expect to get, with the hope that in falling down the
ladder he will grab a rung near the top," the governor admonished. He expected his appointees to be actively involved in

the preparation of their own departmental estimates and even to
"put in a little overtime in the study, an intimate study of
their own budget and make the men they get the facts from
justify them." Once the commissioners had satisfied Smith on
the economical operation of their respective departments, they
were not free to repudiate in their testimony the budget that
he submitted to the legislature, for the very institution of a
cabinet implied a coherence and consistency within the executive
branch. "Above all things," the governor emphasized, "don't
put anything in there and urge it in front of me and be prepared
to take it out when the bill goes upstairs." Such behavior
would give "a black eye to the budget system."[95]

Smith was convinced that a properly functioning executive
budget could rationalize government operations and check legislative extravagance. He enlivened one cabinet meeting on
finances with an amusing account of pork barrel legislation by
the representatives of Schuyler County who ran "on the issue of
how much they could get in the development of Watkins Glen, and
they went so far that they destroyed the natural beauty. When
you come to putting brass rails and concrete stairs down a
chasm, it looks more like a ballroom than a spot of scenic
value."[96] His anecdote expressed a sensitivity to the ideals
of conservation as well as those of efficiency and economy.

The budget reform, which originated in the drive of the
efficiency economy movement for centralization of authority,
inevitably provoked anew competition between executive and
legislature for control of state finances. A number of incidents during Smith's incumbency prefigured the struggle that
eventually broke out when the budget amendment took effect.

In each case, the central issue was jurisdiction over the
segregation of lump sums. For example, the 1924 appropriations
bill, as it emerged from the Republican assembly, required the
concurrence of the governor and the chairmen of the Senate
Finance and Assembly Ways and Means Committees in the itemization of lump sums, a function which the Democratic senate,
acting on Smith's instructions, entrusted to the governor alone.

The impasse ended by inserting in the bill specific items instead of lump sums to be allocated later.[97] In December, 1926
Governor Smith protested to a second Reorganization Commission
against the draft of a provision to involve the legislative
fiscal chairmen in the itemization process, a procedure which
he criticized as "a complete departure from the principles"
and a clear violation of "the letter of the proposed constitutional amendment providing for a State executive budget."[98]
The following year, he complained to his cabinet of a measure
which allowed the two lawmakers to participate in the expenditure of workmen's compensation funds. He resented the chairmen's role as a legislative intrusion into the realm of the
executive in direct contravention of the separation of powers.
Nevertheless in 1927, he was unwilling to disapprove the offensive legislation, because "it seems senseless to get into a
quarrel . . . to the extent of vetoing the whole bill for the
support of government just to carry one little point that
wouldn't be understood by the fellow in the street." Despite—
or perhaps because of—his commitment to the relief of industry's victims, he did veto a similar workmen's compensation
bill in 1928 in the belief "that a warning should be issued to
the people . . . against the increasing encroachments of the
Legislature on executive and administrative matters of this
kind."[99]

The procedural grounds on which the governor vetoed the
bill must be understood in terms of their relation to substantive considerations in the context of New York politics. Republican committee chairmen might use their financial power in
particular to reduce the protection that compensation was affording to the laboring man and in general to undermine or manipulate Democratic programs on the law books. A case in point
is the bitter controversy over state parks in Smith's third and
fourth terms.[100] At any rate, a legislative role in the expenditure of appropriations deprived the executive of the administrative authority that the progressives valued and restored
the legislative intervention that they deplored.

With a fiscal year about to begin, Governor Smith, Senator Hewitt, and Assemblyman Hutchinson met in Albany to segregate the lump sums in the appropriations bill, as the 1928 Democratic convention, which nominated Smith for the presidency, was opening in Houston.[101] After his defeat, Smith assisted in the formulation of the first budget submitted under the constitutional amendment—by his successor, Franklin Delano Roosevelt.

Under Roosevelt, the itemization issue evolved into a test case of the executive budget itself. The battle over the participation of the chairmen of the Senate Finance and Assembly Ways and Means Committees in the segregation of lump sums was rejoined on a larger scale with the new governor taking up his predecessor's position. Eventually, the Court of Appeals decided in Roosevelt's favor in a ruling that interpreted the constitution's new article IV-A as a bar to this kind of assignment of administrative functions to two legislators.[102] The cause célèbre of Roosevelt's first term was essentially a continuation of Smith's struggle with the legislature for the adoption of an executive budget. Had the judiciary ruled differently, it would in effect have nullified the amendment by restoring to the legislature financial initiative and administrative control, which the reformers had intended to vouchsafe to the executive. The outcome assured the integrity of an administration, free from the meddling of legislative fiscal chairmen, and afforded an opportunity for the attainment of a responsible executive.

The progressive program for responsible and responsive government included, not only reorganization and an executive budget, but also a four-year term for statewide officers. The three reforms are closely related, for extended tenure would enable an administration, already made more effective by the other changes, to engage in long-range planning.

What interfered with the adoption of the third reform was disagreement, not so much over the number of years in office, as over the timing of elections. The Hughes commission favored

a four-year term but was noncommittal on when it should begin.
Smith qualified his recommendation to the 1926 legislature for
an amendment by asserting, "and I regard it distinctly unfortunate that there be . . . a combination of elections for
Governor and President of the United States." On the other
hand, the GOP caucus proclaimed that a longer term for state
officials "should be coupled with the provision that the election of such officers should be held at the time of a Presidential election." Democrats and Republicans sponsored competing measures, reflecting the position of their respective
leadership. Inevitably, the lawmakers passed the GOP resolution providing for a four-year term with state and national
elections coinciding.[103] On this issue, the 1927 session was
almost an exact replica of the preceding one.[104]

Having placed its own version of the four-year term before the voters, the GOP experienced divided counsels. Since
many Republicans had opposed any extension, there was pressure
on the organization to come out officially against the amendment, particularly after the defeat of a similar proposal in
New Jersey. The leadership rejected such a repudiation of the
party's legislative record, and Senator Knight confided, "I do
not see how we can afford to run away because Smith threatens
to attack." Instead, the party hedged, preparing to claim
credit in the event of the amendment's success at the polls,
but refusing, in the case of its failure, to consider an alternative with off-year elections. In the latter instance, ". . .
Smith, of course, does not get what he wants," Knight explained.
The Republican platform carried out this strategy by supporting
the amendment, condemning the governor for his opposition and
his alternative, and characterizing his stand as a maneuver "to
perpetuate the hold of Tammany Hall upon the State Government."[105]

In two debates that the League of Women Voters sponsored
between Smith and Knight, controversy centered on the date of
elections specified in the amendment. In the event of its defeat, "the two-year term will be continued," the senator warned

on the first occasion in Buffalo where he admitted the merits
of extended tenure. He defended the holding of state elections
in the years of national contests on the grounds of larger turnout. Carrying the argument to its logical conclusion, the
governor queried "why not elect everybody every four years?"
Smith expounded the progressive theory that separation of elections for the various levels of government would focus each
campaign on the relevant issues. He criticized the amendment
as a device to permit a mediocre candidate to "steal a ride
into the Executive Mansion on a great national issue that has
nothing to do with . . . New York" and derided the quadrennial
voter. When they returned to the fray in Utica, Knight again
declared his sympathy with rural areas where frequent elections
worked a hardship on people distant from the polling places.
Smith gave little credence to this excuse for the GOP plan to
capitalize on people "who vote only every four years and who
vote the Republican ticket." Each man accused the other of
rationalizing partisan political interests.[106]

During the week before election day, Smith repeated his
objections to the GOP version of the four-year term, in an
intensification of his efforts to defeat it at the polls. With
this in view, he made a number of personal appearances in New
York City and delivered an address over radio station WJZ.
Eleanor Roosevelt and Senator Wagner each spoke over the new
communications medium in support of the governor's position.
He, meanwhile, urged the people to deal selectively with the
amendments by voting no on number six and yes on all of the
others, including the executive budget for which he had striven
so vigorously. As if to confirm his influence, eight amendments
won, and the four-year term lost by so wide a margin that it did
not carry a single county.[107]

No sooner had the returns been counted than the two parties renewed their dispute, this time over the meaning of the
figures. They signified a disinclination to hold state and
national elections concurrently but no aversion to the longer
term of office, Smith explained as he called for another refer-

endum with provision for off-year elections. He made these observations on election night in elation over his victory. He
awoke next morning to learn—from Republican sources—that he
had lost. Their state chairman perceived the outcome at the
polls as "a general rout for the Governor and his party and its
principles." The GOP attributed the defeat of the amendment,
not to the provision on the timing of elections, but to the
principle of extending the tenure of office. Although the
governor derided such fallacious logic as showing scant respect
for the intelligence of the electorate, his opponents had deliberately composed their preelection propaganda to fit this
interpretation of the likely results.[108]

In the 1928 session everyone adhered to positions that had
been staked out for the 1927 canvass. Republican lawmakers rejected Smith's idea that they were "morally bound" to submit to
the voters a second four-year term amendment "providing for the
election in a year when there is no election for President of
the United States."[109] The chief executive tried to force the
legislature to do what he conceived as its duty, by arousing
the public to demand a second referendum. In speaking before
business and professional groups, he emphasized the integral
relationship among all three items on the agenda of government
reconstruction and urged its completion with a longer term of
office.[110] As the session waned, he appealed to the electorate,
in a radio broadcast from Albany's Ten Eyck Hotel, and to the
leadership of the Hughes commission, in a well-publicized
letter, to help him prevail upon the legislature. Civic organizations such as the City Club and the League of Women Voters
responded by lobbying for his measure at the state Capitol.
The GOP schism over the efficiency economy movement was again
apparent when Nathan L. Miller rebuked his successor, and
George W. Wickerhsam considered the significance of the 1927
vote on the amendment "an open question" and the proposal for
a referendum on the Democratic alternative "a reasonable request on the part of the Governor." Neither the level of
popular protest nor the prestige of the "federal crowd" was

sufficient to induce the Republican leadership to let the resolution out of committee.[111] Smith retired from office without
gaining the four-year term, which New York finally adopted in
1937 in the form he preferred.

The Smith administration succeeded in restructuring the
state government along the lines of a comprehensive plan, which
included reorganization, the executive budget, and, despite the
delay, the four-year term. To the extent that any one individual can be credited with a complex reform, Governor Smith
effected a shift in the balance of power away from the legislature and to the executive, thereby leading a trend that continued for nearly half a century. By concentrating on those
changes that promoted executive initiative, he put into effect
in New York the program of the efficiency economy wing of the
progressive reformers of government.

In the executive as in the assembly chamber, Smith was
ambivalent toward the progressive goal of direct democracy,
whose relationship to efficiency and economy is a subject of
controversy. The governor's annual messages regularly proposed
such standard reforms as home rule, a more rigorous Corrupt
Practices Act, the initiative on amendments to the state constitution, and a referendum on changes in the federal constitution. He advocated the last item in reaction to Prohibition
which, in his opinion, would not have been ratified, at least in
New York, if the amendment had been put to a vote of the people.
In 1923 after the Miller administration had repealed the direct
primary law of the progressive era, the Democratic senate
passed a bill favored by Smith while the Republican assembly
adopted one acceptable to the Citizens' Union, which then
blamed the governor for the failure to restore primary elections. Since the GOP legislature of his third and fourth terms
did not enact a new primary law, one can only infer that both
parties shied away from a reform which appeared to threaten
their organization.[112] In reconstructing the state government,
Smith registered at best a perfunctory interest in direct

democracy; he invested time and energy and made the greatest
gains in the area of efficiency and economy.

It is misleading to conclude, as some contemporary critics
and recent scholars have done, that reforms carried out in the
name of efficiency and economy were undemocratic. Centralization is not necessarily at odds with democracy, for the concentration of power that limits participation in decisions renders
the decision makers more readily accountable to the people at
the polls. Smith argued cogently that reconstruction would make
the executive more responsive to the voters at the same time
that it made him truly responsible for official action. His
models included parliamentary government as well as corporate
management. The experience of the 1970s with diffusion of
authority has gone far to discredit the conventional wisdom of
the 1960s that equated decentralization with effective democracy.
Before the apportionment decisions of the Warren court, the
state executive commonly represented the majority more faithfully than the legislature with its rotten boroughs. Since the
popular majorities that elected Smith and subsequent Democratic
governors could rarely convert their numerical preponderance
into legislative majorities, it can be maintained that a strong
executive operated as a democratizing rather than an elitist
force in New York. In Smith's case, as subsequent chapters will
demonstrate, he used power for that expansion of the public sector that characterizes the welfare state. Both reformers and
their critics have erred in attributing democracy to structural
forms when democratic government is as much a matter of will
as technique, of spirit as letter.

To bring about structural reform for efficiency and
economy, Smith took advantage of a schism in GOP ranks between
the "federal crowd" and state officials, between progressives
and the old guard. Stimson, Hughes, and Wickersham, who viewed
state politics with a certain detachment, supported Smith,
while Machold, Knight, and Morris obstructed as long as they
could measures that would lessen their power and interfere
with their patronage. The progressive Republicans who assisted

the governor were wary of partisanship, inclined to conceive of
politics as public service, and receptive to the theories of
public administration. Members of the GOP who overcame opposition within their own party combined with Democrats who followed
their governor to effect an essentially progressive reorienta-
tion of government in New York State.

Smith presided only one term over a reorganized administration. When Roosevelt governed New York, he benefited, not
only from consolidation, but also from the executive budget,
while Herbert H. Lehman enjoyed a four-year term after his last
campaign for governor.

In administrative reform, there was far greater continuity
between Governor Smith and President Roosevelt than either man
realized. The members of the President's Committee on Administrative Management were all professionals in public administration whose report to the president was based on progressive
theory. One of them, Luther Gulick, succeeded Charles A. Beard
as director of the training school of the New York Bureau of
Municipal Research, which had generated the reconstruction
program in the state. Federal as well as state plans aimed at
strengthening the executive and bringing under control a multi-
plicity of agencies, which had proliferated partly in response
to the exigencies of economic and social change. Among the
reforms that FDR salvaged from the initial defeat of his reorganization plan was the Executive Office of the President
which, with its goal of administrative and budgetary coordination, bore a strong resemblance to New York State's Executive
Department. Despite the common progressive origins of both
state and federal reorganization, FDR labored under a misconception when he announced, "We have got to get over the notion
that the purpose of reorganization is economy. I had that out
with Al Smith in New York. . . . The reason for reorganization
is good management."[113] Al Smith would not have disagreed.
A study of his fiscal policy will show that to him efficiency
meant the capacity to render service; economy, the elimination
of waste, not diminution of services.

CHAPTER 3

WAYS AND MEANS

One way to resolve the question of the democratic character of the efficiency economy movement is to explore its implications for public finance. In other words, what relationship
prevailed between the terms *efficiency* and *economy*? Did the
reformers conceive of efficiency as a tactic to achieve economy
by reducing government expenditures in order to save money for
middle class taxpayers, or as a process to enable government to
provide better service as a result of economies that counter-
acted wastefulness? In the latter instance, what services and
for whom?

If efficiency and economy were catchwords for retrenchment in the interest of the upper, and to the neglect of the
lower, classes, then the movement would merit the elitist reputation that Governor Smith disclaimed. In the ferment of the
1960s and early 1970s, scholars stressed the undemocratic tendencies in such manifestations of progressivism as government
reconstruction. In the view of Otis L. Graham, progressives
criticized urban government primarily for being "expensive and
immoral—and, quite probably, in that order," desired reform
"chiefly to reduce the taxes paid by property," and during the
1920s transferred their activities from the city to the state
level, for example, in the Smith administration. John D.
Buenker considered Smith something of an exception to the rule
of opposition to administrative reform among urban new stock
politicians who resisted changes that threatened to dry up the
funds on which they depended to meet the needs of the machine
and its constituency. Melvin G. Holli produced extensive evidence of the trimming of budgets—and services—by structural
reformers. On this basis, he contrasted social reform with
structural reform, which Buenker labelled patrician.[1]

The two categories of reform are not necessarily inconsistent as illustrated by the governorship of Alfred E. Smith
who was both a structural reformer and a social reformer.

Acknowledging that efficiency in municipal administration often
involved cutting taxes and appropriations, Martin J. Schiesl
explained that, in public finance, it "did not necessarily mean
economy at the sacrifice of social programs," and identified
a body of administrative reformers who believed "that fiscal
policy should be adjusted to the needs and wants of the urban
masses." Such an interpretation is confirmed by Jane S.
Dahlberg's study of the New York Bureau of Municipal Research
whose professionals "consistently stressed better service
rather than reduced expenditure."[2]

As these conflicting interpretations reveal, structural
reform laid a foundation for two different fiscal policies:
one, involving the contraction of budgets; and another, which
appealed to Smith, the expansion of social services. James T.
Crown, who equated centralization with the advance of democracy
in New York State, suggested that, for Smith as for the progressives, reconstruction was a prerequisite—not a hindrance—
to welfare policies. As he inaugurated a remodeled administration, Smith proclaimed, "The real test of its effectiveness
will not be the perfection of its functioning alone." He
wanted it to be "more than a machine for performing a routine."
"The reorganized government," he insisted, "must be able to
safeguard the health, living, working and business conditions
of all the people, and to care adequately for the unfortunates
who cannot care for themselves." On these things, he was unwilling to stint. In his autobiography, he reflected, "It is
a mistake to think that the people approve of reduced appropriations when in the process of reducing them the state or any
of its activities are to suffer. . . . there is a great difference between large appropriations and waste."[3]

During his legislative apprenticeship, Smith formed the
attitudes toward public finance on which he acted as chief
executive and which he defended in retirement. Under Governor
Hughes, budgets mounted and the public sector expanded in a
precedent that Smith would later follow. The progressive Re-

publican made a deep impression on the young assemblyman even
though the Democratic lawmakers attacked the administration for
its extravagance, a fact that one writer deemed "a better
commentary on that party's conservatism than the GOP's alleged
profligacy."[4] It was less a matter of ideology than a reflex
of a political minority trying to curry favor with the voters
by advocating tax reduction. During the Democratic regime of
the twenties, the criticism continued, but the parties reversed
their positions. The years in the legislature and on its Ways
and Means Committee familiarized the future executive with the
financial affairs of the state.

A decade of experience prompted Smith to propose to the
constitutional convention of 1915 the amendment of certain fiscal clauses dating to 1846. They had been inserted as a corrective to the financial indiscretion of the legislature of the
early nineteenth century. Since then the basic law had prescribed a referendum on all bond issues of more than a million
dollars, thereby giving the voters a veto over their representatives on the creation of substantial debt. The constitution
further restricted each statute for the issuance of bonds to a
"single work or object" in order to spare the electorate the
dilemma of approving an objectionable expenditure or turning
down a desirable one because of the inclusion of both in the
same bill. To stimulate informed consideration of these
matters, the article allowed the submission of only one such
statute at any general election.[5]

Smith urged the convention to liberalize article VII,
section 1, in order to facilitate essential institutional construction. For the word *work* he preferred to substitute the
more general term *purpose*. With this change, the bonds for
several projects could be approved at a single election, instead of at a series stretching over a period of many years.
He argued that "something will have to be done to bond the
State for the alteration, construction and repairs of existing
state hospitals and state institutions" and lamented that "We
have done so little to give the proper care and the proper

attention to the unfortunate people that it is the policy of the State
to take care of." The phrase that seemed to Smith an obstacle to progress appeared to Henry L. Stimson as a protection against meeting expenses by borrowing instead of taxing. The 1915 debate
anticipated the economic controversies of Smith's third term.[6]

    In light of his stand at the constitutional convention, it is
possible to predict Smith's position on public finance throughout his
governorship—but not during the New Deal. Consistent with his
utterances of 1915, during his administration, he supported five
bond measures that vastly increased the magnitude of the state debt.
    Smith's first term ended and his second began with a $45
million bond proposal to finance a bonus to World War I veterans.
Although he had not initiated it, he enthusiastically signed the
1920 bill to hold the required referendum. In the fall the voters
overwhelmingly approved the bonus at the same time that they
turned down the governor's bid for reelection. He was no longer
in office when the Court of Appeals held the measure to be unconstitutional, and its sponsors prepared to circumvent the decision by amending the state constitution.[7] His annual message
of 1923 favored the move, the legislature proposed, and the
voters ratified, an amendment to authorize the debt for the
bonus, which the judiciary had only temporarily frustrated. It
was one of the rare issues on which he found himself in opposition to his frequent allies, the City Club and the Citizens'
Union.[8] If his political instinct told him to back the bonus,
he also shared the sentiment of admiration for the defenders of
the country that made it popular with the electorate. As he
demonstrated at the constitutional convention and several times
in the executive chamber, Smith had no compunction at overriding
fiscal restraints for humanitarian ends.
    Well before the disaster that precipitated the flotation
of bonds for hospital construction, Smith had been sensitive to
the needs of the inmates. He raised with the Reconstruction
Commission of his first term the question that he had addressed

at the constitutional convention about the funding of institutions.[9] On his return to office, he commissioned a survey in
which the State Hospital Commission estimated the money needed
to eliminate overcrowding and fire hazards in its facilities for
the mentally ill. Meanwhile the New York Psychiatrical Society,
"depending on your demonstrated interests in the hospitals and
in the welfare work of the State," approached him with its urgent plea for more generous support, for the establishment of
additional units, and for a bond issue, if necessary to assure
a reliable source of revenue for this purpose. A fire, in
which both patients and employees of the Manhattan State Hospital lost their lives in February, 1923, led to the adoption of
measures that the doctors were recommending and Smith had been
contemplating. The day after the tragedy, he insisted that a
repetition must be prevented, "no matter how much it costs."[10]

Almost immediately the governor asked the legislature to
approve the creation of a state debt of at least $50 million to
finance new buildings. He anticipated no constitutional obstacle to erecting structures for various institutions with the
proceeds, since he defined housing of the state's wards as a
single work or object within the meaning of the document. Louis
Marshall, a prominent attorney, confirmed his opinion on the
constitutionality of the bonds, and the lawmakers passed a bill
to provide for the usual referendum.[11]

What began as an effort to persuade the electorate to vote
for the bonds had lasting consequences for the administration.
The chairman of the State Hospital Commission and the state
architect suggested to Smith an independent survey of the institutions in order, not only to convince the voters of the need
for the money, but also to assure them that it would be wisely
spent. The governor appealed for cooperation to the State
Charities Aid Association, which named a Citizens' Committee on
the Protection of the State's Unfortunates to handle both tasks.
The group campaigned effectively for the bonds before the election and supervised the allocation of the proceeds afterwards.
Smith did his part toward the proposition's overwhelming

victory by obtaining publicity in the *Subway Sun* and by speaking
out himself on the issue.[12]   George W. Wickersham, who chaired
the citizens' committee, and the association, which appointed
it, both praised the governor for his efforts before and after
the referendum.   By his retirement, he could point with pride
to several new hospitals and two psychiatric institutes in
varying stages of completion as well as additions to older
institutions as the fruit of the 1923 bonds.[13]   Furthermore,
the citizens' committee, which contributed so much to the
success of the work, set a precedent of involvement by nonpartisan groups of prestigious laymen to which Smith would
return in the funding of state parks and in the fight for the
larger bond issues of his third term.

The decision to sponsor in 1923 legislation on bonds for
state institutions postponed for a year authorization of a debt
for parks.   Shortly after his reelection in 1922, Smith conferred with leaders of the New York State Association about the
proposal in its brochure, *A State Park Plan for New York*, to
finance development with a $15 million bond issue.   Robert
Moses, who drafted the publication, arranged the meeting.   As
a result, a bill for park bonds was introduced with bipartisan
sponsorship early in the 1923 session.[14]   But the fire on Ward's
Island prompted Smith to urge deferral of this measure to allow
that for hospitals.   "As only one bond issue proposal may be
submitted to the voters next fall," he explained to the legislature, "it is clear to me that the park bond issue proposal
should be postponed in favor of the bond issue for State
hospitals and institutions."   Moses preferred a reversal of
priorities, which probably gave rise to the vignette of him
delivering a harangue on parks while the governor slid lower
and lower in his chair until he disappeared under the desk.[15]

Despite the year's delay, Smith's commitment to the state
park plan was unwavering.   In 1924, nothing interfered with the
routine progress of the park bonds: from the governor's message,
to legislative enactment, to executive approval, and finally
to adoption on election day by a majority of nearly a million,

the largest ever accorded such a proposition up to that
time.[16]

No controversy impeded the authorization of bonds for the
bonus, hospitals, and parks during Smith's second term at a
time when state finance aroused political passion. Politicians
debated the budget with much heat but little reference to the
question of indebtedness. They argued not in economic, but in
moralistic, language over who was wasting and who was saving the
taxpayers' money. This subject first became an issue in the
campaign of 1922 when both candidates had served one term and
their records invited comparison.

During Smith's first administration, the state budget had
shown an increase, which scholars now recognize as representative of a general trend. In an effort to stem the tide, Smith,
like Hughes before him, vetoed countless items of appropriation
such as pork barrel and special claims bills, which legislators
introduce in deference to their constituents but with the
expectation—if not the intent—that the executive will safeguard the public treasury. He alluded to these matters each
year after adjournment when he clarified his economic philosophy
in those annual financial summaries that would become a hallmark
of his career. In many instances, he explained, he was powerless to curtail waste that was vetoproof when incorporated in
appropriations for essential activities. Here he put in a plug
for the executive budget and reorganization as correctives to
such governmental extravagance. The governor did not however,
equate economy with budget cutting, for he justified rising
expenditures to improve the quality of institutional care,
education, and protective labor regulation. "I am entirely convinced," he maintained, "that the people of the State expect an
increase in the cost of government proportionate with the increases along every other line of endeavor. . . ."[17]

The GOP interpreted the will of the people differently,
for its 1922 platform ranked governmental economy first among
the issues and took pride in "living within our means." The

campaign document accused Smith of having accelerated the increase in government expenses and praised Miller for reversing
the trend. In a Cooper Union address, the Republican incumbent
claimed credit for reducing appropriations and taxes and for
increasing the surplus, all without neglecting vital services;
he criticized his challenger for improvidence and an administration that had indulged a "lust to spend." In a number of
appearances, Governor Miller maintained that he had economized
without the structural reforms that Smith was promoting as an
excuse for his extravagance under the existing forms of administration.[18]

Smith, in turn, charged his successor with using the financial issue as a coverup for his defeat of government reconstruction, which alone could produce lasting economies. The
Democratic platform charged Miller with manipulating the
accounts to conceal the actual cost of his administration, and
the Democratic candidate quipped, "figures don't lie, but liars
figure," and asked ingenuously, "If the Governor saved
$14,000,000 where is it?" Not apparent in tax reduction, Smith
implied. Whatever savings Miller accumulated were at the expense of government operations, particularly of the state
hospitals. Hardly a creditable record of economizing, Smith
observed on his upstate tour.[19]

In view of GOP campaign rhetoric, Smith bridled with indignation at the condition of state finances upon his resumption of office in 1923. "I will show by facts and figures that
the attempt at a record of economy on the part of the last
administration is . . . responsible for the size of the appropriations this year," he announced over the radio in June.
Because of Republican parsimony, his own budget was artificially
inflated: with items to make up for the neglect of institutions
and services and with deficiency appropriations (necessary when
the budget of the previous session proves insufficient to support an operation to the end of the fiscal year). "There is
no economy in deferring appropriations. There is no economy in
making inadequate appropriations. There is no economy in

neglecting the known wants of the State."[20]

With these remarks, the stage was set for the contest of 1924, at least in public finance, to be a virtual replay of 1922, with a substitute for one of the earlier principals. Theodore Roosevelt, Jr. excoriated the Democrats who "spend the people's money like water" and their governor who undertook activities regardless of expense. To the incumbent, Republican economy exhibited a callous disregard of human values and urgent needs.[21]

Mutual recriminations obscured a philosophic difference between the parties. The GOP concentrated on the reduction of appropriations. Smith emphasized the adequate funding of state activities. They differed on what constituted appropriate governmental functions, with the governor attributing to the state responsibilities that his opponents preferred to overlook. Both parties wanted credit for the reduction of taxes. But then as now, tax lifting often meant tax shifting, and each organization tried to shift the burden and incidence of taxation from the shoulders of its own constituency. If the clash of interest and ideology becomes clear in retrospect, it was not fully articulate to the politicians who disputed New York's finances during the twenties.

They made an issue of the income tax, for example, without really exploring its social consequences. During their return engagement, Miller implied that Smith's profligacy had necessitated the imposition of the levy.[22] Campaign addresses hardly constitute the most reliable source for economic history, and the Republican's were no exception.

In New York as elsewhere, the state income tax originated in the solution of scholars and reformers to the problems of a maturing economy. Industrialization and urbanization were creating new demands for governmental services while the tax structure failed to produce sufficient revenue. Because of inequities and massive evasion, the general tax on real and personal property rarely yielded enough to meet the rising cost of state and local government. The state income tax offered a

source of revenue that was at once adequate and equitable. Devised by experts in economics, based on the canon of ability to
pay, and collected by a centralized administration, it promised
to furnish the wherewithal to meet the requirements of both the
poor and the middle class for service. In genesis and in
theory, the income tax rose out of the same impulses that led
to the efficiency economy movement in government.[23]

It was however fortuitous that New York began to tax personal incomes during Smith's first administration. Economists
had been agitating for income taxation during the progressive
era when he sat in the assembly. When Prohibition deprived the
state treasury of excises on liquor, the income tax drive culminated in the corporate franchise tax of 1917, the proposals
of a legislative committee of 1918, and the personal income tax
law of 1919. In that year the State Tax Commission, in its
annual report, recommended the levy, legislative hearings on it
attracted surprisingly little attention, and the bill passed
under an emergency message from the governor. Only after receiving a firm commitment of Republican support that would remove the measure from the political arena, did he send the message required when the legislators lacked a final text in print
three days before taking action. Bipartisanship reflected a progressive consensus on the income tax, which a GOP lawmaker
sponsored, a GOP legislature enacted, and a Democratic governor
signed. The 1919 law set the following rates: 1 percent on
the first $10,000 of personal income, 2 percent on the next
$40,000, and 3 percent on everything above $50,000; it established the following exemptions: $1,000 for a single taxpayer,
$2,000 for a married couple, and $200 for each dependent.[24]

The legislative history of the first New York income tax
reveals little consideration being given to the long-range consequences of progressive taxation, especially to its potentiality for the redistribution of wealth. When Governor Smith
inaugurated the activities of the Income Tax Bureau in 1919,
he demonstrated that he was familiar with the ideas of the progressives behind the tax and more sensitive than they to its

political, if not its social, implications. He expected it to
become "a real live issue," and predicted, "The size of the
personal tax will become a matter of political campaign argument."[25]

Not until 1924, did the income tax become a political
football, as Smith had forecast. In 1923, the tax was lowered
without fanfare by the device of raising the level of exemptions.[26] The following year, he proposed tax relief in the form
of a 25 percent across-the-board cut in the personal income
tax. His annual message "was publicly received by the Republican leaders with acclaim and privately referred to in un-
printable language," he recalled in his autobiography. The GOP
preferred to reduce real estate taxes, which bore more heavily
upon its rural strongholds. Henry Morgenthau, Jr., publisher
of the *American Agriculturist*, explained to Smith that his tax
cut "may help city taxpayers. It will not help farmers. . . .
few farmers have taxable incomes, and farmers are in dire need
of tax relief." Urban Republicans like Martin Saxe supported
Smith's proposal; Columbia University's E. R. A. Seligman, the
leading academic in the initial drive for income taxation,
opposed it, for he wanted to eliminate the statewide property
tax instead. A conference between the governor and the legislative leaders produced a compromise: a 25 percent decrease in
both the levy on personal incomes and on real and personal
property.[27] In the gubernatorial campaign that followed, Smith
attributed Republican hesitation over the income tax slash to
a partisan desire to deprive a Democratic governor of the political capital to be gained by such a move. In effect, each
party favored relief for a different constituency, and both
groups benefited. The chief executive submitted the cuts as
evidence of his economical management.[28]

The financial record on which Smith prided himself was
vigorously challenged after his reelection. In 1925, a conflict on economic policy brought together the distinct but related subjects of economy, tax rates, and indebtedness. As a

result, New Yorkers enjoyed from spring to autumn the spectacle
of a continuous debate on public finance, which sporadically
attained a level of distinction in the articulate exposition of
intricate matter.

Much of the animus in the 1925 dispute centered on two
constitutional amendments, which passed without controversy in
the 1924 session and attracted no attention in the gubernatorial
election that year. One had as its purpose grade crossing
elimination, a subject of deep concern to Smith because of the
growing number of fatalities. Before embarking on his second
term, the governor-elect had consulted the New York State Association; it eventually concluded that long-term planning was
essential and that the state should loan to localities and rail-
roads the money for their share of the expense of grade crossing
elimination. Otherwise, the association feared inordinate delay. The recommendations involved two distinct propositions:
a referendum on bonds and a constitutional amendment to permit
the government to make the loans. Smith and his advisers decided to combine the bonding and lending measures in a single
amendment to the constitution. The new article, with provision
for $300 million worth of bonds from the proceeds of which the
state would defray its own costs in grade crossing removal and
make loans for the rest, received its first legislative approval
just before adjournment in 1924.[29]

At the same time that it passed the grade crossing measure,
the legislature adopted a concurrent resolution to amend the
constitution to permit the issuance over a ten-year period, at
the rate of $10 million a year, of $100 million worth of bonds
for construction. Obviously this proposal was embodied in a
constitutional amendment in order to circumvent the constitutional provision restricting each bond statute to a single work
or object. The amendment was formulated at a conference between
Smith and two Republican assembly leaders. Its bipartison origins account for the failure of any message from the governor
or debate by the lawmakers to mark its legislative progress in
1924.[30] Whatever Smith's precise responsibility for the reso-

lution, it coincided with sentiments that he had expressed almost a decade earlier at the constitutional convention.

The governor's annual message of 1925 reviewed his understanding of public finance. He explained that bond proceeds
would distribute the burden of capital expenditures among the
beneficiaries of durable projects while tax revenues should
cover operating expenses. In the spirit of this philosophy, he
advocated approval of the bond amendments initiated at the previous session and continuation of its reduced tax rates because
of a surplus in the current account.[31]

A bitter conflict over the propriety of tax reduction
marked the last month of the 1925 session. It began with a
dramatic move by the governor—a special message, asking the
legislature to recess so that he could confer with its leaders.
The time was running out for executive action on certain appropriation bills, and he wanted them to be recalled and trimmed
in order to make a tax cut feasible. After two meetings
generated nothing but recriminations, with the Republicans
charging that Smith was indulging in "grandstand plays," they
declined to attend a third. The governor then took his case
directly to the people in a radio talk in which he accused his
opponents of padding appropriations in a partisan effort to
undermine his popularity by blocking tax reduction.[32] The
address produced its intended effect. Letters in support of
the governor poured into the Capitol. GOP assemblymen, who
had to stand for reelection annually, sought relief from a
political liability by exerting pressure on the organization to
make concessions. As a result, the majority agreed to go along
with the tax cut if Smith balanced the budget by vetoing appropriations of sufficient magnitude. He denounced the hypocrisy
of the Republicans who claimed to be the party of economical
administration but were "now trying to find every possible excuse for spending the State's money so as to prevent a reduction
in the State income tax." It was now their turn to indict him
for false economy, which must entail neglect of vital government operations. They found no fat that could be trimmed from

the budget. "Nobody is so blind as the man who does not want
to see," Smith retorted as he promised, ". . . I will show them
how to do it."[33]

The chief executive proceeded to list what he deemed un-
justifiable debits in the legislative balance sheet. His deletions included: patronage expenditures on unnecessary positions
and unmerited raises; pork barrel appropriations, particularly
in the record outlay for highways, some designed to produce
votes rather than transportation; and items anticipating the
future with funds for claims not yet settled and programs not
ready to begin. He proposed to halve the amount for indemnities
for tubercular cattle and rationalized the resort to deficiency
appropriations for the second half of the fiscal year on the
grounds that the next session would not be faced with the large
onetime expenses of 1925 and that the period to be covered by
the deficiency appropriations would be only six months—not two
years, as in the Miller administration. Smith also wanted to
remove items for construction and grade crossing elimination as
capital improvements that he planned to finance with the proceeds from the pending bonds. By cutting the budget as he outlined, it would be possible to reduce the income tax without
either impeding essential services or creating a deficit in the
current account.[34]

With considerable reluctance, the GOP acceded to Smith's
plan for cutting appropriations and taxes. Lieutenant Governor
Seymour Lowman expressed his party's skepticism in a radio
address in which he accused his superior of indulging in leger-
demain to conceal the levies necessitated by extravagance:
"He suggests bond issues. . . . deferring until next year appropriations that should be made this year. . . . any thing that
will put off the evil day." Nevertheless, the Republicans cooperated by lowering some appropriations, and Smith vetoed others.
As a result, income and real estate tax rates remained at the
level of 1924.[35] One factor in GOP recalcitrance was a preference for the alternative of affording greater relief to real
estate than to income taxpayers. Smith got the better of his

opponents by the compromise and by his skill in manipulating—
if not in managing—finances. In a broadcast on the budget,
Assemblyman Trubee Davison decried the governor's maneuvers as
"tax shifting" instead of "tax lifting." The chairman of the
Committee on Taxation predicted a deficit as a consequence and
exposed the inconsistency of cutting taxes and floating bonds
at the same time.[36]

If the contestants concentrated their rhetoric on the
politically sensitive issue of taxation, they did occasionally,
like Davison, juxtapose the subjects of taxes and bonds. It
will be recalled that Smith proposed to balance the budget in
part by deleting items for capital outlays, which he preferred
to finance by borrowing. His opponents, on the other hand,
maneuvered to deplete the surplus available for income tax reduction by increasing the appropriations, and shelving the
bonds, for grade crossings. For this purpose, the GOP devised
certain delaying tactics: a joint committee to investigate the
matter of grade crossing elimination, an alternative amendment,
which could not take effect until several years after the one
approved in 1924. When Smith prodded the lawmakers to pass it
a second time, they hedged by adopting both texts. This meant
that the original amendment for grade crossing elimination
bonds would appear on the November ballot along with one for a
public works debt, which passed again without controversy in
the 1925 session, and another for administrative reorganization.[37]

Shortly after adjournment, State Chairman George K. Morris
described all three constitutional changes as organization
measures and predicted "no organized opposition from the Republicans to either of the two proposals for bond issues."[38] The
previous chapter has disclosed the more or less covert efforts
of conservative Republicans to defeat at the polls the reconstruction resolution that their progressive colleagues favored.
Greater unity characterized the GOP position on public finance.
During the spring and summer as the Republicans reviewed the
budgetary actions of the past legislature, they veered more and

more into a posture of opposition, particularly on the debt for
public improvements.

The GOP reversal on the $100 million bonds became apparent
in May during a debate between Smith and Ogden L. Mills at New
York City's Economic Club. The Republican congressman opened
by contending, "There is no economy in reducing taxes by
borrowing to meet recurring expenditures." He charged the
governor with financial irresponsibility: excessive spending,
unwarranted lowering of taxes, and borrowing to meet the inevitable deficit. Tax relief now would only add to the burden of
future generations, which would have to retire the debt and pay
interest upon it. Smith construed Mills's remarks to mean that
"there are two kinds of tax reduction, Republican tax reduction,
which is apparently all right and Democratic tax reduction, not-
withstanding that it reduces, is apparently all wrong." The
chief executive denied the allegations that Democratic tax reduction would lead to a deficit and that the bonds were a device
to balance the budget. According to him, history proved that
under a pay-as-you-go policy, the government's physical plant
suffered neglect, as for example at the Saratoga Spa where the
state was adding fifteen bathtubs a year! Without the continuing commitment which bonds represented, it was impossible
to plan essential capital improvements.[39]

The debate signified a realignment on the public improvement bonds, and each side began to mobilize its forces for the
campaign ahead. With the 1923 Citizens' Committee on the Protection of the State's Unfortunates as a model, Smith intended
to establish a similar committee to work for the adoption of the
$100 million bond amendment and to oversee the allocation of
its proceeds. He therefore invited a group of prominent individuals to an organization meeting on June 2. When it was
abruptly cancelled the day before, on account of the governor's
illness, rumors circulated that he was embarrassed by the number of declinations. If embarrassment was the real reason behind Smith's sudden change of plan, the difficulty came less
from the refusals that he received than from the invitation

that he extended—at their request—to Ogden L. Mills and
Nathan L. Miller to join the gathering in order to speak for
the opposition. The governor subsequently withdrew his invitation to the two Republicans with the explanation that he had
called the meeting, not to consider the wisdom of the amendment,
but to form a committee for its ratification. At the same time
he offered to engage each of them in public debate on the merits
of the proposal.[40]

    During the course of the negotiations, party lines soli-
dified. In addition to Mills and Miller, Root and Stimson participated in the GOP assault on the amendment. The latter took
the trouble personally to explain his objections to Smith. "Now
I have unbosomed myself of my differences with you. I am sorry
to have them come up for I agree with so much that you do and
have such a respect for your character and courage in public
life," he assured the governor. Their disagreement would not,
moreover, interfere with the Republican's support of reorganization and the executive budget. On fiscal matters, both men
were adhering to principles that they had formulated at least
as early as the constitutional convention. Stimson was typical
of the progressive Republicans who backed Smith on government
reconstruction but not on public finance. On the other hand,
the governor enjoyed the support of prominent Democrats such
as Joseph P. Tumulty and Congressman Emanuel Celler, who compared Mills to a chameleon, changing his colors to condemn in
New York the economic policies that he espoused in Washington.
When the coalition that was facilitating government reform disintegrated on the bond proposal, Smith attributed the Republican
defection to political partisanship. Since the GOP could not
disavow reorganization without a split in its own ranks and
opposition to the grade crossing debt would prove fatal in the
event of a spectacular accident, the remaining public works
amendment became the most available campaign issue.[41]

    Publication of the annual statement in which Smith de-
fended his fiscal record led to an exchange with Mills and
Miller over the question. The governor repeated his earlier

complaint that the legislative majority had deliberately inflated the appropriation bill in order to forestall income tax
reduction. "Nothing has been omitted," he assured the electorate, ". . . that cannot be well taken care of at the beginning of the next session from the increased income of the State
without necessitating a single dollar of increased taxation
unless the people . . . reject the proposal to bond the State
. . . for permanent improvements." To Mills, this sounded like
an admission of willingness "to use bond money for current
deficits." Nothing could be further from the truth, according
to the chief executive who reminded his opponents that the constitutional amendment originated in 1924, a year before the
budget that they were claiming it was supposed to balance. The
state was not in the red, but in the black, he insisted. In the
course of epistolary combat in which the politicians accused
each other of falsifying the fiscal condition of the government,
they were making arrangements for the two debates which would
instruct the voters of New York in public finance.[42]

Although Smith was unusually well informed on the state's
financial affairs, with which he had acquired familiarity
during his service on the Assembly Ways and Means Committee, he
prepared carefully for the debates. He undoubtedly relied upon
the work of experts for the theories that he presented and the
data with which he substantiated them.[43]

Carnegie Hall was filled on July 9 for the Smith-Miller
debate, to which an estimated 1.5 million listeners tuned in on
the radio. Charles Evans Hughes introduced the speakers with
the observation that "So long as governors and ex-governors
debate, the State is safe." The incumbent led off with a cata-
logue of pressing needs to be met with the proceeds from the
bonds. He explained the tendency of politicians to court popularity with low appropriations, resulting in the failure to
undertake necessary construction or the even more wasteful
practice of neglecting to complete projects once they were
started. The former governor minimized the unmet needs and
anticipated an endless trail of debt from circumvention of the

constitutional provision for a referendum on each project. He
criticized the amendment as a catchall to induce the voters to
approve questionable items in order to avoid the rejection of
valuable programs. Smith argued that the constitutional restraints, which his opponent so venerated, had not been intended to straightjacket the legislature, for they exempted from
the referendum requirement debts of up to a million dollars, a
not inconsiderable sum in the mid nineteenth century. Miller
exposed the inconsistency between Smith's reliance on the
legislature for wise allocation of the bond revenues and his
distrust of it, on which the executive budget reform was predicated. When the Republican cited him in support of pay-as-
you-go, the governor complained that the passage was taken out
of context. It was like quoting the Bible to vindicate suicide.
Just "turn to one page . . . and at the top it says, 'And Judas
went out and hanged himself.' And then grab a lot of pages and
turn them over, and . . . you will find, 'And Christ said to the
multitude, "Go thou and do likewise."'" Smith favored pay-as-
you-go only for operating, not for capital, expenses. In the
end, he was confident that he had prevailed over Miller.[44]

Many Republicans must have concurred in this evaluation,
despite the fact that their party was closing ranks against
Smith on the bonds. The state chairman who had previously
claimed for the organization proud paternity of the two amendments now abandoned them to the stigma of illegitimacy. Although he objected to indebtedness on principle, Morris singled
out the public works bonds as "especially unsound." Mills experienced misgivings about the contest and wished to divert the
governor's attention from the bonds to reorganization. The
congressman received little encouragement from the titular head
of the Democratic party, the financially conservative John W.
Davis, who defined the issue in terms of necessity and proposed
"to take the word of the executive" on that question.[45]

To demonstrate need, the chief executive relied on the
Citizens' Committee to Support the Public Works Amendment. He
had originally contemplated three such organizations, one to

campaign for each amendment on the ballot.[46] But the Hughes
commission preempted the subject of reorganization, and the
absence of overt opposition obviated any activity on the grade
crossing measure. Only a month before election day, did the
governor reactivate the group whose first meeting had been so
abruptly cancelled in June when the $100 million bond proposal
became controversial. The citizens' committee, which included
among its members two of Smith's successors, FDR and Herbert H.
Lehman, as well as the redoubtable Belle Moskowitz and the ubiquitous Robert Moses, engaged primarily in a public relations
effort. Its pamphlet, *Plain Facts about the Permanent Public
Works Constitutional Amendment*, with an introductory statement
by the governor, contained an itemized schedule of projects,
which enabled him to contend that the bond revenues would be
wisely spent.[47] *Plain Facts* incorporated data from studies
that had been circulating in the administration, on the governor's initiative.[48] In addition to his own citizens' committee,
Smith enlisted the support of the Citizens' Union and the New
York State Association for the public improvement bonds.[49]

On October 22 in Buffalo, Smith came in person to the defense of the bonds in his third public debate of the campaign,
and his second with Mills, over fiscal policy. As usual, the
governor pointed out the needs unfulfilled under pay-as-you-go
and matched that slogan with another, "we do not pay and we do
not go." His opponent, conceding for the sake of argument,
what in fact he challenged, the urgent need for construction,
questioned the wisdom of going into debt to pay for it. How
absurd to borrow and to reduce taxes simultaneously. To Smith
it was paradoxical that the congressman, who in June had condemned the administration for resorting to bonds to conceal a
deficit, in October was suggesting payment for public works out
of a surplus whose magnitude he now acknowledged. Mills objected to borrowing in general because of the added cost of
interest and to the public works amendment in particular because
of its evasion of the normal referendum process with a separate
vote on each project. Giving the legislature a blank check

would only encourage pork barrel and logrolling with borrowed
funds, for no list of projects, however distinguished its pedi-
gree, was binding. According to Smith, the interest charges
would be far less than the losses to the state in unfinished
work and repairs to structures that required replacement. He
justified the constitutional amendment as a unique expedient
to meet an emergency resulting from cumulative neglect.[50]

Between the third debate and election day, the GOP took
advantage of its legislative majority in an effort to undermine
the governor's position. A Special Joint Committee on Taxation
and Retrenchment made a preliminary report on *The Debt of the
State of New York*. The report pretended neutrality on the bond
amendments, and its text offered a well balanced presentation
of both sides of the question. But the timing of the report,
the refusal of Democratic members of the committee to concur in
it, and the tenor of the press release upon its publication, all
contributed to the impression that it aimed to influence the
voters against the amendments. The Joint Legislative Committee
on Grade Crossings staged a hearing on October 27, an opportune
date for testimony inimical to a debt for grade crossing elimination.[51]

The month before the election, Smith spent in countering
Republican attacks and taking positive steps to assure the
success of the bonds. He addressed such diverse groups as the
Westchester County Bankers Association and the City Club of New
York. Upstate and down, he campaigned for the bonds and reorganization, while in the city he also supported the candidacy
of James J. Walker for mayor. Those who seconded the governor's
efforts included State Architect Sullivan Jones, who engaged in
a debate over which Eleanor Roosevelt presided, Owen D. Young
of General Electric, and onetime State Treasurer Addison B.
Colvin, who characterized the propositions' opponents as "just
as well qualified to write about the Commandments—all ten of
them, as they are to discourse on the Amendments."[52] Meanwhile,
the chief executive persuaded the publisher of the *New York
Times* to give space to a feature article to be written by the

state tax commissioner. "What State Bond Issue Would Cost Taxpayers" by Mark Graves appeared appropriately on November 1.[53]

Smith and his supporters based their arguments on a
variety of assumptions that their opponents did not share. He
concentrated on the state's needs and the historic failure to
meet them out of tax revenues because of the politicians' reflex
to accord highest priority to tax reduction. The Republicans
started out by minimizing the deficiencies in the physical
plant and ended up by criticizing indebtedness as an expedient
to overcome them. On the other hand, the governor distinguished
between operating expenses, which should be defrayed from tax
monies, and capital expenses for what he categorized as *permanent* improvements, which should be funded by bonds in order to
distribute more equitably the burden of paying for them. Those
who insisted on pay-as-you-go acknowledged no such distinction.
Since his administration experienced no difficulty in amortizing
and paying interest on the outstanding debt, Smith never clearly
recognized that, carried to its logical conclusion, his practice
could entail deficit finance. If, on occasion, his critics
conceded the validity of issuing bonds, they deplored the proposal on the ballot for circumventing the constitutional language on a single work or object. As long as he held office,
Smith succumbed, neither to the idolization of the constitution,
nor to the economic orthodoxy, that prevailed in the twenties.

Relying on conservatism to defeat the bonds upstate, the
Republicans placed their hopes on reducing the size of Smith's
majority in New York City where Democratic politicians concentrated on getting out the vote. His native city carried both
amendments for the governor: the grade crossing bonds winning
by a vote of 1,032,109 to 859,702; the public works bonds by a
closer margin of 960,385 to 937,990. In New York City 637,920
voters supported the latter amendment while 344,931 opposed it.
Rejoicing in the results of the referendum on the bonds and reorganization, Smith observed that it "provided for a better
state government, for the educational needs of the state and
for . . . the poor, the sick and the afflicted committed to

its care. It was a great day for the State of New York."[54]

It was also a great day for the Republican party, in the mind of Ogden Mills. In the closeness of the race, he perceived an indication of Smith's vulnerability on which the GOP could capitalize in the year ahead.[55] As its gubernatorial candidate in 1926, he revived the fiscal controversy of the earlier year. On this issue, Smith again triumphed over the man who subsequently served Republican presidents as undersecretary and secretary of the treasury.

Governor Smith never hesitated to disregard the conventional wisdom in economics when it threatened to interfere with his humanitarian instinct. He concentrated on the purpose of government expenditures rather than the magnitude, which distressed his Republican critics. In the midst of his presidential campaign, he published *Progress of Public Improvements* with a survey by a committee of his cabinet and an introduction in which he defended bond financing as the only way to overcome the shameful neglect of state institutions. He affirmed his belief in his fiscal policy in the privacy of his cabinet where he disclosed an expedient, even more radical than he was ready to advocate in public. What he had been contemplating was a constitutional amendment to dispense altogether with the requirement for a referendum on indebtedness for charitable and penal institutions. He reasoned that the state treasury needed no protection in the case of these facilities on which everyone was reluctant to spend money. An awareness of the growth in the institutional population combined with a compassion for the inmates to convince Smith of the advisability of loosening the financial restraints that were impeding humane care.[56]

Many strands of administration policy converged in the cabinet to which Smith confessed his financial heresy. The cabinet, which was itself an outgrowth of government reconstruction, provided in the case of the hospital, public works, and grade crossing, bonds the coordination and oversight that the efficiency economy movement anticipated from reorganization.

The official family devoted more time to the construction projects than to any other items recorded in the minutes. His department heads shared the governor's humanitarian impulse,
which lay behind the funding of this work as well as behind
programs on housing and labor. For example, the commissioner
of corrections, in a review of prison construction, considered
the role of the environment in the rehabilitation of convicts.
"We should turn them out, as you have often said," he reminded
his superior, "in as good condition, or better, than when they
went in."[57]

In a recent study of the treatment of deviance in progressive America, David J. Rothman has examined the reform
movement that was the source of Governor Smith's policies on
mental illness and crime. Conscience generated the demand for
reform, and complacency in the validity of the social sciences
dictated its direction. For each case, professionals should
make a diagnosis and prescribe treatment, in an obvious analogy
to medical practice. In criminology, this required greater
reliance on probation, parole, and most of all, on the indeterminate sentence. The reformers wanted to revamp the prisons on
the model of the outside to allow them to serve as schools
where antisocial behavior would be discarded and conformity to
societal norms learned. By implementing their program, they
were confident that "the needs of justice and the aims of
therapy, the welfare of the individual and the security of
society would be satisfied." In the handling of convicts, as
in the regulation of industry, progressives experienced few
qualms about extending the discretionary authority of the state.
It did not occur to them that the convenience of the system
might take precedence over the conscience of its critics to
produce arrangements more repressive and cruel than those they
were condemning.[58]

If Smith was blind to the abuses that could occur in the
name of penal reform, they eluded minds far more sophisticated
than his. He was in complete sympathy with the idealism of the
reformers and deferred as usual to professional opinion. He,

therefore, committed his governorship to extensive reform based
on progressive theories of rehabilitation.[59]

Early in his first term, Governor Smith appointed a Prison
Survey Committee to do the kind of research that progressives
so frequently used as a basis for action. When the committee
exposed deficiencies in the prisons' physical setup, it reinforced the chief executive's conclusions on the necessity of
bond financing for the institutional plant. The committee's
proposal for a department of corrections coincided nicely with
his plans for administrative reorganization. The prison survey
thus complemented Smith's policies on government reconstruction
and public finance. The report was predicated on the assumption
that reformation was the primary purpose of incarceration and
concentrated on productive labor as the most important means to
this end. As a result of the investigation, the following
recommendations were made: classification of prisoners, vocational education, full-time employment, payment of wages, and
most significantly, performance at work as a key factor in
setting a date for release under the indeterminate sentence.
The Prison Survey Committee, which helped to make the Smith
administration a landmark in penal reform, reported too late
for him to act on its conclusions before the expiration of his
first term.[60]

When he returned to office in 1923, the governor took the
initiative that culminated in the enactment of prison reform in
his second term. The legislature cooperated by funding another
study to supplement the work of the Prison Survey Committee.
The law that resulted in 1924 provided for the productive
employment of prisoners, the payment of compensation to them,
and the use of work records in making decisions on parole.[61]
Professionals in the field approved the measure, which Smith
characterized as "the most progressive step in prison legislation ever taken in this State."[62]

In Smith's third term, administrative reform rendered
more effective the earlier legislation for the rehabiliation
of criminals. The State Reorganization Commission fulfilled

the governor's expectations for the unification of all penal
functions in a Department of Corrections.[63] In this way, a
measure of prison reform emerged as a consequence of the reconstruction of the state government.

New York during the Smith administration was typical of
progressive states, which simultaneously adopted humanitarian
and get-tough policies on crime. The latter originated in part
out of the pervasive fear of a crime wave, which was as much
the product of sensational reporting as of the reality of the
situation. Rothman has resolved the paradox of leniency and
severity in a number of ways: judges manifested a class differ-
ential in the sentencing of middle and lower class offenders;
professionals in the criminal justice system coopted reform and
distorted it to suit their own convenience; and most significantly, reformers could not complain of lengthened imprisonment
which, in the case of presumed incorrigibles, carried to a
logical conclusion the principle of individualization in treatment.[64]

When a friend entreated him to assume in the suppression
of crime the leadership that he had demonstrated in administrative reform and low-cost housing, the governor placed his reliance on research. Senator Caleb Baumes presided over two inquiries, the first by a legislative committee that was completing a study on revision of the criminal code when the chief
executive suggested cooperation by the two branches of government in a comprehensive probe of the problem of crime. The
reports of both committees resulted in 1926 and 1927 in a rash
of legislation that gave priority to the interest of the community in law and order over the civil rights of the accused.
Some of the enactments modified judicial procedure to make it
easier to obtain a conviction; others placed constraints on the
granting of probation and parole. The general tendency was to
increase the incidence and length of incarceration, most
notably—or notoriously—in the Baumes Law mandating life imprisonment for habitual offenders.[65]

Smith, whose compassion for the outcast never interfered with his sense of responsibility for the protection of society, resented, in the joint legislative committee's report, the implications that he had shown undue leniency in the exercise of the pardoning power. He moved immediately to set the record straight in a statement in which he at once corrected in detail the misconceptions and attributed them to the partisanship of a GOP majority intent on the campaign ahead.[66]

To counter any negative impact of the report on his own political prospects, Smith appointed George W. Alger, a member of the Prison Survey Committee and of the New York State Association's prison committee, to conduct a Moreland Act investigation into the management of parole and penal institutions in the state. The Moreland Act, which was a legacy from the Hughes administration, contributed to the enhancement of the executive by conferring upon it investigatory authority usually confined to the legislature. The decision to launch the 1926 inquiry came at a time when sensational revelations about Izzy Presser, a parolee with a record of crimes and prison escapes, appeared to reinforce the legislative findings. It was also an opportune moment to improve penal administration in conjunction with the reorganization of the state government. Alger's reports repeated the Prison Survey Committee's recommendations on classification and employment of inmates, favored bond financing of prison facilities, and criticized the practice of granting parole after only the most perfunctory consideration. The study led to the return of Presser to prison, the resignation of the commissioner of corrections whom Smith had originally appointed on the advice of the eminent criminologist, Thomas Mott Osborne, and a change in the administration of parole.[67]

The governor waxed indignant over an exposé of the abuses of parole in *World's Work* for March, 1927 by a consultant to Baumes's New York State Crime Commission. In "Turning the Criminals Loose: Soft Hearts and Hard Yeggs Have Afflicted These New United States with a Great National Plague of Crime," Lawrence Veiller combined sensationalism with an interesting

comparison of American and British practice. Smith protested
to the editor the many distortions in the piece and particularly
the reference to the case of "Bum" Rodgers whose sentence he had
commuted. The governor had been acting at the request of the
trial judge, he wrote, "and I think you will agree with me that
record or no record, the man should not remain in prison if
there is any doubt in the mind of the judge . . . as to his
guilt." In addressing the editor, Smith was dignified and convincing. With "Dear Larry," he showed less restraint in terming
the composition "as complete a crackpot article as I ever
read" and denouncing it for besmirching his reputation with "a
lot of nonsense that has no foundation in fact." When the
journal printed his rebuttal, insiders considered it sound and
praised the governor for his record in criminal justice.[68]

Many experts hastened to commend the governor later in
the year, after his appearance before the crime commission. His
testimony at the hearing revealed his familiarity with professional opinion on probation, parole, and the indeterminate
sentence. In the course of his remarks, he proposed to take
sentencing out of the hands of the judges and entrust it to a
board of professionals, in a radical departure from traditional
practice. The plan, which conformed to progressive ideology,
appealed to academicians like the historian, Harry Elmer Barnes,
who apprised the chief executive that "you will go down in history" for conceiving this reform. From Harvard, Sheldon Glueck,
then at the beginning of a distinguished career in criminology,
praised Smith for his approach to social problems and found it
"most encouraging to students in this field" to receive support
for their cherished ideals from a political leader of his
stature. The psychiatrist, Karl A. Menninger, and the social
worker, Katherine Bement Davis, deemed the proposal appropriate
in the light of their respective professions.[69]

In his testimony, Smith had averred that he would spare
no expense in the humane and effective treatment of offenders.
Given this attitude, he was willing to increase the state debt
in order to improve correctional facilities.

Al Smith's own experience as a youth contributed to the
generosity with which his administration funded both corrections and education. Testifying before the crime commission,
he supported probation "because I personally know . . . coming
from my neighborhood . . . a great many young lads who commit
their first offense, are put on probation and never come into
the courts again." When he urged liberal appropriations for
the schools, he was even more personal in his allusion to the
fact that, "Anybody desiring to have a proper understanding of
the necessity for an education need only talk to the man who
was denied it." As one of those men, in his very first message
to the legislature, he insisted that "whatever curtailment may
be necessary elsewhere, full and adequate provision be made for
the education and training of our children." To a convention
of their teachers, he asserted, "If we can stand $150,000,000
for a canal and $100,000,000 for good roads, we certainly ought
to be able to spend money for education, without which neither
canal nor roads would be worth a quarter."[70]

Although Governor Smith was sympathetic to the demands of
teachers for higher salaries, he was also sensitive to the
pressures from conflicting interest groups. In his first
annual message, he stated that, to maintain the quality of
education, "the teachers should be adequately paid and fairly
pensioned." He was, therefore, pleased with the legislation
of his first term which mandated a minimum salary and, to enable
localities to pay it, increased the state's contribution to
educational expenses. During his third term nevertheless, he
twice vetoed raises for school personnel in New York City:
once on the grounds of the violation of home rule by a state
legislature that did not have to levy the taxes to meet the
obligations to which municipal authorities were objecting; and
a second time, because of the failure of lawmakers to comply
with his recommendation for additional state aid to facilitate
the increases. In his fourth administration, with higher

grants-in-aid pending, he confided to his cabinet, "we want to discourage our school-teacher friends" in the city from lobbying for state legislation to fix their compensation. The principle of home rule forced the governor to balance his concern for municipal employees with his responsibility to city government.[71]

The growth in state aid, which compensated the districts for higher teacher salaries, was only one of the notable advances made in education during Smith's years as chief executive. In educational history, his administration stands out for the increasing proportion of expenses borne by the state, equalization among districts, and centralization of rural schools. As state aid rose, the principle of equalization dictated its allocation in almost inverse proportion to the wealth of the districts in order to make available similar resources for each child in the schools wherever located. The state also awarded grants as incentives to small units to combine.[72]

Edward Paul DeAntoni has focused on centralization in an interpretation of progressive educational reform that parallels Rothman's work on penal reform. According to DeAntoni, school reform was congenial to Smith because of its origins in the same efficiency economy movement that generated reorganization and the executive budget. When professionals displaced laymen and a state department the local authorities in control of the schools, they operated to fit their pupils for their role in an industrial state. In creating more efficient institutions, the reformers often ignored the needs of the individual child and the wishes of rural communities, which opposed consolidation.[73]

It was a manifestation of the progressive faith in experts that four separate investigations influenced the course of educational legislation in New York during the twenties. In 1920, a conference under the auspices of the United States commissioner of education initiated the Educational Finance Inquiry by professional educators and including an intensive study of the Empire State. The same year in New York, agricultural organizations and professional educators cooperated to launch the Rural School Survey by their Joint Committee on Rural Schools. Early in 1925, the Joint Legislative Committee on Taxation and Retrenchment made a crucial report on school finance; at the end of the year, Smith appointed a Governor's Commission on School Finance and Administration. In view of the overlap among the various committees and even more among their professional staff members, it is hardly surprising that they reached similar conclusions, favoring generous appropriations, equalization, and consolidation.[74]

The governor seconded the efforts of professional educators, which culminated, during the second half of his career in office, in a series of significant enactments.[75] In 1924 he called for adoption of the recommendations in the Rural School Survey. When legislative action was not forthcoming, he suggested another study by a commission with representation from the legislature, the educational establishment, and the public, the last to be selected by himself. Instead, the lawmakers referred the subject of educational finance to their Joint Committee on Taxation and Retrenchment, with laymen serving in an advisory capacity on Smith's appointment. The tone of the committee's report was set in its observation that "The state must see that the local units of government are provided with adequate financial resources to pay for the state minimum standard, and it must see that the tax burden . . . is not heavier . . . in different sections of the state." The Cole-Rice Law of 1925 carried out the report's mandate on state aid and equalization and used state funds as a weapon in the fight for centralization in rural areas.[76]

Nowhere is Smith's inclination to defer to experts more apparent than in his support of this legislation, in the face of vigorous rural opposition to consolidation. In response to a regent's commentary on country schools, the governor confessed, "Unfortunately, I am lacking in the intimate knowledge . . ." of the subject, and confided, "I feel that I cannot be guided better than to follow the Commissioner of Education and

the majority of the Regents." How would he decide in the even-
tuality that his authorities disagreed with each other? By
1925, the minority of the regents that had been sensitive to
rural complaints had become a majority of the board that advised the chief executive to veto the Cole-Rice measures. The
educational establishment, which had devised the bills, came to
their defense, with correspondence from school superintendents
running almost unanimously in their favor. The commissioner
of education obviously used his influence with the governor to
obtain his approval of the legislation, which was the product
of professional educators.[77] With Smith's backing, the professionals in the state department prevailed over the laymen
on the board with their connections in the grass roots of rural
New York.

The regions that had protested against the Cole-Rice Law,
under its provisions, received more of the state's bounty than
the cities whose needs prompted additional legislation. To
address their problems, at the end of the year, Smith hosted a
conference of educators and civic leaders, which resulted in
his appointment of the Governor's Commission on School Finance
and Administration. Its chairman, Michael Friedsam, by de-
fraying personally the group's research expenses, spared the
chief executive the jockeying for power between the branches
of government that often accompanied such projects. The
Friedsam commission nevertheless enjoyed the cooperation of
the joint legislative committee and produced a report in line
with the earlier studies. The document contained an interesting reflection on the general issue of public finance in the
observation that "the state cannot consistently plead the lack
of a suitable source of revenue as a reason for declining to
supply the increased state aid recommended in his report if
. . . it refunds to its taxpayers more than $11,000,000 of
income tax." Despite this, Smith gave it his wholehearted
backing. After a year's delay, the legislature enacted the
Dick-Rice Law of 1927, which raised state grants, extended the
equalization principle, and provided relief to the larger

cities.[78]

The laws of 1925 and 1927 established the pattern of
state aid to education that endured in New York as late as
1970. In the decade between 1917 and 1927, expenditures on
public schools approximately trebled while the state's contribution to localities rose nearly tenfold. Looking at the
record, a leading educator described Smith as "an ardent,
powerful, and most effective advocate of a more liberal financial support of public schools," and later concluded, "No other
governor of an American state has ever done so much for public
education as Al Smith has."[79]

Nonetheless, his presidential candidacy aroused apprehension among those who feared for the future of public education
in the administration of a devout communicant of the Roman
Catholic Church with its great investment in parochial schools.
Commissioner of Education Frank Pierrepont Graves, who did not
owe his appointment to the governor, could testify that Smith
"has impressed me as a consistent friend of education and of
the public schools." On the related issue of public subsidies
to parochial schools in New York, Smith avowed, "I am opposed
to any constitutional amendment which would permit the State to
make contributions of State money to any sectarian institution
of any kind." In the pages of the *Atlantic Monthly*, where he
responded to the challenge that his religion disqualified him
for the presidency, he affirmed his stand. In his peroration,
he declared, "I believe in the support of the public school as
one of the corner stones of American liberty. I believe in
the right of every parent to choose whether his child shall be
educated in the public school or in a religious school
supported by those of his own faith."[80]

Under Smith, the operating expenses of the state mounted
sharply, and the proportion spent on public schools rose. In
1920, state aid to education constituted approximately 26 percent of a $72 million budget; for the end of the decade, the
corresponding figures were 48 percent and $203 million respec-

tively. Although Smith had condemned the unreconstructed
government for its wastefulness, reform did not reverse the
trend of higher budgets. Whether or not they would have accelerated even faster without the gains of the efficiency
economy movement is imponderable. A negative answer may be
inferred from the fact that New York's budgets had increased
at an almost constant rate for several decades, and the more
rapid rise of his administration paralleled the experience of
other states. The governor's critics were correct in perceiving a growth in expenditures but erred in blaming him for
it. He was personally responsible only for the increments that
occurred because of his commitment to fulfilling the educational obligations and service functions of the state. The
Republicans were mistaken in predicting insolvency, for he left
the state with a larger surplus than he had found. This happened because revenues and expenditures both increased in response to the same forces: an expanding population and economic growth.[81]

If Smith failed to perceive the long-run economic trends,
he did exhibit a mastery of budgetary detail, according to contemporary observers. Frances Perkins recalled working late on
the budget and returning near midnight to the Executive Mansion where Katie affectionately greeted the governor and served
beer and sandwiches to the weary officials. Perkins drew a
charming vignette of the whole company retiring to the Victorian
pink parlor where Mrs. Smith, "pretty as a pin and prettily
dressed" played the piano to accompany her husband's pleasant
baritone. The overtime work, which preceded the recreation,
focused on the day-to-day costs of running the administration,
not on any theory of public finance.[82]

The closest Smith came to a theoretical formulation was
his distinction between operating expenses to be met on a
pay-as-you-go basis and capital investment to be financed from
bonds. The GOP challenged him on the wisdom of incurring
indebtedness to pay expenses that could be covered by reducing
the surplus. Humanitarian considerations were uppermost in

Smith's mind, whether it came to using current revenues for
schools, or bond proceeds for hospitals, prisons, and grade
crossing elimination. As he expressed it at the groundbreaking
ceremonies for a hospital to be constructed with bonds, "we can
offer no better prayer to God than to press for the proper care
of the poor, sick and afflicted in mind."[83] One may share his
sentiments, even agree that political reality dictates bonds to
assure continuity and timely completion for these projects, and
nevertheless not concede the validity of the governor's logic.
His analogy with corporate procedures for raising capital
breaks down at the point where the investment fails to generate
income for the state. He intended to go into debt only to
finance nonrecurring expenditures on permanent public improvements, but the theoretical difference between current and nonrecurring disappears in practice, and the acceleration of
change shatters the illusion of permanency.

Inevitably, there would emerge new needs, which subsequent governors, following Smith's precedent, would find the
resources to satisfy by sinking the state further into debt.
New York anticipated the fiscal practices of the thirties,
when, in the space of three years, it authorized five bond
issues: for the veterans' bonus, hospitals, parks, grade crossing elimination, and public improvements. Since the state had
previously borrowed, not only for parks, but also for internal
improvements including roads, the grade crossing bonds may be
viewed as an application of earlier practice to the age of the
automobile. It was, however, a departure for the state to
borrow for institutional construction. In a technical sense,
Smith did not engage in deficit financing, for his budgets
balanced with income exceeding outgo, including service on the
debt. But the principal grew so rapidly in the wake of his
administration that the magnitude and added purposes of indebtedness represented new directions that were temporarily obscured by the balanced budgets and the separation of operating
from nonrecurring expenses. The distinction lacked validity,
and the debt remained a fact. As Daniel R. Fusfeld recognized,

public finance under Smith was "closely akin to the 'deficit spending' of the thirties."[84]

Smith did not perceive the continuities between the New York and the federal experience when he attacked the fiscal policies of the New Deal. Roosevelt was not less—nor more—devoted to orthodox finance than Smith. The president's dual budget, with a general budget that balanced and an emergency budget that did not, paralleled Smith's separate accounting for operating expenses and the debt. Both systems fostered the illusion of a balanced budget in the presence of an actual or potential deficit. The president and the governor believed the conventional wisdom of sound finance, from which they deviated only reluctantly to meet urgent needs: recovery and relief in the depression, the plight of the inmates of overcrowded and dilapidated institutions. Scholars understand that FDR neither comprehended nor consciously adopted Keynesian economics, which constructed a theoretical framework that fits the unbalanced budgets of the depression. When the president discussed the deficit, whether in terms of a crisis, of pump priming, or more rarely of compensatory spending, he was not stating an objective but justifying an embarrassing fact. The Smith and Roosevelt administrations resorted to deficit spending because sound finance ranked lower in the scale of values of both men than the humane purposes on which they spent.[85] Their opponents asserted that government should do only what it could afford. The chief executives insisted that it could afford to do what it should.

CHAPTER 4
A STATE PARK PLAN FOR NEW YORK

Accompanying Governor Smith on a tour of projects made
possible by bonds, Robert Moses expressed regret that they had
not floated more than the modest $15 million exclusively for
parks.[1] The administration, nevertheless, financed from tax
revenues in 1923, the park bonds of 1924, and public improvement bonds of 1925, a vast extension of state parks in New York.

The Empire State owed its leadership in the accumulation
of parkland to the preservationist impulse in the conservation
movement. By the time that the movement had acquired a name,
the term, conservation, covered mutually inconsistent intentions:
scientific management of resources to eliminate waste as, for
example, in professional forestry; and preservation of the land-
scape in its pristine state, for aesthetic values and recreation.
If the former was a variation on the efficiency economy drive,
the latter was inspired by Romanticism. Nothing symbolized the
rift in conservation so dramatically as the estrangement between
the friends who had camped together at Grand Canyon, Gifford
Pinchot and John Muir. Despite the forester's influence on
Theodore Roosevelt, the president did add substantially to the
acreage of national parks. His successor held the first conference on national parks. Under Woodrow Wilson, Congress
passed the National Parks Act, and the Senate confirmed the
appointment of Stephen Tyng Mather who continued to direct the
National Park Service until his death in 1928. The progressive
era left the United States with a heritage of preservation,
which persisted in the twenties.[2]

His post in the federal government equipped Mather to
encourage the growth of state parks. He took the lead in
assembling the conservationists who founded the National Conference of State Parks in 1921. The rapid disappearance of undeveloped land to satisfy the demands of a growing population
and economy lent to the very first meeting the sense of urgency
that pervaded Governor Smith's efforts to set aside open space

for parks before it was too late.[3]

By the time of Smith's first inauguration, New York had
advanced further than any other state in the creation of parks.
Here, at any rate, as Eugene James O'Neill has demonstrated,
the preservation of nature for recreational purposes took precedence over the rational exploitation of resources. In the
nineteenth century, a variety of interests had coalesced to
preserve and expand the state domain: those who worried over
the supply of wood and water, some who enjoyed outdoor sports,
and others who placed faith in the curative powers of nature.
After the turn of the century, the groups that had cooperated
to secure the original reservations began to compete. At the
same time that the automobile was rendering the parks accessible
to a large number of urban residents, reformers succeeded in
excluding from their boundaries lumbering operations and railroad transportation. With the triumph of the preservationists,
O'Neill interpreted the movement as democratic rather than
elitist, committed to the conservation of human, rather than
the profitable management of natural, resources. Toward this
outcome, the administration of Governor Hughes, a man greatly
admired by Smith, made a substantial contribution.[4]

The Reconstruction Commission of his first term was a
primary source of Governor Smith's initiatives on parks as on
many vital issues. In the crucial report on the reorganization
of the state government, with which the efficiency economy
drive resumed, the group proposed to place under the supervision of a Department of Conservation all public lands devoted
to recreation, forest, and water supply. A study of parks,
begun by the commission, continued under the auspices of the
New York State Association, after the chief executive lost his
bid for reelection in 1920.[5]

Robert Moses, who went from the defunct Reconstruction
Commission to the newly established civic organization, became
the driving force behind the development of parks in the state.
His biographer, Robert Caro, has charged that in two years
Moses transformed the nonpartisan New York State Association

into a public relations bureau for Smith. In trying to explain
the intimacy between the professional politician and the political scientist, the author suggested that the one was attracted by education and knowledge, the other by the lure of power.
Caro perceived in Moses, during the interregnum, a metamorphosis into a fit example of the adage that power corrupts. At
any rate, the biographer attributed to his subject authorship
of the report that the New York State Association's committee
on parks released just before Smith returned to office.[6]

The New York State Association's *A State Park Plan for
New York* was to the development of recreational facilities what
the Reconstruction Commission's *Retrenchment and Reorganization
in the State Government* was to administrative reform in the
Smith regime. In its pamphlet, the association envisioned "a
really comprehensive and unified state park plan which will
take into consideration the anticipated growth of the state's
population and more particularly . . . of the larger cities."
To fund the program, the association proposed a bond issue,
which has been examined in the context of public finance. To
direct the work, Moses recommended, in conjunction with reorganization, the centralization of authority in a new advisory
commission within a Department of Conservation. In its publication, the civic group suggested the specific allocation of
bond proceeds among the various projects. The state park plan
incorporated the recreational, aesthetic, and ecological goals
of the conservation movement.[7]

From the beginning of his second term, Smith endeavored
to implement the state park plan. As he resumed his campaign
for structural reform, he asked the lawmakers to establish the
park council that Moses had advocated. When the chief executive decided in 1923 to defer the park bonds for a year in
order to give priority to hospitals, he urged the legislature
to make generous appropriations for the parks in the operating
budget. His messages called attention to the simultaneous
shrinking of undeveloped land and expansion of recreational
needs as an outgrowth of modernization and congested living

conditions.[8]

In 1924 Smith began to realize his hopes for public
action to overcome the depletion of open space. The National
Conference on State Parks encouraged him to pursue his program
at the same time that the New York State Association updated
its crucial study of the subject. The executive chamber received an advance copy of the new edition of the report in time
to incorporate its ideas into the governor's communciation with
the legislature on the subject of parks. The revised park plan
included a consolidation of park agencies along regional lines
and stressed the exigencies of the New York metropolitan area.
In view of this, the second edition of the brochure on parks
devoted the bulk of its space to "the development of a comprehensive state park system on Long Island." The lawmakers took
action on Smith's recommendations to establish a State Council
of Parks and regional commissions for Long Island and the
Finger Lakes, to make liberal provision for parks in the annual budget, and to submit to the people the question of bonds
to assure adequate money in the future.[9] The new source of
funds became available after the electorate voted overwhelmingly in favor of the park bonds.

Smith's second term ended with an excellent park plan, an
appropriate administrative structure for its realization, a
design for expansion particularly in the vicinity of urban
areas, and the wherewithal to finance it. It was a signal
achievement and one which contained within itself the potentialities for future progress—and conflict.

The policy of conservation upon which New York embarked
hopefully in Smith's second administration nearly foundered in
his third amid controversy so bitter as to jeopardize the
overall park plan. Although parks and parkways, in general,
enjoyed almost universal support, inevitably the location of
individual projects adversely affected some people and aroused
their hostility. They, in turn, lobbied to protect their interests by legislation that the administration considered

detrimental to the park plan.

Long Island was the scene of the greatest difficulties. The governor appointed to the Long Island State Park Commission Clifford L. Jackson, Townsend Scudder, and Robert Moses, who headed it and, for a time, the State Council of Parks as well. Their proposals for the region originated, according to Caro, in the grandiose vision of their chairman. In its application to Long Island, the commissioners interpreted the park plan as a mandate to open to the public, particularly to the multitudes of the metropolis, areas for outdoor recreation. They believed that this could best be done by the preservation of undeveloped land along the waterfront for parks and by the construction of parkways near the coastlines for access. In the words of their first annual report, issued after a legislative session punc- tuated with controversy over the actions of the commission, it intended:

> (1) A parkway system having the two-fold object of providing access to the individual parks from con- gested centers of population, and also improving the means whereby the residents of Long Island can reach the city and other parts of Long Island on attractive routes. . . .
> (2) The acquisition of as much land upon the shores of Long Island as possible to provide the maxi- mum of park property upon the water at different points upon the north and south shores, and at the undeveloped eastern end of the Island. . . .[10]

To implement these goals, the commission proceeded to map the northern parkway and to acquire park lands from the Taylor Es- tate and on the Montauk Peninsula. The three actions of the commission provoked criticism in the community, litigation in the courts, and obstruction in the legislature when it met in 1925.

Henry L. Stimson and Robert De Forest assumed leadership of the residents of the North Shore who resented the route of an arterial highway through their secluded suburban community. What would today be understood as ecological considerations blended with self-interest in their objections to the Northern State Parkway. Moses consulted them but found their counter-

proposal for the location of the roadway unacceptable. Although De Forest, a public-spirited citizen noted for his efforts on behalf of tenement reform, privately acknowledged the
force of the argument for the commission's route, he nevertheless proceeded to organize the opposition to what he regarded
as an intrusion upon his neighborhood.[11]

Opponents of the Long Island State Park Commission acted
from a variety of motives. In the case of the northern parkway, residents of an older suburb wanted to preserve the in-
tangible values of a community and a way of life from the inroads of concrete and traffic. In other instances, the values
were clearly commercial, which led real estate operators to obstruct the work of the commission.

The profits from speculation in land figured in the challenge to the commission's plan for two parks "at the undeveloped
eastern end of the Island." Carl G. Fisher wanted to duplicate
at the eastern tip of Long Island his real estate promotions on
the southern tip of Florida. The park commission was negotiating for the purchase of two tracts on the Montauk Peninsula
when their owners gave an option to Fisher, who offered a
higher price than the state. With $149,000 available to pay
for the property, the commission exercised the power of eminent
domain to take it on August 11, 1924. For this purpose, it
used the legal process known as entry and appropriation.[12]

In resorting to entry and appropriation, the commission
used one of the alternatives available under the law of eminent
domain. The procedures for taking private property for public
use fall into two categories: administrative and judicial.
In the first instance, the appropriate government agency, for
example, a park commission, formally decides to act, files the
proper papers, takes title immediately, and awards compensation
to the owner. If he is dissatisfied, he can, as a plaintiff,
initiate action for a larger amount. Under the judicial method,
the government agency, as a plaintiff, goes into court first
for authorization to acquire the property and second for the
determination of its worth. Title does not pass until after

the payment is made. Because the second method places the public at an obvious disadvantage, in those jurisdictions where it
is the only statutory procedure, it is circumvented so that
property is taken—in practice although not in theory—by administrative order. Entry and appropriation is an example of the
administrative procedure followed in New York. As early as
1916, the state's Conservation Law contained provision for the
use of this method in acquiring parkland.[13]

Under circumstances somewhat similar to those at Montauk,
the Long Island State Park Commission entered and appropriated
the Taylor Estate at East Islip. The 1,500 acres, used only
for occasional hunting since the death of George Taylor in
1908, belonged to the Deer Range Corporation formed by his
heirs. Already in July, 1924 the commission was negotiating
with the officers of the corporation for the purchase of the
property. By the end of September, the officers were willing
to grant the state an option to buy the tract for $250,000.
The option would run until June 1, 1925, at which time the
commission expected to be in possession of adequate funds to be
appropriated from bond proceeds; in the meantime it would rent
part of the tract for $250 a month. On October 7, the papers
for the transaction were ready, but the commission never obtained the option. When the deal fell through, the authorities
contemplated using the power of eminent domain.[14]

Since the administrative procedure required the governor's approval, the proponents and opponents of a park on the
site struggled for his soul. On October 8, when the officials
of Islip adopted a resolution against locating a state park
within the confines of the town, a local resident wrote to
Smith to see "if in some way the Park Commission could be
steered away from our section." The people of the community,
the governor's correspondent explained, were not "desirous of
having a small Coney Island put right in the middle of our
home sections" and apprehensive that the investment in their
homes "would be very adversely affected by a park of this description." Privacy, as in the case of the North Shore, and

profit, as in the case of Montauk Point, motivated the opposition. On October 9, its leaders, W. Kingsland Macy and Horace
Havemeyer, officers of the adjacent Timber Point Country Club,
offered to pay for the Taylor Estate the same price as the
government and, in addition, one half of the profits accruing
from resale within five years. Moses informed them that the
commission intended to take the property for public use and
Smith that no market for it had existed before the commissioners
showed an interest. The private parties would consummate their
purchase only "if they thought they had enough influence" to
deter the officials from doing their duty to carry out the park
plan. "This seems to me to be clearly an insult to you, . . ."
Moses told the governor. To dispel any misconceptions, the
chairman asserted that the area in question was undeveloped,
not residential as its denizens implied, and that the authorities did not entertain "the remotest idea of making a Coney
Island of the property." He considered the Taylor heirs
"morally bound" to ratify the arrangement with the state and
expected them to do so, for, as he informed Smith, they were
not "the kind of people to crawl out of an agreement."[15]

Moses misjudged the situation, for the owners of the
tract repudiated the work of the agents with whom he had been
dealing. On October 23, the stockholders of the Deer Range
Corporation overruled their officers and rejected the proposition of the state. Then they accepted the alternative offer
from the private parties connected with the country club.[16]

Meanwhile the commissioners again announced to the prospective purchasers their intention to appropriate the property.
The introduction of surveyors on the estate confronted the commission with the disagreeable possibility of subdivision which
could well frustrate their design for a park. At the same
time, the successful outcome of the park bond referendum
apparently assured the funds for the project. At their meeting
on November 26, the commissioners adopted a resolution to enter
and appropriate the Taylor Estate.[17]

Before signing the papers, the governor held two hearings:
the first, an informal interview with Macy and Harry T. Peters
on Sunday evening, November 30 at the Biltmore Hotel where
Smith stayed in town; the second, a public audience the next
day to afford interested parties a chance to present their
views. Although the park's opponents asserted that they wanted
the property for a residential development for members of the
Timber Point Country Club, they denied any intention of pro-
fiting from the resale of the tract. During the subsequent
litigation, Smith recollected that "Mr. Havemeyer wanted to
know if there was any place . . . where a poor millionaire
could go and be left alone, and I told him to go up to the
Harlem Valley Hospital" (a state institution for the insane).
Macy and Havemeyer objected to a park that would attract urban
crowds to their community; at the second hearing, they argued
somewhat inconsistently that the site was not accessible to
city dwellers. Smith indicated that a decision in the matter
properly fell within the jurisdiction of the park commission,
which enjoyed his confidence.[18] In deferring to the discretion of his appointees, he was acting on the theory of public
administration that was implicit in the reconstruction of the
state government.

The witnesses who petitioned him to repudiate his subordinates proceeded to obstruct their efforts. On the very
day of the public hearing, Macy formed the Pauchogue Land Corporation, and it took title to the Taylor Estate.[19]

On December 4, the Long Island State Park Commission
took possession of the property in an act of dubious legality.
The day before, the chief executive had formally approved the
agency's resolution to enter and appropriate. As it was occupying the estate, Smith received word from Irving L. Goldsmith,
who had earlier cautioned Moses that, in his capacity as
deputy attorney general, he deemed it "extremely doubtful
whether a valid appropriation has been made." His memorandum
anticipated the ruling of the courts in finding the availability of funds with which to pay for land to be a prerequi-

site to the lawful exercise of the administrative procedure in eminent domain.[20]

Macy and Havemeyer also challenged the legality of the act of entry and appropriation. On December 31, 1924 they initiated the case of *Pauchogue Land Corporation v. Long Island State Park Commission* when the private parties asked for an injunction to keep the public officials off the Taylor Estate. The foes of the park did not rely exclusively on litigation, for, like the opponents of the parkway, they prepared to mobilize public opinion and legislative votes in their interest.[21]

Because the forces that the Long Island State Park Commission had antagonized in three separate incidents combined to influence legislation, Smith fought a losing battle on a park bill in the 1925 session. His annual message, with its expression of pride in the progress of the park system, particularly on Long Island, showed no awareness of the conflict ahead. It is, however, possible to see between the lines of a special message a few weeks later elements of the approaching controversy. When he outlined the action needed to be taken by the lawmakers, he encouraged them to proceed with dispatch before the rapid disappearance and rising price of open land gave the state less park property for its bond money. He devoted fully half of the text to the technicalities of eminent domain, with an explanation of how the administrative procedure was calculated to subordinate the private interests of speculators and inhabitants alike to the general interest of the state in the rational location of facilities. With some allusion to the Long Island scene, he insisted that "private rights must yield to the public demand."[22]

Attitudes towards the administration's policy on parks varied with the perspective of the observer. After his message on the subject, an editor in far-off Dubuque hailed Smith as "one of the nation's forward-looking statesmen" whom Iowans might well emulate. Unlike the *Dubuque Herald*, the *New York Herald Tribune* sided with the governor's critics when it

charged, "The goal of Mr. Moses seems to be outraged communities and lawsuits—with a minimum of park area. . . ." The
outraged communities found spokesmen, not only in the editorial
offices of a leading newspaper, but also among prominent citizens who authored ostensibly objective studies. It is easy to
see the hand of the landholders along the northern parkway
route in *A Park System for Long Island*, which objected to all
developments in the residential areas of the North Shore, and
proposed locating them instead in the center of the island.
It is obvious how the interests connected with the Taylor Estate expected to benefit from the proposals in *State Parks* to
deprive the Long Island commission of the power of entry and
appropriation and to subject its determinations to the approval
of county government. Speaking for an urban rather than a
suburban constituency, Lillian D. Wald and the residents of the
Henry Street Settlement on the Lower East Side favored the commission and all its works.[23]

Two acrimonious hearings before legislative committees
demonstrated the nature of the alignment on the governor's park
policy. When a Republican assemblyman from Suffolk County
asserted that "we don't want any more State parks down where I
come from," he was contradicted by an inhabitant of East Islip
who apparently represented less influential segments of the
community. Witnesses connected with the county government and
the Pauchogue Land Corporation condemned the power of entry and
appropriation as a menace to home rule and property rights.
They complained of abuse by the Long Island commission. Moses
retorted that he "never knew of persons to come before a legislative hearing with dirtier hands." State officials defended
the administrative procedure in eminent domain and argued, as
Smith had done earlier, that the alternative of condemnation
protected local interests at the expense of the general interest in the park plan. Those who testified against the commission at the hearings affected the course of legislation, for
the Republican majority was sympathetic to their grievances.[24]

As a result, the lawmakers revised beyond recognition the program of the State Council of Parks, and the governor reacted by criticizing the provisions of the Thayer bill with a potential for "ham-stringing the Park authorities" and preventing the development of parks "in a reasonable time and at reasonable expense." On these grounds, he found fault with clauses mandating the judicial procedure in the exercise of eminent domain. He objected vehemently to involving in site selection two agencies whose very existence was inconsistent with the program for administrative reform: the Board of Estimate and Control and the Land Board. What he did not mention, but what all concerned understood, was that the Republican-dominated boards were expected to defer to the interests that were opposing particular locations. Instead, he praised the regional park commissions for having the technical competence and disinterestedness to make proper decisions. If they needed supervision, he would entrust it to the State Council of Parks. The chief executive's message implied the likelihood of a veto, unless the legislature removed from the measure the elements inconsistent with the park plan.[25]

The governor's associates made the threat of a veto explicit when the Thayer bill with its offensive features intact received senate approval. Nevertheless, the assembly passed it the next day, and the legislature adjourned.[26] Smith did not delay in vetoing the bill, despite the fact that his disapproval would deprive the park plan of funds. If he had signed the measure, he asserted, "there would be hardly enough money left to buy a flower garden much less to create a State park system." He preferred to be "responsible for delaying this program for a short time and getting the right principles . . . than to compromise with the principles and accept any such unworkable measure." Although certain lawmakers resented the chief executive's innuendoes, the *New York Times* editorialized, "As for defaming the Legislature, that is an undertaking which the Legislature itself has made superfluous." In contrast, the *Herald Tribune* found the parks "plunged into politics," not by the enactment of the legislature, but by the action of the executive.[27]

If the legislature had succeeded in enacting the Thayer bill, Republican agencies would have prevented the Long Island commission from implementing the park plan in the face of local displeasure. Since the chief executive disapproved the bill with its provisions for the appropriation of proceeds from the park bonds, the shortage of funds had a similar effect. After adjournment, the Pauchogue Land Corporation filed an amended complaint in which it noted the failure of the session to appropriate money for the Long Island State Park Commission and claimed that it "has no funds from which it could now pay the fair market value" of the Taylor Estate.[28] The vetoed legislation or no legislation appeared equally to serve the purposes of the foes of individual projects.

The governor supported the commission in its proposals for Long Island against an opposition with a strategic advantage in legislation and a distinction in public service that he himself admired. When he toured the sites later in the spring, he affirmed his commitment, not only to a park on the Taylor Estate, but also to the controversial northern parkway. He agreed with the commissioners that the public interest required parks at the shore and parkways parallel to it. To the skeptical editor of *World's Work*, Smith explained that it would be only too "easy for them to plan out park developments in out of the way places," where they would offend few and serve fewer. Henry L. Stimson suspected that Moses was the real author of these sentiments and intended to express an opinion of him to the governor "that I shouldn't like to put in writing." There was something disingenuous in the indignation of the lawyer who was an anonymous source of publicity detrimental to the commission. In his approach to the governor, Stimson criticized Moses and his colleagues for their dictatorial attitude in overriding the wishes of the local inhabitants. The arguments failed to shake Smith's confidence in the wisdom of the commission when he replied, "I want to do what is best for all

around but I do want to get a system of parkways that will meet
the demands."[29] Despite their disagreement, Smith and Stimson
retained their mutual respect for each other. They continued
to cooperate on reorganization and the executive budget at the
same time that they were engaging in combat over the financing
of public improvements and the location of parks and parkways.

Smith tried to bring Stimson and Moses together in order
to overcome their differences on the northern parkway. Although the two were reluctant to meet, they were willing to
comply with the wishes of the chief executive. "On the fundamental issue of getting a good park system . . ." the attorney
assured him, "good citizens do not really differ, and even we
who live on Long Island and who are opposing Mr. Moses' present
plan believe that we are good citizens and not merely selfish
obstructionists on account of our own interests." What Stimson
was impelled to deny was exactly what the commissioner believed as he informed his chief, "when these people suggest
compromise they simply mean that we must keep away from their
places entirely and turn our parkway into a broad road in the
middle of the island . . . where we would not be justified in
constructing a parkway at all." More clearly than Smith, the
two Republicans recognized the incompatibility of their respective positions as expressions of divergent ideas and interests.[30] Stimson represented the island's past; Moses pressed
the claims of the future population of city and subdivision to
access to remaining undeveloped land. The exercise of eminent
domain inevitably produces this kind of conflict, for the power
itself implies a clash between private property and public
policy.

The Thayer bill had resolved the conflict in favor of
private property; the governor's veto had spoken for public
policy; and the resultant impasse would deprive the park sys-
tme of funds for an entire year, unless a special session of
the legislature should appropriate the money. Even as the unsatisfactory measure was advancing to its final passage,
rumors circulated of the governor's intention to summon the

lawmakers back to Albany. His veto memorandum hinted at the
possibility. Questioned about it, he admitted that there was
"a good deal of talk," and parried, "but I am not going to do
any of the talking."[31]

The regional park commissions were decisive in persuading
him to call a special session. The members, who gave their
time without compensation as a public service to the community,
were predominantly Republican. They encouraged him to arrange
a conference at which they hoped to reach an accord with the
legislative leadership on an acceptable measure. In advance
of the conference, he was informed that the park officials rejected any interference in their work by the Land Board, preferred to retain the autonomy of the individual commissions,
but were willing to compromise on supervision by the State
Council of Parks. At the meeting, he retired discreetly into
the background while they fought it out with the GOP lawmakers
who remained committed to the Thayer bill. Although the conferees failed to come to an agreement, Smith still responded to
queries on a special session with "I do not know." The governor could count on the prestige of the park commissioners, the
rumored conversion to their point of view of the Westchester
County Republicans, and the editorial support of Frank Gannett's
chain of upstate newspapers to aid him in his campaign to
mobilize public opinion and to obtain legislation to his
liking.[32]

On June 10, Smith issued the call for a special session;
the following evening, he took his case to the people over the
radio. Senator John Knight presumably received equal time to
answer him the next day. The executive urged his listeners to
defend their interest in the park plan while the legislator
blamed the governor for the delay on parks and the expense of
an extra session. Their quarrel concentrated on site selection
for which they both adduced the Taylor Estate as a horrible
example. Smith affirmed his confidence in the regional commissions and the State Council of Parks as the proper authorities to determine location. The Land Board was interjected

into the process to enable the Taylor Estate litigants and others to exclude parks from neighborhoods where the public interest required them. Quite the contrary, Knight described the East Islip section as unsuitable for a park, its acquisition as illegal, and the governor's disapproval of the Thayer bill as a desperate move to extricate the Long Island commission from an embarrassing lawsuit. With telling force, the senator argued, "If the taking of the Taylor property was legal, Governor Smith's entire argument is unnecessary because . . . the State would now own the property. If illegal, the necessity of supervision by the elected Land Board has been conclusively proved." To Smith, with regard to the bond money, the question was: "Will it buy choice park spots and locate parkways where there is fine air and scenic beauty or will money, power and influence compel the State to buy for the people that which nobody else wants?" Circumscribing the commissions would deliver the park plan "into the hands of the very men who now desire to weaken it in the interest of the few," he contended.[33]

Between the delivery of his radio address and the convening of the special session, Smith used all of the resources at his disposal to assure a successful outcome. The members of the park commissions who rallied to his support included two chairmen who were subsequently aggrieved by the behavior of Moses. The Republican, Alphonso T. Clearwater, resisted pressure from Stimson "to put brakes" on "a rather arbitrary young man" and authored the resolution of his own Niagara commission, endorsing the governor's stand. Writing as head of the Taconic commission, Franklin Delano Roosevelt publicized the administration view in letters to the editors of upstate newspapers, but succeeded no better in convincing Senator Wadsworth "to use your influence . . . to keep their parks out of politics" than Stimson did in his endeavor to convert Judge Clearwater.[34] Groups such as the Parks and Playgrounds Association and the City Club supplemented the efforts of officials. Since the embattled Long Island parks meant a great deal to the inhabi-

tants of New York City, its organizations and mayor were
natural allies of the governor in this affair. Timed as it was,
to avert a move by Smith to deny renomination to the mayor, his
support was self-serving as well as of service to his community.[35] Whether the maneuvering would affect votes remained to
be seen.

New York awaited a battle royal on Monday, June 22, when
the session opened. On Sunday, Speaker Joseph McGinnies predicted adjournment by Friday when "we will send the Thayer bill
to Governor Smith for such action as he deems proper." If the
Republicans expected him to sign it in order to avert additional
delay, he counted on forcing them to reconsider. A special
session offered a hope of success because all attention concentrated on a single issue whose merits would become apparent
without the distractions of regular business.[36]

On the appointed evening, Smith addressed a hostile
legislature and a sympathetic gallery, filled to overflowing.
He began by denying, on his part, any fight with the legislature. The quarrel lay between the proponents of the Thayer
bill and the members of the State Council of Parks which he
praised as disinterested, nonpartisan, and technically competent, in contrast to the Land Board—and overwhelmingly Republican. It was an adroit maneuver to remove the issue from
party politics. But he could not avoid antagonism when he
turned to the crux of the difficulties on Long Island which he
described as "a natural park" and "a natural outlet for the
great seething masses of people that are gathered in the city,"
particularly when he alluded to "a lot of people on Long Island
who would like to keep it all for themselves." As an example,
he reviewed the history of the Taylor Estate on which he had
sought a briefing from park officials. The liberal in him
warned, "Be careful that you do not give the soap box orator,
the wild-eyed socialist, the Bolshevist and the anarchist a
chance to be able to say that when wealth and great power and
great influence is interfered with, all the plans . . . of a
great democracy have to be brushed aside." In maintaining

that the way to curb radicalism was to remove the grievances on
which it thrived, the speech against the Thayer bill was typical of the governor who so courageously resisted the Red
Scare.[37]

The day after the address, Smith suggested a compromise.
His proposal would reconstitute the State Council of Parks by
placing at its head the conservation commissioner, and by including in its membership certain elective officials but
leaving them in a distinct minority. The suggestion originated
with the chairman, Robert Moses, who was prepared to sacrifice
himself on the altar of his own park plan. The governor, who
never wavered in his admiration for Moses, was willing to
yield on any point but the Land Board. His concessions to the
Republicans were symbolic, for they failed to change materially
the nature of the decision-making authority in the acquisition
of land. Therefore, it is hardly surprising that the GOP rejected them. By the middle of the week, the chief executive
acknowledged the futility of his effort to reach an agreement.[38]

An ugly episode marred the discussion of compromise.
Smith accused Senator Charles Hewitt of inserting in the Thayer
bill an appropriation far in excess of the value of the land
for the proposed Fair Haven Park in his county. The senator
called the governor a liar and disclaimed all interest in the
project. But the State Council of Parks turned up evidence of
Hewitt's prior intercession for the project. Smith pointed to
the item in the Thayer bill and remarked, "Some one had to put
it in. The porter at the Ten Eyck Hotel didn't." Smith did
not frequently descend to the ad hominem argument. Here he
used it as an example of "the sort of political logrolling we
will have unless the Park Council is left in complete control
of park land purchases." John Knight, who had come perhaps too
quickly to his colleague's defense, said of the governor, "If
he were sincere he would not charge Senators with improprie-
ties. . . ." Then the president of the senate reverted to the
principle of proper supervision over expenditures. "That's
not what he wants," Smith retorted. "He wants what he said

himself— . . . a court of appeals to which aggrieved persons
could present their grievances. . . . He meant to be of service to a small group of wealthy men on Long Island. . . . and
that's why he wants a political land board substituted for the
Park Council."[39]

Smith charged the GOP with enforcing party discipline to
keep its members in line behind the self-serving measure. He
could find no other explanation for their refusal to recognize
the justice of his proposal. In his own colorful words, "They
are helplessly tied hand and foot, bound and gagged. Their
watchword is 'It is better we have an organization, even if we
have to lie in the gutter. . . .'" The legislative leaders rejoined, "If the Governor says it was a caucus, he lies in his
teeth." His failure to receive anticipated support in the
Westchester delegation, only confirmed his suspicion of the
pressures being exerted to maintain regularity. He also disclosed the Thayer bill's inducement to the representatives of
the city's northern suburbs to go along with the organization:
the exemption of the Westchester County Park Commission from
the unwelcome oversight of the Land Board. The joker substantiated his accusation that his opponents were unable to consider the bill on its merits.[40]

All the accumulated bitterness of the special session
welled up on the closing day in debate on the floor which
changed few votes. Senator James J. Walker took the lead in
assailing, "these lonely, fox-hunting, multi-millionaires,
who . . . came to you and did pretty well at the expense of
the poor people of New York City, where they had made their
millions out of the poor, despised Kikes and Wops of the
tenements whom . . . they are now seeking to shut out from good
sunshine and a restful day in the country." A Republican
lamented that, "people in Long Island have been afraid to go
to bed for fear that when they woke up in the morning they
would find their property seized by Robert Moses." A Democrat
retorted that if Long Islanders did not retire, "it is because
the bed sheets may be in use elsewhere,"—a reference to the

Klan. After both parties had vented their hostility, the
Thayer bill passed again, with only a handful of Republicans
defying the organization.[41]

If the Republicans assumed that Smith would not dare to
withhold funds from the parks any longer by vetoing the measure
again, they were sadly disappointed. In record time, just one
half hour after receiving it, he rejected it with the comment,
"The same reasons which led me to veto the bill then, [in April]
lead me to do the same thing now."[42]

Evaluations of the special session varied predictably.
When the governor took his family to the circus, a reporter
asked him to compare the Big Show with the one in the legislature. Readily he replied, "there is no comparison. The animals
are very intelligent." The *New York Times* derided the GOP for
"Politics But No Parks" in an editorial that echoed Smith's
speeches and messages. Stimson had tried to set the editor
straight by blaming Moses for the difficulties and deploring
his influence upon the governor. The lawyer's case was more
persuasive to the editor of the *Herald Tribune* which, throughout the controversy, sided with the Republicans as the *Times*
did with the Democrats. Caro, who judged the *Times* unfair in
its reporting of the subject, condemned Moses and Smith for the
impasse which cost the state dearly in the loss of some potential parks and higher prices for others.[43]

The summer of 1925, Smith and the Republicans were engaged in conflict, not only over state parks, but also over
public finance. Whereas no organized opposition had contested
the incurring of indebtedness for parks, the GOP was intent on
defeating the creation of a new debt of $100 million for public
improvements. It is ironic that the governor was assuring the
voters that the revenue from a bond issue for unspecified
public works would be spent judiciously at the same time that
he was caught in a spectacular imbroglio over the application
of the proceeds from the park bonds.

At the moment of the special session, the most controversial project was the park on the Taylor Estate. The govern-

ment's title to the property had been questioned by the attorney general and in a civil suit on the grounds that the Long Island State Park Commission lacked the money to pay for the land that it had acquired by eminent domain. Under the terms of the vetoed Thayer bill, the Land Board would have blocked any subsequent action by the commission to retain the estate.

In order to keep the site, Smith appealed, during the summer, to August Heckscher for money to buy the park, which now bears his name. The philanthropist responded with a donation of $262,000 to cover the 1924 asking price plus 6 percent interest from the time of the original entry and appropriation. With funds at hand, Smith asked the Pauchogue Land Corporation to reconsider its refusal to sell to the government. The plea was turned down peremptorily by Kingsland Macy who interpreted the governor's approach as a ploy "to rescue your appointee [Moses] from the extreme embarrassment and personal liability under which he now rests," and the private munificence as "a virtual confession that the Commission had no right to seize this property." Macy also tried to dissuade Heckscher from putting up the money.[44]

Upon receipt of the gift, the Long Island State Park Commission again resolved to enter and appropriate the Taylor Estate. Before giving his official sanction, Smith conversed with Macy in an effort to induce him to abandon his intervention. Then the chief executive signed the papers. On September 24, 1925, the commission for the second time concluded the formalities for the exercise of eminent domain with regard to the Taylor Estate. Counsel for the Pauchogue Land Corporation, which was contesting the validity of the first resolution of entry and appropriation, condemned the second as illegal, for "If the first appropriation of the property was good, there would be no reason for a second."[45]

The plaintiffs were ready to try their case, not only in the courts of law, but also before the court of public opinion and in the state and county legislatures. Macy's attorney proposed that Ogden Mills take the opportunity of his second de-

bate with Smith to inject the park issue into the referendum on
the $100 million bonds by arguing the possibility of their
being used to facilitate the work of the Long Island commission.
The Suffolk County Taxpayers' Association, led by Marvin
Shiebler, found the officials of their county more receptive
than those of Nassau to efforts to emasculate Moses' agency on
the grounds that it was favoring New York City at the expense
of the suburbs.[46] The administration must have faced the 1926
legislative session with mixed emotions: confidence at the
outcome of the bond election, marred by concern over the continuing park litigation and the influence of the Long Island
lobbyists on the Republican majority.

For the legislature, the Suffolk junto had prepared two
bills to allow interested groups to control the development of
parks on Long Island. The first set up a county commission in
Suffolk to assume, within its jurisdiction, the functions of
the Long Island State Park Commission. Henry L. Stimson recognized that it "goes quite far in asking the State to give up
all initiative," but refused to concede that "it goes too
far." He suggested an alternative to accomplish, by indirection, the aim of home rule. The second measure reconstituted
the state commission by adding two representatives each from
Nassau and Suffolk and by requiring their approval for acqui-
sitions within their respective counties. When a print of the
bill appeared without the section on county veto, Stimson was
indignant over what was "nothing more than an elaborate trap to
deliver Suffolk, tied hand and foot, over to Moses and his
friends of Nassau County." The attorney succeeded in restoring
the crucial provision with which opponents of particular projects hoped to obtain leverage over the decisions of the commission.[47]

Shiebler was not sanguine about executive approval when
he urged Stimson to intercede with the governor. That the
lobbyist's fears were well founded was demonstrated by a
scathing veto of a similar proposal for Monroe County. Smith
quickly disapproved the proposal for a Suffolk County park

commission with the observation that "it seems clear from the acknowledged origin of this bill that its purpose was to embarrass the state park program." Likewise, he disapproved the measure for enlarging the Long Island State Park Commission and filed a veto memorandum containing the verbatim objections of Commissioner Townsend Scudder. The memorandum condemned the bill for subordinating general to local, and public to private, interest in a manner suggestive of western obstruction of national park policy, and for threatening to exclude parks from scenic and waterfront locations attractive to private enterprise. The document identified the groups at Wheatley Hills, East Islip, and Montauk that the bill was designed to serve.[48]

In 1926, Smith vetoed, not only the park commission bills, but also two versions of a claims bill drafted to oblige the Long Island interests. To understand the reasons for his disapproval, it is necessary to review the alternatives available to a landowner whose property was taken by entry and appropriation. He could challenge the official action in a court of record, as the Pauchogue Land Corporation was doing, or he could ask the court of claims to award him a higher price than the state proposed to pay, but he could not pursue both remedies simultaneously, because that would place him in the logically inconsistent position of seeking more money for real estate that he was trying to retain. Furthermore, the statute of limitations allowed only two years for the initiation of either action. The new measure would change that by extending the time in which to file a claim for six months beyond the conclusion of unsuccessful litigation for the recovery of the property. A law that would encourage private parties to engage in dilatory tactics in order to gain a windfall from appreciating land values was neither in the public interest, nor in the interest of justice, as the governor understood it. To avert any injustice resulting from the protracted litigation over the Taylor Estate, the park commission had already agreed to a stipulation allowing the plaintiff to make a claim after

it had exhausted the remedies for recovery of the parkland.
But the litigants at Montauk Point who stood to benefit from
the current bill deserved no such consideration in Smith's view,
because they had waited nearly two years before contesting the
exercise of eminent domain. Legislation that would enable them
to profit from the delay "is entirely too much corn beef for a
nickel," Smith insisted to Judge Proskauer, who questioned the
fairness of the vetoes.[49]

Whereas the vetoes of 1925 had resulted in an impasse,
those of the following year protected the Long Island parks
without impeding further development. In 1926, the governor
signed measures that enabled him to proceed with the park plan.
The compromise of 1926 was to some degree a by-product of the
reorganization of the state government. The Hughes commission
recommended and the State Departments Law provided for a
division of parks within the Department of Conservation and
the supervision of the State Council of Parks and its constit-
uent regional commissions by the head of the department. The
new statute met Republican objections to the autonomy of the
park officials at the same time that it subjected their budgetary, spending, and eminent domain, functions to the approval
of the conservation commissioner whom Smith had suggested,
during the special session, as the appropriate official to
have this responsibility.[50]

The Land Board, to which Smith objected so strenuously,
remained but without its potentiality for mischief. His quarrel
with the board antedated the conflict over parks. Just before
he returned to Albany for his second term, the agency, in a
"midnight" move, which he could only regard as a giveaway to
the Santa Clara Lumber Company, had abandoned the state's claim
to a substantial forested tract in the Adirondacks. His administration resumed the legal contest over the property. At the
height of the dispute over the role of the Land Board in park
affairs, the state appeared to be winning a case (which it
ultimately lost) from which to infer that the agency had violated its trust.[51] Despite Smith's protest, the Hughes com-

mission did not eliminate the Land Board, but the State
Departments Law placed gubernatorial appointees in a majority
and required the approval of the chief executive for all land
grants. As a result of reorganization, the Land Board would
no longer serve as the focus of the governor's fears and the
legislature's hopes.[52]

With the metamorphosis of the Land Board, administrative
reform became one of the factors that facilitated the park compromise of 1926. In his annual message, the governor could
"confidently expect" the Hughes commission to "point the way to
a solution of the bond issue difficulty." The Thayer-Moore
Act, making appropriations from the proceeds of the park bonds,
passed early in the session, before the release of the report
on reorganization, but the absence of the Land Board suggests
that the bill's sponsors were privy to the deliberations of
the State Reorganization Commission. Caro attributes the GOP
willingness to make concessions in part to the fact that the
party's obstructionist image was becoming a political liability,
for opposing parks was tantamount to opposing motherhood. Caro
puts even more weight on the transformation of Robert Moses
into a power broker dealing out what George Washington Plunkitt
called honest graft to Long Island Republicans in exchange for
legislative votes. The anguished appeals of Suffolk's leading
lobbyist to prominent Republicans in and out of the legislature
confirm some of the author's explanations for the easy passage
of the park statute.[53]

The governor and the legislative majority compromised in
the Thayer-Moore Act by subjecting the park plan to the dual
control of two groups with the ability to check each other.
Under the new provisions, all expenditures on land required
the assent, both of the State Council of Parks, and of three
individuals: the governor, and the two legislative fiscal
chairmen. In the language of the law, no development could
take place until the maps and estimates for it "shall have been
submitted to the governor, the chairman of the senate finance
committee and the chairman of the assembly ways and means

committee in such detail as they shall require and shall have
been approved by them." The law divided jurisdiction over the
location of projects between the State Council of Parks that
Smith preferred and the three-man review that the Republicans
substituted for the Land Board.[54] Since their party usually
predominated in the legislature, the device of a triumvirate
afforded the GOP at least a negative in park affairs. The process was analogous to the one devised by the majority for the
participation of the same two lawmakers in the segregation of
lump sum items in the budget. In both cases, the involvement
of the chairmen of the Assembly Ways and Means and Senate
Finance Committees appeared to Smith to be unwarranted legislative interference in executive functions and Republican partisanship in obstructing a Democratic administration.

Any evaluation of the Thayer-Moore Act must take into
account its failure to assure the governor power commensurate
with his responsibility for the park plan. The law violated
the concepts of public administration on which Smith based his
reform of the government. Like his political opponents however, he too could no longer afford to delay the program by
intransigence. He saved face by the elimination of the Land
Board, and the park plan by the introduction of the State
Council of Parks, in site acquisition. Although the law gave
the Republicans a chance to check developments unacceptable to
them, it left the chief executive in a strong position to bargain for what he wanted. If the lawmakers should block his
plans, he could retaliate against projects dear to their
hearts—or to their constituents. He gained from the act a
greater measure of control over the system of parks than the
legislature had been willing to grant him in the bill that he
twice vetoed. The compromise enabled noncontroversial projects
to proceed and offered the Republicans ample opportunity to
interfere with disputed ones. What could be inferred from the
law would be confirmed in practice.

The legislature had not yet adjourned when Governor Smith,
Senator Charles Hewitt, and Assemblyman Eberly Hutchinson met

with members of the State Council of Parks to review its plans.
There was more than a slight difference of opinion upon the
function of the hearing. Smith and the park officials expected
the governor and legislators to approve or reject general plans,
once the park council had gone over the details. Hewitt and
Hutchinson insisted on receiving in writing specific facts on
each individual project. In framing rules to enable them to
obstruct certain developments, they were fulfilling the legislative intent when it provided for the participation of these
two legislators in the executive process of park administration.
The governor agreed with the members who charged that the rules
would hamstring their regional commissions and inflate the
price of parkland. To Townsend Scudder, it appeared that the
procedure "might make it very difficult for the Long Island
State Park Commission to function at all, and of course . . .
there is no such intention on the part of you gentlemen." By
the time the hearing ended at midnight, the triumvirate had
approved a number of uncontested plans and deferred action on
others on which Hewitt and Hutchinson overruled Smith.[55]

To no proposal did the lawmakers devote more attention
than that of the Long Island commission for the Northern State
Parkway. If Shiebler implored the fiscal chairmen to resist
the commission's usurpation of the authority to map highways,
Stimson protested specifically against a route through the area
where he and De Forest made their home. Both Hewitt and
Hutchinson assured him of their determination to be more than
a rubber stamp for the commission. When a tour of the neighborhood rendered the two lawmakers receptive to the arguments of
Stimson and De Forest, they hoped to bring the governor around
to their point of view with a second outing. Stimson criticized the chief executive's attitude that the legislators
should assent without question to the commission's designs as
something symbolic of the autocracy which "prevailed when Baron
Haussmann was laying out the boulevards of Paris for Napoleon
III" and attributed to Moses a Napoleonic complex.[56] Dissatisfaction with Moses led Stimson to encourage legislative inter-

vention in administration at the same time that, on the Hughes
commission, he was laboring for reorganization based on assumptions of executive responsibility.

Not only the power of Hewitt and Hutchinson, but also
respect for Stimson and De Forest, inclined Smith towards compromise on the route of the northern parkway. The chief executive urged the commission to devise acceptable alternatives and
the leading residents of the North Shore to cooperate with the
officials. He told the critics, "It seems to me that there
must be some way in which public spirited people representing
the State could get together with public spirited people like
you in a matter of this kind." Judge Scudder personally presented the compromise to Stimson and De Forest, both of whom
reacted favorably. De Forest assured Smith, ". . . I will
cooperate in anything I deem for the public good, even if
against my private interest." The governor wanted to bring all
the parties together to explore the possibilities for agreement. As he put it, "I will be the Referee. Eight ounce
gloves will be used and the match will be conducted under the
Marquis of Queensbury rules." Stimson returned the chief executive's banter with a reference to the gloves as "a concession
to my age in view of the youthfulness of Chairman Moses." The
contending parties toured the alternative sites, which Stimson
admitted to be satisfactory. Never diffident where his official duties were concerned, Moses proposed that residents of
the area "anchor" the new route with the dedication of appropriate rights-of-way. Stimson bristled at what might be construed as a threat or a bribe. The commissioner instantly disclaimed any such intention. Stimson, who considered the compromise superior to the commission's original plan in avoiding
damage to the area, remained skeptical of the idea of a northern parkway.[57]

Although Stimson and De Forest eventually came round,
the GOP, acting through the fiscal committee chairmen, stalled
progress on the Northern State Parkway. With their veto over
the segregation of lump sums in the budget and over expendi-

tures for parks and parkways, they could withhold funds, as
they did in 1928, from necessary surveys. At the start of his
presidential campaign, Smith engaged in an acrimonious exchange
in which he accused Hewitt and Hutchinson of blocking recreational development for the many in order to accommodate the
wealthy few. They, in turn, charged him with bad faith in circumventing the legislature and violating an agreement to defer
work on the northern, until the completion of the southern,
parkway. Smith used the contest as another horrible example of
the folly of including legislators in financial administration,
a practice that he predicted would end with the effective date
of the constitutional executive budget. Meanwhile, Heckscher's
benevolence again enabled the governor to overcome obstruction
on Long Island by providing funds for surveying gifts of land
and buying small parcels along the route.[58]

Smith used the power of his office to lay out highways
near the coasts as the Long Island State Park Commission proposed instead of in the center of the island as its detractors
desired, but the Northern State Parkway detours for eleven
miles around the estates of Dix Hills and Wheatley Hills. The
first loop resulted from the negotiations recounted above; the
second in the Roosevelt years, from a similar contest, which
one writer has called "The Battle of Parkway Bulge." The ultimate route reflects, according to Caro, the inordinate ambition
of Moses who made concessions of questionable morality—if not
legality—to those with the wealth and clout to stand in his
way while ruthlessly exercising the power of eminent domain on
the property of small farmers who lacked the resources to protect themselves.[59] Smith certainly, and Moses probably, did
not see it that way, for the governor viewed the implementation
of the park plan on Long Island as a triumph of the people over
selfish interests, and any deviations from the grand design as
only the give-and-take of the real world of fallible human
beings.

As chief executive, Smith backed the Long Island State
Park Commission, not only against legislative interference with

the parkways, but also in the face of legal threats to Heckscher, Montauk, and Hither Hills State Parks. The two law-makers, who under the terms of the Thayer-Moore Act had the authority to veto the acquisition of new sites, were powerless to interfere with these parks—if the state already owned the land. Since litigation was in progress to challenge the government's title to all three tracts, the decision on the parks rested, not with the executive or the legislature, but with the judiciary.

In May, 1926 the New York Court of Appeals handed down the most significant decision in the case of *Pauchogue Land Corporation v. Long Island State Park Commission*. Two regular sessions and one special session of the legislature, in which the lawsuit was a cause célèbre, had elapsed since Macy and Havemeyer initiated the action to recover the Taylor Estate. Although the judges of the state's highest tribunal were techni-cally ruling only on preliminary motions, their unanimous opinion, heavily weighted with obiter dicta, prefigured the administration's ultimate success in the complex litigation.[60]

The way the court reasoned led to the conclusion that the first occupation of the Taylor Estate was invalid; the second, valid. The judges found that the law allowed the Long Island State Park Commission to exercise the power of eminent domain only when it possessed the money with which to pay for the property taken. In the words of the decision:

> The only basis of the right of appropriation is the inability to agree as to the purchase price when the Commission has funds to pay if the compensation were agreed on. No funds, no negotiations; no negotiations, no appropriation.

In 1924 when the commission acted in anticipation of the reve-nue from the park bonds, "The appropriation of and entry on the lands was illegal. . . ." Did August Heckscher's donation overcome the legal impediment to the park? The opinion ex-plained, "But if an appropriation of money is made available a lawful reappropriation of the lands will terminate their il-legal acts and the action will be one for damages only." With

that, the court implied that the second seizure of the Taylor
Estate, of which it could not then take official cognizance,
was lawful, but that the commissioners were liable for damages
resulting from their original lawless action. What if the estate were worth, not the $262,000 of the Heckscher gift, but the
$800,000 at which the plaintiff was now appraising it? Would
that mean that the commission had lacked the resources to compensate the owners and that the second appropriation of the
Taylor Estate was also unlawful? The court answered no, for
the state was bound to pay amounts awarded by its Court of
Claims.

> It by no means follows that if the amount of
> money . . . is inadequate fully to pay the judgment
> of the Court of Claims, compensation is not sufficiently
> provided for to meet constitutional demands and that an
> act of appropriation of lands is therefore, *ultra vires*
> and void. . . . Public officials are presumed to act
> within their authority. . . . Otherwise the whole plan
> of appropriation by entry or condemnation would be de-
> pendent on the infallibility of the public officials
> in estimating the true value of the property taken by
> them for State purposes.[61]

From this decision of the state's highest court, it is
possible to predict the outcome—except for one strange interlude. On June 3, the very day of a final ruling by the Court
of Appeals, *Pauchogue Land Corporation v. Long Island State
Park Commission* went to trial in the Supreme Court of Suffolk
County. The defendants' attorney, who at the time was arguing
an appeal elsewhere, withdrew when the proceedings resumed on
June 7, because having begun in his absence, they were preju-
dicial to his clients. The plaintiff won $22,000 in damages
and the tract of land from the unrepresented commissioners—
but not for long. Their appeal resulted in a new trial.[62]

The second trial took place in December and lasted, not
two days, but three weeks. Governor Smith took the witness
stand to testify on his firsthand knowledge of events that this
chapter has recounted. He told of the private interview and
public hearing at which the plaintiff had criticized the proposed park because of its adverse effect on local residents, of

a visit that had convinced him of the superb recreational facilities of the area, of his initiative in obtaining the Heckscher
gift for its purchase, and of his final effort to persuade the
officers of the corporation to sell the property before his
authorization of the second act of entry and appropriation.
The judge found none of this germaine to the case before
him.[63]

What was at issue was the damages incurred by the commissioners for their trespass upon the Taylor Estate. The decision of the Court of Appeals forced the defense to concede
the unlawfulness of the first exercise of eminent domain.
Counsel found in the same opinion warrant for a presumption of
the legality of the second taking of the site. The defense
argued that the Pauchogue Land Corporation suffered no material
injury from the deprivation of its property between the two
dates and, therefore, was entitled to no more than nominal
damages. The lawyer explained that the owners had long
carried the property at a loss, that the corporation had bought
it in the knowledge that eminent domain proceedings were
pending, and that the plaintiff had contributed to the wrong
of which it was complaining by lobbying against the provision
of funds to pay for the park. According to the other side, it
deserved compensation for losses sustained when standing in the
way of official lawlessness. Plaintiff fought for the recovery
of the property and the award of substantial damages. On the
former count, it was necessary to disprove the validity of the
second act of entry and appropriation; on the latter, to demonstrate financial losses caused by the defendants' illegal
activities. Attorney for the corporation challenged the legitimacy of the second seizure on the grounds that the commissioners did not act in good faith in offering $250,000 for an
estate which he valued at a much higher figure. If this was
one way of measuring his client's loss, another was in terms
of the potential profits from subdivision during the period
of litigation.[64]

Given the opinion of the Court of Appeals, the presiding judge held the first, but not the second, entry to be unlawful, in view of the presumption of official good faith. He found the plaintiff entitled to legal damages for a legal wrong. It was up to the jury to decide the extent of actual damages—if any. After several hours of deliberation, it awarded the nominal amount of six cents.[65] With this verdict, the administration won a victory and the people, a park on Long Island's southern shore.

Although the 1926 decision of the Court of Appeals determined the outcome and the second jury trial dramatized it, the case dragged on for three more years. When New York's highest tribunal upheld the judgment of the trial court, Governor Smith, who was then running for national office, was understandably "very well pleased" with the decision. He had backed the commissioners on the park "because I was convinced that they were right." It had been worth the struggle "to vindicate the principle that no group of men, however influential, can for purely selfish and temporary ends, block an important and permanent public work." After the United States Supreme Court denied the appeal of Macy and Havemeyer for review, the Court of Claims awarded the Pauchogue Land Corporation $275,000, a sum not far in excess of the amount donated by Heckscher for the purchase of the Taylor Estate.[66]

Pauchogue Land Corporation v. Long Island State Park Commission served as a precedent for *Flagg v. Moses* involving disputed tracts on the Montauk Peninsula. In 1928 a court affirmed the state's title to the area in a decision that applied the tests of official good faith and reasonable adequacy of funds. The judge found the plaintiffs without legal standing to sue. After the governor's veto of the bill to extend the statute of limitations for their benefit, they had filed a claim that placed them in the logically inconsistent and legally untenable position of asking a higher price for property that they were trying to recover. The decision cleared the way for the establishment of Montauk Point and

Hither Hills State Parks.[67]

Governor Smith implemented the New York State Association's park plan, which on Long Island resulted in the parks
at Montauk and East Islip and in the parkways parallel to the
north and south shores. In the process, he overcame the selfish interests bent on influencing, not only the location of
facilities on the island, but also the very character of legislation to provide for the expenditure of funds raised by the
bonds. The chief executive vetoed bills drafted to serve these
special groups at the same time that he compromised on the
Thayer-Moore Act that allowed him to proceed with the park plan
in the public interest. To assist him, he chose officials with
a conservationist point of view and a sensitivity to the recreational needs of the entire New York metropolitan area. He respected their judgment, and they could count on his support in
resisting local pressures. In sustaining the park commissioners, he was adhering to the same principle of executive
responsibility that sparked the drive for reorganization.

The governor, who defended the park authorities against
outside interference, also stood by Moses in instances where
dissension within the administration presented a challenge to
his leadership. Because he enjoyed Smith's confidence, Moses
was able, not only to maintain the integrity of the park plan
that he created, but also to determine priorities in implementing it. The availability of limited resources for a multi-
plicity of worthy projects inevitably led to competition and
discord among the commissions.

Certainly, the question of precedence among developments
was a factor embittering the relations between Moses and many
of the unpaid commissioners, including those on the Commission
of the State Reservation at Niagara whose president, Alphonso
T. Clearwater, was one of the firmest friends the park plan
ever had. Moses himself attributed to the Republican judge
the unprecedented affirmative vote on the park bonds in rural
Ulster County. In turn, Clearwater profoundly admired

Governor Smith because "he has the courage to place himself at
the head of a most enlightened Park program, which will commend
him not only to the people of the State, but of the Nation."
During the tribulations of 1925, the jurist sided with Smith
and worked actively against the endeavor of his own GOP to gain
control of the state parks through the Thayer bill.[68]

Yet Clearwater's group did not receive its anticipated
share of the bond revenue that the compromise of 1926 released
for use by the park commissions. Robert Moses inspired, within
the administration, criticism of the Niagara commission for
lack of comprehensive planning to protect the Niagara shoreline
and for improper relations with a power company. Although the
members convincingly refuted these allegations, the misgivings
they generated undoubtedly influenced the governor and the
State Council of Parks when it came to the disposition of funds.
Increasingly, they withheld approval from the expenditures of
the Niagara commission and applied pressure upon it to transfer
appropriations to the Erie County Park Commission. Ironically,
Moses objected to the presence on the Niagara commission of men
who were not resident in the region, although his own Long
Island commission had come under fire in this respect.[69]

The commissioners, who felt aggrieved by unfair treatment, correctly perceived Moses as the source of their difficulties. Ansley Wilcox, who as acting head of the commission
during the illness of its president, defended it against the
implications of ineffectiveness and impropriety, accused Moses
of seeking revenge on Clearwater, De Forest, and himself because of their occasional disagreement with him over policy.
Just as their respect for Smith continued undiminished despite
their distrust of his subordinate, the governor remained un-
shaken in his confidence in Moses. Yet Clearwater retained "a
great admiration and a sincere affection" for the chief executive who possessed "all the elements of greatness and few of
its limitations." The judge regretted that "Unfortunately,
some men greatly his inferior . . . have his confidence which

unhesitatingly they abuse. . . ." The criticism of the conduct
of the affairs of the Niagara reservation prompted Robert De
Forest to assure the governor that "the Niagara Commission was
functioning," also that "Judge Clearwater is functioning," and
in addition that "the public interests have never been neglected." Shortly afterwards, it was Clearwater's turn to praise
De Forest, to blame his resignation on Moses, and to cast aspersions on Smith's adviser. It was Moses who drafted the
reply in which the governor explained to the judge, "you have
perhaps misunderstood the motive" behind the actions of the
State Council of Parks. Although the letter encouraged Clearwater to remain in office, a year later, when he complained
about Moses violating civil service regulations, that official
was again trying to ease the octogenarian off the commission.
In his definitive and perceptive account of the Niagara commission's difficulties, Robert Caro concludes, "that Moses had
determined to hound . . . elderly men whose only crime was
their refusal to allow him to exercise unbridled power . . .
and to remove them from control of the park they loved, the
park that one of them had created, the park to which they had
given so much of their lives."[70]

There is an instructive parallel in the relationship of
Moses to the elderly judge and to the aspiring politician,
Franklin Delano Roosevelt, who also headed a park commission in
the Smith administration. Despite unquestioned devotion to the
park movement, both upstate men clashed with its leading New
York spokesman. FDR, who had earlier expressed an interest in
creating a park in the region, was named in 1925 to the newly
established Taconic State Park Commission and immediately
chosen as chairman. To the news of his election, he responded,
"of course I shall be delighted to serve though I think it
would be far better to have a Chairman who could get around
without crutches and attend meetings." Their roles in park
development fostered an antagonism between Roosevelt and Moses
that was one factor in the estrangement between Smith and his
successor.[71]

On both the Niagara and the Taconic commission, the dissatisfaction with Moses dated from the disbursement of park bond proceeds in 1926 and flourished under a growing sense of deprivation in the allocation of resources to the region. The very first year, chafing at the holding up of certain funds, FDR appealed to the governor's secretary, "Can you find out where the shoe pinches or who has died!" only to be met with strictures on economy. Although there may be some truth to the report that Roosevelt and Moses clashed over the former's intention to find a sinecure for Louis Howe on the staff of the commission, their basic disagreement occurred over policy—not patronage.[72] Roosevelt unfolded to Smith for the Taconic region, a vision not unlike that of Moses for Long Island. As chairman, he understood the function of his commission to be the development, not only of the tristate park, but also of a scenic parkway extending from Westchester to northern New York and providing access to facilities for outdoor recreation within the state and in New England. Moses ghosted the response in which the governor admonished, "you must keep in mind that only limited funds are available and that there is tremendous pressure," and acknowledged, "Of course this program looks away into the future . . . and we cannot expect to do all these things at once."[73]

A year—and a budget—later, the disagreement over the scope of the commission's mandate revived with FDR's protest, "I know all about the need of cutting appropriations. Try just for once making the cut on somebody else—I decline the honor." To "Dear Frank," Al patiently explained "the first and most important claim" on revenues, of those regions "closest to population centers where . . . we have had to purchase land immediately if we are ever going to have it." Roosevelt resented the concentration on Long Island and accused Moses of cornering appropriations for his own Long Island region at the expense of the Taconic. To "Dear Al," Frank expostulated, "When all is said and done, I wasn't born yesterday!" He traced to its source, the commission's frustration. "I am sorry to say," he complained to the governor, ". . . that Bob Moses has played fast and loose with the Taconic State Park Commission since the beginning." Funding would have been available, "if Bob and you had gone after it" for the program to which they had earlier committed the administration. Smith blamed the legislative leaders for the cutbacks. The chief executive, who assured FDR, "I know of no man I have met in my whole public career who I have any stronger affection for than for yourself," nevertheless supported Moses when the two men quarreled.[74]

The antagonism between Moses, on the one hand, and Commissioners Roosevelt and Clearwater, on the other, was a matter of personality and policy. Robert Caro, in his exhaustive examination of the character and career of Robert Moses, identifies the Smith years as the turning point in a transformation "from the idealist who put his faith in truth and reason to the pragmatist who put his faith in power." Wielding power ruthlessly, deviously, he inevitably came into conflict with those who were not powerless and who learned to distrust him. Yet Smith supported Moses, even against men whom the governor esteemed highly. In some of the controversies, the adviser possibly misled his mentor.[75] Smith appears not to have questioned the justice of what Moses was doing. But the aggrieved commissioners often acknowledged that official's unsurpassed contribution to the system of state parks that Smith valued so dearly. To the extent that he controlled the allocation of finite resources, Moses was bound to disappoint, if not to anger, the backers of slighted developments. Giving priority to the New York metropolitan area was rational, in view of the density of the population, and appealing, to a governor who grew up on the Lower East Side. Smith stood behind Moses because he believed in the park plan that the younger man was following and because he administered the state by delegating almost unquestioned authority to his immediate subordinates as the efficiency economy movement prescribed.

New York under Smith served as a model for the emerging
state park movement. He governed a state in which recreation
had early received recognition as a reason for protecting and
enlarging the public domain. Building on the past, he provided
for the future by increasing the number and extent of state
parks and improving the ease of access to them. What was
notable about this growth was, not only its magnitude, but also
development proceeding according to a prearranged plan, the
state park plan of the New York State Association.

To adhere to the plan, the governor—and Moses—had to
fight for it. Everyone favors parks in the abstract, but when
it comes down to concrete projects, pressure groups try to take
the determination of the location of a park or the route of a
parkway out of the hands of officials. The efforts of Long
Islanders, for example, placed the entire plan in jeopardy because of their ability to influence legislation. Although
Smith, in resisting the Thayer bill, enjoyed the support of the
prominent Republicans on the park council and commissions, the
alignment in the legislature was essentially partisan. In
following party lines, the cleavage between Democrat and Republican reflected a deeper division between executive and
legislature, city and country, public welfare and private
property. Smith always attributed the impasse of 1925 on park
appropriations to "selfish interests on Long Island, bent on
preventing the establishment of parks and parkways in the
vicinity of golf clubs and big estates and determined to build
a wall between the City of New York and its most natural recreation area."[76] By protracted litigation and strategic
vetoes, the chief executive kept the park plan from being
gutted on Long Island, and possibly elsewhere, by a legislature
with a majority responsive to those interests.

In the eyes of the governor, the park plan was worth
fighting for, because it meant "welfare, health, and happiness"
for city people who now lived within motoring distance of the
countryside that the administration was endeavoring to preserve

for them. Smith placed conservation in the larger context of
social welfare when he observed: "Our institutional program
is mostly cure. Our recreational work is prevention. As our
life becomes more artificial the need for great areas where
natural conditions remain is a vital necessity."[77] To make
them available to the urban masses, he struggled to create the
system of parks to which his successors have added.

Governor Roosevelt, in his second term, exhibited his
commitment to conservation with the expansion of the Adirondack
State Park, which he described as "one of the world's great
natural playgrounds and health resorts—larger indeed than the
great Yellowstone Park," and with the Hewitt amendment to the
state constitution, which authorized a debt of $19 million for
the purchase and reforestation of marginal lands. As the
referendum neared, Smith called for the defeat of the proposition in what was his first public attack on FDR. Smith's
opposition was inconsistent with his own earlier stand on public finance and on parks. As the *New York Times* explained, the
disagreement between the two Democrats "concerned the presidency more than it did conservation."[78]

On conservation, as on public finance, Smith's significance lies more in what he did in the twenties than what he
said in the thirties. His administration in New York anticipated the New Deal in conservation in Washington. There was
more continuity between the two governors than Smith's condemnation of the Hewitt amendment implied. The tilt of the conservation movement towards aesthetic values and recreational
purposes, which was exhibited in the work of New York's State
Council of Parks and of the National Park Service during the
1920s, gained momentum when FDR went to Washington. President
Roosevelt used work relief programs to improve both national
and state parks. A study by his National Resources Board gave
to the state park movement in the thirties the impetus that
the New York State Association's park plan, which Smith
adopted, had generated in the preceding decade.[79]

For his contributions to the cause, the National Conference of State Parks, meeting in 1927, applauded Governor Smith and greeted him as "the next President of the United States." With characteristic aplomb, he agreed to "accept the nomination of the Bear Mountain Convention, having already been nominated at Coney Island." Early in the following year, the Albany reporters put on a skit in which Secretary of State Moses proposed to President Smith the annexation of Canada as a national park.[80]

CHAPTER 5
A HOME, EVERYONE MUST HAVE

Governor Smith's policies on housing accorded a growing
recognition to the public sector in maintaining the quality of
life that the state parks enhanced. He would commit the state
to the growth of parks, to the amelioration of institutional
life, and—if he had his way—to the subsidization of housing,
and to the generation of hydroelectricity. The bonds that
financed the first two embroiled Smith in controversy: over
the expenditure of proceeds on parks, over the wisdom of a debt
for public improvements. To avoid the problems associated with
bonds, he suggested the device of a public corporation to meet
the government's objectives for housing and water power.

The housing problem that Smith proposed to alleviate by
this means was not a new one.[1] It had evolved through a century of rapid urban growth. In the 1800s, private enterprise
did construct dwellings for the poor at a profit to the producer, but at a cost that the community became increasingly
unwilling to pay. The slums of New York City were notorious:
for congestion, unsanitary conditions, and fire hazards. When
reformers managed to set minimum standards in order to combat
these social ills, they often drove up the cost of building to
a point where the private sector ceased to create new units at
a price that the lower classes could afford. The trickle-down
process failed to meet the housing needs of a growing portion
of the city population.

If Smith grew up in a section of the city where the problem was acute, he acquired familiarity with proposals for its
solution when he sat in the assembly. The remedy most in
keeping with the freewheeling capitalism of the nineteenth century was model tenements built by limited-dividend corporations.
In theory, investors were supposed to accept a modest rate of
return in exchange for a reduced risk and the satisfaction of
contributing to communal well-being. In practice, such projects housed too few people to meet the needs and charged them

rent well beyond the means of the poor. In view of these limitations, progressives turned to government regulation to uphold minimum standards of construction and maintenance for
multiple dwellings. Governor Theodore Roosevelt supported the
investigation that culminated in New York's epochal Tenement
House Law of 1901. Assemblyman Smith cooperated with Lawrence
Veiller in bringing under its jurisdiction the smaller cities
of the state. Veiller, a professional bureaucrat and reformer,
and Robert W. De Forest, a philanthropic attorney (both of whom
figured in earlier chapters), administered the first agency in
New York City to enforce the law that they had been instrumental in enacting. Progressives like Veiller, who found the
regulatory approach congenial, did not intend to undermine
private enterprise but only to rid it of unacceptable practices.
He, therefore, opposed any suggestions for municipal housing on
the European model or for government subsidies.

Even some of Veiller's contemporaries realized that the
progressive achievement in regulation "may prevent the worst
housing from being erected, but cannot guarantee a sufficient
supply of good housing at rents (or costs) suited to low-income
or even middle-income groups." It would take a form of socialism or subsidy to reach the second goal. President Theodore
Roosevelt's Homes Commission favored government loans; the reformer, Edith Elmer Wood, approved of, not only subsidies, but
also municipal construction, to assure decent shelter to what
she described as one-third of a nation, ill housed. World War
I moved the federal government to take action, which some
leaders had been urging in vain, for the extension of credit
and the building of units to accommodate war workers. At the
close of hostilities, Washington hastily liquidated its investment, and housing reverted to the domain of private enterprise.[2]

The states were left to cope the best they could with a
housing shortage when Smith entered upon his career as governor
of New York. Wartime demographic and economic dislocation
added a new dimension to an old problem. Migration to the
cities increased the demand at the same time that a temporary

halt in construction curtailed the supply of dwelling space.
As its price rose precipitately, city residents protested by
forming tenants' associations, holding mass demonstrations, and
conducting rent strikes.[3] The agitation confronted Smith with
an urgency that drew his attention to the question of housing.

If the number of agencies investigating a problem give a
measure of its significance, housing had reached a critical
point at the beginning of Smith's governorship. Soon there
were three official groups in the field: his own Reconstruction Commission, the [New York City] Mayor's Committee on Rent
Profiteering, and the Joint Legislative Committee on Housing.

Both wartime dislocation and longstanding difficulties
concerned Smith when he appointed the Reconstruction Commission
and charged it, among other things, with formulating policy on
housing. A perceived emergency led the commission, in May, to
make a preliminary progress report in which it dismissed recommendations for rent control because, "The rising rents are
merely a symptom. The disease is lack of sufficient houses."
The report, therefore, emphasized new construction for which
the commission intended to rely on private enterprise, possibly
in the form of limited-dividend companies.[4]

Acting on the advice of the commission, the governor met
with members of the financial community in order to encourage
them to invest in residential building. In his after dinner
remarks at the Metropolitan Club on May 16, he refused to
countenance proposals for relaxation of the Tenement House Law
for the purpose of increasing the number of units by lowering
standards. In the progressive tradition, he assigned to
government only a regulatory function in the economy when he
asserted, "There is no legislation that will make houses grow
on empty lots." He identified the need as "*more houses*" and
called upon his listeners to perform "a patriotic duty" by
supplying them.[5]

"Moreover, I fail to see why it was necessary to bring
the Governor from Albany in a matter which could have been dis-

posed of by business men in half an hour without the flare of
trumpets," protested Nathan Hirsch, the chairman of the mayor's
committee. Hirsch, who was highly critical of the governor,
led his committee in an endeavor, popular in a city where
tenants predominated over homeowners, to check the postwar rise
in rents. The mayor's committee also felt free to press for
subsidies for building—for which the state would supply the
funds.[6]

Nowhere is the tension between city and state more obvious than in the relationship between the mayor's committee, on
the one hand, and the governor's commission and the legislative
committee, on the other. The two state agencies cooperated with
each other, but the city group antagonized both. On the day of
the release of the Reconstruction Commission's report, the members of the Joint Legislative Committee on Housing met to organize and elected Senator Charles C. Lockwood as chairman.
Smith hastened to proffer to him the services of the Reconstruction Commission which he, in turn, praised for its achievements. In contrast, efforts to coordinate the work of the city
and state committees foundered, when Samuel Untermyer, speaking
for the former, denounced the legislators for whitewashing the
monopolies that were limiting the supply of housing.[7]

All three groups did cooperate, however, in obtaining
action at a special session of the legislature in 1919. Shortly
after adjournment of the regular session, the mayor's committee
requested the governor to summon an extraordinary session to
pass legislation against rent profiteering. The expressed
aversion of Smith and his Reconstruction Commission to such
laws was seen—mistakenly, it would seem—as a refusal. When
the chief executive did call a special session to ratify the
Nineteenth Amendment to the United States Constitution, Hirsch
immediately asked him to place housing on the agenda. Both
Governor Smith and Senator Lockwood turned out to be amenable
to having the session consider the question, if accord existed
on specific measures to be taken.[8]

Meanwhile the legislative committee and the executive commission agreed to pass the buck to the federal government by calling upon it to relieve the crucial shortage of capital for residential construction. With this in view, the lawmakers advocated a federal home loan bank; the governor's task force, income tax exemption for holders of mortgages and bonds of the State Land Bank. Smith offered to use his influence with New York's congressional delegation to press for the proposals, had a letter drafted supporting the tax exemptions, but apparently never mailed it to the representatives.[9]

Reconsideration of the letter reflected the governor's growing inclination to refer the problem of housing to the special session. What apparently decided Smith to place it on the legislative agenda, was the unanimous agreement of the three committees and other experts on four bills. He reversed himself to join with the Charity Organization Society and the Tenement House Department in supporting an amendment to the Tenement House Law. It is significant that two groups intimately associated with these regulations, the first largely responsible for their enactment, and the second, for their enforcement, acquiesced. A second proposal dealt with the shortage of capital by making housing a legal investment for savings banks. Two bills addressed the plight of the tenant in a lessors' market by granting a limited delay before eviction. The Lockwood committee recommended, not only the enactment of this legislation favored by the governor, but also the adoption of two resolutions calling upon Congress to set up a home loan bank and to allow tax exemption for State Land Bank bonds—but not for mortgage income.[10]

The legislature passed the four bills, adopted the two resolutions, and ratified the woman suffrage amendment in a record-breaking three and one-half hours. Smith expressed satisfaction with the session, but by midsummer Belle Moskowitz failed to detect any letup in the housing crisis.[11]

By midwinter, when the legislature reconvened for the regular session of 1920, housing conditions had deteriorated

enough to elicit a special message from the chief executive.
Although he deplored the greed of certain landlords, he concentrated, not on the temporary—if sensational—matter of exorbitant rents, but on the permanent shortage of moderately priced
dwellings. Alluding to the impact of the war, he discerned "a
willingness to consider new responsibilities for the State differing somewhat from our deep-rooted policy of individualism."
He concluded by appealing to the lawmakers to assume their responsibility by enacting the measures that the Reconstruction
Commission had recommended to him a few days before.[12]

The Reconstruction Commission influenced Smith's thinking
and framed his policy on housing as on reorganization and parks.
Through its housing committee, it conducted field studies that
resulted in an understanding of the chronic, rather than temporary, nature of the shortage of working-class accommodations.
The commission, therefore, lacked enthusiasm for the "popular
indoor and outdoor sports" of "rent regulating and landlord-
baiting," which would add nothing to the supply of low-cost
units. Although the committee was unanimous in recognizing a
need for government involvement, the members differed on the
form it should take. A majority favored both loans to limited-
dividend corporations to subsidize the construction of model
tenements and also the more radical expedient of municipal
housing. "So far as dwellings for working people. . . , the
Reconstruction Commission has offered the only solutions," its
secretary, Belle Moskowitz, asserted. She assured Smith, "you
have offered definite remedies, that would go far toward
solving the situation."[13]

They were not enacted into law, for the legislative
appointees, who were concentrating on the immediate emergency,
exerted a greater impact upon their colleagues than the executive panel. The Lockwood committee, which was more favorable
to business than to labor, was reluctant to approve direct
government aid to increase the supply of housing. Its members
were more sympathetic to the construction industry than to
landlords because, as politicians, they could not be insensi-

tive to the outrage of tenants who formed a large part of their
constituency. Their preliminary report excoriated "speculators
who do not build and lessees of buildings who take over proper-
ties solely for the purpose of making excessive profits out of
tenants," and recommended measures to curb rent profiteering.
Although Smith was not partial to rent regulation, he did send
the emergency messages to facilitate its adoption. An opponent
of the bills predicted their passage "because election day is
not far off." As if to confirm his political analysis, they
passed, just a few days after the formation of a tenants' organization at a meeting punctuated by threats of rent strikes and
riots, and a week after a tumultuous hearing marked by the presence in Albany of a delegation of a thousand tenants. Representing their interest, Fiorello La Guardia, flamboyant successor to Smith as president of the Board of Aldermen, de-
claimed "that I come here not to praise the landlord but to
bury him." In contrast, Senator Lockwood observed, "We want to
be fair to the landlords. . . . but we must be fair to the
tenants. . . . and we are going to adopt such legislation as
we think will meet that situation."[14]

    With its emergency rent laws, the Lockwood committee in-
tended to moderate the rise in rents by curbing the legal recourse and unscrupulous practices of landlords that, in the
opinion of the investigators, bore some responsibility for the
emergency. Chapter 139 of the Laws of 1920 denied to the
lessor repossession of premises through summary proceedings for
nonpayment of rent, unless he could establish that "the rent
. . . is no greater than the amount paid by the tenant for the
month preceding the default . . . or has not been increased
more than twenty-five per centum over the rent as it existed
one year prior." Although the legislature expected to confine
the rise to 25 percent a year, the wording of the first clause
left latitude for a more substantial increase, if not initially
resisted by the tenant. The legislative intent is confirmed
by debate on the bill, by subsequent legislation, and by another law enacted simultaneously. Chapter 136 allowed the

tenant, in an action for the recovery of unpaid rent, the defense that the rent was unreasonable, and created a legal presumption of unreasonableness when rent had risen over 25 percent a year. Chapter 137 empowered the courts to stay issuance
of a dispossess warrant for as long as a year where the tenant
was holding over without the landlord's consent but could not
find suitable accommodations, and continued to pay a reasonable
rent. This statute gave the judiciary some discretion in the
determination of rent. Two measures relieved a tenant in dispossess cases of liability for substantial damages and permitted him to collect an award in the event that he successfully
contested the action against him. Besides controlling rents
indirectly by inhibiting the resort to legal remedies for dispossession and for recovery of rent, the laws intended to prevent the landlord from exacting higher rents from new lessees
by a turnover of tenants who were forced to move against their
will. One statute made it an offense to suspend vital services; another transferred from the landlord to the court the
decision that a tenant was objectionable where this was grounds
for termination of a lease. The law that presumed a duration
of a year rather than a month for unwritten agreements lessened
the frequency of possible rent increases for the most defense-
less apartment dwellers. As a consequence of these enactments,
the regular session of 1920 imposed a degree of rent control on
the metropolitan areas of New York for two years.[15]

All of the emergency rent laws "merely scratched the surface of the housing problem," whose solution required measures
to stimulate the construction of low-cost dwellings, according
to the Citizens' Union. Both the Citizens' Union and the City
Club favored the recommendations of the Reconstruction Commission for municipal projects and for state loans to limited-
dividend corporations. Shortly after adjournment, the two
civic groups urged the governor to recall the legislature to
reconsider the housing proposals, labor legislation, reorganization, and the executive budget. Belle Moskowitz, who joined
the clamor for a special session in New York, pressed Smith to

work for a plank in the Democratic platform, committing Congress
to housing subsidies, when he attended the national convention
at which his name was first placed in nomination for the presidency.[16]

Smith deferred, until his return from California, the
decision to place the Reconstruction Commission's program on
housing before a special session. His deliberations were complicated by an episode in the Red Scare. During the regular
session, the assembly had first suspended and then expelled its
Socialist members. The proceedings, which he denounced at the
time, deprived of representation five districts in which the
housing crisis was acute. The fact that an extraordinary session would confront the governor with the question of whether
or not to fill these seats goes far to explain his reluctance
to reconvene the legislature. In the end, he made the principled, but politically inexpedient, choice of holding special
elections.[17]

Early in August, Smith confided that he was "unable to
see how we can get away from an Extraordinary Session, in view
of the . . . housing situation." It appeared more likely when
Clarence Stein, the Reconstruction Commission's housing expert,
testified at a committee hearing. On the twelfth, the governor
issued the call and immediately left Albany on vacation. Towards the end of the month, when he addressed the New York State
Federation of Labor, he displayed a cautious optimism on the
prospects for constructive legislative action. By the beginning
of September, he recognized that there was legislation that
could make houses grow on empty lots. At a conference with the
Lockwood committee, when a real estate lobbyist objected to
state aid as a violation of the tenets of Jeffersonian Democracy, the chief executive retorted, "But there was no shortage
of houses in Jefferson's time." In a speech to civic groups
in New York City, he backed the Reconstruction Commission's
program and complained of inaction by the regular session:
"They did what they thought was right. . . . they didn't think
much about it. . . . The question of extending the credit of

the State toward the building of houses is debatable. . . . the question was not even debated."[18]

As the special session approached, the governor's office received a large volume of mail, which did debate the entire issue of housing. His staff prepared a digest of this mail, which canvassed all of the housing proposals that were considered by the administration—and many that were not. They ranged all the way from a version of Henry George's single tax to a special surtax on rents. Among the writers, Royal S. Copeland, Congressman Jefferson Levy, and William Church Osborn favored such government assistance as the Reconstruction Commission had advocated. Real estate interests divided on the commission's recommendations, which one trade organization denounced as socialism. Most of the realtors preferred tax exemptions and the repeal of the rent laws that other correspondents sought to strengthen. Smith dismissed a suggestion for producers' cooperatives as too controversial for a special session. He had ample advice from which to frame his message to the returning lawmakers.[19]

In his address, Smith expressed regret that the regular session had disregarded the proposals of the Reconstruction Commission and confined itself to the emergency rent laws. Now, however, he favored rent regulation as a way of mitigating the hardships that the housing crisis was inflicting on families in modest circumstances who "have managed to protect themselves from other forms of profiteering, but they are helpless to deal with this one, because a home, everyone must have." To the critics of rent control, he offered an opinion "that only those who seek to live outside of the moral law have any great fear of State regulation." He wanted to plug the loopholes in the rent laws, however, only as a preliminary to a more comprehensive program to stimulate construction and engage in long-range planning. The specifics included municipal projects, subsidies in the form of state loans and tax exemption, antitrust action to reduce the price of building materials, and the establishment of a new agency to direct the housing effort.[20]

As before, the Joint Legislative Committee on Housing
was more conservative in its recommendations than the governor.
It deemed state credit and municipal housing inappropriate subjects for a special session: the former, because it clearly
required a constitutional amendment; the latter, because of
possible constitutional obstacles. In view of the convergence
of legislative and executive opinion on rent control, more
rigorous regulation emerged as the major achievement of the
session.[21]

In order to understand the new legislation, it is necessary to review the legal status of landlord and tenant in New
York before the extraordinary session suspended the conventional
relation between the two parties.[22] Under normal circumstances,
renewal of a tenancy depends upon an offer extended by the landlord and accepted by the tenant. Unless both of these conditions are fulfilled, a tenant, remaining in possession, holds
over without the consent of the landlord. The landlord may have
recourse to summary proceedings or action in ejectment, to dispossess a tenant holding over without consent. Or the landlord
may hold the tenant for a renewed term; in this case the tenant
is deemed by virtue of holding over, to have assented to any
new conditions specified by the landlord, including a change in
rent.

As Smith implied in his message, holdover proceedings were
being used to circumvent the rent laws. A tenant continuing in
possession and exercising his rights under the laws enacted at
the regular session, could avert rent increases of more than 25
percent per annum. With a change of tenancy, the landlord was
free to raise the rent almost at will. Under the prevailing
conditions of scarcity, a new tenant presumably might agree to
a rent more than 25 percent above that paid for the premises in
the preceding year and pay at least one month's rent before
occupying the dwelling. After that, if the new tenant balked
at the rent, the landlord would be in a position to succeed in
summary proceedings for nonpayment of rent because he could
prove "that the rent . . . is no greater than the amount paid

by the tenant for the month preceding the default." Under
these conditions, landlords found it to their advantage to refuse to renew tenancies, institute summary proceedings on the
grounds that the occupants were holding over without the landlord's consent, dispossess tenants, and replace them with new
ones willing to pay higher rents. The landlord's right to rent
or withhold premises at his own discretion and therefore to dispossess tenants for the reason that they were holding over
against the will of the landlord, made possible the circumvention of the rent laws of the regular session of 1920. This
legislation, therefore, failed to provide the intended relief.

In September, the lawmakers framed provisions to close the
loopholes. Where the regular session had limited dispossessory
remedies on the grounds of nonpayment of rent to cases where
the rent was reasonable, the special session went further by
clarifying what was reasonable and by permitting tenants to remain as long as they did not default. As a result, in much
residential property, the landlord lost his discretionary power
to change tenants, the holdover status was virtually eliminated,
and in its place a statutory tenancy created with the right to
continue in possession as long as a reasonable rent was paid.
The crucial provisions were those which, for all practical purposes, halted dispossession for the cause of holding over and
allowed a tenant to occupy the premises while remitting a
reasonable rent. The special session redefined reasonable in
order to remove the possibility of raises of 25 percent a year.
Under the new statutes, any increase established the presumption of unreasonableness; therefore, in the metropolitan areas
to which they applied, it was no longer feasible to dispossess
a tenant for nonpayment or collect the amount in default, in
the event of any raise. By suspending dispossession of tenants
for holding over, and preventing it for default on increased
rents, the legislation stabilized rates for tenants who did not
move. In effect, the special session froze rents in urban
areas where the vacancy rate was abnormally low.[23]

Given the distress caused by a housing shortage, it was all too human to find a scapegoat—or two: landlords who raised rents and monopolies that inflated the price of new buildings. No sooner had Smith announced the special session than Samuel Untermyer suggested to him that the legislature attack the combinations in the construction industry, which were increasing the cost, and the investment policies of the insurance companies, which were diminishing the capital, for housing. The financial world was vulnerable because of the revelations of the Hughes investigation in New York at the beginning of the progressive era and of the Pujo committee, with which Untermyer had been associated, at its close. The governor acted on this information by referring it to the Lockwood committee, the attorney general, and the superintendent of insurance, only to learn that the crusading attorney lacked confidence in the officials. Untermyer insisted he had "no taste for the task that I have said I would be willing to perform if called upon to do so" and soon thereafter joined the staff of the Joint Legislative Committee on Housing, where he carried on an investigation in the sensational tradition of irresponsible committees with little respect for witnesses and less for facts. There was a second misunderstanding between Untermyer and Smith, this one over the policy to be pursued in correcting the evils of monopoly in housing. The lawyer took a Rooseveltian approach, condoning combination under effective government supervision to protect the public interest. The reference to monopoly in the governor's message to the legislature was Wilsonian, implying the restoration of competition to bring a downward adjustment in prices. The special session did nothing on monopoly beyond authorizing the Lockwood committee, and petitioning Congress, to study the problem.[24]

Smith was less evasive when he intervened to keep the session from adopting Lockwood committee recommendations about which he entertained misgivings. In his opening address, he had been as sanguine as the legislators about amending the Tenement House Law to facilitate an increase in the number of

dwelling units without any decline in the standards of accommodation. Robert De Forest, the Charity Organization Society,
and other social organizations combined to convince him that although the state would not gain much housing, favored landlords
would reap profits, and the poor would suffer, from relaxation
of the regulations. The governor reversed himself and used his
influence against any revision. In acknowledgment of his cooperation, a leader of the COS hastened to "express my appreciation of the manner in which you dealt with the proposals to
amend the Tenement House Law."[25]

Smith probably dealt in the same manner with the proposals
of the legislative committee to amend the income tax law, in
order to encourage investment in mortgages by making the return
tax-exempt. He consulted Mark Graves, who argued against the
exemption on the grounds that it would set a precedent for
opening loopholes in the law without substantially increasing
the capital available for housing. The governor's official
papers contain statements by two authorities on the subject, a
professor at Columbia University and a retired tax commissioner,
both of whom gave the same advice as the head of the income tax
bureau. The chief executive expressed his reservations to the
legislature where neither the bill for relief from the state
tax, nor a resolution asking Congress for an exemption from the
federal income tax, passed. The only measure that the special
session adopted to increase the supply of housing did use the
device of tax abatement as an inducement. Both the governor
and the Lockwood committee agreed on the desirability of allowing local governments to relieve new construction from real
estate levies for a limited period of time, and the legislature
took the required action.[26]

Evaluations of the special session differed, but Professor Samuel McCune Lindsay considered real estate tax abatement
the only constructive measure to emerge. The political scientist reviewed the year's legislation on housing in a study that
condemned the rent laws as counterproductive for tending to discourage the maintenance of old, and the construction of new,

units. Smith, who had been persuaded of the need for these
statutes, was more inclined to "feel that some good comes from
the special session." He did not, however, conceal his disappointment at the failure of the legislature, either to give
serious consideration to his comprehensive program for increasing the supply of moderately priced housing, or to take
action "looking toward a permanent solution of the housing problem." During his campaign for reelection, he acknowledged
the responsibility of the state to stimulate building in order
to assure decent accommodations within the means of all the
people.[27]

This was the theme of an address prepared by Belle
Moskowitz to represent Smith's views at the Governors' Conference in December. The paper measured the distance he had
traveled in his thinking on housing during his first term. The
chief executive, who initially had been skeptical of rent control and placed his reliance on private enterprise, now
approved of the emergency rent laws and recognized the inade-
quacy of the private sector. In the name of humanitarianism,
he ascribed to government the responsibility of assuring decent
accommodations for all of its citizens by such forms of economic
intervention as municipal construction, state subsidies, and
planning agencies.[28]

Despite Smith's predilection for attacking the causes of
the housing problem, rent regulation, which only alleviated the
symptoms, was the main achievement of his first administration—
and one that his Republican successor did not reverse. Before
he left office, the Democrat took steps to ward off a challenge
to the constitutionality of the rent laws. During the Miller
regime, they were upheld in the courts and extended by the
legislature to February 15, 1924, on the recommendation of its
joint committee.[29]

The Lockwood committee gave way to a new housing agency
in 1923. When Smith returned to Albany, both Lockwood and
Untermyer urged him to use his influence to prevent the legislature from terminating the committee whose research had sub-

stantiated the emergency on which the constitutionality of the
rent laws was predicated. The belligerent attorney held Smith
accountable for the action of the Democratic senate; he, in
turn, disclaimed any part in the proceedings of the other
branch. In the end, it was the assembly, with its Republican
majority, that declined to extend the life of the committee.
The outcome could hardly have been displeasing to the governor,
since the lawmakers did establish a Bureau of (later, Commission
on) Housing and Regional Planning, which he had been advocating
since the Reconstruction Commission first made the proposal.
The new bureau, which replaced the defunct committee, could defend the rent laws equally well and had the distinct advantage
of being under executive, rather than legislative, jurisdiction.[30]

From the time of its establishment, the bureau framed
Smith's policies on housing in general, and on rent control in
particular, with a few exceptions where political expediency
interfered. In 1923, he disapproved a bill to extend the rent
laws beyond their expiration date in February, 1924, on the
grounds that the commission's report would be available to guide
action at the next session. The veto was unpopular, particularly among tenants in New York City. He justified it by the
need to prove an emergency in order to prevent the courts from
finding any extension unconstitutional and reassured a protester,
"I have no doubt that the situation is still acute and that . . .
its report will be able to demonstrate that fact."[31] It is
significant that even in 1923 he did not use the same logic
when he signed measures extending rent control to certain upstate cities and to tenancies beginning after the passage of the
protective legislation. The two situations are not strictly
analogous, for the courts had been handing down conflicting
rulings on the applicability of the laws to new occupants, and
the Rosenman bill clarified the legislative intent. Assemblyman Samuel I. Rosenman, known in later years as FDR's speech-
writer, argued persuasively for his measure at the hearing
where the governor's ambivalence appeared in his remarks that

"You can't go on indefinitely invoking the police power of the State to permit tenants to virtually fix their own rents."[32]

In 1924, nevertheless, the governor put the weight of his office behind continued rent control. Its investigation led the Commission on Housing and Regional Planning to advocate a two-year extension, the chief executive endorsed the findings, and the legislature unanimously converted them into law.[33] Just as he had approved the inclusion of cities in the capital district in the absence of any investigation by the commission in 1923, the following year he signed a bill to include the villages of Westchester County, despite the objections of the agency. One of those who favored the inclusion was Julius Henry Cohen, who figured prominently in the governor's subsequent housing policy. Smith was more responsive to the needs of a potential constituency in the working class of the area than to its real estate interests.[34]

Similar political considerations affected the process of decontrol, which began with the expiration of the 1924 legislation. The Commission on Housing and Regional Planning and its successor, the State Board of Housing, recommended, the legislature enacted, and the governor signed in 1926 and 1927 measures for the gradual phasing out of the emergency rent laws. It was to be accomplished by renewing them for a year at a time while progressively excluding from their jurisdiction more expensive quarters, less densely populated localities, and new tenancies.[35] By 1928, partial decontrol had proceeded far enough to prevent undue hardship upon the termination of rent regulation, and the emergency that had justified the program no longer existed, according to the State Board of Housing. Therefore, it did not favor extending control when the current law expired on June 1. The motives were obvious that led the politicians to discard the report, as the legislature enacted and the governor approved another year's extension. Both were currying favor with a significant group of voters. Republicans, who had been reluctant supporters of the legislation, found a chance to embarrass Smith by forcing him to choose between the

advice of his experts and the interest of numerous tenants. A
spokesman for realty, writing "as an individual, a Roman
Catholic, a Tammany Democrat, and one who is ardently desirous
of seeing your excellency . . . elected to the Presidency of the
United States," warned of the adverse political effect of a
failure to uphold the rights of property in this situation.
Smith justified his signature as necessary to mitigate the difficulties of low-income renters.[36]

In the case of the emergency rent laws, it is hard to tell
where Smith's humanitarianism left off and his politics began.
He always recognized that the legislation was only a palliative
and never a cure for the shortage of moderately priced housing.
Like all direct controls, it created some inequities while relieving others. New York was hardly alone in imposing rent
regulation, which thirteen states and many foreign nations
adopted after World War I.

Although rent control remained in attenuated force until
after Smith's retirement, the housing effort shifted during his
tenure in office. The emergency rent laws originated in his
first term; a pioneering measure to stimulate the construction
of low-cost housing passed in his third. The issue of monopoly
dominated the consideration of housing in 1923 at the start of
his second administration.

Samuel Untermyer, the flamboyant attorney, who, as
counsel to the Lockwood committee, had begun investigating combinations in the housing industry about the time of Smith's defeat, was pressing for legislative action when the governor won
reelection. Although the housing committee did submit the first
of two reports on the problem of monopoly in time for consideration during the interregnum, the Miller legislature proved unsympathetic to its proposals. The committee attributed the
housing crisis to combinations, which raised the price and
limited the supply through typical monopolistic practices. Its
investigation uncovered restraint of trade in three areas:
building materials and the construction industry where trade

associations, so characteristic of the decade, artificially maintained prices; the building trades' unions, with their limited
membership and restrictive practices that increased the cost of
labor; and the financial world where the manipulation of securities intensified economic concentration and where the reluctance
to invest in mortgages inflated interest rates and prices. Both
reports contained accounts of the successful prosecution of illegal activities, at the instigation of the committee, and suggestions for remedial legislation against the abuses of all
three factors: entrepreneurial, labor, and capital. The committee proposed the establishment of a state regulatory agency
analogous to the Federal Trade Commission and the more rigorous
enforcement of antitrust law. Untermyer favored a measure to
open union enrollment, prohibit featherbedding, and eliminate
the obstruction of technological innovation. On capital, there
were bills regulating the securities' exchanges and requiring
certain financial institutions to place a specified proportion
of their resources in housing. To encourage such investment, the
committee recommended that the legislature finish the work begun
by Hughes in the progressive era, by refusing any extension of
the time in which insurance companies were required to divest
themselves of corporate stockholdings. As Smith began his
second term, the Joint Legislative Committee on Housing was
ready to introduce bills with the effect of substantially regulating the state's economy.[37]

The fate of this legislation was a factor in the plea of
Lockwood and Untermyer to the chief executive to intercede on
behalf of the committee. In the combinations to be regulated,
they perceived a threat to both the bills and their sponsors.
The counsel hinted at "powerful lobbies intent on strangling
committee" while the *Times* reported on the prominence within
the Democratic organization of contractors and union leaders in
the building trades, which were resisting any regulation.[38]
Under these circumstances, the Lockwood committee and its proposals died during the 1923 session. The lineup on the bills
was similar to that on the resolution to renew the mandate of
the committee, with the governor professing neutrality, the

Democratic senate approving the measures to regulate industry
and finance—but not labor—and the Republican assembly rejecting the legislation and the resolution. What Smith's noncommittal position really meant was the subject of speculation.
One leading Republican, Senator Clayton Lusk, accused the governor of opposing the bills; another, Ogden Mills, condemned
Smith for support of them, which could be inferred from the
senate action.[39] A hearing revealed what his common sense told
him, that each interest group resented the measures by which it
would be affected.[40] His hands' off policy left the proposals
to the mercies of a legislature, no less sensitive than he to
the political implications. Indeed, the wholly Republican
state government of his predecessor had made short shrift of
them. Governor Smith, with his sympathies for labor, was unenthusiastic about anti-union and antitrust legislation.

Untermyer, who drafted it, reflected what Richard
Hofstadter has analyzed as progressive discontent with organizations that were raising the cost of living. Smith was not
particularly susceptible to the antimonopolistic or individual-
istic outlook in progressivism.[41] It was an aspect of the movement with which he, as an organization politician, did not
identify.

In the year that Untermyer's antimonopoly crusade petered
out, Smith renewed his efforts to implement the Reconstruction
Commission's program, which culminated in the State Housing Law
of 1926. He viewed the subject of housing as "one of the fundamental questions we must solve because of its effect on the
public health and welfare." As a first step, he promoted the
establishment of the Commission on Housing and Regional Planning. The governor assured its chairman, Clarence S. Stein,
that his agency represented "the first move on the part of the
State toward a permanent solution of the housing problem."
Stein, who had earlier worked with the Reconstruction Commission, brought to the administration the perspective of experts
in both the social service and technical professions who

favored active intervention by the government. His experience
with the Hudson Guild Settlement, the American Institute of
Architects, and the newly formed Regional Planning Association
of America guided him in his leadership of the commission. As
a result, Smith's policies on housing came to reflect advanced
opinion in social work, architecture, and the fledgling craft
of city planning.[42]

Always inclined to follow expert advice, the governor
viewed the research of the Commission on Housing and Regional
Planning as a blueprint for legislative action. When the
bureau's first report advocated the use of public credit to
facilitate low-priced housing, Smith reminded the lawmakers
that it "confirms in every respect the recommendation of the
Reconstruction Commission." Several times, he called upon the
1924 session for approval of constitutional amendments to allow
state and local governments to provide money for this purpose.
The Democratic senate adopted the resolutions, but the Republican assembly refused. The following year, after the complexion
of the legislature had changed, neither house took favorable
action.[43] By then, the bureau had substantiated its conclusions
with an exhaustive study that proved housing to be "a permanent
problem" because "At all times and in all places private enterprises has been [sic] unable to supply adequate housing to meet
the needs of the underlying population." Since the cost of
financing placed decent shelter beyond the means of an estimated
two-thirds of the people, the commission again proposed to reduce the price through subsidies in the form of loans to non-
profit corporations and of tax relief.[44]

Smith's conception of the program, which the two reports
recommended, was recorded in his answer to a United States
senator who inquired whether or not it would involve the government in the business of building. The chief executive responded in the negative and explained, "there is nothing in the
report of the Housing Commission or in my recommendation that
intends to put the State or any of its municipality [sic] in
the business of building houses." He made a distinction be-

tween government enterprise in construction and his own proposal
to authorize the state only to "lend money on the proper regulation and restriction to those who would build houses."[45]

In 1926 the governor finally succeeded in gaining legislative approval of a modified version of the commission's proposals—but without the crucial element of public credit. He
opened the session by insisting that for New York "to maintain
its position in the front rank of the progressive commonwealths
of the country," it would be necessary to use government resources to assure its people decent housing. Elements of his
program for achieving this goal were already in operation on a
small scale in the form of real estate tax abatement and
limited-dividend companies for the purpose of new residential
construction. A law to allow tax relief dated from Smith's
first term; to permit insurance companies to build housing projects, from the interregnum. The Commission on Housing and
Regional Planning had supported the renewal of both measures
before their expiration in 1924. Developments undertaken,
under this legislation, by the Metropolitan Life Insurance
Company served the governor as a model on which to base his
plans for public and private cooperation in housing.[46]

Julius Henry Cohen drafted a bill to carry out the policies enunciated by Smith and formulated by the Commission on
Housing and Regional Planning. Clarence S. Stein turned to the
lawyer whose experience with the Port of New York Authority
qualified him to adapt to housing the concept of a public
authority, which Smith was then striving to apply to water
power. In its original version, the housing measure provided
for a state housing bank in the form of a public authority of
a type familiar to Americans since the rise of TVA. A public
authority is a corporation organized for a public purpose but
with certain advantages of incorporation normally associated
with private business. As a corporation, the proposed bank
would be able to raise capital for housing by floating bonds
to be self-liquidating from the projects' revenues and to contract with private enterprise for construction and management.

One advantage of a public authority was the possibility of funding through the statutory procedure of chartering a corporation instead of the more onerous process of constitutional
amendment, which would be required in the case of a state loan
for housing. Joseph Proskauer agreed with its author on the
bill's constitutionality. In a progress report to the governor,
Cohen exulted, "I like this baby quite as much as I liked the
Port Authority. She'll be a more popular child anyway when
she grows up." If she never reached maturity, it was through
no fault of the chief executive. He recognized the failure of
private enterprise to find low-cost housing profitable as he
called upon the legislature to assure decent accommodations to
the working class by following the recommendations of the
housing commission and enacting Cohen's bill.[47]

The measure relied on the police power to justify government involvement in housing. The text opened with a legislative finding to the effect that substandard housing constituted
a hazard to the health, safety, and welfare of the public that
private enterprise proved incapable of abating. Consequently,
the bill provided for a number of expedients designed to bring
the cost of new accommodations within the means of those who
could not afford the market price for decent shelter: a public
authority, eminent domain, limited-dividend corporations, and
real estate tax abatement. Central to all the calculations was
the state housing bank which, as a public corporation with tax-
exempt securities, was expected to raise money at interest below the going rate for mortgages. The bill contemplated a combination of public and private enterprise in which the housing
bank held title to developments built and managed by the private sector. Ownership by a public entity would permit use of
eminent domain to assemble tracts large enough to produce
economies of scale. Participation by limited-dividend corporations in raising one-third of the capital for the projects that
they would construct and operate offered a further reduction in
cost in what was normally a very speculative industry. Whether
or not a lien on the property provided sufficient security to

induce investors to accept the restricted return remained to be
seen. The housing commission acknowledged the difficulty when
it suggested that local governments purchase stock in the companies. Municipalities were encouraged to cooperate in the
venture also by granting exemption from real estate taxes for a
limited period of time. To see that the savings were passed on
to the occupants, the bill specified maximum rents and reduction below the statutory limit if warranted by the company's
financial condition. The bill envisaged a new housing board
with regulatory authority over projects established under its
provisions and with general jurisdiction in the field.[48]

Smith's housing policy received favorable notice in many
quarters. The *American City Magazine* quoted the governor at
length, while the University of Michigan's student newspaper
evaluated his plan as "the most sane of recent examples of social
legislation." The editor explained to his readers that the program "is not socialistic," but he did not see "why it would
necessarily be objectionable if it was." Although Norman
Thomas agreed that it was not an example of socialism, he nevertheless indicated his approval.[49] The director found it conducive to the efforts of his Association for Improving the Condition of the Poor. Even some realtors wrote words of praise
for the governor and his measure. Congressman Fiorello La
Guardia sent him an article from the Italian-language press,
which was gratifying—if unintelligible—to the chief executive.[50]

After Senator Bernard Downing and Assemblyman Maurice
Bloch introduced the housing bill, the administration rallied
to its support. To publicize their case, members of the
housing commission prepared an exhibit in the Capitol corridor.
Belle Moskowitz worked behind the scenes while Cohen and Stein
testified at a legislative hearing. In an interview with Silas
Bent of the *New York Times*, the governor explained the device
of a housing bank and voiced a sense of responsibility for the
welfare of those who would benefit from its operation. He justified government intervention in housing because, "Shelter is

more important than a public utility; it is a public necessity."
In response to GOP criticism, he offered to compromise. "If
the Republicans in their wisdom can think of a better way,"
he remarked, ". . . let them go to it. . . . They can plaster
it all over with the Republican label and hang their pictures
all over it, and I shall be satisfied. I do not care whether
it is done with a Democratic or Republican bill, as long as the
thing is done."[51]

Although the GOP was responsive to a popular demand for
action on housing, it was reluctant to accept the governor's
measure. Republicans criticized it as unconstitutional, radical, and unfair to business, which would bear the burden, take
the risks, and profit little. As they were composing an alternative with more incentive to private enterprise and without
the housing bank, Smith publically professed "an open mind."
The way was paved for compromise on the Nicoll-Hofstadter bill
that the majority party introduced only a few days before an
assembly committee buried the Downing-Bloch bill.[52]

From the publicity that accompanied the preparation of
the GOP measure, it was apparent that it would not be satisfactory to the chief executive. He was briefed on its defects
by an official of Metropolitan Life, which had pioneered in
housing development, and by Julius Henry Cohen, the latter in
terms so critical of the Republicans that Smith destroyed his
communication. The bill drafter warned against legislation
that was merely window dressing, and his boss concurred, "we
can't let them put over something that is useless and then go
before the people and claim that they helped solve the housing
problem." The governor assured Cohen, ". . . I am relying very
strongly on your advice."[53]

The lawyer's analysis enabled Smith, in a presentation to
the legislature, to compare the two bills, to the detriment of
the Nicoll-Hofstadter. Although both parties had designed
their measures to create a supply of moderately priced dwellings
by reducing the cost of borrowing, limiting the profit on development, exempting it from certain taxes, and using eminent

domain, the two differed substantially. The GOP text suffered
fatally, in Smith's eyes, from the omission of the housing
bank. Instead, limited-dividend companies would raise all
the capital and hold title to the projects that they built and
managed. As public utilities, they would submit to regulation
by a state housing board. The administration criticized this
alternative on several grounds. The state would grant substantial privileges, exercise of eminent domain and exemption from
taxation, to private enterprise rather than to a public authority responsible to the chief executive and ultimately to the
electorate. Should the courts overturn the regulatory provisions or should the projects change hands, the state would have
given valuable considerations without receiving the quid pro
quo. The companies might not be able to perform the function
of low-cost financing in case investors failed to find their
bonds attractive at the specified interest rates or the federal
government rejected the legal fiction that made them instrumentalities of the state for the purpose of issuing tax-exempt
securities. Behind the divergent texts lay a philosophical disagreement on government intervention in the economy. The Democrat believed that the state would have to play an active role
in financing and planning, if the housing needs of the working
class were to be met; his Republican opponents entrusted both
of these functions exclusively to private enterprise with public assistance and under public regulation.[54]

    In an effort to obtain a compromise acceptable to him,
Smith invited the framers of both proposals to a conference.
In accepting for the GOP, Assemblyman Samuel Hofstadter denied
the implication in the governor's remarks that the Republicans
intended only to counteract a Democratic initiative by presenting their own measure. The legislator found the executive
misinformed on its contents and expected their meeting to convince him that, in contrast to the Downing-Bloch measure, "the
bill sponsored by us meets the requirements of sound government policy, correct economics and constitutional principles."
On the contrary, Cohen judged the Nicoll-Hofstadter bill to be

deficient in all three respects as he helped the governor to prepare for the conference. On closer analysis, the lawyer discovered objectionable provisions under which some of the companies would benefit from the financial incentives without being subject to the rent and profit limitations that were their justification. "Look what we have found about the private limited dividend companies. . . ," he exclaimed. The Republicans had resorted to "an old legislative method with which you are familiar, to make you think you're getting it when you're not," he informed the governor. "One section gives it to you but another leaves it out. This will bear your close scrutiny." The irrepressible and indefatigable Mr. Cohen planned to arrive in Albany in time to confer with Smith before the armistice negotiations.[55]

Smith opened the hearing on April 7 with the remarks, "Now, we are sitting around the table here today to see how we can put these two bills together, retaining the best features of both, the way we consolidate our newspapers. . . ." He pointed out that the measures differed primarily on the question of a state housing bank. With an occasional assist from the governor, Cohen conducted the defense for the commission's bill with provision for the public authority. At one point a Republican conferee announced that the party leaders insisted upon the elimination of the bank, which they regarded as an entering wedge for socialism. And while some of his best friends were socialists, Republicans would never vote for a socialist measure. To Smith this was "more enlightening than any of the discussion of fine constitutional points that has gone before. . . . We cannot have the bank. . . . No use of beating around any longer. The constitution is one thing, but the boss is another." Afterwards, in summing up the hearing, Smith concluded that any housing bill would not be a compromise but, "the Republican bill with whatever changes counsel for the Housing Commission can induce the Republicans to accept in order to make it a better bill."[56]

After a second meeting with Republican leaders, Cohen was
more sanguine as he reported to the chief executive, "The bill
is now very much improved. The features which we regarded as
vicious are gone." Specifically, Courtlandt Nicoll agreed to
include in his measure provisions setting maximum rentals and
limited returns on capital for all of the companies. Although
Cohen acknowledged that the conference had remedied the worst
defects in the Nicoll-Hofstadter bill, he still objected to it
on principle, because it relied on private enterprise rather
than a public agency and placed the investors' interest above
the public interest. He subsequently repudiated even this
mildly favorable evaluation of the bill.[57]

Consequently, the governor encountered conflicting advice shortly before passage confronted him with the necessity
of deciding whether to sign or veto the measure. Cohen informed
him of the detrimental changes that the Republican had made
in the bill during its legislative progress. The attorney now
held a more negative attitude than he had following the conferences. He complained that the latest version of the text
relieved the private limited-dividend corporations of rent
regulation by the housing board, thereby restricting them only
to the statutory maximums, and even opened the way for them,
under certain conditions, to exceed these limits. Nevertheless,
they would continue to enjoy the privilege of tax exemption.
Nicoll interpreted the print differently than Cohen. The
senator reminded the governor that he would appoint the members
of the regulatory agency with authority over the companies'
operations. Removing their rent from its jurisdiction was
defensible in order to afford management the flexibility to
function profitably. Nicoll denied the contention that any
corporation could charge more than the statutory levels while
retaining its tax-exempt status. The apparent inconsistency
arises from emphasis on different sections of the measure.
The legislator was referring to clauses on rent control; the
governor's adviser, to provisions for a fair return to investors. Contrary to Cohen, the Republican assured Smith that

recent revisions in the text were verbal rather than substantive.[58]

In a gesture toward the courts that would test its constitutionality, the bill reaching the governor's desk began with an assertion of the need to exercise the police power in housing and a description of the companies operating under its provisions as instrumentalities of the state, organized for a public purpose. The law created a State Board of Housing to initiate and regulate projects wherever people of modest means lacked decent shelter. The board would facilitate developments by certain corporations. They would provide equity capital equal to one-third of the value of the project by issuing stock with dividends limited to 6 percent. They would raise the remaining two-thirds of the money through mortgages at interest rates not above 5½ percent. The bill itself stipulated maximum rentals, varying from $9.00 to $12.50 per room per month in different localities. In its final form, however, it empowered the board to regulate the rents of all of the companies involved and to reduce them below the maximums where conditions warranted. On the other hand, rents might exceed the statutory limits, if the board could find no other way to protect the investors' right to a fair return. These corporations and their securities were exempt from applicable state taxes, and localities might relieve their property of real estate levies. The limited-dividend corporations fell into two categories: public and private. In return for more thoroughgoing supervision, the public corporations enjoyed the exercise of eminent domain, unavailable to the private. In contrast, the latter had greater freedom in the acquisition and disposition of their property, subject to the proviso that tax abatement would end if title were no longer vested in a limited-dividend corporation under the board's jurisdiction.[59] The legislation aimed to stimulate the production of low-cost housing by facilitating savings and offering inducements to investors. In effect, they represented an indirect subsidy. In order to prevent abuse, the state subjected the recipients to regulation.

The session that undertook to subsidize residential construction through the State Housing Law also consummated reorganization in the State Departments Law and ended the impasse
on parks with the Thayer-Moore Act. The administration reached
the peak of its legislative creativity in the year 1926, which
brought to fruition many of Smith's major programs for reform,
including a watered down version of his housing proposal.

It was a foregone conclusion that the governor, whatever
his reservations, would sign the housing bill. Cohen, who in
his disappointment over the elimination of the housing bank had
been suggesting a veto, recollected his chief to remark, "I
find that the fellow who insists on getting his bill through
without a change is a fellow who does not really care enough
to get the main thing." It is a sample of the homely wisdom
that made Smith effective as a politician and reformer. The
attorney, who had incorporated his idea for a housing bank in
the defunct Downing-Bloch bill, remained skeptical of the success of the alternative in raising funds at low enough rates of
interest. Nevertheless, he was reconciled to it as "a great
step forward in the social enlightenment of our community" on
its responsibility to make decent dwellings available to the
working class. "You and I know from our early experience," he
reminded Smith, "what it meant for our parents in the way of
struggle to bring up a family." Although the governor affirmed
his faith in the measure's potentiality for relieving the hardships of the poor, he readily acknowledged, "This legislation
is not perfect, nor do I believe we have said the last word on
the subject. . . ."[60]

The legislation of 1926 gave less state aid to low-cost
housing than Smith had long been requesting. The postwar
crisis had made him acutely aware of the failure of private
enterprise to provide adequate dwellings for New Yorkers in
modest circumstances. He backed the Reconstruction Commission
and the Commission on Housing and Regional Planning when each
in turn recommended the extension of public credit to reduce
the cost of shelter. At first, he contemplated amending the

constitution to permit the state to make loans for this purpose.
Under Cohen's tutelage, he substituted a public authority in
the form of the state housing bank, which the legislature could
incorporate by statute, as the instrument for borrowing funds
at below market rates. The opposition of the GOP, which preferred regulated private, to public, enterprise, killed the
housing bank. Compromise resulted in a law providing the indirect subsidies of tax relief and eminent domain to limited-
dividend corporations, building model tenements under the
regulation of a housing board.

For its effectiveness, the law depended on the cooperation of the business community to invest in housing projects
and of municipal authorities to exempt them from property taxes.
New York City, where the housing shortage was most acute,
stalled repeatedly. The State Housing Board negotiated with
city officials, and the governor conferred with the mayor, but
action was not soon forthcoming. More than a year elapsed between the enactment of the State Housing Law and of the appropriate city ordinance for real estate tax abatement.[61] Mayor
Walker was promoting a charter amendment for excess condemnation to allow the city to apply to low-cost housing any land
remaining unused after the exercise of eminent domain for other
purposes. Implementation of the state program might dissuade
the electorate from adopting his proposition. In an example
of the conflict that is endemic in the politics of New York
between the chief executives of the state and its metropolis,
the governor and the mayor were each apprehensive that the
other's policy would divert resources from his own. Just as
Walker made a belated concession on tax abatement, Smith, on
the eve of the 1927 referendum, gave charter revision a qualified endorsement while asserting that "new tenement-house
building on any large scale can only satisfactorily take place
under the State housing statute by the organization of limited
dividend corporations."[62]

Smith used all the influence of his office to promote
the companies in order to guarantee the law's success. In

anticipation of its passage, he could make no better suggestion
to a friend who offered to cooperate, than to engage in the
business of building under the auspices of the measure. In
public as well as in private, he took advantage of every opportunity to solicit investments in limited-dividend corporations.
The dinner of the new State Housing Board was one such occasion when a number of financiers responded liberally to the
governor's appeal. He, himself, bought stock in a firm incorporated to improve housing in Brooklyn and approached the party
leadership in the borough to assist in raising funds. The
chief executive's concern with housing did not stop with the
passage of the bill but extended to all phases of its operation.[63]

Judged by its results, the 1926 statute was hardly a
success, for it met only a minute fraction of the need for good
low-cost dwellings. Under its provisions, eleven limited-
dividend companies erected fourteen developments with approximately six thousand living units. If it had included the
housing bank, which Smith proposed, it is reasonable to assume
that these totals would have been significantly higher. Nevertheless, they would have been far below what was required to
eliminate substandard housing, as subsequent experience demonstrates. Judged in the wider perspective of social welfare,
the New York housing law was a pioneering measure at a time
when few jurisdictions recognized the existence of the problem
and fewer were willing to do anything about it. Louis Pink,
a member of the housing board, and the promoter of one limited-
dividend corporation, understood this when he published *The
New Day in Housing* during Smith's last year in office. The
law, "disappointing as are its results," the author admitted,
"points the way to substantial progress and is the most hopeful
legislation of its kind, yet enacted in this country." The
governor, in his introduction to the book, was more optimistic
about the future as he recorded his impression that "Homes
built under this plan already have made happier, healthier
living possible for many hundreds of moderate income families."[64]

Governor Smith was convinced that the way to this goal
lay through the stimulation of new building rather than through
the relaxation of standards in order to encourage the multiplication of units in existing structures. Although he acceded to
the latter approach during the crisis of his first year in
office, in 1920 he intervened to keep the legislature from
amending the Tenement House Law, and in each of his subsequent
terms he vetoed attempts at unwise revision. Despite his recognition of the need for additional dwelling units, he refused
to countenance measures that could produce "a renewal of the
conditions that the Tenement House Act was intended to wipe
out." He insisted on preserving in full force the progressive
regulatory legislation. Valuable as it was however in eradi-
cating the worst abuses, it contributed nothing to the supply
of low-cost housing, on which Smith concentrated his energies.
He was unwilling to have the housing board created by the act
of 1926 diverted from its basic work of generating new accommodations, by a study on the updating of the Tenement House Law,
a task that he preferred to assign to an ad hoc committee. "I
would much rather have your Commission," he explained to its
chairman, "stick close to the big job, which I consider more
important than anything else that the State has undertaken in
a long while."[65] Although the governor respected the progressive achievement, he advanced beyond progressivism in his efforts to overcome the troublesome housing shortage.

There is significance in the fact that the predecessor
to the State Housing Board was named Commission on Housing and
Regional Planning. In the Smith administration, the planning
movement was represented in the New York bureaucracy by
Clarence Stein, and in the ranks of distinguished citizens to
whom the governor looked up, by Robert De Forest. The chief
executive's remarks to the first annual state conference on
planning revealed the influence of the planners, both when he
extolled the vision of the garden city, and when he averred,

"The planning of communities and the planning of the State is
probably the greatest undertaking we have before us." Nevertheless, planning was honored more in theory than in practice
during his years in office—with the notable exception of the
park plan. The planning movement, which had gained impetus in
the heyday of progressivism, received encouragement from Smith,
and flourished under the New Deal in such agencies as the
Tennessee Valley Authority and the National Resources Planning
Board.[66]

Although he was ahead of his time, Smith's interest in
planning was secondary to his concern with housing. He gave
recognition to planning but took action on housing. The
planners, who expressed an interest in the improvement of
housing, were generally inhibited by economic orthodoxies from
contemplating realistic measures for its attainment.[67] The
more pragmatic Smith was ready to experiment with various forms
of state aid. Out of a humanitarian compassion for the slum
dwellers and out of a political instinct for government expedients, he fashioned a program that served as a model to subsequent administrations in state and nation.

Even the limited success that the governor scored in
housing would have been impossible without the consistency with
which he adhered to humane ends and the flexibility with which
he devised legislative means. To prevent the poor from being
forced into more congested and substandard quarters, he overcame his initial reluctance to rent control. The chief executive who had once asserted that "There is no legislation that
will make houses grow on empty lots," later proposed to provide
by law the "home, everyone must have." If the State Housing
Act of 1926 constituted his major achievement in this direction,
the public authority, for which he struggled unsuccessfully,
served as a model long after his retirement. His record led
Edith Elmer Wood to conclude, "The most important *efforts* to
obtain state housing credits have been those in New York, with
which the name of Governor Alfred E. Smith has been identified."
In the depression decade, the Empire State adopted the policies

of municipal construction and government loans, which he had long been advocating.[68]

In the thirties, the state assumed additional responsibility for housing partly in response to the incentives offered by the federal government. Two groups of New Yorkers who had influenced the Smith administration were instrumental in framing New Deal legislation on housing: members of the State Housing Board and social settlement workers. The National Industrial Recovery Act and Robert Wagner's United States Housing Act included elements of Smith's program such as government subsidies, local authorities, and public corporations. Primarily because of Smith's role in promoting the idea of the public authority, a recent scholar has dubbed his administration "a staging area for New Deal reform."[69]

If neither Governor Smith nor President Roosevelt were able materially to alter a situation which found one-third of the population ill housed, it is to their administrations that we owe much of our understanding of the problem and many of the experiments to solve it. On the Lower East Side, where he grew up and from which he entered politics, the Alfred E. Smith Houses stand as an appropriate monument to the governor's efforts to improve the living conditions of the poor.

CONSERVATION OF HUMAN RESOURCES

Governor Smith's housing policy grew out of his concern for the working class. In his introduction to *The New Day in Housing*, he made explicit the connections among the various elements of a comprehensive program to improve the quality of life by "our system of State parks, housing laws, our labor code and the laws protecting women and children in industry."[1] They added up to what a later generation would recognize as a welfare state.

The administration derived its labor and welfare legislation from the progressivism of the reformers who were so influential during Smith's years in the assembly. Although the historiography of American history affords few topics more controversial than progressivism, there does exist a considerable body of scholarship to document the progressive sources of the welfare state. As the progressive movement neared its close, Benjamin Parke De Witt analyzed its three components, including one that "has to do with the extension of the functions of government—city, state, and national—to relieve, as far as possible, the distress caused by social and economic conditions." Subsequently, Russel B. Nye located midwestern progressives "in the middle, between the laissez-faire conservative and the socialist," because they proposed "to extend the power of the state . . . positively, to use it to promote and protect the public social and economic welfare." John D. Buenker traced urban liberalism back to its progressive origins in eastern industrial states among new stock Democratic politicians, men like Smith and Wagner, with "a desire for government intervention in the economy to protect the less fortunate, the welfare state." Turning from political to social and intellectual history, Robert Bremner discovered a body of progressive reformers who hoped to eliminate poverty with measures involving "limitations on private-property rights and extension of public authority into areas previously regarded as the

exclusive preserve of individual initiative." More specifically,
the settlement workers whom Allen F. Davis studied, "helped to
extend the social welfare function of government"; he found
these progressives "less paternalistic and more genuinely sympathetic to the cause of organized labor," and in addition, "more
genuinely committed to the city" than the revisionists would
imply. All of the works cited revealed progressive support for
the welfare and labor legislation associated with Smith's
governorship in New York and the New Deal in Washington.[2]

To characterize progressives as committed to social legislation and receptive to trade unions is not to deny that there
were those who were differently inclined. If some progressives
preferred laissez faire or favored economic intervention only to
serve the interests of corporate enterprise, objected to labor
organization or opposed welfare measures,[3] it is important to
remember that others—who influenced Governor Smith—dedicated
themselves to social justice. The social progressives made substantial gains, which did not end abruptly in the twenties, at
least in New York.

If, nevertheless, the progressive achievement in labor
legislation suffers by comparison with Europe, it is necessary
to remember that the practice of judicial review inhibited the
Americans. The judiciary set the parameters of labor law; the
executive and the legislature were restrained both by the
actual decisions of the courts and in anticipation of how they
would rule. The ambiguity of the precedents complicated the
process of prediction. In the example of state legislation
restricting the hours of labor for men, by the time Smith became
governor, this kind of regulation had been upheld in the case of
hazardous occupations, overturned where the trade could not be
so classified, and subsequently upheld in a case where the distinction from earlier decisions was not clear. The courts
generally left the states free to prescribe maximum hours for
women and children and to ban child labor. The rulings implied
that a minimum wage was constitutional for women—but not for
men. It was possible for lawmakers to draft workmen's compen-

sation laws to meet the constitutional scruples of the bench.
On the one hand, the freedom-of-contract doctrine constrained
the lawmaking authority; on the other, the judges abated its
rigors by a sexual classification that enabled them to uphold
labor legislation designed to protect women, but in reality
often depriving them of job opportunities. The brooding presence of the courts explains why the wage and hour proposals of
the progressive era and the Smith administration tended to apply
only to women and children.[4]

Constitutional impediments did not prevent the states from
giving serious consideration to a large volume of social legislation in the progressive era and adopting a substantial number
of measures. Leading the way were the voluntary organizations
such as the American Association for Labor Legislation and the
National Child Labor Committee, which could derive satisfaction
from enactments setting a minimum age for leaving school and
entering the labor force, and barring children from dangerous
trades and night work. Legislatures moved to protect working
women and children from exploitation with statutes, not only on
maximum hours, but also on minimum wages. Wage laws assumed one
of two basic forms: the first, based on the example of Massachusetts, which relied on voluntary cooperation and publicity
to deter employers from paying substandard wages; and a second,
with greater appeal to Smith, which used the authority of the
state to compel the payment of a minimum wage. Reformers also
advocated social insurance to protect working-class families
from poverty arising out of circumstances beyond their control.
Workmen's compensation gained the widest adoption, perhaps because it engaged the self-interest of employers by limiting
their liability at the same time that it afforded some security
to their injured employees. Many states provided mothers'
pensions to enable widows to support their children at home
instead of consigning them to orphan asylums. Progressives campaigned vigorously, but without success, for health and unemployment insurance. Nevertheless, the commitment to social
justice was so pervasive at the end of the progressive era,

according to a study for the United States Department of Labor,
that "More important legislation affecting women's work was put
on the statute books . . . than in any other period of corresponding length."[5]

The fact that trade unions frequently opposed labor legislation indicates the ambivalence in the relationship between
the progressives and organized labor. Even in California where
reformers in Los Angeles and Sacramento were obstructing unioni-
zation, progressives in San Francisco proved more sympathetic
to labor. Republican progressives in Wisconsin, who were
pressing for "the conservation of human resources," and Democratic progressives in Ohio, both acknowledged the right of
labor to organize and inserted in party platforms planks condemning the use of injunctions to defeat strikes. In both
states, unions endorsed progressive politicians; in the second,
labor leaders were active in the progressive movement. Hull
House exemplified an attitude common among settlement workers
when it employed only union labor, opened its facilities to
union meetings, and lent support to striking workers. Like the
pro-union progressives, Smith was cordial to organized labor,
but, unlike its leaders, gave priority to social legislation
and preferred to see disputes settled by mediation rather than
strikes.[6]

In New York, neither the progressive, nor the labor movement was monolithic, as Irwin Yellowitz has pointed out. Social
progressives favored labor legislation that their more conservative colleagues deplored and on which labor leaders divided.
If a middle-class mentality made unions suspect, even in the
eyes of advanced progressives, labor felt more secure in gains
won by collective bargaining than by legislation. Nevertheless,
cooperation between the two groups placed on the statute books
protection for working women and children and workmen's compensation. The administration of the progressive Republican,
Charles Evans Hughes, was noteworthy, not only for the enactment
of many of these laws, but also for their effective enforcement.[7]

With the resignation of Governor Hughes, the torch of progressivism passed from Republican to Democratic hands. The divisions wedged by progressivism in the GOP enabled the organization of Smith and Wagner to capture control of the state government in the elections of 1910 and 1912. Together, they chaired the Factory Investigating Commission, which inspired a new wave of social legislation. Smith was part of the legislative leadership responsible, not only for adopting mothers' pensions and workmen's compensation, but also for carrying out the recommendations of the factory commission. It resulted in more stringent regulation of the workplace, new child labor legislation, and a fifty-four hour law with provision for a six-day week. In debating against an exemption for canneries, Smith quipped, "I have read carefully the commandment, 'Remember the Sabbath Day, to keep it holy,' but I am unable to find any language in it that says 'except in the Canneries.'" He spent his last years in the legislature working to prevent the commission's achievements from being gutted at the hands of a resurgent Republican majority.[8]

Frances Perkins was lobbying for the fifty-four hour bill when she made the acquaintance of Assemblyman Smith and gained an introduction to political life that would eventually lead her to Washington as secretary of labor and the first woman to hold a position in the cabinet of an American president. The New Englander had graduated from Mount Holyoke College where a guest lecture by Florence Kelley inspired a vocational interest in serving the underprivileged. While teaching at a private school in a suburb of Chicago, Perkins spent her leisure time in the city's famous settlements. From there, she went to Philadelphia as general secretary of a research and protective association formed to safeguard the multitudes of young women arriving in the metropolis in search of opportunity. She took a course at the University of Pennsylvania with Simon Patten, a political economist who was challenging the conventional wisdom of his day, and continued her studies of the social sciences

at New York's Columbia University. Employment by the Consumers'
League and by the New York Committee of Safety, which was
funding investigations for the factory committee, brought her
into contact with Smith for whom she conceived a liking and
respect. In her judgment, service on the Factory Investigating
Commission "was the turning point in Al Smith's life," both because it broadened his understanding of social legislation and
demonstrated his ability in a way that furthered his career.[9]

From the reports of the factory commission, it is possible
to anticipate the labor policies of the Smith administration.
Although the commission supported the nine-hour law, it acknowledged that "The goal of working people themselves throughout
the world is the eight-hour day." Economic activity could not
proceed "without ultimate injury to society" if the remuneration received by working women and children were calculated on
the assumption that they "do not need to be paid wages sufficient for self-support." The commission, therefore, recommended
a minimum wage statute on the Massachusetts model, with a back-
up of compulsion, should voluntarism prove ineffective in establishing a living wage. Hoping to see "the human resources
of the State more adequately conserved," a majority favored
social insurance and public employment agencies. Even as it
began its work, the commission recognized the need for a "comprehensive system of legislation" based on the experience of
the more advanced jurisdictions at home and abroad.[10]

The Factory Investigating Commission filed its final report in 1915, the year that the struggle over labor conditions
shifted from the legislature to the constitutional convention,
which Smith attended as a delegate. There, a plan surfaced to
insert in the basic law language that would, not only nullify
the advances made on the initiative of the commission, but also
ban future social legislation. The Barnes amendment consisted
of three clauses, each of which barred the legislature from
taking action: "to establish a wage for service to be paid to
any employee by a private employer"; "authorizing the expenditure of any public money to be paid to any person except for

materials furnished or services rendered"; "granting to classes
of individuals privileges and immunities not granted equally to
all members of the State." William Barnes, Jr. aimed his first
provision against minimum wage proposals; the second, against
mothers' pensions and social insurance; the third, against protective labor legislation in general. With his amendment, the
Republican leader intended to incorporate in the state constitution the doctrines of laissez faire economics and conservative
Darwinism. Nowhere did Smith speak more eloquently for social
justice than in opposition to the measure on the floor of the
convention.[11]

Echoing the Darwinian tones of the opponents whom he reproached for their willingness "to reduce the basic law to the
same level of the cave-man's law, the law of the sharpest tooth,
the angriest brow and the greediest maw," Smith rejected the
appeal for minimal government. In contrast to his adversaries,
he viewed the state, not as an abstraction to be feared, but as
the community organized for the service of its citizens. He
defined it, not in physical terms of "fields and rivers and
lakes and mountains and cities," but in human terms. "It is
the people, all the people of the State," he expostulated, "and
anything that tends to make the members of the State strong
and vigorous in turn helps to make the State so . . . ." What
the Barnes amendment would foreclose, "has been for the general
good and could in no way be described as a privilege," he
assured his listeners.[12]

Smith did not share what he perceived as his conservative
colleagues' vision of the law as "the expression of some divine
or eternal right," standing as a barrier to social legislation.
"I am unable to see it that way," he confessed. "My idea of
law and Democracy is the expression of what is best, what fits
the present-day needs of society, what goes the farthest to do
the greatest good for the greatest number." Disavowing the
assumptions of the mechanical jurisprudence, he understood the
law to be an instrument of power rather than an impediment to
its abuse, a device to be used in advancing social justice.

Towards the end of the convention, he was even more explicit in
his rejection of the substantive interpretation of due process
that was posing a grave threat to the constitutionality of
vital reforms.

> The great trouble in this State to meet the present
> day problem is that we should not have any such
> language as "liberty" and "preserving property and
> liberty by due process of law." That word "liberty"
> in there does not mean what our courts have of latter
> years construed it to mean. The gentleman from Albany
> [Barnes] knows that himself. That word "liberty" means
> physical liberty, the right to walk around and not be
> detained in any one place, and they have stretched it
> around all over the map to make it mean liberty of
> contract.

Urban problems were defying solution, he complained, for they
"cannot be met by the legislative bodies here because they find
themselves tied up by some language in the Constitution that was
never intended to apply to that situation."[13]

From the record of the constitutional convention, it is
clear that Smith, whatever the deficiencies of his formal education, was conversant with the intellectual currents of his
day. He handled them selectively, accepting those such as
legal realism, institutional economics, and reform Darwinism,
which were consistent with his political purposes. His mastery
of social theory contributed to his defense of social legislation as a delegate to the constitutional convention and to his
efforts to extend its scope as governor of the Empire State.

In his first campaign for the governorship, Smith reminded
the electorate, "no man in all the State's history devoted as
much time to the study and passage of laws in the interest of
men, women, and children that labor, as I did." Put on the defensive by Whitman's disparaging description of him as a professional politician who never earned his livelihood by the work
of his hands, Smith contrasted his own youthful experience at
the Fulton Fish Market with that of the incumbent as a student
at the elite Amherst College. Given his background, the
challenger could truthfully aver, "I know labor's needs. I

have lived and worked all my life among men and women who labor
for their daily bread. . . ."[14]

Following his election, in his first annual message,
Governor Smith called upon the legislature to meet the needs of
labor. Specifically, he recommended a statute "to lift labor
out of the category of commodities or articles of commerce,"
expansion of workmen's compensation coverage, the factory commission's minimum wage bill, more extensive regulation of the
conditions of employment for women and children, and health and
maternity insurance. Although the details of his program
changed with the times, its theme of providing "adequate protection for workers" reverberated throughout his four administrations.[15]

Smith did not wait passively for the legislature to act,
but took the initiative available to the chief executive in
promoting the reform of workmen's compensation. When he was
running for office, Smith condemned the GOP for lessening the
protection of the compensation law by instituting direct
settlements. Where the original statute had required official
supervision of all settlements, subsequent amendment permitted
adjustments without the Industrial Commission's intervention
between the insurer and the claimant, frequently to the disadvantage to the injured party. In February, Smith initiated
a Moreland Act inquiry into the administration of workmen's
compensation in general and of direct settlements in particular
and appointed Jeremiah F. Connor, a former official, to conduct
it. In accordance with his instructions, Connor hastily surveyed the record of direct settlements and, within a month, was
able to inform the governor's secretary that the evidence "on
this question alone will fully justify his investigation."[16]
A week later, long before the completion of his comprehensive
study of workmen's compensation, the commissioner submitted a
special report on direct settlements "because existing conditions are so shocking as to require immediate remedial legislation." The probe uncovered underpayment in 50 percent of the
cases investigated; therefore, Connor recommended the abolition

of direct settlements and a review of all cases in which they
had occurred. Smith followed up the report by calling upon the
legislature and the Industrial Commission to take the recommended action. They both complied, and the provisions that he had
criticized as inequitable to the workingman were repealed as a
result of the Moreland Act inquiry.[17]

Satisfaction over the termination of direct settlements
gave way to misgivings from right and left when the investigation extended into other aspects of the system of compensation.
The governor himself convinced a Republican businessman that
the purpose of prolonging the inquiry was not "to replace the
experienced men with deserving Democrats." On the other hand,
a labor lawyer expressed suspicion that additional revelations
discrediting the state fund would only redound to the benefit
of private insurance companies. To the chief executive, he
confided that Connor "at friendly poker games, . . . and in my
presence has shown that his attitude was consistently one antagonistic to State Insurance." As if to confirm these apprehensions, Connor released an exposé of the state fund in a second
preliminary report, with the observation that it was "only a
scratch on the surface" and a recommendation that "the whole
State Insurance Fund be investigated from start to finish."[18]
Yet Miles Dawson, the actuary whom Smith chose to do the technical study, had been an early advocate of workmen's compensation
and approached his task in a constructive spirit. Connor indicated a primary concern with the rights of injured workers who
were being underpaid, which was undoubtedly what had motivated
Smith to authorize the probe in the first place.[19]

The report filed at the completion of the Moreland Act
investigation, which found both public and private insurance
carriers victimizing workers, did not suggest the abolition of
the state fund. It was not only solvent, but also competitive
with the private companies and able to charge lower premiums
because of a lower expense ratio. Increasing the volume of
its business would reduce the unit cost of workmen's compensation even further. These considerations led Dawson to conclude

in favor of a state monopoly and the elimination of private
enterprise from this form of insurance.[20]

The facts on the state fund were somewhat obscured by the
sensationalism inherent in a report that concentrated on the
wrongs to claimants and insureds alike. For example, in
setting rates, the fund classified its clients in special and
general groups with what the investigator suspected as favoritism to the former. He alleged that for the special groups,
premiums and dividends were calculated upon the basis of their
own favorable experience, but in case of a deficit, they drew
upon the overall resources, while the general groups were not
credited with their own surplus in the determination of rates
and dividends but even paid the price of rebates to the others.
Many companies in the special category subscribed to the
Wyncoop Service on the basis of a contingent fee, which varied
inversely with their premiums. Wyncoop apparently served his
clients primarily by minimizing the claims of their employees
and extracting favors from officials like the one whose wife
received a gift—or a bribe—of an expensive automobile. The
report also questioned the relationship between the bureaucracy
and the insurance companies on the one hand, and Dr. Meyer
Wolff to whose clinics they directed injured workers. Entre-
preneurs, insurance companies, and corrupt officials all pro-
fited from depressing awards below what was the workers' due.
The investigators uncovered cases in which individuals extorted
a portion of the awards under the pretense of expediting
settlements. The Industrial Commission, which administered
workmen's compensation, denied the charges and justified its
practices by explaining, for example, that Wyncoop specialized
professionally in accident prevention and Dr. Wolff, in industrial medicine. Nevertheless, the inquiry resulted in a number
of resignations and prosecutions. In their report, Connor and
Dawson recommended, not only remedies to curb the abuses, but
also liberalizing the benefits of workmen's compensation.[21]

Having rushed his first report in order to promote the
abolition of direct settlements in 1919, the Moreland Act

commissioner submitted a definitive study at the end of the
year, in time for a legislative overhaul of workmen's compensation at the 1920 session. Just before it convened, Smith
arranged a conference to review the findings. Where the Industrial Commission agreed, the governor recommended, and the
legislature adopted a variety of measures designed to check the
practices that the inquiry revealed to be depriving workers of
their rights, to improve the administration of workmen's compensation in general and the state fund in particular, and to
increase the benefits paid to claimants. The chief executive
demonstrated where his sympathies lay when he characterized the
raise as "progressive legislation" and "an act of justice to
the workingman and his family."[22]

On his own initiative, Smith succeeded in giving workers
additional protection against on-the-job hazards. He convinced
the legislature to enact laws including occupational diseases
under workmen's compensation and providing rehabilitation services in conjunction with federal grants-in-aid. Frances
Perkins, who broke new ground for women in government with her
appointment by Smith to the Industrial Commission, found him
"very anxious to have the workmen's compensation law made as
broad and liberal, and given as wide coverage as possible."[23]

Nevertheless, he demurred in 1920 at some of Dawson's
more radical suggestions. Smith rejected universal coverage on
the grounds that workmen's compensation was not needed in
relatively safe occupations. The Industrial Commission advised
against a requirement to place employers without adequate
insurance in the state fund, lest the difficulties undermine
its solvency. Divided counsels deterred the governor from
sponsoring a bill to make the fund a monopoly in his first term,
when even its proponents on the commission did not consider the
time ripe. In his subsequent administrations, the Democratic
leadership regularly introduced such a measure, which the knowledgeable *New York Times* categorized as part of the governor's
program.[24]

Smith had run for office on a platform calling for the reform of workmen's compensation, but after his election the problem of unemployment demanded his immediate attention as a result of the postwar recession. In the spring of his first year,
the Reconstruction Commission made no fewer than three reports
on the subject. The administration's persistent concern with
a problem, for whose solution many contemporaries relied upon
the automatic operation of the market, arose out of a sensitivity to hardship and a sense of responsibility for its allevia-
tion. If the commission was perceptive in its recognition of
the chronic nature of unemployment and advanced in its willingness to formulate "A Permanent Employment Program" for the state,
it was less venturesome in its specific proposals. In its
recommendations, it shied away from active government intervention and deferred, to an indefinite future, unemployment insurance coupled with labor exchanges on the British model. For
the short run, the commission recommended state employment
offices to replace those that the federal government had closed,
consultation to encourage local officials to undertake public
works, and a speedup of state projects. Belle Moskowitz lined
up support for the successful measure to expand the employment
service; the governor invited local officials to confer with
him on the coordination of construction projects. Smith's first
term was noteworthy for its consideration—not its solution—
of the problem of joblessness, which diminished with the return
of prosperity.[25]

Unemployment and inflation contributed to labor unrest
and a rash of strikes in 1919, which governmental agencies
joined in suppressing. Since organized labor associated police
forces with strikebreaking, the New York State Federation of
Labor opposed the creation of the state police. Sympathetic to
trade unions, Smith entered office committed to the abolition
of the state troopers, but the bill for that purpose failed to
pass in his first year. To a defender of the force who urged
him to reconsider, he responded, "I have never taken a position
from which I was not willing to retire when proven wrong."

George F. Chandler, the superintendent of the state police, convinced him that he was wrong, and he reversed himself. He came
to have such a high regard for Chandler that he appointed sight
unseen the man whom the retiring chief desired as his successor.
If the new commander was extremely punctilious in calling at
the Executive Mansion, as its occupant reminisced, ". . . I was
probably the last one in the official family to discover a ro-
mance between the government and the household of the governor."
It ended in the elaborate wedding of Emily Smith to John A.
Warner in the Cathedral of the Immaculate Conception in Albany.
Under his leadership, the force retained the high reputation
for fairness in labor disputes that his predecessor had established in 1919.[26]

During the strikes of that year, it was customary for
employers and sympathetic local officials to apply for the dispatch of state troopers to their community. Smith was reluctant
to comply, and when he did so, insisted that the constabulary
act with impartiality in keeping the peace. In the words of
Chandler, *Never . . . did we try to use the troopers as strike
breakers.*[27]

His contention is borne out by the events of that first
postwar year of industrial unrest. In March, the mayor of
Hornell requested the protection of the state police for the
operations of a struck textile mill; upon the advice of
Chandler, the governor refused.[28] A similar petition did bring
the constabulary into Auburn for a few days in June during the
stoppage at a diesel engine plant, but the troop withdrew even
before the New York State Federation of Labor could register a
formal protest.[29]

Frances Perkins took the lead in the settlement of a prolonged strike at the metalworking plants in Rome, where the
chief executive had been reluctant to deploy the state police.
He dispatched them to avert violence among the contending parties, after Chandler's reassurance that he "was not going to
shoot anybody." At the same time, the governor insisted that
the employers negotiate, which explains Perkins' presence in an

official capacity. A friend, who was in the city in July, reported enthusiastically, "your Commissioner Miss Perkins made
a 'Ten Strike.' Al, she's a Diplomat." Smith acknowledged that
even a representative of Associated Industries, which had opposed her confirmation, praised her performance in this situation.[30]

As the year waned, new strikes arose and, with them, calls
for the aid of the state police. The officers whom Smith
ordered to Olean in August during a traction strike arrested
the scabs—not the strikers—for fomenting disorder.[31] In
September, he turned down a request from a state senator for
troopers to patrol Amsterdam, where glovers were on strike,[32]
and another from the mayor of Beacon, where hatters had walked
off the job. In the second instance, he acted on the recommendation of the constabulary which, on investigation, found the
strikers engaging in no unlawful activities, but the mayor exhibiting a partiality to the employers. Whereupon, Smith read
him a lesson on the function of the state police: "they take
no sides one way or the other, and . . . to have them brought
there for the purpose of intimidating strikers, should be dis-
couraged."[33] At Buffalo as at Beacon, Chandler preferred to
keep his men outside the city, but fatalities in the steel conflict brought troopers on the scene. To a union leader who protested against their conduct, Smith insisted that they "have
been instructed to do nothing but preserve order, and they are
there for your protection equally with everybody else." He
personally heard labor's charges of police brutality, but the
force claimed to be restraining acts of violence by both company
agents and strikers. It was withdrawn after consultation with
Chandler towards the end of December, and the governor resisted
all appeals to return it as a check upon an incoming Socialist
regime.[34] In its early years, the New York State Police did not
warrant the apprehensions of the trade unions because Governor
Smith recognized the right of labor to organize, to bargain
collectively, and to strike, and resisted the excesses of the
Red Scare.

If Smith took an advanced position for his time when he declined to suppress strikes with all the power at his command, he preferred to have disputes settled through mediation or arbitration rather than walkouts. To facilitate this in a year of unprecedented work stoppages, the Reconstruction Commission arranged a conference on industrial relations, for which Belle Moskowitz secured the indispensable cooperation of the New York State Federation of Labor. The governor opened the conference in September by emphasizing the importance of preventing halts in production. The meeting concluded, as its planners had intended, with the creation of a tripartite agency comparable to the War Labor Board in its composition of labor, management, and public, representatives. During the remainder of Smith's first term, the Reconstruction Labor Board intervened successfully in a number of disputes, including the one in Beacon, where he refused to summon the state troopers, and several in the garment industry, so crucial to New York City's economy. That the governor's personal involvement contributed to the outcome in a number of these cases, testifies to his rapport with organized labor.[35]

Despite their good record in industrial relations, the governor and his aides were less effective on occasion when they found themselves in the middle between contending forces within a union. A case in point is the 1919 printers' strike in which the workers struggled against their employers; New York City locals, against the international union; and Perkins labored in vain to produce a solution acceptable to all parties.[36] The achievements of Smith's first administration in bringing peace to the garment industry could not survive the deterioration of its unions into warring factions.

In 1920, Smith intervened in a clothing industry with a pattern of collective bargaining that had evolved through the progressive era. Negotiations extended beyond the usual issues of wages and hours to certain aspects of the business that fell within the realm of what management typically considers its exclusive prerogatives. The stable businesses and the unions cooperated to minimize the threat of competition from a kind of putting-out system in which jobbers subcontracted work to small, nonunion shops with lower overhead and labor costs than the "inside manufacturers" who provided steadier employment. When the employers refused to reopen a contract, the workers, whose wages were being outpaced by postwar inflation, protested by engaging in wildcat strikes. Appalled by the waste and suffering caused by stoppages in the city's major industry, Governor Smith personally presided over a conference in January at which he extracted concessions from both labor and management. The union ordered its members back to work, while the employers agreed to arbitration of the wage dispute. To decide the issue, the chief executive appointed an ad hoc committee, resembling the Reconstruction Labor Board in structure and overlapping it in personnel. The board granted a raise in the hope that it would not be passed on to the consumer in the form of higher prices, but absorbed by the industry through a gain in productivity. For his part in the outcome, the governor earned the appreciation of the union leadership.[37]

Faced with the threat of a strike in 1924, the governor duplicated his efforts of an earlier year to maintain peace in the garment industry. He personally interviewed the contending parties again, before appointing a fact-finding commission whose recommendations formed the basis of a settlement. If it required compromise, it did go far towards meeting labor's demands for unionizing all segments of the business and renewed the efforts to promote "inside manufacturing" over subcontracting. Leaders of management and labor joined in praising the commission and the governor who appointed it. He prized and intended to preserve for his posterity a message from Morris Hillquit, counsel to the International Ladies' Garment Workers' Union, rejoicing in the settlement and assuring Smith that "the credit is due primarily to your personal intervention."[38]

That many members did not share Hillquit's satisfaction with the agreement, explains in part why the Smith administration was powerless to prevent the outbreak of economic warfare

in 1926. ILGWU was deeply divided between a conservative wing
that espoused business unionism and a militant element that resented government interference in the strikes with which the
working class could secure its own advancement. The factions
suspected each other of undemocratic tactics to gain control of
the organization, and each accused the other of selling out:
the right, to management and government; the left, to commu-
nism.[39] The Governor's Advisory Commission, which had framed
the earlier settlement, presented its new recommendations to a
union torn by dissension, in which the left was philosophically
opposed to mediation and the right was turning to militance to
counteract the appeal of its opponents. In its report, the
commission proposed to strengthen the "inside shops," a goal in
line with the interest of the workers, but by a method that
they inevitably rejected, of making the favored manufacturers
more competitive by allowing reorganization once a year with
the dismissal of up to 10 percent of the employees. ILGWU considered the prospective loss of jobs and the denial of a forty-
hour week unacceptable, and it struck on July 1. Smith met with
the different parties, but the jobbers and the union both turned
down his suggestion for arbitration. After several months, the
walkout ended on terms less advantageous to labor than those of
the governor's commission.[40] This time, he proved unable to
reconcile the conflicting interests in the garment industry as
successfully as in his preceding administration.

By engaging in mediation efforts, Smith took a stand
popular with the right, but not the left, wing of ILGWU; by
promoting social legislation, he adopted a policy with considerable support among labor leaders in New York, but not nation-
wide. He placed his faith in the law to improve the quality
of life of the working class, as already demonstrated with regard to housing and parks.

In 1919, Governor Smith's program of social legislation
consisted of measures on wages, hours, and health insurance,
as well as the abolition of direct settlements in workmen's
compensation, a topic considered above. His first annual

message repudiated the economic theory that treated labor as a
commodity to be priced by the operation of the law of supply
and demand. In alluding to the forty-eight hour and minimum
wage bills, he found it "just as cruel to underpay a woman as
to overwork her." On the subject of health insurance, he advised the lawmakers to learn from the successful experience of
other industrialized nations.[41] The Factory Investigating
Commission, on which he had served, was the source of Smith's
ideas on wage and hour regulation; the American Association
for Labor Legislation, on the health plan. By the time he
became governor, the medical profession, which had initially
acquiesced in health insurance, had moved overwhelmingly into
opposition. The New York State Federation of Labor and the
Women's Joint Legislative Conference joined AALL in supporting
the governor's three bills, while the Women's League for Equal
Opportunity objected to the labor regulations, which would protect females by discriminating against them,[42] a position that
the chief executive, like the social feminists, had difficulty
understanding.

     Smith's welfare program had a curious legislative history
during his first session as chief executive. The three bills
passed the senate where progressive Republicans joined the
Democrats in voting for them. The governor delivered an eloquent plea for a living wage for women, which may have stimu-
lated action in the upper house but exerted no effect upon the
lower. By holding the measures in the Rules Committee,
Speaker Thaddeus Sweet prevented their consideration on the
floor of the assembly where, he presumptuously explained, he
was sparing his colleagues the embarrassment of voting against
popular, but unwise, legislation. Its proponents tried to
frustrate him by keeping the legislature in session until he
allowed debate on the controversial proposals. In the senate,
the coalition of Democrats and insurgent Republicans that had
adopted the bills twice defeated a resolution for adjournment,
on one occasion filibustering to delay a tally until the
arrival of their absent cohorts. The tactic appeared to con-

firm Sweet's apprehension that a majority of the assemblymen,
if required to stand up and be counted, might vote for what he
denounced as socialism. Only a few days later however, the
senators capitulated, and the legislature decamped on schedule
on April 19. It is clear, neither why the progressive lawmakers submitted, nor why the chief executive, whose policy was
at stake, failed to use the powers of his office to detain the
legislative branch. Informed observers speculated that concession was required in order to retain bipartisan support for
the income tax bill, which the progressives also favored. Perhaps they too harbored misgivings about the outcome, if their
program came to a division in the lower house.[43]

Hoping for greater success in the future, Smith and his
allies made every effort to strengthen their case for the welfare measures. Frederick M. Davenport, the Republican sponsor
of health insurance, suggested that they collect information on
the British experience to buttress their position. In the
autumn when Congressman Sol Bloom was going abroad, the governor requested the future chairman of the House Foreign Affairs
Committee to investigate health care in England. A month later,
in its report on public health, the Reconstruction Commission
advocated compulsory medical insurance in the form of the
Davenport-Donohue bill that had received senate approval.[44]

The governor's annual message of 1920 recommended passage
of the health insurance, wage, and hour bills introduced the
year before. He warned the legislature against "smoke-screens
from the reactionary interests" and "specious propaganda directed to appease selfish interests" that were standing in the way
of the general welfare. If Smith referred in generalities to
the forces obstructing his policy, the League of Women Voters
identified Associated Industries of New York and its spokesman,
Mark Daly, as primarily responsible for the defeat of social
legislation. It was a vigorous lobby with which Smith would
have to contend in subsequent administrations as he renewed his
efforts in behalf of labor. The legislative situation of 1920
resembled that of his first year as governor. Insurgent Repub-

licans still lacked sufficient strength to overcome opposition
in the ranks of the majority to welfare proposals, the GOP caucus decisively rejected them, and the three bills again died in
committee in the assembly. In the years of the Red Scare,
smearing the measures with the Bolshevik label contributed to
their defeat. The hysteria did not divert Smith from his
course on welfare legislation, whose supporters appreciated the
efforts of a governor who kept the issue alive.[45]

Smith campaigned on that issue when he ran in 1920. As
a friend of labor, he criticized the Republicans, not only for
their opposition to the welfare bills, but also for the tactic
that kept them from coming to a vote. Nathan Miller objected
to the minimum wage provisions as inflationary. In the rhetoric
of Social Darwinism, the GOP candidate intoned, "Life is a
struggle. . . . All human progress has been brought about in
that way," and warned labor that "those who urge you that the
world owes you a living are not your friends." His oratory reminded Smith of "the old-time reactionary attitude toward social
welfare." It was characteristic of the argument for the Barnes
amendment at the constitutional convention. A victory for his
opponent would jeopardize all the progress made since the investigations of the factory commission, the governor feared. As
the founder of the Henry Street Settlement, Lillian D. Wald
worked for the reelection of Smith because of their shared commitment to "a program of progressive social welfare."[46]

Although the victorious Miller did not reverse the legislative gains of the progressive era, he did undermine the labor
law by unsympathetic enforcement. In their return engagement,
Smith criticized the incumbent, not only for his administration
of the Labor Department, but also for his unwillingness to
support bills for shorter hours and a minimum wage.[47] The
governor condemned the proposals of his opponent in the same
spirit of Social Darwinism that he had manifested in their
earlier campaign as he remarked, "If the State undertakes to
hold crutches under . . . its citizens, it will develop a race

of cripples." Furthermore, he claimed to have improved the administration of the Industrial Commission by ridding it of
"labor politicians whose chief interest in labor consists in an
effort to live without labor." In rebuttal, the Democratic
candidate stood "for the restoration to the Labor Department
of full power to administer and enforce the labor laws and the
Workmen's Compensation Act."[48]

As he began his second term, Smith asked the legislature
for additional funds for the department's activities and conferred with its newly appointed head, Bernard Shientag, on the
means to increase its effectiveness. The results enabled the
governor to open the 1924 session by pointing with pride to the
rehabilitation of the unit, which was evident in the improvement of factory inspection, the speedy settlement of compensation claims, and the revival of the bureau of women in industry.[49]

Barely a week after he had expressed satisfaction with
the restoration of the Labor Department, the governor received
from Associated Industries a request for a Moreland Act inquiry
into the state agency. The business group charged the department with inefficiency, waste, and political patronage in its
operations. Union leaders, on the other hand, suggested that
it might be more appropriate to investigate the manufacturers'
lobby. The idea apparently crossed Smith's mind when he decided to conduct the probe himself and subpoenaed the directors
of Associated Industries to appear before him. "I guess the
labor laws are being enforced too strictly to suit these people
and the shoe is beginning to pinch," he mused. His opinion was
confirmed in communications from the state Federation of Labor,
which assured him that the Labor Department "has never been in
a better condition than it is at the present time," and from
the National Consumers' League, which praised the industrial
commissioner as "the ablest and most efficient head" in the
unit's history. As a member of the Industrial Commission,
Frances Perkins, who was briefing the chief executive, declared,
"I am very glad, indeed, that you are to make this investiga-

tion yourself."[50]

The governor put Associated Industries on the defensive
in two days of hearings at the end of January. Under sharp
interrogation by Smith, the organization's representatives, including its general secretary, Mark Daly, who had initiated the
complaint, were forced to retract. The chief executive disposed
of the allegations one by one, which ranged from general incompetence in the Labor Department to specific deficiencies in
workmen's compensation. Daly, who had originally charged that
the state insurance fund was exceeding its legal expense ratio,
confessed that he founded his accusation on nothing but hearsay
evidence from a source so dubious that he refused to disclose
it. Under questioning, he acknowledged that he could not cite
any cases of the delay and inefficiency of which he had complained in the settlement of compensation claims. Such an
admission of ignorance provoked Smith to expostulate, "That is
as much as to say that you based all of this upon information
and belief and you haven't got the evidence. . . ." In contrast, department officials produced facts and figures to
demonstrate improvement in the handling of workmen's compensation since Smith took office. Perkins argued convincingly
that an administrative requirement for better fire protection
in certain buildings, to which the manufacturers were objecting,
was both morally and legally justifiable. The exchanges revealed that the administration and the businessmen were
reasoning from conflicting sets of assumptions, for Smith had
obtained additional funds and personnel for the department in
order better to protect labor, while Associated Industries interpreted any increase as prima facie evidence of the inefficiency and extravagance it had alleged. The lobby failed to sustain its charge of patronage in a department where most
employees gained their posts through civil service examination
and where many of those in the exempt category were Republican
holdovers from the previous administration. As Smith dismissed the accusation of politics in the Labor Department, he
entertained a suspicion of politics in the complaint of

Associated Industries. In his opinion, the demand for an inquiry
indicated a disposition to interfere with the enforcement of
existing labor laws and the adoption of new ones, as he disclosed "a notion in my head that the whole thing was done to
create an atmosphere around this building against pending legislation."[51]

Because the hearing vindicated the administration and discredited Associated Industries, the episode enhanced the prospects for welfare legislation. Daly conceded that he had received "a very thorough and substantial spanking" for his
errors, and Smith, showing a capacity to endear himself even
to his opponents, rejoined, "Executive clemency issues forth-
with." As the primary spokesman for the manufacturing interest
in the state, Daly's organization functioned negatively rather
than positively: to impede regulatory activities and prevent
the enactment of legislation to which its members objected.
Democrats like Smith, who favored government intervention in the
economy, inevitably faced opposition from this pressure group.[52]

After the interregnum, Smith returned to Albany with a
determination, not only to revitalize the Labor Department, but
also to resume the struggle for welfare legislation that had
distinguished his first administration. Before each session of
his second term, he conferred with officials of the New York
State Federation of Labor whose legislative agenda largely coincided with his own. Consequently, the program that he presented
to the lawmakers embraced a minimum wage and forty-eight hour
limitation for working women and minors, restrictions on the
resort to injunctions in labor disputes, aid to dependent
children, and provisions for public health.[53]

Each year, the governor's wage and hour bills passed the
Democratic senate, only to remain in committee in the Republican assembly. In 1923, he personally urged his party's leadership to make a last-ditch effort to pry the forty-eight hour
measure loose from the Rules Committee of the lower house; in
1924, he admonished its members, "when we hear so much of the

conservation of natural resources, do not overlook our human resources."[54]

Although Smith never faltered in his adherence to the principle of a minimum wage, a 1923 decision of the United States Supreme Court impelled him to revise his legislative proposal on the subject. Because of his commitment to wage regulation, he was interested in the challenge to the constitutionality of the minimum wage legislation for the District of Columbia. Therefore, New York's attorney general prepared to enter the case as a friend of the court with a brief that cited passages from the governor's messages on the subject. Smith had always preferred a mandatory to a permissive statute because he believed that penalties were more effective than moral suasion in inducing business to pay a living wage. But the ruling in *Adkins v. Children's Hospital* forced him to change his tactics. After the Court overturned the D.C. provisions, which were similar to those Smith had been advocating, Bernard Shientag advised, "In view of the decision . . . I do not see any use in attempting to put through our original minimum wage bill." In order to give the most exploited segment of the labor force the modicum of protection that the judicial ruling allowed, the industrial commissioner proposed a substitute conforming to the Massachusetts model whose constitutionality was not in doubt. His advice to the chief executive was similar to that which Felix Frankfurther gave at the time to a gathering of civic leaders and social workers. After consultation with Shientag, the governor appealed to the legislators to enact the revised measure to establish a commission with the power to determine an adequate wage and to publish the names of employers who were paying less than the specified amount.[55] As indicated earlier, the assembly failed to respond to his pleas for labor legislation in his second term. He deplored the legislature's conservatism and the judiciary's substantive interpretation of due process, both of which impeded but did not halt his quest for social justice.

During his second term, Smith enjoyed more success with health than labor legislation, despite the fact that he held office at a time when organized medicine was in retreat from the flirtation with social reform that had nurtured the public health movement. When the reformers were in the ascendancy, Assemblyman Smith and Senator Wagner had shepherded through the legislature the statute that one authority has called "the most important landmark in the history of state health administration in the United States since the creation of the first state health department." New York was fortunate in securing the services of Dr. Hermann Biggs, an authority of international repute, to direct its efforts in public health. When his term expired in 1920, Governor Smith automatically reappointed him. Upon his death, the watchdog of New York politics, the *Times*, editorially commended the choice of a successor as "beyond criticism."[56] The commissioners of health inspired the administration's initiatives in this field.

As in the case of government reorganization, the Reconstruction Commission derived from professional and progressive opinion a plan of action on public health. The same report that recommended medical insurance proposed the establishment of health centers, which Dr. Biggs favored as a means of overcoming the shortage of physicians in rural areas. In asking the state to support clinical facilities, both Biggs and the governor's task force were extending the concept of public health to embrace the treatment as well as the prevention of illness. Although Smith backed a bill to establish the centers, organized medicine assured its defeat in 1920 and again in the Miller administration.[57]

With the return of a sympathetic regime to Albany, New York resumed its progress in public health, beginning with a meeting between Smith and the leaders of the medical profession early in 1923. Although he placed a variety of topics on the agenda for the afternoon, he concentrated on medical centers to improve rural health care, since the conference grew out of the Health Department's concern with deficiencies in this area.

Dr. Biggs, who tried to disarm the opposition by his own resistance to sickness insurance, argued for the health centers. He
received support from the governor who observed, "If we once get
it established as a matter of State Policy, that we propose to
subsidize a township or a county for proper hospital facilities,
and that the State proposes to see the doctors are there if
they cannot bring them in any other way, we have established the
whole principle." The president of the Medical Society of the
State of New York appeared to assent when he responded, "There
is no difference between the profession and the State Health
Commission." The ambience of the executive chamber momentarily
repressed a basic philosophical conflict between the physicians
in the service of the state and those in private practice.
Their differences surfaced in the *Journal of the American
Medical Association,* which labelled the health centers "unacceptable to the medical profession." Nevertheless, both the
AMA and its New York counterpart praised the governor for his
interest in public health and his sensitivity to professional
opinion.[58]

The conference ended in the appointment of the Governor's
Medical Advisory Committee to assist in the formulation of
policy. If the committee's report was susceptible of varying interpretations, it exposed the disagreement between health officials and private practitioners that the conference had temporarily obscured. The former were exaggerating the shortage of
medical personnel, in the opinion of the latter, who believed that
"there is no indication for the adoption of a state subsidy
program." In its devotion to classical economics, the committee
relied on the law of supply and demand to regulate the availability of health care and analyzed the market to show that "it
requires more patients to support a doctor today than it did
formerly." Elsewhere, the document admonished the state government to prod local jurisdictions into providing the necessary
physical plant in view of the fact that "certain communities
and districts up-State are now lacking in adequate medical
care." Focusing on such passages, Smith assured the committee,

". . . I shall make specific recommendations to the Legislature
in line with your opinion that it is necessary to increase the
hospital, nursing and laboratory facilities in country communities." A spokesman for the group tried to correct the governor's misconceptions by deploring public subsidies for rural
medicine "before an actual need . . . shall have been established," and referred to the report for "evidence on hand which
indicates that state intervention is unnecessary." Where the
doctor considered the deficiency of health care a hypothesis,
necessary—and unlikely—to be proven, and the undesirability
of government intervention, a demonstrable fact, the chief
executive accepted the shortages as factual, and state aid as
an experiment to remedy lamentable conditions.[59]

Drawing from the report conclusions that its authors dis-
avowed, the governor sponsored legislation for health centers
and expanded laboratory facilities upstate. The lawmakers
offered state grants-in-aid to supplement local expenditures
for both purposes and authorized the Health Department to extend its laboratory services. At this juncture, the New York
State Medical Society pressed for a veto of the health center
bill, while its champions in the department reiterated their
approval. Smith's signature came as a fitting climax to the
career of Dr. Biggs and kept New York in the forefront in
public health.[60]

With Smith's encouragement, New York State took action in
1923 to match, not only local, but also federal funds for public
health. When Congress in the Sheppard-Towner Act of 1921
provided grants-in-aid to the states, the Miller administration
declined to establish a qualifying program for the improvement
of maternal and infant care. New York remained a holdout until
Smith regained the governorship. Although he objected in
principle to federal involvement in what he deemed a matter of
state jurisdiction, he reasoned that the grants were comparable
to those for highway construction and persuaded the lawmakers
in Albany to adopt the appropriate legislation. The social
feminists, who were leading the campaign, credited Smith with

contributing substantially to their success. Under his guidance, New York participated in a welfare effort that has been rightly characterized as "both an example of the persistence of progressivism in the 1920s and a link between the progressive era and the New Deal."[61]

In contrast to the conservatives who considered health exclusively a personal matter, the governor affirmed, "I believe it to be the business of the State because the State itself cannot be healthier than its people." The enactments of 1923 implemented Smith's belief and reflected Dr. Biggs's conviction that "public health is purchasable," which the governor often cited, on one occasion adding, "and I believe we have demonstrated it." At a time when the medical guild was deeply divided between physicians in public service and academe, who despite their heresies in medical economics commanded professional respect, and private practitioners, who dominated the New York State Medical Society, Smith took advice from the former without antagonizing the latter. The society valued his devotion to public health even when it questioned the governor's policies. Commenting on his administration in its journal, the group considered it "unique for a Governor to take a deep interest in health, and still more so to demonstrate a broad understanding of the subject and a grasp of the point of view of medical men." As he prepared to seek higher office, the state's doctors welcomed him to their annual convention as the guest of honor, in "appreciation of his service to public health."[62]

New York made important advances in public health and aid to dependent children during Smith's second term as governor; in both cases, he had laid the foundations during his career in the assembly. Mothers' allowances, which were a forerunner of the present welfare system, grew out of a progressive impulse that historians have variously interpreted as conservative or humanitarian in motive: to regulate the poor or to enable widows to keep their children out of institutions. It was the second motive that inspired Smith to speak so eloquently

on behalf of the mothers' pension bill that he moved his fellow
lawmakers to an unwonted demonstration. Few aspects of public
life touched the religious core of his nature so deeply as when
he told the house that, by enactment of the measure, "we're
sending up to Him a prayer of Thanksgiving for the blessings
He has showered upon us, particularly in the light of the words
of the Saviour himself who said, 'Suffer little children to
come unto Me, and forbid them not, for of such is the Kingdom
of Heaven.'" The 1915 statute authorized localities to establish child welfare boards with the resources to grant pensions to deserving widows for the support of their children.
The relation between mothers' pensions and social insurance was
ambiguous. From one point of view, the payments fell somewhere
"between charity and social justice."[63]

As governor, Smith supplemented the work on behalf of
dependent children that he had begun in the assembly. In his
first term, the Wilson administration convened a White House
Conference on the subject, a decade after a similar event sponsored by Theodore Roosevelt. Acting on the recommendations of
this second gathering, in 1920 New York established a Child
Welfare Commission. Without waiting for it to report, the
chief executive advised, and the legislature amended the original mothers' pension statute by making participation of local
governments mandatory rather than optional and by expanding
coverage, for example to certain cases where homes were deprived
of a father, not by death, but by institutionalization.[64]

After the interregnum, progress accelerated, for the
Child Welfare Commission viewed outdoor relief as a right
rather than a privilege and was ready to acknowledge Smith's
help in securing it. They would be only doing their duty, not
engaging in charity, he told the lawmakers, when he asked them
to carry out the recommendations of the commission. The same
religious tone that had characterized the debate on initiating
mothers' pensions was present in the words of the annual message, calling on the state to provide from its bounty for the
support of dependent children, which "will have the blessing

of Almighty God Himself and no amount of money can buy that."
Spurred by the reports of the commission and the messages of
the governor, the legislature of his second administration expanded the program of allowances to cover additional contin-
gencies: the guardianship of children bereft of both parents,
physical disability of the father, offspring of certain aliens
ineligible under earlier legislation, and the desertion of the
family by the husband. Opposition to the payments to guardians
arose from two sources: social and civic workers who anticipated the exploitation of orphans by recipients being "paid for
nursemaids and farm hands," and New York City officials who objected to the expense. If the amounts provided were inadequate
to support the number of children in need, they did represent
a humane approach to a problem whose solution remains illusory.[65]

The payments would have been more generous if Smith had
had his way. He began his second administration by proposing
that the state contribute to mothers' pensions in proportion to
the amount raised by each community, in order to encourage more
liberal allowances. The device of matching funds was the same
one that he used successfully for public health. The Child
Welfare Commission accepted his suggestion and drafted a bill to
put it into effect. But neither the encouragement of the commission, nor the repeated requests of the governor, moved the
legislature to supplement local revenues for aid to dependent
children.[66]

The Child Welfare Commission, with which Smith worked so
closely, went on record as favoring the federal child labor
amendment. Congress had proposed this amendment to the Constitution in order to recover the authority twice denied it by the
Supreme Court in overturning successive Child Labor Acts. In
the New York gubernatorial election of 1924, both parties campaigned on platforms pledged to ratification. After his reelection, Smith refused to renege, explaining to a Democratic
functionary that "to my mind, it is a question of keeping faith
with the people themselves."[67]

Whether or not he kept faith has become so controversial
that it is necessary to examine in detail the governor's
handling of the child labor amendment at the 1925 session.   In
his annual message, he stated:

> I am in hearty accord with what is sought to be done
> by this amendment because I believe that children are
> a national asset and their proper care and early
> training must be guarded by the Nation while there
> exists a disposition to ignore this problem in some
> of our commonwealths which prevents action for the
> conservation of child life by the States themselves.

Having affirmed his commitment to ratification, he proposed a
special election for a referendum "in time for the present
Legislature to act in accordance with the will of the people
. . . when the question can be decided on its merits free from
confusion with other political issues." With that, he clearly
went on record against deferring the matter to the next general
election. He did not expect New York to follow in the foot-
steps of Massachusetts, where the voters had already registered
their disapproval, for he insisted, "I have no doubt about the
favorable attitude of the people of this State. . . ." If
Smith was hedging, the GOP leadership was veering towards out-
right opposition to the amendment. Introduced by Democrats, a
resolution for ratification and a bill for a March election
died in committee in both houses; even a Republican-sponsored
measure for a November referendum succeeded only in the less
conservative senate. But by then, the question was academic,
for on January 27 the thirteenth state rejected the amendment.[68]

Because of the injection of the referendum issue into the
debate on the child labor amendment, some of its supporters
believed that Smith was double-crossing them, and subsequent
historians have too uncritically taken their word for it. The
governor evidently had intended to call for immediate legislative ratification until he got wind of a GOP plan to defer
action, pending a referendum in November. He reasoned that the
amendment stood a better chance of approval at a special election than at the general election when a larger turnout in
rural Republican strongholds would work to its disadvantage.

Calculating that a favorable vote, while the lawmakers were still in session, would force their hand, he opted for a March canvass and prepared to campaign publicly for the child labor article. On the basis of her intimate knowledge, Frances Perkins tried to disabuse the governor's critics of their conviction that he had deserted the child labor cause.[69]

An interpretation of Smith's role in his state's failure to ratify the amendment depends primarily on the proposed referendum and hinges specifically on expectations of its outcome. He had suggested the procedure initially in objecting to the Eighteenth Amendment, which probably would not have carried urban regions in a popular vote. With considerable justification, he anticipated that New Yorkers, if given the chance, would join him in rejecting national Prohibition and accepting federal regulation of child labor. It is true however, that the governor's mail in favor of the referendum ran heavily against the amendment.[70] In killing the referendum, the GOP at least displayed a lack of confidence that the results would justify the party in repudiating its platform plank on ratification. Responsibility for the state's inaction rests, in any case, with the Republican majority in the legislature, not with the chief executive.

His critics attributed the Democrat's putative turnabout to states' rights and religion. It is wrong to assume that he operated in the twenties from the same perspective on federalism that he manifested in the thirties. The governor was neither doctrinaire on states' rights, when he reversed his predecessor with regard to the Sheppard-Towner Act, nor submissive to the hierarchy of his church, when he took a stand on public education and civil liberties. Frances Perkins is perhaps the best source on the conjectural influence of the Roman Catholic Church in the child labor issue. Not long after the 1925 session, she testified that the clergy had refrained from approaching Smith on the subject since he was on record in favor of the amendment. Only later when she came to record her memoirs, did she describe a dramatic scene in which the gover-

nor rebuked a priest who presumed to instruct him that child
labor legislation violated the teachings of the church. It is
fair to suppose that her memory was more reliable several
months, than several decades, after the event. The amendment
was not a matter of faith or morals on which he was bound to
obey, as shown by such prominent exceptions to the church's
overwhelmingly negative stance as Senator Thomas J. Walsh,
Monsignor John A. Ryan, and the editors of the *Milwaukee
Catholic Herald-Citizen* and the *Catholic Worker*, published in
New York City.[71] Despite the ambiguity of his situation,
Governor Smith belongs in that group. A refreshing candor
marked the entire political career of this man, who never feared
to take positions unpopular with his church or the general public, as for example when he defended civil liberties at the
height of the Red Scare. Why not believe what he said on the
child labor amendment? As chief executive, he was consistent
in his willingness to use the power of government to assure the
welfare of children.

Protective labor legislation had been a primary issue in
the statewide election of 1924, in which both parties endorsed
the child labor amendment and each gubernatorial candidate proclaimed himself the friend of the working class. As a result
of Republican administrations, New York led the nation in promoting the welfare of its workers, according to Theodore
Roosevelt, Jr. Crediting his own party with the adoption of
the state's fifty-four hour law, he affirmed GOP intentions
to reduce the permissible work week for women and children even
further, to forty-eight hours. Smith too, took pride in the
state's progressive record but ridiculed his challenger's
account of the GOP contribution. The governor described the
labor laws as originating mostly in Democratic administrations
and passing "over the vigorous and forceful protest of Republican legislators." Smith criticized Roosevelt's speeches as
wildly misinformed on the history of labor in New York and his
record in the assembly as hardly calculated to inspire confidence in the laboring population. Echoing as a refrain the

colonel's promise to deliver the goods, Smith asked, "To whom did he deliver the goods when he abandoned the minimum wage bill. . . . when he voted against the 48 hour bill. . . ?"[72]

The candidates were reproducing the dispute implied in the platforms where each organization viewed itself as labor's benefactor and cast aspersions on the other. Looking to the future, both parties promised to lower the maximum number of hours; the Republican, in a text that read, "We favor the enactment of a law providing a forty-eight-hour-week for women in industry, with suitable provisions for safeguarding seasonal employment."[73]

In his third and fourth terms, Smith shifted the emphasis in welfare legislation to the question of wages and hours, first by calling on the 1925 session for forty-eight hour and minimum wage laws for women and minors. In regard to hours, two alternatives received legislative consideration: the Mastick bill, which conformed to the governor's recommendations by reducing the basic work week from fifty-four to forty-eight hours; and the Joiner bill, which authorized the Industrial Board to make the reduction for those occupations where it determined the longer hours to be "detrimental to the health of females so employed." At a legislative hearing, Eleanor Roosevelt testified in favor of the Mastick bill in the conviction that it enjoyed the support of "a great majority of working women," while the National Woman's Party opposed both measures on the grounds that protective legislation, unless applied equally to both sexes, would deprive females of employment opportunities. While the measures were pending, Smith denounced the Joiner bill as a fraud and described it as absolutely worthless. With GOP endorsement however, it passed both houses, while the Mastick bill, which the governor preferred, languished in committee in the assembly. In both chambers, progressive Republicans bolted in order to vote for the stronger measure, but only in the senate, did they, in combination with the Democrats, command a majority. Just before adjournment,

Smith made a last-minute appeal to the assembly for passage of
the Mastick bill as the only one in keeping with the campaign
promises of both parties. But the session ended by sending him
only the Joiner bill, which he had already threatened to veto.[74]

Before taking action, the governor conducted a hearing
at which the *Times* compared him to Marc Antony, coming not to
praise but to bury the Joiner bill. He held the meeting, not
for the purpose of consulting the public, but of justifying the
decision that he announced unequivocally, "Of course, I will
veto this bill," as a measure introduced "in bad faith" and only
with the intention of providing "an excuse for side stepping
a genuine forty-eight-hour bill." The measure's only defender,
Mark Daly of Associated Industries, confirmed the accusation
when he admitted, "We want you to sign the Joiner bill because
it will finally dispose of the question . . . from the standpoint of a political issue. . . ." Contrariwise, in disapproving it, the chief executive anticipated, "we shall see an
end of the attempts to hoodwink the public on this subject."
The bill would accomplish no reduction in hours, the veto
memorandum explained, "but only a series of lengthy litiga-
tions, investigations, arguments and public hearings and that
by no possible process can the women workers of the State benefit under this act." The vetoed measure afforded no better
protection than the existing fifty-four hour maximum, which he
would persist in attempting to lower effectively.[75]

Smith returned to the subject at the next session when he
admonished the legislature to brook "no further delay" in
adopting the forty-eight hour standard. Nonetheless, the lawmakers delayed yet another year. The conservative Republicans
and business lobbyists, who had foisted the innocuous Joiner
bill on the previous session, now suggested a thorough investigation before enacting any additional labor legislation. For
this purpose, the GOP leaders proposed an Industrial Survey
Commission to report to the next legislature. Their resolution
to establish it easily passed the senate, where the impression
prevailed that the forty-eight hour bill was exempt from the

moratorium on new labor law. The State Federation of Labor protested to Smith against deferring the reduction of hours and
the liberalization of workmen's compensation that both parties
had promised. He, in turn, renewed his call for action because
"No good that I am able to see can grow out of any further legislative investigation of these questions." By the time the
assembly debated the motion, it was clear to the Democrats that
it was "a sham and a lie and is intended primarily to sidetrack
the forty-eight hour bill for another year." The resolution
faced rougher going in the lower house where it took the casting
vote of the Speaker to break the tie that occurred when progressive Republicans combined with Democrats in opposition to
the survey. The prospective inquiry enabled the lawmakers to
evade the issue of maximum hours and leave the bills on the
subject in committee.[76]

In a significant exception to the standstill on labor, the
legislature increased the size of the Industrial Board, as Smith
had been recommending in order to facilitate the handling of
compensation claims. This change occurred as a by-product of
the overall reorganization of the state government and in compliance with the report of the Hughes commission from which the
lawmakers hesitated to deviate.[77]

Enjoying the confidence of the majority party, the Industrial Survey Commission, like the Reorganization Commission before it, anticipated the adoption of its recommendations, including the abbreviated work week, for which Smith had been contending. Although the joint legislative committee recognized
that "a more important question to women is the obtaining for
them of wages more nearly approximating the wages of men," it
reported to the 1927 session in favor of a forty-eight hour
measure comparable to the earlier Mastick bill. With its
passage, New York restricted the hours of women in factories to
forty-eight a week and eight a day, with the exception of
limited overtime to compensate for the addition of a half-
holiday to the required day of rest and to accommodate business
in periods of peak activity. Despite these compromises, the

statute enjoyed support from organized labor and aroused anxiety
in the National Industrial Conference Board. Like the business
organization, the National Woman's Party relied on classical
economics in criticizing legislation, leading to "in many
instances the loss of a job, and in every instance reduced
earning power and unequal opportunity" for women. The lineup
indicates that the law conformed better to the governor's ideal
of social justice than the one that he had vetoed two years before. He approved the bill with considerable satisfaction and
only one regret, "that its benefits should have been withheld
for so many years."[78]

The governor's veto worked as an even more effective
tactic in the case of the forty-eight hour law than in that of
state parks. In 1925, by disapproving both the Thayer bill for
park appropriations and the Joiner bill, Smith denied his legislative opposition the semblance, without the reality, of
achieving the stated goals. The vetoes, which temporarily
halted progress on park expansion and labor standards, denied
the GOP the luxury of verbally supporting, while legislatively
sabotaging, the chief executive's policies. Delay proved more
of a liability to the Republicans than the Democrats, and the
majority compromised with the governor on parks and surrendered
to him on hours.

Legislative investigation postponed action but did not
defeat the governor's proposals either for maximum hours or for
workmen's compensation. Taking pride in the protection gained
by injured workers from his second administration, Smith began
his third by advocating measures to increase benefits under
workmen's compensation, limit employers' appeals, and add members to the Industrial Board responsible for handling the cases.
Instead, an unsympathetic legislature determined upon an inquiry
to discover whether delays in the payment of claims were resulting from deficiencies in the law or in the executive
branch.[79] Little came of the Whitley committee's brief probe
except where Republicans agreed with Smith on a measure to
discourage dilatory tactics by adding interest to awards de-

layed by appeals. On the other hand, he vetoed a bill for additional personnel, which would have been self-defeating by requiring two officials to make decisions where earlier one had
sufficed.[80] The 1925 session ended in a stalemate between the
governor, who gave priority to the interest of labor in adequate
and speedy payments, and the GOP majority, which placed more importance on protecting management from invalid claims through
procedures designed to facilitate successful appeals.

The Whitley committee set a precedent for the creation of
the Industrial Survey Commission in 1926, which enabled the GOP
to stall for another year, before complying with Smith's recommendations on the forty-eight hour law and the liberalization
of workmen's compensation. If the report of the commission
signified the acquiescence of the Republican lawmakers in these
particular policies of the governor, it concluded, in deference
to the business community, by advocating a five-year moratorium
on subsequent labor legislation. First, however, the 1927
legislature enacted the measures for improving compensation
coverage that the executive had urged and its own committee
favored. Although the commission uncovered some abuses, it
attributed delays to the adversary process rather than maladmin-
istration. In general, the report rated New York highly on its
system of compensation and contained words of praise for the
officials who were administering it as well as for the state
insurance fund.[81]

In the light of these findings, the allegations of commission members, which prompted two new inquiries in 1928,
appear as a ploy to embarrass Smith politically in anticipation
of his presidential nomination. The charges led first to an
executive investigation when Smith announced, "If what Assemblyman Cornaire said is true, nobody is more anxious for the facts
than I am," and added, "If what he said is not true, the people
of the State ought to know it." To find out, the chief executive appointed Professor Lindsay Rogers, Columbia University
political scientist, as a Moreland Act commissioner. The GOP
reacted with the hasty introduction of a resolution for a

legislative probe, despite the fact that earlier in the day its
spokesmen had disclaimed any intention of taking such action.
Smith suspected the Republicans of making their sensational
charges of fraud and incompetence "for the purpose of blocking
all progressive legislation that has to do with labor and workmen's compensation at this session." The atmosphere around the
legislature is suggested by the following exchange in which a
prominent Republican was asked, "Are you trying to beat the
Governor to it?" The legislator responded, "Perhaps the
Governor is trying to beat us to it." Just one day after the
appointment of Rogers, the chief executive declared, "I told
him to step on the gas and get started. . . ." As a member of
the department under investigation, Frances Perkins expressed
confidence in the Moreland Act commissioner and assured Smith,
"It was a brilliant idea to appoint him."[82]

    While Rogers was still engaged in his research, the
Industrial Survey Commission completed its study of workmen's
compensation. There was a twofold division over the legislative
investigation: between Democrats who opposed it and Republicans
who supported it; and between Republicans who preferred to cooperate with the executive inquiry and those who chose to compete with it in an effort to discredit the administration. The
GOP organization engineered a compromise that prolonged the life
and expanded the investigative authority of the joint legislative committee. In March, the report of the commission reflected the ambiguity of its mandate. The new evaluation was
more negative than that of the preceding year, although the two
documents differed more in emphasis than substantive content.
The later report concentrated on difficulties upon which the
earlier one had lightly touched, for example, abuses in workmen's compensation reminiscent of those uncovered by Connor in
Smith's first term. What the commission recommended in the way
of remedies such as the licensing of claimants' representatives
and the penalizing of conflict of interest, and also in added
coverage, the legislature generally enacted. The session ended
without fulfilling either all of Smith's hopes for greater

benefits or his fears generated by the extended inquiry.[83]

After adjournment, when the governor traveled to North Carolina for rest and recreation, he invited his Moreland Act commissioner to join his party. On his holiday with Smith, Rogers has reminisced, "I played golf with him, sat up and held his hand at night, and he never asked me a damned word about whether my report was going to be embarrassing to the administration or not!"[84]

The report, which the professor submitted in three installments between June and December, was painful to all concerned. The Industrial Survey Commission came under attack when he questioned the propriety of the participation of interested parties in its work. They included the ubiquitous Associated Industries and the commission's executive secretary, Henry D. Sayer, former department official and current corporate executive doing business in compensation. In the words of the document, "The familiar analogy of Dr. Jekyl and Mr. Hyde is not sufficient. Mr. Sayer's role is trivalent." Under his questionable influence, the lawmakers adopted legislation which "does not excuse, but it at least explains" many of the deficiencies that Rogers uncovered in his study. He started out by dismissing the charges of corruption, which had spawned the two probes, and by exonerating the Labor Department. His report, however, became progressively more critical of the administration of workmen's compensation and particularly of the performance of Smith's last industrial commissioner, James A. Hamilton, who had failed to rectify the abuses that the investigation revealed. All of the efforts since Smith's first term had been insufficient to suppress the exploitation of claimants by runners and to eliminate the arrangements whereby the insurance companies diverted compensation cases to favored doctors predisposed to minimize the extent of injury. Despite their differing and respective biases, the legislative and executive inquiries disclosed the same shortcomings in the operation of workmen's compensation. "I believe that Rogers made a good job of it . . ." the governor acknowledged as he commended to his successor the scholar's proposals for corrective legislation.[85]

Smith's administration ended as it began with an investigation of workmen's compensation and with recommendations for
legislation on improved benefits, a minimum wage, and a legal
redefinition of labor to distinguish it from articles of commerce. The extent to which he reverted to the same problems is
a measure of the degree to which his aspirations outran his
achievement. Nevertheless, from the interregnum to his retirement, he made substantial legislative gains in compensation
coverage, the reduction of hours, the limitation of child labor,
public health, and mother's pensions. The annual message of
1928 was a valedictory in which he reviewed the advances in
welfare under his stewardship and voiced the need for state aid
to dependent children, anti-injunction measures, and a minimum
wage, on all of which the politicians of the next decade would
legislate.[86]

Governor Smith and President Roosevelt both extended the
ideal of conservation from natural resources to human resources.
Conservation of human resources was a goal of the labor and
welfare legislation that was proposed successively by the social
progressives, New York's Democratic governors, and the national
administration of the thirties. These programs involve Smith
in the continuity between the major reform movements of the
first half of the century.[87]

What obscures the similarities and accounts for some of
the differences between Smith and FDR is that the former administered New York during a period of prosperity and the latter presided over a nation in the throes of a depression. Smith did
however end his governorship as he began it, by displaying concern over the rise in unemployment that would reach catastrophic
levels in the downturn ahead. Having directed his Labor
Department to investigate the facts, he deprived himself of the
luxury, available to more complacent politicians, of denying
the realities of joblessness. Sensitive to the distress behind
the statistics, he tried to stimulate employment by encouraging

state and municipal authorities to accelerate their public works
projects. In response to Smith's suggestions, the mayor of
Buffalo declared it "characteristic of the Governor of our State
to be among the first to interest himself in . . . the unemployment situation"; the chief executive of Long Beach lauded the
governor's action as "another proof that your knowledge of
economics should be utilized by the whole Nation."[88]

Organized labor in the Empire State, which had invariably
supported Smith in his campaigns for governor, in 1928 endorsed
him first for the Democratic nomination and then for the presidency. Assembled at their annual convention, members of the
New York State Federation of Labor greeted with acclaim William
Green's praise of their governor. Although the AFL president
observed that the workers of the state had shown their approval
of Smith "by voting for him almost unanimously in every campaign
in which he has figured," the national union declined to give
the Democratic candidate the backing that he received from its
New York affiliate. By the retreat to neutrality, the national
federation managed "neither to reward its 'friend' nor to attack
its 'enemy,'" in the words of a labor historian.[89] In many
parts of the country however, trade unions did follow the lead
of New York toward an alignment that culminated in the New Deal
coalition. Consequently, another scholar reached "a conclusion
seldom given in general accounts of the election: substantial
elements in the American trade union movement supported in 1928
the candidate of one party—the Democratic party—well before
the New Deal and . . . labor partisanship for President Franklin
D. Roosevelt."[90]

An officer of the New York State Federation of Labor
explained its enthusiasm for a Smith presidency by the governor's contribution to "the enactment of progressive legislation
and a sympathetic administration of the labor laws." The
governor sided with unions on the crucial issue of limiting the
use of injunctions to curb strikes. His friendship for labor
made Governor Smith a featured speaker at union conventions.
On one such occasion, he defended economic intervention by

explaining that the due process clause was not designed "to prevent the State from enacting legislation to safeguard the health
and welfare of the people"; on another, he vindicated the rights
of unions by observing, "Of course, we all believe in organization. The Government itself is organized. The Church is highly
organized. Business is organized. . . . there is nothing left
for labor to do but to organize." If Roosevelt showed less
understanding of organized labor than Smith, the governor's old
friend, the senator from New York, made the New Deal responsive
to union needs.[91] Smith and FDR received the votes of labor
because in office they did not neglect the economic interests
of labor.

With Robert F. Wagner in the United States Senate and
Frances Perkins in the president's cabinet, the Roosevelt administration drew heavily on the New York experience in the realm
of labor and social welfare. It has been said of Perkins that
"from 1925 to 1945, on social legislation hers was the knowledgeable, dominant voice at the ear of the leader of the Democratic party." As a result, the New Deal derived some inspiration from the Smith regime for the labor provisions of the
National Industrial Recovery Act, the Fair Labor Standards Act,
and the Social Security Act.[92]

Perkins could not imagine the New Deal of President
Roosevelt without the pioneering of Governor Smith, to whom she
attributed the beginning of the welfare state and "the progress
. . . of democratic liberalism" in the United States.[93] Smith
arrived at his liberal convictions in the assembly of the progressive era, defended his persuasion against the old guard at
the constitutional convention, molded his programs in the
crucible of his experience as chief executive, and left a
legacy to be improved upon by the New Deal. Writing in retirement "that the government must look to the betterment of people
who have no other resource or methods of helping themselves,"
he expressed an attitude that motivated many New Dealers. Interpretations of reform that emphasize the social component of
progressivism, its survival in the twenties, and its resurgence

in the thirties offer a perspective on Smith's behavior before
1929. Social workers like Perkins, whose pursuit of social
justice began under the impetus of progressivism and culminated
under the patronage of President Roosevelt, played an important
role in New York politics in the Smith era. The governor himself is a prime example of the new stock politicians who created
urban liberalism, despite the fact that he abandoned it in the
thirties.[94] As governor, his contribution to the conservation
of human resources forged one of the connecting links between
progressivism and the New Deal—but, paradoxically, Alfred E.
Smith was at home in neither.

CONSERVATION OF NATURAL RESOURCES: WATER POWER

In promoting social and labor legislation, Governor Smith frequently drew an analogy between the conservation of human resources and the conservation of natural resources. The two goals were interrelated, for the preservation of land and water resources would improve the quality of life for the people of the state. From the expansion of state parks, subject of an earlier chapter, they would gain access to recreational sites; from the public development of water power, cheap energy. The idea of governmental responsibility for human and natural resources came to Smith from the progressive movement.

In the historiography of progressivism, the conservation movement is as controversial as the efficiency economy drive and social legislation and is often identified with one of the two in scholarly debate. Samuel P. Hays defines conservation as the efficient management of resources, associates it with administrative reform, and classifies the reformers as elitist. He insists on viewing the movement "from the vantage point of applied science, rather than of democratic protest" and its politics as arising "out of the political implications of applied science rather than from conflict over the distribution of wealth." In contrast, J. Leonard Bates interprets conserva- tion, not as "a matter of efficiency as such, but a fighting, democratic faith," and one "concerned more with economic jus- tice and democracy in the handling of resources than with mere prevention of waste." He notes the movement's trend toward public enterprise and its commitment to subordinate private profit to the public interest in the national domain. His con- servationists intended to lessen monopoly in production, widen access to resources, and lower prices to consumers. In agree- ment with Bates, Judson King reviews *The Conservation Fight* as a struggle for public power, which began in the administration of Theodore Roosevelt and culminated in the Tennessee Valley Authority. As one of its participants, he recalls, "They sought to halt the frightful waste of all natural resources and thwart private monopoly in their utilization."[1]

Theodore Roosevelt's conservation effort moved Hays to classify him as a technocrat; King, as a democrat; and a recent biographer to state, "In none other did the President blend science and morality quite so effectively. . . ." Here science refers to considerations of efficiency; morality, to intimations of democracy in the vetoes of giveaways, the attacks on monopoly, and the solicitude for reasonable electric rates.[2] If the motives behind the progressive drive for conservation included both efficiency and democracy, to deny the second is to distort the movement and to overlook the aspect of it that led Alfred E. Smith to support public power.

George W. Norris offers an example of a progressive whose position on water power reflected the democratic ethos, which in the twenties moved him and Smith along first a parallel, and then a converging, course. Already in Norris' first term in the Senate in the waning of the progressive era, "it seemed to me that the development and conservation of these resources ought always to be under public control, public ownership, and public operation," he explained in a memoir, which recalled the events of these years as a battle of consumers against the trusts. Recent scholarship confirms his interpretation of his activities during the Wilson administration. The senator supported the Hetch Hetchy project as a source of municipally distributed hydroelectricity for San Francisco and proposed a dam on the Potomac with similar advantages to the national capital. In condemning the Shields bill for long-term leases of power sites as a giveaway to private interests, he took a stand that Governor Smith could appreciate when he opposed similar legislation in New York. The division of the progressive vote in Congress on water power at least suggests the danger of defining the movement so narrowly as to exclude its democratic implications.[3]

Likewise in New York, the lines on water power were not as clearly drawn in the progressive era as in the twenties when

the Democratic party advocated public development; the GOP,
private. The Hughes administration, which alternately favored
public regulation of private enterprise in the name of efficiency and state generation of electricity from water resources
in the public domain, unequivocably resisted the exploitation
of public lands without adequate compensation to the state, as
in the case of a prospective license to the Long Sault Development Company to produce electricity from the Saint Lawrence
River. By his defense of the public interest, Hughes made a
lasting impression on Assemblyman Smith. Nevertheless, the
future governor did not compile a consistent record on water
power during his years in the legislature. On one occasion,
he backed for private industry the type of grant that he would
later condemn. Before he left the assembly however, he evi-
denced the conversion to public power that characterized his
subsequent political career.[4]

At the constitutional convention, Smith saw himself as
carrying on the tradition of Governor Hughes to whom he attributed a more advanced position than the justice had in reality
taken. Crediting the Republican with inspiring a provision
that he was seeking to insert in the constitution, Smith observed, "There is the meat in the cocoanut, under State ownership and control." Just as Norris denounced the utility companies for blocking Hetch Hetchy, Smith perceived similar
forces obstructing his plan for New York. "But there is some
power in this State, some place—I am unable to say where—that
is interested in grabbing the water power of this State, and
evidences of their activity continually crop up . . ." he
complained. The Democrat objected to a clause being drafted
for the purpose of inhibiting the efforts of the state to
generate electricity.[5] The delegate, who displayed ambivalence
to the efficiency economy drive for administrative reform, overlooked its implications for conservation, which he interpreted
primarily in terms of public power.

By the time that he became chief executive, Smith was
even more firmly convinced of the wisdom of having the state

produce hydroelectricity from its water resources. A potential
for such development existed on the Saint Lawrence and Niagara
rivers, forming a boundary between New York and Canada, and on
inland mountain streams, largely in the forest preserve.

In his very first message to the legislature, Smith
announced, "this is the proper time to begin development of our
unused water powers." Toward this end, he promoted a measure
to authorize the Conservation Commission, not only to generate
hydroelectricity, but also to transmit it to municipal distributors and directly to consumers. Like his bills on wages,
hours, and health insurance, the one to amend the Conservation
Law failed to emerge from committee in the assembly but passed
in the senate, where a coalition of Democrats and progressive
Republicans filibustered to delay adjournment in the hope of
forcing the lower house to consider the matters.[6] With the
surrender of the insurgents, the only legislation on the issue
to reach the governor's desk called innocuously for an investigation on water power. He vetoed it with a reminder that previous inquiries had "collected enough data upon this subject to
fill any room in the Capitol" and out of reluctance to condone
"the expenditure of more money" and "the waste of more time."
What was obstructing progress was not a lack of know-how but a
dispute over who should produce the energy, and he sided with
those who favored public over private enterprise.[7]

At the following session, the governor outlined the alternatives on water power: transfer of the sites from the
public domain to private ownership and their exploitation for
profit; government ownership and regulated private operation
under long-term leases—as advocated by the efficiency movement
to assure conservation; and public ownership and operation. He
dismissed the first summarily and the second because experience
proved that "nobody has benefited but the individuals who have
been lucky enough to secure the rights." Only the third option
would work to the advantage of the people to whom the resources
rightfully belonged, he insisted. The Republican majority dis-

agreed, and as in the preceding year, a bill for public power died in committee.[8] At the same session, a measure to facilitate leasing to private industry received legislative but not executive approval. With his veto, the governor affirmed his commitment to the utilization of the water supply "by the State for the benefit of the people" and declared, "I am opposed to its development by individuals or corporations as a private enterprise."[9]

The federal Water Power Act, which President Wilson signed in June, contained features that Governor Smith had condemned in the state legislation that he disapproved in May. The act of Congress provided for the leasing of waters to private producers and the regulation of their activities by an administrative agency of the federal government. In view of the divided counsels among progressives in Congress, it is not surprising that historians have variously interpreted the statute as a triumph or betrayal of the conservation movement, depending upon whether they emphasized the regulatory authority or its ineffectiveness, the fees for use of the public domain or the abandonment of public power, the goal of efficiency or that of democracy.[10]

The act of Congress served as a model for state legislation in New York during the interregnum when Republicans controlled the executive branch and both houses of the legislature. A growing divergence between the parties on water power policy had prevented action by the divided governments of the closing years of the progressive era and of Smith's first term. After the Democrat lost his bid for reelection, Nathan L. Miller secured the adoption of the New York State Water Power Act of 1921. It established a Water Power Commission chaired by a gubernatorial appointee, the conservation commissioner, and including two statewide officers, the engineer and surveyor and the attorney general, as well as two legislative leaders, the president of the senate and the Speaker of the assembly. The basic and most controversial function of the commission was to grant licenses to generate hydroelectricity from the public

domain. While making some concession to municipal utilities
and providing for the regulation of rates, the law contemplated
placing development primarily in the hands of private enterprise, an intention confirmed by Governor Miller in advocating
it. The measure authorized the commission to charge its
lessees a fee based on the state's administrative costs and the
value of the undeveloped land—but not of the energy produced.
If the licensee defaulted, the state, in order to recover the
property, was bound to compensate for any improvements—at re-
production cost. Furthermore, the commission could agree to
pay for improvements at the expiration of the lease before the
property reverted to the state.[11] Under the provisions for
recapture and fees, the state assumed the risks, and business
enjoyed the profits, of development. It was questionable
whether or not the enactment served the public as well as the
investor.

Smith raised the question during the campaign of 1922 when
he denounced the Republicans for favoritism to the utilities
and repeated his own commitment to public enterprise "for the
benefit of all the people in order to bring about cheaper light
and cheaper power." He ran on a platform that opposed the
private exploitation of natural resources in general, and in
particular, the Ferris amendment, "which would deliver State
resources to private monopolies." The GOP, on the other hand,
deemed private enterprise to be in the public interest and took
credit for ending an era of inaction with a constructive energy
policy. On public power, Miller jibed, "They have been talking
that for more than a quarter of a century, and not one step has
been taken to develop one kilowatt."[12]

With some justification, Smith interpreted his victory
at the polls as a mandate for public power and intervened to
prevent the licensing of private operation in the interval between his election and his inauguration. The canvass assured
him a majority on the crucial Water Power Commission when he
resumed office. Learning that the lame duck commission, which
had been quiescent for several months, was meeting to consider

applications for a project on the Niagara River, the governor-
elect requested it to defer to the new administration "in view
of the decision of the people at the polls following the campaign in which this subject was a distinct issue." To the suggestion that his interference was without precedent, he responded, ". . . I am quite willing to establish one." The officials
involved denied any inclination to act precipitately and complied with his wishes. Moved by the incident, the poet, Edwin
Markham, who described himself in the words, "I am from the
crowd," applauded Smith for faithfully representing the common
people.[13]

Smith kept the Niagara River out of the hands of corporate
interests at a time when George Norris was battling to protect
the Tennessee River from private exploitation. As the governor
returned to Albany, in Washington the senator was leading the
opposition that frustrated the plans of two administrations to
lease Muscle Shoals to Henry Ford. Their efforts in the cause,
led one authority to describe Norris and the progressives as
"heirs of the Roosevelt-Pinchot conservation movement, making
alliances with remnants of the reform element in the cities."[14]

If Al Smith typified the urban progressives, his second
term demonstrated that he was better positioned to obstruct
private than to foster public development of water power. He
recommended to the lawmakers that they repeal Miller's legislation, with its provisions for leasing state lands to business
corporations, and replace it with a measure for government
generation and transmission of hydroelectricity from the Saint
Lawrence and Niagara rivers under the direction of the state
engineer and surveyor. Smith's policy enjoyed support in the
City Council of Buffalo and the Conference of Mayors and Other
City Officials—but not in the New York State Assembly. The
lower house refused to take from committee the governor's bill,
sponsored by Senator Ellwood M. Rabenold and approved by a
majority of the senate.[15] The 1923 session ended, therefore,
in the failure of the efforts to reverse the decision of the

interregnum in favor of private enterprise. On the Water Power
Commission, a Democratic majority now blocked development under
the terms of the 1921 law by declining to consider applications
from the private sector; in the assembly, GOP control prevented
adoption of the executive's plan to produce energy in the public sector of the economy.

As a result of Smith's election to a second term, private
interests lost an opportunity to profit from the hydroelectric
potential, not only of the boundary rivers, but also of certain
inland streams. Development of the interior waters threatened
the integrity of the forest preserve and antagonized many conservationists who turned to the governor for assistance in
blocking the Ferris amendment and river regulating districts.

To understand these issues of the Smith administration,
it is necessary to review the background of conservation in New
York. Late in the nineteenth century, the state had created a
forest preserve and protected it by constitutional provisions
that it "shall be forever kept as wild forest lands," which
"shall not be leased, sold, or exchanged." The reserve consisted of all publicly owned land in a large area upstate,
which was delineated by a blue line on the map of New York.
To ward off intrusions upon it and to prevent any tampering
with the clause, early in this century, a group of citizens
with substantial property in the region formed the Association
for the Protection of the Adirondacks. It did not, however,
resist a 1913 constitutional amendment to permit the use of no
more than 3 percent of the territory for water supply, navigation, and flood control. Shortly afterwards, the Machold
Water Storage Law authorized the Conservation Commission to
approve river regulating districts pursuant to the amendment.
The measure set a precedent for the state Water Power Act by
basing rental charges on the value of the unimproved land at
a level that meant a windfall to lessees who generated hydroelectricity. Because the law did not specify energy production as a reason for establishing the districts and article
VII, section 7 of the constitution made no mention of it,

opponents of public and private power alike alternately argued
against specific projects on the grounds that they were unconstitutional.[16]

Governor Miller took steps to overcome the obstacles to
development and enable private parties to proceed with the
organization of river regulating districts. He wanted to
apply to the forest streams the same policy of long-term
leases that prevailed in the state Water Power Act. With this
in view, the Republican administration secured a law to transfer jurisdiction over river regulation to a Water Control Commission composed of the conservation commissioner, the attorney
general, and the state engineer and surveyor and also sponsored
a constitutional amendment to include water power among the
acceptable uses of the forest preserve. At the session that
established the commission, the Ferris amendment gained passage
for the first time, with the Democratic minority in opposition.
The platform on which Smith ran in 1922 expressly condemned the
amendment that the incumbent had initiated.[17]

Following the election in which Democrats gained control
of the senate, the Ferris amendment appeared to have no prospect
of success in obtaining approval a second time. Its passage
in 1923, therefore, left one member of the party questioning,
"why if we felt so strongly in opposition, we should not have
killed the measure when we had the chance." In April, Senator
Ellwood M. Rabenold learned that he "might find the Democratic
attitude . . . different from last year." James Walker, who as
minority leader had led the fight against the amendment when
Miller proposed it, as president of the senate shifted to an
enigmatic stance and then voted in favor of what he had
originally tried to block. In the end, only five members of the
upper house opposed the measure: the progressive Republican,
Frederick Davenport, and four Democrats led by Rabenold who
served as sponsor of Smith's water power legislation. Sensitive
as well as principled, the lawmaker suffered acutely from "the
abuse heaped upon me during the debate." As the proceedings
reveal, the Democrats, whatever their official posture, divided

over the issue. The amendment did not come up for consideration until the closing hours of the session, when discipline
was loose, vigilance relaxed, and legislators could disclaim
responsibility on the grounds that they did not know what they
were doing in the frantic haste to adjourn.[18] Probably, the
utilities exerted enough pressure to influence many Democrats
to do in obscurity what they would disavow under publicity.

The vote in the senate invites speculation over the role
of Governor Smith as the acknowledged leader of his party. Did
he, like his fellow Democrats in the upper house, condone in
private what he would condemn in public? The reflections of
Senator Rabenold, who was in a position to know, suggest the
contrary. Such hypocritical behavior was not characteristic
of the man, nor consistent with his record as governor on conservation, nor plausible in the light of what followed. More
likely, he was unaware of the maneuvers to revive the amendment
or momentarily lost control of an unruly organization.
Rabenold proceeded on the assumption that the governor was uninformed.[19]

If Smith remained ignorant of the move to promote the
Ferris amendment until too late to interfere with its passage,
the same cannot be said of his official family. James A.
Parsons evidently cooperated with the measure's supporters.
The governor's counsel, who misjudged the situation to the extent of expecting Rabenold to sponsor the resolution, may have
mistaken the chief executive's intentions as well. At the same
time, an official with a history of advocating public power
professed dissatisfaction over "the form in which the resolution is drawn," but raised "no objection to the general object."
In an effort to bring the matter to Smith's attention in the
hectic last days of the session, Senator Rabenold called at the
executive chamber, but its occupant was out, and the two failed
to communicate. Shortly after adjournment, the senator
appealed to the governor to undo the damage of the legislature
by calling on the voters to reject the measure at the polls,
despite the fact that he would find it "embarrassing to cam-

paign against the proposal in the face of our submission."
While assuring the governor, "you have no executive responsibility in connection with the passage of the amendment,"
Rabenold insisted that "the only way we can atone for the
action of the Democratic Senate is to make absolutely certain
that the amendment is defeated in November."[20]

If Rabenold stood alone in the spring in alerting Smith
to the unanticipated action of the legislature, in the summer
prominent people with a stake in the Adirondack region added
their voices calling upon the governor to combat the Ferris
amendment. Louis Marshall approached him with the expectation
that "your personal influence can unquestionably defeat it."
Cognizant of the administration's devotion to public power, the
Republican argued against the provisions on the grounds of the
potentiality for private developers to reap windfall profits
from the public domain. A distinguished member of the bar, he
had been instrumental in protecting the forest preserve at two
constitutional conventions. He built a summer camp on Saranac
Lake, promoted the establishment of the College of Forestry
at Syracuse University, and fathered a son who graduated from
the institution to become a leading professional worker in the
field of conservation.[21] When another attorney, John G. Agar,
speaking for the New York State Association, protested against
the amendment, Smith declared his own hostility to it and
averred that "at the right time, I propose to oppose it publicly." On the advice of Robert Moses, the chief executive
spoke out a fortnight later in a response to Agar, which was
intended for publication.[22]

The chief executive cooperated in many ways with the
nonpartisan groups that mounted the drive to prevent ratification of the Ferris amendment. He used his influence to obtain
a condemnation of the proposition from the Water Power Commission where Walker, who in May had cast an affirmative vote
in the senate, again reversed himself. On the campaign trail
in Troy, Smith spoke in favor of the institutional bonds and
against the Ferris amendment for subordinating public to pri-

vate interest in the forest preserve. "That great big natural
park is the property of the people of this State," he reminded
his audience, as he insisted "and if water power is going to
be developed from it, it should be developed for the people
themselves, and not for the private owners. . . ."[23] After the
referendum in which the opponents outnumbered the supporters
by a margin of nearly two to one, Marshall assured the governor
that "your action with regard to the amendment unquestionably
brought about its defeat."[24]

By rejecting the Ferris amendment, the voters blocked
plans for the creation of a Raquette River Regulating District.
Earlier, the formation of the Black and Hudson river regulating
districts had encountered little resistance, but the new proposal antagonized the forces of organized conservation. The
petition for a Raquette River district, which in the process of
generating hydroelectricity would flood land in the forest preserve, was pending before the Water Control Commission at the
time of the balloting on the Ferris amendment to legitimize
water power as a purpose of development within the wilderness.
Marshall contended that, without the amendment, the proposed
district was unconstitutional; even in the event of ratification, illegal because the primary purpose was not river regulation but production of energy. The amendment's opponents all
suggested to Smith that it was inspired by the very interests
that were applying for the river regulating district, which
was seen as a giveaway of public property to the utilities.
Smith, who before election day offered to intervene with the
commission, afterwards seemed "satisfied that all of the proceedings for the creation of river regulating districts were
violative of the Constitution." Marshall, as a constitutional
lawyer unwilling to let rights accrue by default, prodded the
administration until the petitioners withdrew the application
for the Raquette River district.[25]

Abandonment of the Raquette River plan did not end the
threat of private power in the public domain. Power companies
would try again for a river regulating district after Smith

failed in repeated efforts to gain legislative approval of public power.

While retaining the essence of public enterprise, the
administration's policy on water power assumed a new form in
1924 with the proposal for a power authority. Smith derived
the idea from the Port of New York Authority. It was a public
corporation with many of the attributes that have since become
familiar in the public sector of mixed economies. It operated
terminal and transport facilities, where necessary established
new ones, charged fees for their use, raised capital by the
flotation of its own bonds, and retired its debt with the
revenue from its activities. The preliminaries to its establishment began at the time of Smith's brief career in city
government, continued through his first administration in
Albany, and culminated during the interregnum with ratification
of the interstate compact and approval of the comprehensive plan
for the port. On appointment by Governor Miller, Smith served
as one of the original commissioners of the authority. He remained loyal to it despite opposition in his own party, particularly from the Hylan administration in New York City. Two
experts on whose judgment Smith frequently relied, the attorney,
Julius Henry Cohen, and the social worker, Belle Moskowitz, contributed instrumentally to the success of the agency. The conception of a public authority, modelled on one in London, originated with Cohen, who would apply it later in drafting the 1926
housing bill with provision for a public corporation in the
form of the abortive state housing bank. A public authority
enjoyed certain advantages over the state officials on whom
Smith had originally intended to confer responsibility for the
production of hydroelectricity. As a corporation, it possessed
resources for financing its operations without burdening either
the taxpayers with additional government debt or the political
process with a referendum to authorize it. On the other hand,
the authority could expect to provide cheaper energy than private enterprise because as a public entity it would benefit
from lower capital costs.[26]

Smith himself conceived the strategy of a public corporation to supply hydroelectricity and turned to Cohen for a study of its feasibility. As a result, the attorney formulated the administration's policy on water power for the 1924 session. He demonstrated, not only the constitutionality, but also the financial viability, of a power authority and extolled the benefits of "complete control of the power by the State's own agency, the title being substantially in the state throughout, not alone to the real estate but to the transmission lines, power stations and the like." Robert Moses and Henry Moskowitz relied on Cohen's legal and economic arguments in mid-December when they presented the plan for a power authority to a group of interested legislators and other officials. In contrast to the lawyer, the two spokesmen implied a willingness, on the part of the executive, to concede to existing utilities a role in the transmission of electricity produced by the authority.[27]

Preparation of the proposal for an authority enabled the governor to be more concrete in his remarks on water power in 1924, than in earlier years, when he delivered his annual message. In it, he interpreted the recent election, in which the voters had rejected the Ferris amendment, as a mandate for public power. His enthusiasm for electrification as a stimulus to progress was tempered only by apprehension at the "possibilities for evil if this development of power is not publicly controlled at the source and regulated in the interests of the people." He deplored the control of energy by private enterprise for fear that "a monopoly may be created more powerful and more sinister than any which this country has known before." To avert this unpleasant possibility, he urged repeal of the state Water Power Act, which authorized the leasing of resources to private developers, and recommended its replacement by a new measure to charter a public corporation to exploit the rapidly flowing rivers. Equally inconceivable to Smith was profit making by private parties, whether from hydroelectricity, or from the transportation facilities already under the jurisdiction of the Port Authority, which served as a model for the

projected power authority. As a result of its operation, he
envisaged reducing the cost of energy to the consumer.[28] The
concern with price and the strictures on monopoly in this message imply that Smith espoused conservation as a democratic reform. A willingness to use the state government to improve the
living standards of the less advantaged runs as a thread through
the governor's policies on water power, labor, social legislation, housing, and parks.

    With the device of a public corporation, Smith injected
into the debate a new element, which briefly raised hopes of
resolving the impasse on water power. A public authority was
less vulnerable to charges of socialism than direct government
operation; as a corporation, it could raise capital without
adding to the state debt. The second consideration influenced
H. Edmund Machold to announce, "I am glad to see that Governor
Smith has changed his mind about permitting the credit of the
State to be used for private business." A conference at which
Smith and the Republican leadership agreed in principle on a
power authority justified the optimism that the assembly
Speaker had engendered. In the spirit of compromise, the administration modified its bill. As Rabenold originally drafted
the measure after consultation with Cohen and others, it not
only set up a public authority holding title to the water resources in the public domain, but also empowered the agency to
generate and transmit electricity, or to sell it, giving preference to municipalities and contracting for resale under conditions designed to protect the ultimate consumer. The subsequent version made no mention of transmission in the provisions for a public corporation authorized—not to proceed with
development—only to submit a plan for approval by the following
legislature. Midway through the session, Moses had "every reason to suppose" that the watered-down draft "will be agreed on
next week."[29]

    The illusion of harmony was dispelled by a conference
between the governor and the Speaker, which grew more acrimonious as it dragged into the wee hours of a winter morning. No

legislation for a power authority could overcome their basic
divergence on the issue of public power. The GOP was willing,
as in Smith's preceding administration, to sanction another
inquiry, and even to put it under the auspices of a power
authority, but not to vest title to the natural resources and
improvements with the express provision that they "shall not be
sold, leased, exchanged or conveyed to any private corporation,
individual or agency, but shall always continue under public
control." Without that concession, his opponents had "taken
the carburetor out of the engine," Smith complained.[30]

The following day, the introduction of competing measures
signalized the failure to reach a compromise. The senate acted
favorably on proposals to repeal Miller's and adopt Smith's
policy, but the Democratic bills remained in committee in the
assembly, which accepted a Republican version of the power
authority without the crucial clauses on public control. It was
a repetition of the performance of earlier years, even to the
governor's futile appeal to the lower house on behalf of his
own program. Since he failed to move the assembly, his second
term ended as his first, without any progress on water power.[31]

Republican campaign tactics in 1924 tended to obscure the
issue that divided the parties and prevented concurrence on a
course of action. Sounding like the governor, Theodore
Roosevelt, Jr. described himself as "unalterably opposed to
alienating the water power of this State from the possession of
the people." In his address in Middletown, he said nothing at
variance with the GOP line. What his party stood for was
technically not alienation of the state's natural resources,
but their rental—not sale—to private enterprise for exploitation. Critics analyzed this as a distinction without a difference because of the capitalization of the public domain for
private profit and because of the cost and difficulty of re-
capturing the resources with their improvements. The candidate
tried to overcome these objections when after renouncing
alienation, he specified, "nor will I sanction its equivalent
in the form of long leases." With that, he apparently repudi-

ated the Republican position. Going along with his party however, he voiced objections to government enterprise requiring
a large number of employees. To resolve the apparent contradiction, he speculated on two alternatives: franchises of indefinite duration, and public generation combined with private
transmission. Where the candidate shifted in an effort to
please the advocates of public and private power alike, the
Republican platform studiously evaded the issue.[32]

        "The man that wrote the water power plank in the Republi-
can platform knows as much about water power development in
this State . . . as I know about the rise and fall of the tide
in the China Sea," Smith observed in Rochester in a speech devoted exclusively to the subject. As for Roosevelt's devotion
to conservation, on another occasion the governor inquired, "Did
the Republican candidate . . . display any conspicuous fitness
for responsible public office when he played such an important
part in the delivery of the naval oil reserves to private interests—and afterwards . . . testified that he knew little or
nothing about the details?" The incumbent charged the GOP and
its candidate with doing everything within their means to hand
over the boundary rivers and the streams of the forest preserve
to the power interests. Reviewing the history of water power in
New York, Smith defined for his Rochester audience the issue
that his opponents were obfuscating:

        The Republican party believes in private develop-
    ment under private ownership and private control for
    private profit.
        The Democratic party believes in public develop-
    ment under public ownership and control for the
    benefit of all the people, the real owners of the
    property.[33]

        Their disagreement explains the impasse on water power
that persisted through the next four years under a Democratic
executive and a Republican legislature. The altered political
complexion of the legislature in 1925 rendered it less responsive than earlier to Smith's pleas for the establishment of a
power authority and for the repeal of existing legislation under
which administrative agencies might grant franchises for private

operation. The refusal of the New York lawmakers to rescind
the licensing authority coincided with the lame duck session of
Congress when Senator Norris, by an adroit parliamentary
maneuver, killed the Underwood bill to lease Muscle Shoals to
private interests.[34]

Smith was no more successful in 1926 than in 1925 in
gaining legislative approval for his water power policy despite
revision to make it more acceptable to the GOP. Until the
middle of his second term, he had insisted on public generation
and transmission. Somewhere in the process of formulating the
plan for a power authority, he reconsidered his stand on transmission. As eventually introduced, the power authority bills
provided for production of hydroelectricity but left the mode
of distribution undetermined. The absence of specific provisions opened the way for distribution by private enterprise.
For two years, the governor concentrated on the generation of
electricity by a public corporation in order to keep the
natural resources in the hands of the state and said little
about transmission. The concession, implicit in his silence,
became explicit in the 1926 annual message when he referred to
the power authority. "It does not mean" he answered his
critics, "that the State is going into the business of dealing
in electrical energy. All that is required" he explained, "is
that the State itself shall own, control and develop water power
at the source." He now conceived the power authority in terms
of public production and private distribution. A month later,
the chief executive renewed his appeal to revoke Miller's water
power legislation and replace it by adopting a measure for a
power authority.[35]

At this session, the governor's bills managed to generate
controversy, but not electricity. Their sponsor in the assembly
accused the GOP opposition of intending to "make some new
millionaires in the northern part of the state," who would profit at public expense. Smith viewed the conflict as a reprise
of the progressive struggles against the same vested interests.
Condemning the administration plan for a power authority as

"economically unsound," Senator John Knight phrased the Republican attitude in a classic formulation: "It should not be the
policy of the State to engage in business, but rather to encourage business by private capital on a fair basis, yielding
a reasonable return to the State, and protect the consuming
public against any increase in rates for electrical power." It
should be obvious to "any student of political economy in the
High Schools of our State," Smith retorted, that consumers would
fare better in purchasing energy from a public authority than
from profit-making utilities. The chief executive denounced
long-term leases as the "equivalent of a gift" of the property
of the many to the privileged few. Rate regulation could not
safeguard the public interest, he explained, because of the complexities of valuation of the investment entitled to a fair return. Ontario furnished him with an illustration of low rates
and excellent service supplied by the provincial government.[36]

While a former Democratic governor praised Smith, a would-
be governor took up the Republican cudgels against him. Ogden
L. Mills, who a year earlier had opened the 1926 campaign by
his attack on the public improvement bonds, now promoted his
candidacy by criticism of public power. Speaking before a
gathering of his party, the GOP hopeful professed it "hard to
determine where the bad economics end and the shrewd politics
begin" in Smith's design for water power. The Republican disputed both the success of the Ontario experience and the failure
of regulation. Affirming his faith in individualism, Mills
condemned Smith's policy as socialist and made a comparison,
whose negative implications were not lost on his audience, between the progressive senator from Wisconsin and the governor
of New York.[37]

While the politicians were debating in public, consulta-
tions were proceeding behind-the-scenes that led to the compromise of 1926 in which Smith yielded on the matter of private
transmission with the prospect of gaining legislative approval
for public generation of hydroelectricity. The negotiations,
which ultimately failed to achieve their object, dated to an

overture by Owen D. Young, as Smith resumed office after the
interregnum. The chairman of the board of General Electric,
which depended on abundant energy, reflected that "if you assume
the worst which the Government ownership people say of private
interests, or if you assume the worst which the private ownership people say of Government development," everyone had a
stake in realizing the potential of water power. To achieve it,
he suggested a combination of government and private ownership
for the purpose of supplying electricity cheaply. Whether or
not the industrialist outlined the terms of the later compromise
already in their 1923 conference, a concrete proposal for government production and private distribution, drafted by the man
behind the Ferris amendment, did reach the governor's desk as he
was preparing for his third administration.[38]

Young intervened actively in the futile effort to advance
power authority legislation along these lines in 1926. As the
session began, Julius Henry Cohen acknowledged, "last year's
bill not drawn with appreciation of business point of view"
and suggested involving the magnate at a time when a Conservative ministry in London was contemplating a public corporation
for energy. With regard to the British example, Smith commented,
"I don't know who thought of it first but I hope they are
copying us." The governor encouraged the contact between Cohen
and Young that led to a meeting between him and Smith at which
"we found that we were not very far apart." Consequently, the
businessman lent his support to the plan for a public authority
so long as it floated its own bonds instead of depending on the
government for financing and relied on existing companies for
the distribution of its power. Under these circumstances, "I
see no objection, but on the contrary, I can see some advantages . . ." to the generation of hydroelectricity by a public
corporation, Young asserted.[39] He was unable to persuade the
Republican leadership, and his attempt to effect a compromise
failed as the party caucus affirmed its adherence to Miller's
water power policy.[40]

The decision of the GOP in February signified that the
1926 legislature, which later in the session rejected the
housing bank, would not accept the power authority, despite
Smith's persuasive arguments on behalf of a public corporation
in both cases. To no avail, he demonstrated that the market for
port authority bonds proved the financial viability of a public
corporation, anticipated that the low interest rates on its
securities would be passed on to the consumer in the form of
moderate priced housing and electricity, and asserted that public enterprise offered the only way to generate water power
without privilege. The Republicans remained unconvinced, and
the Democrats lacked the strength to dislodge his water power
bills from committee.[41]

At their annual stunt dinner, the Albany correspondents
showed that their sympathies lay with the governor. Simon
Legree Smith chastised the Uncle Tom Republican legislature for
allowing Eliza to escape with her Water Power Baby into the
domain of the special interests. "As the scene closed, Uncle
Tom informed Legree Smith that his body may belong to the
Governor, but that his 'old black Republican soul belongs to
Senator Jim Wadsworth.'" Earlier in the skit, "Legree
threatened to sell Uncle Tom or consolidate him with a State
Department . . ." in an obvious allusion to reorganization.[42]

The festivities took place during the session's last
month, which the legislature devoted to translating the Reorganization of Government report into the State Departments Law.
Administrative reform enabled Smith to gain some action on parks,
labor, and water power to which the Republicans had been unwilling to accede in the give-and-take of daily politics.

If H. Edmund Machold rather than Charles Evans Hughes had
chaired the Reorganization Commission, it would not have made
possible even the limited success on conservation. In working
behind the scenes against the choice of the GOP organization,
the governor secured the commission's leadership for a man
identified with the progressive wing of the party, administrative reform, and conservation. Richard S. Childs, who lobbied

for Hughes among his fellow members of the commission, objected
to Machold because of a conflict of interest between the power
companies with which he was affiliated and the Conservation Department whose destiny lay in the hands of the reorganizers.
To allow the former Speaker to chair the commission "would be
quite improper," the reformer concluded.[43] With the chairmanship of Hughes, Smith and his allies delivered the commission
from the foes of reorganization and from the foes of conservation, who might manipulate reconstruction for the benefit of
vested interests.

In accordance with the principles of public administration,
the Hughes commission lodged the supervision of all natural
resources in the Department of Conservation and of all water
resources in a departmental division of water power and control.
To head the division, the report recommended a single Water
Power and Control Commission, which would consolidate the functions of the two existing independent agencies and would consist of the conservation commissioner, the superintendent of
public works, and the attorney general. Furthermore, the State
Departments Law required approval by the governor for the exercise of the commission's authority to license water power development and to create river regulating districts. Through his
appointive power, the chief executive would name a majority of
the members of the commission, and through his veto power, he
could control its actions. Consequently, when the new statute
took effect on the first day of 1927, a governor in favor of
public power would be in a position to block exploitation of
the state's water resources by private enterprise.[44]

Throughout Smith's third term, Republicans, sympathetic
to private development, predominated on both the Water Power and
the Water Control Commissions, which enjoyed complete autonomy.
Facing a change in personnel and a loss of authority, both
agencies experienced a sudden spurt of activity in 1926.

In order to understand the events of that year, it is
necessary, not only to keep in mind the progress of reorganization, but also to review the record of the Water Power Com-

mission. It began its career in the Miller administration by
preparing to lease boundary waters to industrial corporations
as it was authorized to do by law. At this time, the commission
received applications for the exploitation of the Niagara River
and went so far as to grant preliminary permits to guarantee
priority to two petitioners for use of the Saint Lawrence. The
election that Miller lost placed the Democrats in a majority on
the commission during Smith's second term. For two years, the
commission refused to proceed with the licensing of private
enterprise under a law that the governor could not induce the
assembly to repeal. Although the Republicans, who regained control of the commission as a result of the election of 1924,
announced their intention of restoring its function and rein-
stated the earlier applications, they dragged their feet in the
first year of their return to power.[45]

Not until after the November election that made reorganization a certainty, did the Water Power Commission move vigorously to carry out its stated intention of granting franchises
for the boundary rivers. When the commission made public its
plans at the end of January, 1926, the governor declared himself
"unalterably opposed to giving permits to these big corporations." He criticized the commission as an anomaly in violation
of the principles of public administration underlying the pending reconstruction of the state government. The report of the
commission and the introduction of the governor's bills for
public power provoked in the legislature a lively debate in
which a leading Democrat pronounced it "unseemly that in its
dying hour this Water Power Commission should be in such a rush
to give away" natural resources to various monopolies "without
awaiting the report of the Hughes commission." Coming to the
defense of the water power commissioners, one of them, Senator
John Knight, explained that government policy "is expressed in
the existing law and not in something which the Governor thinks
the law should be." Another, Albert Ottinger, expanded on the
idea that the agency was "compelled to live up to the requirements of the law" by licensing applicants to exploit the

rivers. Smith challenged him "to tell the people of the State
of New York just who the applicants for these valuable water
power rights are." Dismissing the implications of impropriety,
the attorney general responded with a question of his own, "who
will be back of public construction and of public operation."
Not the people, but "the politicians feeding at the public crib
for fat jobs at the expense of the people," he alleged. Hearings
at the end of February answered Smith's question by revealing
the involvement of such corporate giants as General Electric and
Aluminum Company of America, while various sources brought to
light the financial interest of prominent Republicans such as
Machold and Mills.[46]

Adverse publicity caused the officials to hesitate.
Echoing the Democrats in the executive and legislative branches,
both the prestigious New York State Association and an ad hoc
committee of prominent women, including Eleanor Roosevelt and
Rose Schneiderman, impugned the proceedings of a commission
that, in its existing form, would not survive reorganization.
Not long afterwards but just before a hearing, which Smith described as a "farce comedy," the agency itself showed an inclination to refrain from making any decision prior to the report
of the Hughes commission. After the legislature adjourned, the
Water Power Commission resumed its deliberations amid conflicting estimates of its intentions. Although rumors circulated
that it would issue no licenses until after the November election, for fear of voter retribution against the GOP, Ottinger
gave assurances of prompt action as soon as the commission
possessed the requisite information. With proper timing, the
two courses were not mutually exclusive. At the end of June,
the state engineer and surveyor detailed the conditions for
leasing, in a report favorable to private enterprise. Not until the end of September, did the commissioners meet to approve
it. A month later, they reviewed competing applications for
the Saint Lawrence franchise and, at the conclusion of their
hearing, recessed without setting a date for reconvening, but

with every indication of postponement until after election day.[47]

While the Water Power Commission was contemplating hydroelectric projects on the boundary rivers, the Water Control
Commission took under consideration a proposal for an inland
stream. The projected Salmon River Regulating District resembled the Raquette River Regulating District that the administration had quashed in 1923. Louis Marshall, who had been instrumental in foiling the earlier petition, informed Smith in July
of the new proceeding of which "the real, but concealed, object
is to construct a reservoir solely for power purposes," and
which was therefore of questionable legality under provisions
for the regulation of the flow of streams. Not long afterwards,
the governor intervened with the commission to procure a delay
in order to permit the attorney to present the case against the
district. Toward the end of October, the north country conservation groups, which had fought the Ferris amendment and the
Raquette River district, protested against power installations
on the Salmon River "that will destroy the beauty of the
Adirondack Preserve." Smith insisted that he would "never be
found willing to alienate the State's power resources in any
such fashion as this" and stated, "I have been opposed to the
river regulating districts on the Raquette River and I am firmly
opposed to the Salmon River Regulating District."[48]

The governor criticized both commissions in his last campaign for reelection. He referred to the application before
the Water Control Commission as "a water power grab, pure and
simple" of natural resources, and accused his opponent of
willingness to "give them away to private interests for a song,
that they may make private fortunes from their development."
On another occasion, he charged the Water Power Commission with
deliberately stalling on the leases for "fear of the political
consequences if the people should later wake up to find that
this commission had alienated . . . the last line of our great
natural resources."[49]

In 1926, as two years before, Smith chose Rochester as
the location for a speech devoted exclusively to water power,

which he identified as "the greatest single issue" of the contest. Where the governor discussed the issue in terms of public versus private interest, his opponent, Ogden Mills, interpreted it differently as "whether government is to enter the
business field and operate vast business enterprises, or whether
we will continue to place our reliance on the American system of
individual initiative, enterprise and opportunity." The Republican candidate equated the power authority with the first
alternative which, to him, meant "inefficiency," "waste,"
"extravagance," "patronage," a "spoils system," and a "listless
bureaucracy." It raised the specter of socialism.[50] Smith derided the allusion to radicalism as "political hypocrisy and
bunk." If his water power policy made him a socialist, it
placed him in the impeccable Republican company of Theodore
Roosevelt and Charles Evans Hughes. The chief executive defended his program of public generation and private transmission as
the way to safeguard the interest of the people as the owner of
the natural resources and the consumer of electricity. He was
the recipient of information on Mills's investments in power
companies, which was used on at least one occasion to point out
the connection between personal gain and the power policy of
the Republican.[51]

Smith won easily over Mills despite the efforts of the
utility corporations to bring about the governor's defeat. A
congratulatory note regaled him with an amusing anecdote about
how the Niagara Falls Power Company provided free transportation
to the polls for one hundred fifty people, all of whom reputedly
"voted the straight Democratic ticket."[52]

His victory assured Smith of control over the disposition
of water power resources in the reorganized government after
January 1. These facts justified him in his appeal to the Water
Power Commission not to use the interval to take irrevocable
action on hydroelectric franchises. Complimenting the governor
on his presence of mind, a New York attorney observed, "No
executive position is too important or too large for such a
man to fill." On December 10, Smith's correspondent exploded

with indignation, "When I wrote you on November 4th, it appeared inconceivable that any move to thwart the popular will would be attempted by a commission whose official life could not continue with the new administration."[53]   By then, much water had flowed over the unbuilt dams.

The Water Power Commission set December 8 as the date of a meeting to decide between the alternative proposals for the Saint Lawrence franchise. A majority was determined not to permit a replay of the scene of 1922 when Smith, interpreting his election as a mandate for public power, had dissuaded the commissioners from making an irrevocable commitment during their last month in office. This time, four of the commissioners intended to act while they still had the authority, on the grounds that failure to do so would delay development indefinitely in a repetition of the impasse of Smith's second term when the executive blocked private exploitation; the legislature, public power. They were unwilling to allow his antipathy to render inoperative a law unlikely to be repealed by the incoming administration. To induce Smith to go along, they offered to insert a clause, making the lease contingent on the failure of the next session to authorize public power. They called his bluff. No amount of righteous indignation could conceal the fact that the proposition rested on an analysis of political reality. The governor scored his strongest point with regard to the morality of a lame duck commission giving away the bulk of the state's remaining water power potential. "I certainly cannot agree to any such absurd deal . . ." he objected when "as Governor and as Governor-elect," he renewed his request for a moratorium on grants.[54]

Smith prepared to take legal action to keep the commission from issuing the license. When Daniel F. Cohalan advised him to apply for an injunction in New York City, the chief executive reminded him that jursidiction lay in the courts of Albany, not the metropolis. The judge, who acknowledged the inevitability of a change of venue, explained, "This would take, how-

ever, a day or two at a time when days count for your opponents." Dilatory tactics could hamstring the commission until
the end of the year. Nevertheless, the governor's special
counsel, Samuel Untermyer, planned to seek the restraining order
in the capital.[55]

A show of determination enabled the chief executive to
block the franchise without going to court. The administration
had retained Untermyer because it could hardly expect help from
a Republican attorney general who sat on the commission and
sided with its majority. On the advice of his special counsel,
Smith communicated with the commission to challenge the legality
of its prospective grant on the grounds that its recapture provisions, in their generosity to private enterprise, neglected
the public interest and that the document in question constituted, not a lease, but an option unauthorized by law. At the
same time, he warned both the Frontier Corporation and the
American Super-Power Corporation that they proceeded at their
own risk in accepting any license from the agency. Both companies backed down amid speculation that they were withdrawing
in response to private overtures from the commissioners desirous
of extricating the GOP from an embarrassing situation. In any
case, the license had become a financial liability to the corporations, in view of probable litigation and the hostility of
the administration, and a political liability to the Republican
party, in view of the general opposition of the press and the
adverse reaction of the electorate. The outcome allowed the
Water Power Commission to save its face—but not its franchise.[56]

On the eve of his fourth term, Smith duplicated his feat
of 1922 in preventing the Water Power Commission from initiating
private development during its last month in office. If the
agency had not yielded, whether the judiciary would have upheld
Untermyer's challenge to the validity of the lease, is dubious;
whether the process of litigation would have afforded the delay
necessary to checkmate the commission, is problematical. The
agency was entitled to act literally until midnight, December 31.

Smith was on firmer moral than legal ground, for the commission
had compromised itself by deliberately putting off the grant
until after election day, and the terms were extraordinarily
favorable to business in which influential Republicans had a
personal financial stake.

The governor interceded with the Water Control Commission
in a situation with striking parallels to that of the Water
Power Commission. Between midsummer and early December, the
Water Control Commission had appeared in no hurry to approve
the petition for a Salmon River Regulating District, which
Smith denounced in the autumn campaign. In the midst of the
controversy over the Saint Lawrence franchise, he responded to
the appeal of conservationists to deter the unit from acting on
the Salmon River proposal during its final month in office. He
requested the lame duck commission to leave the matter to the
new administration. On the same day that they presided over
the withdrawal of the Saint Lawrence applications, the conservation commissioner, the attorney general, and the state engineer and surveyor, in their capacity as water control commissioners, heard counsel for the Malone Power and Light Company
rescind the Salmon River petition. Louis Marshall, who was
representing the governor in the case, was indifferent to the
proceedings of the commission. After the failure of the
Ferris amendment, the violation of the forest preserve for the
generation of electricity remained unconstitutional; therefore,
he was confident of success in reversing any action the commission might take to establish a Salmon River Regulating District.[57] Consequently, Smith stood on sounder legal ground in
obstructing the Water Control than the Water Power Commission.

His simultaneous victory over both commissions augured
well, not only for the governor's policy on natural resources,
but also for his future in politics. A Brooklynite exulted,
"Three cheers and a tiger for your stand on the water power."
While the publisher of the *New York World* congratulated Smith,
the usually staid *Times* editorialized that the state "contains
within its boundaries a seemingly inexhaustible store of elec-

tric energy popularly described as Superpower or Smith Power."
The editor continued:

> Strenuous efforts to dam up and control Smith
> Power . . . for the purpose of feeding the Republican
> State Utilities have resulted in serious casualties
> among the construction personnel. . . . licenses and
> leases to Republican candidates for office are issued
> with a cancellation option to the licensee in case
> Smith decides to run again. . . . The Republican
> engineers and road gangs have been warned that if
> they fail to establish control over the Smith Power
> in New York it will spill over beyond State bound-
> aries and electrify the rest of the United States.[58]

Smith's fourth term appears as a lull between the presidential campaign ahead and, behind, substantial achievements in
reorganizing the government, financing public improvements, conserving parkland, promoting low-cost housing, extending welfare
legislation, defending civil liberties, and conserving water
resources. It was a time for the consolidation of gains already made rather than for innovation. The governor suffered
disappointment when his defeat of corporate interests in 1926
did not eventuate in public power in 1927-28. At the very moment of his success in immobilizing the two water commissions,
Senator Knight had predicted that "there will be no development
on the St. Lawrence for a long time to come" and discounted the
possibility of legislative approval for administration policy
on water power.[59]

In 1927 the chief executive opened the legislative session, as he had been doing since 1924, with a plea for a power
authority. This time, Julius Henry Cohen supplied data to support Smith's argument on the advantages of government operation
over government regulation of private business in hydroelectricity. Judicial rulings, which inflated valuation with
watered capital, allowed utilities to charge consumers rates
far in excess of what a public corporation would set. To give
the people the benefit of cheap energy from the public domain,
the Democrats, as in earlier years, put in the hopper a bill
for a power authority.[60]

With a show of seeking a compromise, the lawmakers considered a variety of alternatives. The Republicans, to whom a
power authority was unacceptable, proposed to set up an impar-
tial commission of experts to investigate the comparative advantages of private and public development. Smith no longer considered this an open question, for he interpreted recent events
as a mandate for public power. He referred to the inquiry as
a joke, since the selection of personnel would predetermine the
conclusions. He modified his stand to bring it slightly closer
to the GOP in a revised power authority measure, which authorized the public corporation to prepare a comprehensive plan for
legislative approval, before undertaking generation as provided
in the original draft. He countered the Republican proposal
for the settlement of the issue by putative experts with his
own for a popular referendum. This is a device that he was
willing to use also on the child labor amendment and Prohibition, where he felt confident of finding in the electorate the
majority that he lacked in the malapportioned legislature. The
Democrats who had introduced the bill for a power authority
also presented one for a referendum. The Republicans derided
it, for the only electoral mandate that they acknowledged was
one "to beware of unsound economics." Each side accused the
other of obstructing development by political posturing. In
the course of debate, Senator Bernard Downing insinuated that
"the same interests that blocked the Boulder Dam and Muscle
Shoals legislation in Congress" were determined to defeat
Smith's power authority measure in the New York State Legislature. There was no room for substantive compromise, because
the political parties held mutually exclusive views on whether
a public or a private corporation should generate energy from
the swiftly flowing waters, and each contestant made concessions only on procedural details that would not sacrifice its
basic goal. Consequently, the Republican majority accepted
only the bill for an investigatory commission, which the governor promptly rejected. With a gesture reminiscent of his first
term, he accompanied his veto with a memorandum that consisted

of a single sentence declaring that the bill "would waste the public funds and accomplish no useful purpose."[61]

No water power legislation even emerged from committee in the 1928 session at which the lawmakers turned a deaf ear to Smith's appeals for a power authority or a referendum on public power.[62] His administration ended as it began with an acute awareness of unutilized potential and an unheeded call for public development of hydroelectricity.

Although the majority declined to consider general legislation on water power in Smith's last year in office, it did attempt by indirection to facilitate private exploitation of inland streams. This was the hidden agenda in two bills, which passed in the last month of the session: one to exclude river regulating districts from certain sites in the forest preserve and a second to authorize a study of the return to the state from property used for such districts.[63]

Just what these measures implied invited speculation, which led to dissension in the conservation movement. The governor initially assumed that the first was drafted to protect the wilderness and its resorts; the second, to assure proper remuneration for the use of the public domain. These were the purposes stated by the bills' supporters such as the Adirondack Civic Association, but the Association for the Protection of the Adirondacks, with its own conservationist credentials, disagreed. If the opponents charged that the bills were no more than a subterfuge for private development of hydroelectricity, their legislative sponsor admitted as much when he told the chief executive, "it seems to me that the resulting fact of more power at reduced costs to the consumers of the locality affected must be taken into consideration." Louis Marshall, who condemned the legislation as the opening wedge for private power, was as influential as anyone in dissuading the governor from signing it. The attorney argued that to ban the districts from some locations was to legitimate them in others and to increase the fees for entry on state land was to imply its rental, not for public purposes such as

flood control, but for the profitable production of energy.
Without the Ferris amendment, to whose defeat he had contributed, the constitution barred water power development in the
forest reserve, he insisted. Smith incorporated the lawyer's
arguments in the veto memorandum with which he carried on the
tradition that he had established by opposing the Ferris amendment and the Raquette and Salmon river regulating districts.[64]

Smith criticized his last legislature for its defeat of
public power and its favoritism to private interests "in the
face of the national scandal growing out of the alienation of
the country's natural resources." For the first time in 1928,
Senator Norris, who had earlier taken advantage of the reaction
to Teapot Dome to introduce a public power bill, was able to
guide legislation for government operation at Muscle Shoals
through both houses. In Washington, Congress approved public
power, and President Calvin Coolidge vetoed the measure.[65] In
Albany, the legislature encouraged private enterprise, and
Governor Alfred E. Smith disapproved. As the presidential campaign neared, water power was one of the issues that separated
progressives from conservatives in state and nation.

Concentrating on a single theme in each campaign address,
Smith chose Denver for the presentation of his views on water
power. His talk suggested the implementation on a national
scale of the policies that he had formulated out of his New
York experience. Stop the leasing of natural resources to
private developers. In its place, he stood for the generation
of hydroelectricity by government at the appropriate level and
sale to transmission companies under contractual safeguards to
protect the public interest in reasonable rates. As for the
principles underlying his recommendations on water resources,

> I view them as God-given resources of the country.
> I make the claim that the benefit of their develop-
> ment should accrue to the people themselves and that
> we should not permit them to fall into private hands
> for private development, which means private gain at
> the expense of all the users of the energy.

Specifically, he proposed government operation at Boulder Dam and Muscle Shoals.[66]

Although he was a Republican, Senator Norris, who almost singlehandedly blocked private enterprise at Muscle Shoals, endorsed Smith in 1928. A year before the contest, the Nebraskan had predicted, "The West will vote for Al Smith or some other progressive rather than for an 'Eastern reactionary.'" The New Yorker's "liberal and farsighted position" on water power impressed the senator and led to his defection from the GOP. The ambiguities of the Hoover campaign ended in an administration that favored the policy of leasing and vetoed the second Norris bill for public power at Muscle Shoals to clear both houses of Congress.[67]

What success Smith and Norris enjoyed at this time was the essentially negative one of checking private interests; the positive achievement of public power eluded them, for the governor's plans were subject to veto by a Republican legislature; the senator's, by a Republican executive. Smith could not overcome legislative resistance despite the flexibility with which he tailored his program to meet GOP objections. Initially, he had proposed public generation and transmission of energy, administration of the program by a unit of the state government, and funding of the operation through the normal channels of public finance: tax revenues and government bonds. In its final version, his bill confined itself to government generation under the direction of a public corporation with the capacity to raise capital by its own indebtedness, to be serviced from the revenues of the projects. With the reconstruction of the state government, New York's chief executive acquired over natural resources the jurisdiction that allowed Smith to prevent private exploitation in his last term; before reorganization, he had relied on the prestige of his position to interfere with GOP arrangements for private production. The impasse that resulted delayed the development of water power in New York but averted an irretrievable commitment to special interests.

Ideology and interest dictated the partisan cleavage on
water power during the Smith administration. The GOP upheld
the ideal of free enterprise in arguing against government
intervention in the economy, when involvement meant state
operation of—not state aid to—business. In contrast, Smith's
positions on water power and welfare reflect the influence of
institutional economics, which he assimilated unconsciously in
much the same way as the related ideas of reform Darwinism and
legal realism. If these social theories were democratic in
their implications, so too was a conservation policy that
placed the interest of the mass of consumers above that of the
electric utilities. Campaigning in Denver, Smith denounced the
lobbying activities of the power corporations. Investigation
would reveal how closely allied were New York's utilities to a
Republican party many of whose leaders benefited financially
from the connection. In a classic example of conflict of
interest, a state senator in the pay of one company reported
services consisting, less in the enactment of new laws, than in
"the fact that many detrimental bills which were introduced we
were able to kill in my committee."[68] Few words explain better
the fate of the governor's water power legislation.

The very interests that thwarted Smith did not abate
their hostility to public power under Governor Roosevelt, but
the altered political climate rendered them less effective. In
his gubernatorial campaign, FDR assured conservationists that
he was "in full accord" with the outgoing executive in objecting to river regulating districts that would generate hydroelectricity in the forest preserve. Roosevelt fought a long
and hard, but successful, battle to implement the plan that his
predecessor had devised for a power authority. At one point
in the struggle, the new governor informed the old of the
favorable prospect for preliminary legislation "which seems to
accept the great basic principle for which you and I have
fought so long" and received in return, "Happy congratulations
on your victory." FDR's experience in New York convinced him
of the need, not only for public production, but also for

public distribution of water power.[69]

The New Deal in hydroelectricity derived largely from the New York of Governors Roosevelt, Smith, and Hughes, for FDR applied in the presidency what he had learned in the governorship. Although the Tennessee Valley Authority went far beyond the New York State Power Authority in regional planning, each was organized as the public corporation that Smith had envisioned for the production of energy. He championed public power in the spirit of the progressives in the conservation movement, and, in the words with which they have been described, was "more concerned with economic justice in the handling of resources than with the mere prevention of waste."[70]

Governor Smith spoke out on behalf of public enterprise
both in hydroelectricity and urban transportation. Reformers
who favored the first were likely to support the second, according to a scholar, who has discerned in the corporate world of
interlocking power and traction companies a common enemy of
both reforms. In cities as distant from one another as San
Francisco, Cleveland, and Jersey City, progressive mayors committed themselves with varying degrees of success to municipal
ownership of public utilities, transit among them.[1] When Mayor
John F. Hylan of New York encountered obstacles to his plans
for municipally owned and operated subways, William Randolph
Hearst blamed the governor and charged him with hypocrisy.
Municipal ownership was a major consideration in the sensational feud between Smith and Hearst.

Both men emerged on the New York political scene in the
heyday of progressivism; contemporaries recognized young Hearst
as a progressive when they did not fear him as a radical or
distrust him as a demagogue.[2] In retrospect, he fits into the
category of social progressives who distinguished themselves
by their sensitivity to the working class and urban immigrants.
In the roles of publisher and politician, he backed reform
candidates and took up the progressive cause in the battles of
the first decade of the century: against political corruption
and for direct democracy; against child labor and for labor
legislation; against the trusts and for government ownership of
utilities. If he made a fetish of public ownership, he held
the monopolies responsible for the high cost of living and the
deprivations of the poor. Unsympathetic scholars have suggested that he wielded the issue "like a kind of Damocles'
sword" over the head of each official whom he supported but who
invariably lacked the means to implement public ownership, a
fact that "would always afford a convenient ground for attacking him later if that proved desirable." The publisher used

this tactic in his relations with Alfred E. Smith.[3]

The governor thereby joined a company of politicians whom Hearst had supported, only to turn against them, and whose ranks include both Roosevelts, John Purroy Mitchel, and Samuel Seabury. Historians disagree on the extent to which Hearst's political behavior was motivated by principle and by ambition. Through his newspapers, he could inform the masses and activate them politically at the same time that he promoted his own candidacies. He fashioned his journals into organs of the muckraking tradition, but critics alleged that "much of the muck which he raked up was muck which he himself deposited."[4] The too frequent disregard for truth, the sensationalism, and the class consciousness of his press offended those who questioned the propriety of an officeseeker controlling the media for his own benefit. His papers enjoyed wide circulation in the Democratic constituency, and he used this leverage to manipulate the party. Although he ran for office on its ticket, when it suited his purpose, he rarely hesitated to abandon the organization or to foster a third party to divert enough votes to assure a Democratic defeat. A severe ambivalence characterized the relation between the publisher and New York Democracy during the years when Smith was rising through its ranks from clubhouse to statehouse.

A year before Smith went to the assembly, Tammany Hall sent Hearst to Congress and launched the political career of the publisher who would fight for control of the organization. Charles Francis Murphy refused to encourage Hearst's presidential aspirations at the Democratic convention of 1904. The very next year, the congressman, having decided against seeking a third term, ran as the candidate of a third party, for mayor of New York City. He came in a close second to the Democratic victor—in the official returns—in an election that authorities generally concede he would have won in an honest count. Murphy, who respected the power of the Hearst press more than its publisher, engineered his nomination for governor in 1906, but Charles Evans Hughes defeated him in a contest in which his

running mates on the statewide ticket all succeeded in gaining
office.   Voting patterns suggest that, not Murphy, but his
Brooklyn counterpart sabotaged the Hearst campaign.   Nevertheless, Hearst blamed the Tammany leader, for he retaliated in a
move with far-reaching consequences, by unsuccessfully backing
a challenger to Tom Foley, Al Smith's mentor, in a race for
sheriff of New York County.   Turning against his original
choice for mayor, William Jay Gaynor, in 1909 the journalist
headed the ticket of the Civic Alliance, for which he earned
the sobriquet, William ALSO-RANdolph Hearst.[5]   Although Gaynor
won the mayorality, his organization lost its majority on the
Board of Estimate.   The third party tactic that weakened the
Democrats in the city failed to stop their sweep of the state
government in 1910.   A few years later, when Governor Sulzer
was under attack by Tammany, Hearst came to his aid against the
machine; from one point of view, the impeachment of Sulzer was
another episode in the struggle between Murphy and Hearst.   In
1916 the publisher deserted his earlier ally, the reformer,
Samuel Seabury, and backed a Republican for governor in another
attempt to rule or ruin the Democratic party.

Hearst returned to the Democratic fold in 1917 to hand-
pick the party's nominee for mayor.   In the now familiar pattern, the journalist wished to deny a second term to the reformer, John Purroy Mitchel, the Fusion candidate whom he had
enthusiastically endorsed four years earlier.   The nomination,
which Hearst again coveted, would be useless if Foley and his
adherents carried out a threat to retaliate against the newspaperman for his frequent defections.   Caught between the regular Democrats, who detested the publisher, and Hearst, who held
the party hostage by his command of publicity, Murphy designated John F. Hylan, a man eminently acceptable to the journalist.   Although Hylan had worked his way through law school, he
labored under the reputation of being little better than a
mouthpiece for the clever, if unscrupulous, Hearst.   Hylan had
been fired from a job as a motorman on the elevated, and the
two men shared an aversion to the traction trust.   "Taken quite

apart from the influences promoting his candidacy," the Citizens' Union deemed Hylan "the most unfit candidate for Mayor presented in recent years." If Hearst used the new mayor as the instrument of his own ambitions to lead the liberal wing of the Democratic party, they were frustrated in the first decade of the century by William Jennings Bryan; in the second, by Woodrow Wilson; and in the third, by Alfred E. Smith.[6]

Hearst was a serious contender for the gubernatorial nomination that Murphy procured for Smith in 1918. After the organization candidate issued a statement to the effect that "experience has taught us the wisdom of Government ownership and operation of public utilities," he received the publisher's blessing in the primary contest. The Hearst press advised its readers to cast "a vote for progress and against reaction" in the general election by marking their ballots for the Democrat. Several times during the campaign, Smith spoke out in favor of municipal ownership.[7] His election as governor made him a competitor to Hearst for political preferment and a victim of the inconstancy that the publisher had shown in his relations with other politicians.

For the time being, Hearst could derive satisfaction from the passage on public ownership of utilities in the governor's first annual message. Reasoning like the institutional economists, Smith explained that "whatever is of necessity a monopoly, should be a public monopoly." The very day that these words were being read in the legislature, newspaper headlines announced the bankruptcy of a private monopoly, the Brooklyn Rapid Transit Company.[8]

By 1919, BRT and IRT (Interborough Rapid Transit Company) had come to dominate New York City's system of transportation, whose history illumines the terms of the debate on municipal ownership in which Smith engaged with Mayor Hylan and Mr. Hearst.[9] Here as elsewhere in the nineteenth century, competition had yielded to consolidation, paving the way for monopoly as exercised by the two corporations. If New Yorkers

benefited from the integration of competing lines into two systems, each charging only a single fare for a ride covering a
considerable distance on its component routes, the city paid a
high price. In the process of unification, insiders made a
killing by the financial manipulation familiar to students of
industrial combination. Interborough, for example, in 1903 had
leased Manhattan Elevated Railway on terms favorable to the
lessor and in 1906 negotiated a merger extraordinarily profitable to Metropolitan Street Railway. Promoters saddled the
companies with watered capital and huge debts, which added to
the problem of high fixed costs inherent in the technology of
the transportation industry. In the inflationary economy after
World War I, IRT and BRT were no longer able to meet all of
their obligations. Potential income from expansion failed to
materialize when rising construction costs led to delay, and
receivership ensued. At the time, BRT owned some of its facilities, but both companies were operating surface or elevated
lines leased from private enterprise, often at extortionate
rents, and subways belonging to the city.

The granting of lucrative franchises to business corporations, which had produced the elevated and surface lines,
proved unacceptable in the case of the subways, and they developed through a combination of public and private enterprise.
Shortly after the turn of the century, the city negotiated
contracts no. 1 and no. 2, whereby it provided the capital for
construction but left the building and operation of the subways
to companies organized for that purpose. The city owned the
subways, and the companies, which operated them under long-
term leases, paid rent just about sufficient to service the
municipal debt incurred in financing them. Having strained its
borrowing capacity, in 1913 New York resorted to different
arrangements in order to gain badly needed extensions. Under
the dual contracts, no. 3 and no. 4, the city assumed responsibility for new construction, but the operating companies shared
its cost. Consequently, IRT, in Manhattan and the Bronx, and
BRT, in Manhattan and Brooklyn, each operated a unified transit

system consisting of publicly owned subways and privately owned
elevated and surface lines. Operating revenues from the systems were assigned to meet obligations in the following order
of priority: (1) operating and certain fixed expenses, including rent to private lessors and to the city for the original
subways built under contracts no. 1 and no. 2; (2) preferential
payments to IRT and BRT in lieu of profits earned on privately
owned lines and for the amortization of the debt for construction under the dual contracts; (3) service on the municipal
debt under the dual contracts; (4) profit sharing between the
city and the operating companies. If funds were inadequate at
any time to cover a category of high priority, in subsequent
years, it was necessary to meet the cumulative deficiency before using revenue for categories below. To the time of
Smith's retirement, income generally sufficed for the first two
classes of payments, thereby amortizing much of the private,
but little of the public, indebtedness for subway extension.

Although the city did not get a good deal financially in
the dual contracts, they contained certain compensating features. Like the earlier agreements, they prescribed a five-
cent fare for a single ride throughout a system with free
transfers among its component parts. Not only were the dual
contracts of shorter duration than the original, but they also
included recapture clauses to enable the city to take over subway operation, prior to the expiration of the agreements, upon
stipulated payment to, or default by, the lessees. The provisions for fares and recapture were controversial in the
twenties, when the companies petitioned for higher fares and
Mayor Hylan proposed municipal operation of the subways.

When Smith took the helm of state, the city administration was trying to maneuver the corporations into a position of
default, while the Hearst press engaged in a campaign of publicity for recapture of the subways. Writing in the *American* on
the operators' petition to raise the fare, Arthur Brisbane de-
claimed, "This effort to put hundreds of millions of watered
stock, all pure H_2O, upon a self-supporting basis will be the

first test of New York's new Governor." As for the end in
view, Hearst himself editorialized, "let the traction companies
abandon the contract and turn the city's property over to the
city to be run for the benefit of the citizens." The Board of
Estimate acted to force the companies' hand by aggravating
their financial embarrassment. It was justified in denying the
rate hike, which would have gone to meet the cumulative deficit
in preferential payments to the corporations without any quid
pro quo to the city. Municipal officials, however, were violating the contracts by withholding funds for construction.
Every delay worsened the companies' position by depriving them
of potential revenue from subway extension. Caught in the
middle, Smith admonished both parties "to stop quarreling and
get together, vote the necessary money, and then get on with
the subway." His personal intervention influenced the city
government at the end of January to abandon a tactic of dubious
legality and to abide by its contractual obligations.[10]

When the legislative session addressed the transit problem, Governor Smith would neither condone a solution that favored the companies at the expense of the city, nor waver in
his commitment to the principle of municipal ownership. Two
measures of equal but opposite effect came up for consideration
in 1919, and he supported the one for city ownership. Drafted
by the state's Conference of Mayors, the Fowler bill made provision for public enterprise in local utilities. It shared the
fate of the governor's proposals on water power and labor that
passed in the senate, only to die in committee in the assembly
where the Republican caucus exerted firmer control. By contrast, the Carson-Martin bill to which Smith objected passed
in the lower, but not the upper house. The GOP sponsored this
measure to authorize the Public Service Commission to set
rates in excess of the maximum prescribed in a franchise. Such
a one-sided proposal assured business a profit while transfer-
ring to the city all of the risk. If adopted, the law would
have deprived the municipal administration of a counter with
which to extract concessions from the corporations in return

for increased fares. Whatever chance it had in the senate evap-
orated with the revelation of an attempt to bribe a senator to
vote for it. Amid calls for an investigation, the session
ended without materially changing the relative strength of the
parties to the dual contracts.[11]

The legislature that rejected public ownership did comply
with the governor's recommendations affecting the regulation of
New York City transit. Since the Hughes administration, two
Public Service Commissions, one with jurisdiction exclusively
in New York City, had regulated utilities in the Empire State.
On taking office, Smith proposed two changes: first, to separate the regulatory from the entrepreneurial function with regard to the subways and entrust the latter to a transit construction commissioner; second, to replace the regulatory commissions with a single official in charge of each agency. Although Smith justified this suggestion on the same theory of
executive responsibility that undergirded reform of the state
government, the Citizens' Union, which favored reorganization
in general, denounced the amendments to the Public Service Commissions Law as ripper legislation. Nevertheless, the lawmakers acted on Smith's proposals for the city by restructuring
the Public Service Commission for the First District and by
creating a new Office of Transit Construction Commissioner.[12]

Since the Hearst press attacked Smith over transit fares
and milk prices, it is important to note that he was not insen-
sitive to the hardship resulting from high-priced necessities.
His first annual message, which called for municipal ownership
of utilities, termed expensive milk "a public menace." Sounding ironically like the *Journal's* editor, the governor declared, "Thousands of poor people and especially children, are
deprived of sufficient nourishment. . . ." In the role of consumer advocate, the newspaper chain could disregard the interest of the producer and the distributor, while the chief executive faced the dilemma of protecting each interest group, "but
not at the expense of the others."[13]

What provoked the governor to comment was a strike that caused a shortage of milk at the same time that the bankruptcy of Brooklyn Rapid Transit threatened to disrupt public transportation in New York City. The Dairymen's League, an organization of producers, halted deliveries of milk in protest against the low price offered by the distributors' organization, the Milk Conference Board. Smith showed his concern by appointing representatives of both associations and of the general public to the inevitable tripartite committee and by conferring personally with the contending parties. Satisfaction over the resumption of normal supplies late in January was diminished by a feeling in the city administration that the dairy farmers and middlemen had composed their differences at the expense of the consumer.[14]

The milk strike presented the chief executive with a challenge to do something about the problem of monopoly. District Attorney Edward Swann of New York County explained that officials were powerless to protect the consumer of this commodity from price fixing because the dairy industry had obtained an exemption from the state's antitrust laws. At the mere mention of repeal, organized agriculture flooded the executive chamber with protests, including one from a Democratic functionary, who cautioned Smith, "If Dooling and Hylan get by with the repeal of the Donnelly anti-trust act, your Up State Democratic organization is killed as far as the Farm vote is concerned." Political considerations were uppermost, for the governor acknowledged the force of the argument for repeal and explained his inaction on the grounds that he lacked the votes in the legislature. But the absence of a majority rarely inhibited him, as it did this time, in addressing the lawmakers on a policy in which he believed.[15]

Smith was more willing, but less able, to correct deficiencies that the milk strike exposed in the Department of Farms and Markets. It was charged with collaborating with the interests it was supposed to regulate, in order to raise the price of milk. Information on incompetence and patronage within the agency had reached the governor-elect. But the department, which was ruled by a council that the legislature chose, was impervious to influence by the chief executive. All he could do was to recommend in vain to the legislature a series of reforms suggested to him by a Republican state senator.[16]

Milk and transit figured prominently in the editorial assault on the governor that began in the *New York American* in the month after adjournment. The paper criticized gubernatorial appointments and alleged a conflict of interest between the corporate associations and official duties of the men named, for example to the Public Service Commission. A writer who condemned Smith for appointing officials of the Dairymen's League to a milk commission distorted the situation, for they were designated to serve on an ad hoc committee consisting of representatives of interested parties—not in a regulatory agency, as the article implied. On one occasion, Hearst denied publicly that his criticism of judicial appointments resulted from the failure of his own candidates to receive a nomination and declared that he had not sought patronage from Smith, "for I have never been quite convinced of the sincerity of his professions of progressive principles." The political implications of the pieces became explicit in an editorial that warned "unless a Governor shows by his appointments early in his term" and "unless Governor Smith turns over a new leaf and does much better in the future he will fail as many other men have recently failed in this city and State."[17]

In July the *American* found fault with Smith for the PSC decision to allow a two-cent charge for transfers on street railways. Mayor Hylan appealed to the governor to use his influence to avert the fee so that New Yorkers "who are already overburdened with an additional charge for milk and other necessities of life, will at least not be further burdened by an increase in fare." Without the additional income, however, the bankrupt corporation could not pay the rent on its leased lines, which would then revert to the lessors. In view of this alternative, the commission approved the transfer fee as "the

lesser evil," in order to prevent disintegration of the system
at even higher cost to riders who would have to pay a full fare
at each change of line.   Reluctantly, Smith acquiesced in a departure from the politically sacrosanct single five-cent fare.[18]
He was convinced that the PSC "is accomplishing all that can be
accomplished under the existing statutes."   The commission resented allegations of favoritism to corporate interests as "not
only unfair and unjust but . . . also wickedly false and un-
true."   On the other hand, as the *American* interpreted the new
transfer provisions, "One party is thus permitted to withdraw
from its contract, without condition, and the other party,
thanks to Governor Smith, is temporarily helpless."   Ignoring
the legal complexities, the editor perceived in the traction
company's financial embarrassment an opportunity to promote
municipal ownership, to praise Hylan, and to blame Smith.[19]

     Hearst's *New York Evening Journal* echoed the evaluation
in July in a series of editorials, which held Smith responsible
for increases in the cost of living that a well-intentioned
mayor was depicted as powerless to prevent.   At the end of the
month, the editor juxtaposed the issues of milk prices and
streetcar fares when he described the governor as suffering
from paralysis on one side, that of the people, but sound on
the other or corporate side.   In the words of the paper:

> When a poor mother with a starving child appeals
> for relief from outrageous over-charges for what her
> baby must have to live the Governor is perfectly help-
> less.
>   But when a corporation . . . asks him to legalize
> a 40 per cent increase in carfares, off comes his coat
> and the thing is done.[20]

The *American* cast aspersions in graphic form in a series
of cartoons with the title "Trusteroodle Film Co. Presents" in
which Smith appeared as the villain of the piece.   Frederick
Burr Opper drew the governor as the lackey of the traction and
milk trusts, and the executive chamber as a home mortgaged to
the same interests.   In one frame, Smith played Hamlet, standing by the grave of free transfers, fingering the skull of the
public, and declaiming, "Alas, poor New Yorik I'm too busy to

help him just now." In "The Great Robbery Scene," Detectuff
Smithlock Holmes turned the other way as the criminal traction
and milk trusts escaped.[21]

   With fewer intellectual pretensions than the morning
paper, the evening *Journal* concentrated on the milk issue with
a demagogy hard to match in the annals of American journalism.
A typical cartoon showed two pitiful infants clutching empty
bottles and wailing, "Save us from the milk profiteers"; the
caption over the executive chamber read "Nobody Home." In a
constant refrain, almost daily editorials declared that the
governor "does nothing while thousands of babies are suffering—
many of them dying—from lack of sufficient food in order that
the Milk Trust may fatten its pocketbook." What he could do,
the writer studiously refrained from indicating. The editor
implicated the governor and absolved the mayor in the evils
under exposure, although it was never clear what power over
price levels the one possessed that the other lacked. Nevertheless, the *Journal* held Smith responsible "for the starving
and dying children who cannot have milk at the present unwarranted prices," and "for the multiplication of the little
mounds in the graveyards and the added death dollars in the
Milk Trust's treasury." Amid the barrage of uncomplimentary
publicity, the single point worthy of serious consideration was
the reluctance of the chief executive to press for the removal
of the milk business's exemption from antitrust regulation.[22]

   With less justification, the newspaper published a story
on conflict of interest under the headline, "Smith Lets Milk
Ring Pay State Officers." The legislature had declined to act
on his suggestions for reform of the Department of Farms and
Markets, whose leadership was subject to legislative—not executive—appointment. In reaction to the continuous criticism
in the Hearst press, in August the governor launched a Moreland
Act inquiry into the affairs of the department by Commissioner
of Education John H. Finley and former Governor Martin H. Glynn.
They implied that the high price of milk could be attributed in
part to monopolistic practices and concluded that, if other

expedients failed, the dairy industry should be regulated as a
utility in order to protect the public against exorbitant
charges for a vital commodity. Smith followed up on the report
of his commissioners, who also recommended a second, more
thorough investigation of the department than they were willing
to undertake.[23]

As the new Moreland Act commissioner, George Gordon
Battle, began his probe of the department, the *Journal* editorialized, "A Governor influenced by sincere motives would have
cleaned house and endeavored to keep it clean." In contrast,
the investigator reported, "The law gives to the Governor no
authority whatever over the administration of the Department"
or the appointment and removal of officials within it. Battle
did, however, substantiate the newspaper's charges against
Commissioner Eugene H. Porter who, in his official capacity,
furthered the interest of the Dairymen's League, with which he
was affiliated, at the expense of the public, which he was
appointed to serve. Early in October, Battle filed a preliminary report for the express purpose of presenting the evidence
to justify the dismissal of the offending bureaucrat. But the
Council of Farms and Markets was unresponsive to Smith's request to discharge Porter, who remained in office at the year's
end; as Battle explained, there was nothing that the governor
could do.[24]

The Moreland Act probe coincided with the inquest of the
runaway grand jury, both of which embittered relations between
Smith and Hearst. Impaneled in the summer of the Red Scare,
the special grand jury was investigating criminal anarchy when
District Attorney Swann diverted its attention to criminal
conspiracy to raise prices in the milk and traction industries.
His allegations were identical with those made by Mayor Hylan
and publicized in the Hearst newspapers. When the jurors
questioned the validity of the evidence and started to investigate its source, they found Swann uncooperative and petitioned
the governor to provide counsel, "absolutely free from bias,
sinister newspaper and political influence." The option of

inviting the Republican state attorney general to go on a
fishing expedition in the troubled waters of a Democratic city
administration did not appeal to Smith, who explained that he
lacked the authority to supplant a local official in the absence of formal charges. Smith was as reluctant to replace the
district attorney as the jury was to prefer charges, although
it did not hesitate to accuse the governor of interfering with
the administration of justice. Both parties dragged their feet
until February, 1920 when the jury filed a complaint and Smith
complied with its request.[25] If the jurors suspected Swann of
impropriety, he in turn believed that they were unscrupulously
trying "to find something on" Hylan and Hearst. At the time of
the origin of the controversy in the fall, the *American* had
concurred in the governor's hands' off policy, but insinuated,
"To what extent the impending election was a factor . . . may
never be known."[26]

     During the summer of 1919, Hearst had engaged in a strug-
gle with regular Democrats over nominations for the bench. Indignation at Tammany Hall over the journalistic vendetta
against Smith prevented Murphy from conciliating the publisher,
with the result that the organization wiped his candidates from
a slate that conspicuously included men he had attacked. At
issue was, not only the prestigious posts, but also the patronage at the disposal of the judges; in his efforts to deny it
to Tammany, Hearst was competing with the leadership for control of the party. In the campaign, in which an editor on the
Evening Journal denounced the judicial ticket, a cartoonist in
the *American* depicted Murphy as an auctioneer, selling a
judge's robe; as a thief, stealing it; and as a legal expert,
qualified by long experience tending bar. As the assault began, a friend exclaimed, "Al, it's damned near time that Murphy
went to the mat with Hearst."[27] It was Al who was destined to
wrestle with the journalist.

     At a reception to the Democratic judicial candidates,
Smith threw down the gauntlet to Hearst. "I think that the
greatest thing that can be said for our ticket," the chief

executive gibed, "is that it has been nominated and that it
will win without his assistance." The politician challenged
the publisher to a debate with the condition that "he can ask
me any question he likes about my public or about my private
life, if he will let me do the same"—an allusion to Hearst's
political and marital infidelity that was not lost on the Democratic audience. Before any encounter could occur, renewed
muckraking goaded the governor to admonish the mayor, "If unclean milk is being sold in New York City, your Commissioner of
Health ought to know that fact. If . . . an unclean newspaper
is again misrepresenting facts, the public should know that
fact."[28] The journal's publisher refused to meet Smith in debate, "as I find no satisfaction in the company of crooked
politicians." The pattern of alliance followed by defection
surfaced when Hearst denounced as faithless to a pledge of
municipal ownership the chief executive whom he had endorsed
for office the year before. An audience of his friends would
consist of "the Milk Trust and the Traction Trust and the politicians they own and the Judges they are seeking to control."
Hearst concluded by taunting, "if you gentlemen are going to
hire Carnegie Hall every time my papers expose rascally politicians, you would better take a long-term lease on the property."[29]

Smith exploited the dramatic possibilities of his soli-
tary appearance on the stage of Carnegie Hall. If he stood
alone, the situation marked his opponent as a coward with a
liver "whiter, if that could be, than the driven snow." The
purpose of inviting him to share the platform was "to show him
that he is a liar." Smith was able to document for his listeners the distortions of the Hearst press because someone had
compiled for him an annotated review of its references to the
administration. To accuse him, as Hearst had done, of back-
sliding on municipal ownership was grossly to misrepresent the
proceedings of the legislative session. The governor reserved
his fury for the milk issue, for it wounded him deeply as a
humane individual to be blamed for the afflictions of children.

It was downright dishonest to imply that he could lower the
price of milk, and the journalist who "never utters a word until it is well scrutinized by an array of lawyers to keep him
away from libel suits" knew better, said the speaker, adding "I
defy him or his lawyers to challenge that cold, straightforward
statement of mine, that no power exists in my hands . . . to
fix the price at which anybody can sell anything in this State,
whether it is milk . . . or anything else." To undermine faith
in government for one's own advantage, as Hearst was doing, was
truly subversive, observed the chief executive, who even at the
height of the Red Scare realized that "the wildest anarchist,
the most extreme Socialist, the wildest radical that you can
think of, may at least be sincere in his own heart." A person,
however, who sows "discontent and dissatisfaction to help himself . . . and to destroy, as he said himself he would, the
Governor of the State, is a man as low and as mean as I can
picture him." That his adversary was such a man who regularly
discredited others in order to advance himself, Smith inferred
from the columns of his journals where "no man can be trusted
in this country after he is put into public office." In conclusion, the governor appealed to the audience "to stay the
danger that comes from these papers," so that "we may get rid
of this pestilence that walks in the dark."[30]

The Carnegie Hall address created such a sensation that
it almost obscured the electoral contest that occasioned it.
In a subsequent campaign speech, Smith evoked the image of a
cuttlefish, which emits inky black vapor, to describe Hearst
and his newspapers, one of which the governor christened the
Mudgutter Gazette. In the paradoxical outcome of the election,
the loser won and the winner lost. The Hearst press influenced
the returns in which Democrats failed to retain many judicial
and executive posts in the city and declined in strength both
on the board of aldermen and in the state assembly.[31] On the
other hand, Hearst never recovered his political fortunes,
while Smith gained prominence, to emerge as a figure of national stature.

Hearst could not even consolidate his victory in the
short run when the legislature organized for the 1920 session.
He backed a "progressive" challenger in a race for minority
leader of the senate against James J. Walker, whom the *American*
characterized as a reactionary tool of the traction trust, the
milk monopoly—and Governor Smith. The publisher widened a
rift in the Democratic organization between the Brooklyn
leader, John H. McCooey, who joined forces with him, and
Charles Francis Murphy, who picked the winner. One senator
identified the issue as "whether Hearst is to control the
Democratic Party in New York City." His influence merely delayed for a day the decision of the caucus to choose Walker.[32]

Once the legislature was organized, the governor presented his program for dealing with the question of milk. He
had already reached the conclusion that the commodity affected
the public interest and consequently required regulation "even
to the extent of fixing the price." He had also contemplated
the alternative of empowering local governments to enter the
milk business. What he recommended to the lawmakers in 1920
was state regulation, not municipal distribution, of milk; they
however, refused to adopt his proposal, which represented "the
unanimous opinion of all those who have made any study of the
subject."[33]

Smith was referring to the results of four separate
studies: by the Reconstruction Commission, two Moreland Act
commissions, and the Fair Price Milk Committee, which originated at the suggestion of Finley and Glynn and which favored
regulation of the dairy industry "from the cow to the consumer."
The investigators all agreed that the price of milk affected
public health, that the public interest and monopolistic practices made the milk business a public utility, and that the
state should supervise it through a regulatory agency of the
type that had proliferated in the progressive era.[34]

George Gordon Battle, the Moreland Act Commissioner who
had first recommended a shakeup in the personnel of the Department of Farms and Markets, subsequently advocated its reorgani-

zation on the principles underlying the ultimate reconstruction of the state government. In detailing some of the consequences of official malfeasance, his report read like passages out of *The Jungle*. Smith supported Battle's recommendations except that for a separate agency to protect the consumer of agricultural products. But the differences between the two were purely academic, for the Republican lawmakers showed no inclination to relieve the department of legislative domination. Smith was powerless to do more than disclaim responsibility for the performance of a unit beyond his control.[35] Even the Hughes commission failed to make any essential changes in this administrative monstrosity.

The 1920 session ignored the governor's messages on all three subjects on which the Hearst press accused him of inaction: the abuses in the Department of Farms and Markets, the regulation of milk prices, and municipal ownership of transit. In interpreting the feud between the two men, biographers of Smith have emphasized the milk issue, for the memory of his mother, crying in the delirium of illness, "My son did not kill the babies," haunted him, to make reconciliation unthinkable. Writers on Smith have tended to overlook the transit issue that biographers of Hearst perceived because of its recurrence in his relations with politicians.[36] The two men did not differ so much on policy as in their understanding of how to implement it, for the publisher attributed to the chief executive an authority that actually reposed in a legislature dominated by the party of the opposition. In any case, the *American* began its assault on the governor over a matter of patronage, and its proprietor challenged Democratic candidates in 1919 in the hope of assuming control of their organization.

With apparent inconsistency, Hearst backed Harding for president and Smith for governor in 1920. At the climax of the feud in New York, the publisher's endorsement of Smith seemed inconceivable. In January, 1920 the *American's* correspondent in Albany had indulged in wishful thinking to the ex-

tent of reporting that the chief executive, rejected by party
and public alike, would retire in disgrace at the end of his
term to avoid certain defeat.   Running for reelection contrary
to the prediction, the governor reaffirmed a policy of municipal ownership, which his Republican opponent denounced as a
scheme "to turn the transit systems of this city over to
Tammany Hall."   Only a few days before the canvass, Hearst
switched his support from a third party candidate, with no hope
of success, to the Democrat, who represented the lesser of
evils.[37]

During the interregnum following his defeat, Smith maintained the political connections that enabled him to stage a
swift comeback.   Although he distrusted Hylan for his intimacy
with Hearst and had little regard for the mayor's intellect,
Smith campaigned for his reelection in 1921 out of loyalty to
the party.   As its titular head, the ex-governor talked of
those qualities that he honestly found praiseworthy: the
mayor's sympathy for the common man and his devotion to urban
home rule.   Looking back at Hylan's 1921 victory, the governor
later insisted, "if I say it myself,   I made more intelligent
speeches for his election than he was able to make himself."
Smith delivered that assessment publicly only after the mayor
had shown his gratitude by promoting Hearst for the gubernatorial nomination in 1922 and Smith had not only captured the
governorship, but also kept the publisher from running for
senator on the same ticket.[38]

Once Smith gained his party's designation, the differences between a Democratic and a Republican administration inevitably rendered utilities regulation and public transportation important issues in the return engagement between Smith
and Miller.   During the interregnum, the GOP had consolidated
the two Public Service Commissions into one and replaced the
Office of Transit Construction Commissioner with a Transit
Commission whose members were chosen by the governor and confirmed by the senate but whose expenses were charged to the
city.   The new legislation revived the principles of the dis-

credited Carson-Martin bill by conferring on both commissions
the authority to set rates above those specified in utility
franchises.   Power tilted away from the city toward the state.
Reflecting Miller's own emphasis on the quasi-judicial role of
the PSC, his appointees were readier to assure a fair return
to the investor than a fair price to the consumer.[39]

On the campaign trail, Smith reproached the incumbent for
policies that disregarded home rule, the contractual obligations of the utility companies, and the public interest.   The
Democrat charged Miller with structuring the regulatory agencies to fit "his own desire to serve the traction companies."
Each man posed as the champion of lower fares, while the Republican laid claim to being able "to supplant obstruction with
construction" of subways.   Although Miller repeated his warning
of two years before that the election of his opponent would
open the way for Tammany Hall to take over rapid transit, the
voters returned Smith to office.[40]

In the municipal election of 1923, Hearst perceived an
opportunity to take revenge on the Democratic party for his
exclusion from the statewide ticket the preceding year.   He
formed the Citizens' Independent party for the purpose of en-
ticing traditionally Democratic voters to cast their ballots
for the Republican judicial aspirants on the line of a third
party, without having to support the GOP.   If Tammany's candidates suffered defeat, "there would soon be new leaders in the
place of Boss Murphy and Boss Foley," a Hearst editor suggested,
as he assured his readers, "You CAN BE A GOOD DEMOCRAT and still
vote against Glucose and Bucketshop."[41]   It required little
subtlety to infer that the publisher aimed to succeed the
leaders to whom his writers referred in such uncomplimentary
language.   The editor was alluding to the bosses' legal difficulties, for a grand jury had indicted Murphy for his activities in the glucose business and Foley for connections with
bucketshops or brokerage houses that were systematically de-
frauding their clients.   For want of evidence however, a judge
dismissed charges against the former, and a district attorney

declined to prosecute the latter. Moreover, in the case of
Foley, it appears that Hearst's employees were making some of
the news that they reported, for they tampered with witnesses
in the effort to incriminate the Democrat. Meanwhile, the
American, capitalized on the episode to describe the sachems
as criminals and their candidates as minions of big business.[42]

The campaign resembled the midterm election four years
earlier when Smith had intervened actively in New York City in
order to frustrate Hearst's designs on the Democratic party.
Addressing the faithful at Tammany Hall in 1923, Smith attributed the publisher's opposition to disappointed ambitions
rather than zeal for reform, since his silence "made the sphinx
over in Egypt look like Gallagher and Shean" when the governor
was pressing for progressive legislation. At Town Hall, the
politician denounced the journalist as "a politically ambitious
owner of what very few intelligent people dignify as newspapers" and as "the leading agent for the dissemination of political bunk." As in Smith's first term, the feud between the
two men overshadowed the issues, to become itself an issue, but
this time the outcome was different. A Democratic landslide
vindicated the governor. On election night, a jubilant campaign manager pronounced the publisher's epitaph: "The victory
of the Democratic judiciary ticket means that Hearst is dead
politically" because "Governor Smith put the tag on him. . . ."
In an editorial postmortem, the *Times* reflected that the Republicans "got down in the dirt for nothing when they made up
their judicial ticket in alliance with the Hearst newspapers."
Murphy publicly excluded the offensive journals from his household.[43]

His sudden death in the spring of 1924 intensified the
struggle between the regulars and Hearst's allies for control
of Tammany Hall. What was at stake was not only the leadership of the wigwam, but also the political future of New
York's governor and mayor. When the insurgents authored a
resolution to endorse the nomination of Smith for president and
Hylan for mayor, the regulars defeated it in order to avoid a

commitment to Hearst's protégé. With no greater success, Hylan
opposed the choice of James A. Foley for the position that his
late father-in-law had occupied. The regulars lost ground when
the surrogate, who had been reluctant to assume the responsibilities, resigned after twenty-four hours with the implication
that his health could not take the strain of the anticipated
row with Hearst. A makeshift regency reigned until after the
national convention, when Smith's forces named George W. Olvany
to fill the vacancy.[44]

If Murphy had lived, Smith may not have gotten the presidential nomination in 1924, but it is also unlikely that the
convention would have deadlocked for 102 ballots. Smith suffered, not only a personal, but also a political loss, and his
tries for the presidency floundered in miscalculations inconceivable with the boss's advice. Tammany returned to the dis-
reputable state from which Murphy had rescued it with political
acumen and candidates of Smith's caliber.[45]

Hearst, who had aligned with the anti-Smith forces at the
national convention, urged the state's Democrats to deny renomination to the governor. Smith retorted that the party
"will admire his literary effort, but it has not any use for
his advice," and announced as an afterthought, "When it needs
advice it will go to Democrats for it, and not to either demagogue or crackpot." Neither the threat of editorial opposition,
nor the specter of a third party impeded the inevitable designation of Smith for a third term.[46]

Hearst failed in 1924 to drive the governor into defeat
or to force him into submission. Since the publisher instructed his editors to remain neutral, the *American* lamented, "The
progressive, independent voters have no candidate for Governor
this year in New York." It was merely a technical neutrality
that inspired the editor to write that a Demcorat loyal to the
tradition of Jefferson, Jackson, and Cleveland, "might just as
well vote for Mr. Roosevelt." The columns portrayed Smith as
"an avowed friend of the people" but "the secret servant of
the big private interests" and one who has "protected the mo-

nopolists that seek the private control of our matchless water
powers." A subsequent editorial called upon him to pledge his
support to legislation to abolish the Transit Commission and to
finance a city-owned-and-operated subway system, in language
that implied either a threat or a promise: "Governor Smith
still has five days in which to declare himself on this supreme
transit issue. . . ."[47] He, however, no longer responded to
such blandishments. He was reelected in spite of—or perhaps
because of—Hearst.

Despite their claim of neutrality in the campaign that
placed Smith in the executive chamber for a third time, the
Hearst newspapers distorted the record of his second term on
water power and transit. He had begun his second administration, not only by reasserting his commitment to public ownership, but also by moving closer to Hylan on the subject of
regulation. Although, in his first term, he had adhered to
the principle of state regulation of public utilities, now in
the name of home rule, he favored city regulation of intra-
urban facilities. He called for the repeal of Miller's legislation that permitted the raising of rates beyond the level
specified in companies' franchises and also for the abolition
of the Transit Commission and the transfer to the city government of authority over subway construction. When the measures
that had passed the senate stalled in the assembly, he pressed
the lower house for action.[48]

Smith achieved a modicum of success at this session, for
only his proposal to restore the contractual limitations on
utility charges passed both houses to become law. With regard
to the subways, the immovable object of Hylan met the irresis-
tible force of the Republicans. Following his customary procedure in a legislative deadlock, the chief executive conferred
at length with the opposition. The GOP insisted on setting
certain conditions for municipal subway operation that the
mayor found unacceptable: that fares be high enough to make it
self-sustaining in order to avoid a shift in costs from the

straphanger to the taxpayer; that a state commission retain
regulatory authority to protect the private companies from
being driven to the wall by city manipulation. If the Republican position reflected distrust of the Hylan administration,
his objections derived from a somewhat unrealistic vision of a
municipal system that would offer better service at lower cost
both to the riders and the government than the existing arrangements. He consequently denounced the Republicans, who broke
off the negotiations, which Smith had considered promising.[49]
When the *American* extolled the mayor as "an honest public servant" in the same columns that denounced the governor as "the
compromiser, pretending to be for the public, but yielding the
public's rights to the corporations," it only confirmed the
suspicion that Hearst was responsible for Hylan's intransigence.[50]

By 1924, Hylan reluctantly agreed to the compromise whose
wisdom Smith had recognized the year before. The GOP drafted
legislation containing the safeguards on which the party had
insisted earlier, and the mayor advised Smith to sign the bill
on the grounds that "it is better to accept this morsel which
the Republican Assembly grudgingly gave us" than nothing at
all. Coming in the form of an amendment to the Public Service
Commission Law, the Republican measure established a new Board
of Transportation to be appointed by city officials to build
and operate subways and required the board to charge fares high
enough to cover specified expenses. Under this enactment, New
York City eventually constructed and managed its independent
subway system. Since the lawmakers failed to heed Smith's
plea for home rule in utility regulation, they left the state's
Transit Commission, with Miller's appointees, as the agency
with regulatory authority over city transportation.[51]

After the legislature refused to relinquish state regulation, Hylan determined to get rid of the Transit Commission
by ousting the commissioners. City and state officials had
been unable to cooperate, for they were proceeding from mutually exclusive sets of assumptions. Acting within the given

framework of a mixed economy, the commissioners expected concessions from both the traction companies and the city in order
to protect the interest of each. The mayor, on the other hand,
planned to expropriate the corporations and create a municipal
monopoly of public transportation. After obstructing the work
of the commission for a number of years, in a dramatic move in
October, 1924, the city government filed charges against the
commissioners and demanded their dismissal. The formal complaint held them responsible for deficiencies in service and
accused them of approving financial arrangements that yielded
unwarranted profit to private enterprise at the expense of the
riders. A member of Hylan's administration subsequently confirmed the suspicion that the mayor had timed the issuance of
the charges to embarrass Smith in his bid for reelection. As
the campaign was drawing to a close, the *New York American*
called upon the governor, who in his second term had recommended an end to the commission, to state "whether or not he is
in sympathy with the demand of the Mayor and the Board of Estimate that the Transit Commission, culpably negligent in the
performance of their duty . . . shall be removed, and their
power entrusted to a New York City body that will protect the
lives of the people, and not the profits of the corporations."[52]

A few weeks after his election, Smith responded by instituting a Moreland Act investigation of the Transit Commission.
Before taking action, he had agreed to confer with a lawyer for
the commissioners, who protested against the injustice of subjecting them to the strain and expense of defending themselves
against charges that were politically motivated. Consequently,
the governor named an appellate judge, John V. McAvoy, to conduct an inquiry into the operation of the Transit Commission
and its conflict with the municipal administration. The procedure angered Hylan, who had anticipated, not a general probe
under the Executive Law, but under the Public Service Commission Law, a trial followed by dismissal of the offending commissioners. Unable to see himself as others saw him as a
party to the controversy, Hylan viewed his own role as that of

a prosecutor, but the governor clearly did not accept his accusations at face value. The decision to proceed under the Moreland Act raised the conflict with Hylan and Hearst to a new
stage and suggested to one politician that Smith was about to
demonstrate "that he is the sure enough leader of his party in
this State by naming the next Democratic candidate for Mayor."[53]

Meanwhile, McAvoy, whom a wag described as a Latin scholar, "hearing all about sick transit," produced a document
highly critical of Mayor Hylan. The judge concluded unequivocally "that the charges are without foundation and that no
cause exists for the removal from office of the Commissioners."
In his report, he blamed, not the Transit Commission, but the
municipal government, for the delay in subway construction, for
city officials had deliberately obstructed the work of the commission. Despite his reservations about the incumbent municipal administration, he did advocate more home rule in transit
matters. Specifically, he favored an amendment to the state
constitution to enable the city to float the bonds needed to
finance new subway lines and also repeal of the provisions permitting the state-appointed commissioners to act for the city
in negotiating revision of existing contracts.[54] Although he
discredited the charges against the commission, McAvoy acknowledged the right of the city to be free from state interference
in its public transportation.

The governor expressed satisfaction with McAvoy's report,
and the legislature complied with his recommendations for enlarging the borrowing capacity of the city and restraining the
authority of the Transit Commission. Recognizing however, "a
sharp distinction between the removal from office of individual
Commissioners upon charges of misconduct and the abolition of
a Commission itself," Smith urged the lawmakers to take the
second step, which he had advocated in his previous administration. They were unwilling to abdicate all state jurisdiction,
and he admitted that displeasure at its continuance "should
not and can not be urged in extenuation of the conduct of the
Board of Estimate and Apportionment in its persistent refusal

to cooperate with the Transit Commission."[55]

Although they presumably read the same document, it led
Governor Smith to blame the Hylan administration, and the
American's editor to hold the Transit Commission responsible,
for the lack of subway construction. The Hearst press, which
criticized McAvoy, was surprisingly conciliatory toward the
governor during the 1925 legislative session. If the *American*
assumed that the Moreland Act report would improve Hylan's
chances for a third term, a civic leader reacted by declaring,
"The city dominated by four years more of a Hylan-Hearst combination is unthinkable. . . ." At the same time, a correspondent confided in Smith, "Down in your heart we know what you
must think of Mayor Hylan, who is not competent mentally to be
at the head of this great City," and suggested that deposing
him would demonstrate fitness "for higher honors."[56]

If the Moreland Act investigation of transit implied that
Smith was ready to break with Hylan and defy Hearst, the publisher's editorial pages indicated that he was seeking a reconciliation with the governor in order to reelect the mayor. At
the end of May, Hearst preached party unity in a letter to his
own editor, cleverly playing on Smith's presidential ambitions
in an effort to obtain support for Hylan without really guaran-
teeing the quid pro quo. Dissension in Democratic ranks,
Hearst explained, would be of no advantage either to Smith or
Hylan, both of whom could expect to gain office with a united
organization behind them. If it held firm, the author predicted the election of "a Democratic Mayor, a Democratic
Governor, a Democratic United States Senator, and a Democratic
President." After raising the question, "Who is going to upset
the apple cart?" the journalist concluded, "Certainly not the
gentlemen who are sitting pretty on it."[57] Even had Smith been
less sensitive to the continual breaches of party loyalty,
common sense and self-interest would have kept the governor
from putting faith in the frequent turncoat and his equivocal
statement.

As the brouhaha over the Transit Commission was reaching a climax, an incident involving the Port of New York Authority intensified Smith's distrust of the mayor and his journalistic supporter. The authority, which Smith had encouraged from the outset, faced constant frustration at the hands of the Hylan administration and frequent criticism in the Hearst newspapers, which stood alone among New York City dailies in their opposition to the interstate agency. At this time, the public corporation was attempting to buy the Hoboken Shore Line Railroad from the federal government, which had taken over during the war. The governor was instrumental in getting Congressman Ogden L. Mills to sponsor the appropriate legislation. It did not pass because of the objections of the city's congressional delegation, acting under the influence of Mayor Hylan. The Republican confided to Julius Henry Cohen his embarrassment at discovering "that John Hylan, and not Alfred E. Smith, is the real Boss of the Democratic Party." Whereupon, the lawyer repeated the remarks to Smith with the observation, "I know this will make you mad . . ." and the admonition, "I am afraid we shall have to go to the mat with the gentleman in the City Hall."[58] If these comments were hardly the sufficient cause, they were followed shortly by the desired effect.

Smith took the initiative in the repudiation of Hylan and thereby precipitated the definitive rupture with Hearst that Murphy had so cautiously avoided. Where the boss had been subtle and calculating, unwilling to relinquish any electoral advantage, the officeholder was more direct and less compromising. The chief executive reacted more emotionally than the sachem to the vilification that they, along with innumerable politicians, had endured at the hands of the newspaperman. An uncooperative administration at City Hall handicapped the governor in policymaking. With Murphy gone, Hearst's infiltration appeared as a more ominous threat, first to the integrity of the party, and then to Smith's presidential ambitions. For these and other reasons, Smith decided that the elimination of Hylan outweighed the risks of the discord it would generate in the Democratic organization.

What was at stake in the mayoralty nomination was nothing
less than control of the Democratic party in New York City and
State; the outcome would determine who would rule, not only at
City Hall, but also at Tammany Hall. The contest proceeded on
two levels: between Smith and Hearst; and among the county
chiefs to fill the vacuum left by Murphy's death. With
Hearst's support, John H. McCooey of Brooklyn was challenging
the leadership of George W. Olvany of New York County and
Edward J. Flynn of the Bronx, both of whom agreed with Smith on
the desirability of replacing Hylan. When the leaders met to
choose the organization candidate, Queens and Richmond aligned
with Brooklyn to give Hylan a majority of the boroughs, although his opponents represented a greater number of potential
voters. Facing the possible loss of the Democratic designation
in a primary fight, Hylan intimated that in any case he would
run in the general election, and Hearst declared his willingness to support an independent candidacy.[59] Although many
Democratic politicians hesitated to deny Hylan the nomination
for fear of a third party, Smith did not take the threat seriously. He and his allies in Manhattan and the Bronx considered
a third term for the mayor more damaging than a third ticket in
November. Smith, Olvany, and Flynn decided to enter the primaries to contest the organization's choice of Hylan who eventually consented to abide by the will of the Democratic voters
as expressed at the polls.[60]

The effort to dump Hylan confronted Tammany Hall with the
same dilemma it had faced on the death of Murphy: to find a
suitable replacement. In each case, an unfortunate decision
paved the way for future disaster. Olvany, the new chieftain,
and his candidate, James J. Walker, each resigned prematurely
not long after Smith's retirement. He preferred either Foley
or Wagner for the office of mayor, but both refused to leave
the security of the bench for the vagaries of municipal administration. At this juncture, Olvany asserted his authority as
Murphy's successor and, with the help of Flynn, insisted on

naming Walker, despite the governor's reservations. Singing
"We'll Walk in with Walker," celebrities from the world of show
business boosted his candidacy. The state senator enjoyed a
reputation as an adroit legislative leader, a gifted orator,
and a notorious playboy. Smith evidently felt a fatherly affection for the charming Walker while disapproving of the er-
rant behavior that made him a fit symbol of the Roaring Twenties. He promised the governor to abstain from wine—in public—and women—except Mrs. Walker—but not song. That pledge,
along with the contrast between Walker's ability and Hylan's
ineptitude, reconciled Smith to Tammany's selection. Once it
was announced, the governor had no choice but to campaign
vigorously for Walker's nomination.[61]

The Hearst papers capitalized on the shortcomings of
Walker, who would resign the office of mayor during proceedings
before Governor Roosevelt for his dismissal. Alluding to the
senator's career in Tin Pan Alley, the *Journal* editorialized,
"It is no time for song writers, no time even for the prettiest
tunes or the smoothest, most promising words." Referring to
his lyrics for "Will You Love Me in December As You Do in May,"
the editor predicted that the traction companies would not love
him in November as they did in August because in defeat he
would be useless to them. The *American* reasoned that the repudiation of Hylan in the primaries would undermine confidence
in the party that had twice elected him and would result in a
Republican victory in the general election.[62]

Although the names of Hylan and Walker appeared on the
Democratic ballot, the principals in the contest were Hearst
and Smith. The governor campaigned as actively as if he himself were running in the primary, while the publisher, in his
statements, and his editors, in their columns, attacked the
chief executive. The campaign, which was one of the dirtiest
in a city not exactly famed for the gentility of its politics,
degenerated into an exchange of insults, with little rational
discourse on the issues.

Smith fought the opening rounds in the enemy territory
of Brooklyn and Queens. He attributed the conflict between the
state and city administrations to the domination of the mayor
by Hearst, who served as "the keeper of his conscience and the
director of his political will." Their relationship was simply
another indication of Hylan's inability to cope on his own initiative with municipal problems. The speaker appealed to his
listeners, "before you go to bed, and you kneel down to say
your evening prayers, . . . look into your consciences, and ask
yourselves whether you have any right or not to expect even an
attempted solution . . . from the man who is now in the city
hall." Calling for his defeat, Smith contrasted the incompetence of the mayor with the ability and experience of his challenger. Sharing a platform with the governor the next day,
Walker promised to expand transit facilities and taunted his
opponent, "For digging subways, you need a pickaxe, not a
thorax." Resentful of being blamed for fare increases beyond
his control, Smith conferred upon Hylan the title of "past
grand master of the Order of Insinuation and Innuendo."[63]

The mayor broadcast two campaign addresses over WNYC before the courts enjoined the use of the municipal radio station
for partisan purposes and he spoke a third time on a commercial
outlet. His reelection was necessary to assure municipal operation of transit and to prevent "an increased carfare and a
wide-open town," Hylan told the radio audience. He denounced
the Moreland Act investigation as a whitewash of the Transit
Commission and accused the governor of ingratitude to Hearst—
for his political support.[64] Touring Staten Island, Smith defended McAvoy and his conclusion that "not only did Hylan not
build subways, but he stopped everybody else from doing it."
After the mayor charged Smith with permitting the sale of adul-
terated milk, he retorted that Hylan's speeches were composed
in Hearst's editorial rooms. When the mayor substantiated his
allegations of collusion between Smith and the traction companies with evidence of a conference that had never taken place,
the governor exposed the error as typical of the distortions to

be found in Hylan's oratory and Hearst's journalism. Introduced at the Brooklyn Academy of Music as a man who is "loved
for the enemies he has made," Smith urged the crowd to resist
becoming "the conquered province of an editor in California
that says himself he is not a Democrat, and he never will be
while we can keep him out."[65]

The governor, who clashed in oratorical combat with the
mayor, engaged in an epistolary exchange with the publisher.
It began with a letter to the editor of the *American* in which
Hearst suggested that friendship for Wall Street motivated Smith
to unseat Hylan. The governor responded that nothing would
handicap Hylan more in the upcoming election than the backing
of Hearst, "the last man in the world who should attempt to be
the judge of what is undemocratic, un-American or unpatriotic,
unless he is prepared to point to himself as the shining example." After the correspondents had called each other liars,
the journalist characterized his opponent's epistle as "a vul-
gar tirade that any resident of Billingsgate or any occupant of
the alcoholic ward in Bellevue could have written . . . with
more evidence of education and intelligence." The two argued
over the significance of the Democratic National Convention
where, according to Smith, Hearst had cooperated with the Klan
to block the New Yorker's nomination, and according to Hearst,
Smith had conspired with corporate interests to advance the
candidacy of John W. Davis. In regard to the primary over
which the writers were contending, the governor asserted:

> Mr. Hearst has the nerve of a Bengal tiger, to
> be loafing in the splendor and grandeur of his pala-
> tial estate on the Pacific coast and attempting to
> dictate the politics of the greatest city in the
> world. He has no interest in the Democratic party.
> He never supports its candidates except when to do
> so serves his own selfish purposes. This primary
> fight in the Democratic party is none of his business.
> He does not belong to the Democratic party.

While Smith read him out of the party, the publisher, who
prided himself on his independence, declared:

> I cannot be a Democrat . . . while a brazen instru-
> ment of the traction companies sits in the Governor's
> chair. . . . I cannot be a Democrat when an honest
> Mayor like Mayor Hylan is opposed by Tammany because
> he is honest and because while he is Mayor Tammany
> cannot further its nefarious schemes and feather its
> illicit nest by "delivering" the administration of
> New York City for the benefit of the profiteering
> interests that are willing to pay the price.[66]

It was the consensus among Democratic politicians that the Walker landslide signalled an end to whatever influence Hearst had wielded in party affairs and concomitantly a rise in Smith's standing in the state and national organization. Wearing a gray fedora in place of his customary brown derby, the governor accompanied the senator the few blocks from Tammany Hall, where they had been listening to the returns, to the ballroom of the Hotel Commodore, where the faithful hailed the victor and greeted Smith as the next president. Walker and his citywide ticket carried not only Manhattan and the Bronx, where the leadership had backed them, but also Brooklyn, to the distress of the McCooey machine.[67]

If Hylan had reneged on the promise that he made upon entering the primary and run on a third slate, he might have turned Walker's success into a Pyrrhic victory. Although Hearst encouraged such a move, the mayor announced his retirement to private life. In the aftermath of the bitter campaign, Smith could not resist the ungracious comment, "Well, that's tough on private life, but I don't see how he could be kept out of that." The publisher, in his determination to make the primary an empty victory, proposed that Congressman Fiorello La Guardia enter the mayoralty race as an independent. When he, too, declined, the threat of a third party collapsed.[68]

The most that could be expected from a third party was the diversion of Democratic votes and a Republican mayor; consistency would have led Hearst, after failing to launch a third candidate, to support the GOP. He nevertheless endorsed Walker and his running mates because he preferred the transit plank in their platform. Even his qualified enthusiasm for Democrats stopped at the city line, and his newspapers vigorously op-

posed the referendum measures that the governor had placed on
the ballot. Smith triumphed anew on election day with the
prospect of a sympathetic administration at City Hall and the
ratification of constitutional amendments providing for reconstruction of the government and the financing of public improvements and grade crossing elimination. In reporting the
event, the usually staid *Times* employed a delightfully mixed
metaphor, "A new feather adorns Governor Smith's far-famed
brown derby."[69]

Smith proved himself a master of electoral politics in
1925, not only by bringing to fruition his major administrative
and fiscal reforms, but also by ridding himself of a political
liability. He moved against Hylan for various reasons, not the
least of which was a conviction that the mayor was incompetent.
After appointing him a judge of the juvenile court, Walker remarked that "the children now can be tried by their peer." A
Hylan administration meant placing at the disposal of Hearst
the city government's patronage with which to build a machine
in competition with the regular organization. An organization
capable of fulfilling the publisher's ambitions represented a
threat to Smith's presidential aspirations.[70] Whatever the
merits of the case, the defeat of Hylan and Hearst demonstrated
its author's capacity for seeking higher office.

Paradoxically, the Walker administration, which owed its
existence to Smith, embarrassed him in his last campaign for
governor. The new regime at City Hall began well enough by
investigating the corruption that had allowed the sale of adul-
terated milk and by prosecuting offenders against whom it possessed evidence. By summer however, the Citizens' Union, suspicious that wrongdoers were escaping justice and jeopardizing
the purity of the city's food supply, asked the governor to
place the state attorney general in charge of the inquest.[71]
When no action was forthcoming, in the fall the civic group,
which professed an inclination "not to inject itself into a
State Campaign," renewed its request. Smith took the position
that it was inappropriate to supersede the district attorneys

of the counties, unless requested to do so by municipal authorities or presented with proof of malfeasance.[72]

Despite the disclaimer of the Citizens' Union, Smith's
antagonists used the milk question against him in the campaign
of 1926. Hearst backed Wagner for senator and Mills for governor. The *New York American* asked rhetorically, "would it not
be a good idea to have a Republican Governor like Ogden Mills
appoint a special prosecutor under no obligations to Tammany
Hall to do all the indicting and prosecuting?" It was reminiscent of 1919 when the paper's editorials held Smith responsible for events outside his jurisdiction and inveighed in muckraking tones, "When poisoned milk is fed to babies . . . all to
the profit of certain Tammany leaders—that issue becomes not
only a political issue but a domestic issue. . . ." Campaigning in a rural area, the Republican suggested that the state
administration was abetting the government of the metropolis
in the coverup of a milk scandal. The *New York Times*, which
dismissed the charges as a figment of yellow journalism, rebuked him, "What shall it profit him to gain a few votes, if
he does gain them, and lose his own hitherto high reputation?"[73]

Smith perceived the milk issue as evidence, not of continuing corruption in the city government, but of an unholy
coalition between Mills and Hearst. The Democrat reminded the
voters that the wrongdoing had occurred under a mayor whose reelection he opposed and the publisher favored. Because they
found little to criticize in his administration, the Republicans latched on to the issue of milk, the incumbent declared.
Had it not been for his progressive record, the GOP "would have
had the issues and there would be no occasion for the cultured
son of an aristocratic family to go down into the mud gutter
and seek a companionship with the despicable Hearst."[74]

The Citizens' Union continued to harbor suspicions of
the Walker administration and after the election, again pressed
Smith to order his attorney general to conduct a grand jury
investigation of the New York City Department of Health. Convinced that the district attorneys were faithfully performing

their duty, in exasperation Smith suggested that the civic
leaders be subpoenaed to present the evidence that warranted
a new probe. After hearing them, the grand jury found no
reason to proceed further.[75] Although Smith worked with the
Citizens' Union on many policies, most notably reorganization,
he refused to cooperate in this case because, to him, the
charges lacked credibility in view of their origin in the
Hearst press. In addition, he faced a dilemma similar to that
of Governor Roosevelt a few years later, for both men needed
the support of Tammany, which stood behind Walker, and of the
independents, who were insisting on a cleanup. There was, however, one crucial difference in the situation of the two chief
executives: in Smith's day, unlike FDR's, the mayor's derelic-
tions were far from proven.

Power, more than policy, explains the feud between Smith
and Hearst. How they differed substantively on the issues,
even that of municipal ownership of transit, is far from clear.
The columns of the *New York American* and the *New York Evening
Journal* were better calculated to discredit the governor than
to reverse his policies.

What was at stake in the struggle for power between Smith
and Hearst was office, which the one held and the other coveted,
and leadership in the party that controlled access to office.
In pursuit of these goals, the publisher as a young man had
established a pattern to which he adhered in his relations
with Smith: initial cooperation based on mutual interest,
followed by defection out of self-interest. Once attacked,
Smith took the offensive, using the Democratic convention of
1922 to keep the newspaperman from running as the candidate of
a party to which he had been conspicuously disloyal, and the
primary of 1925 to prevent him from manipulating the party to
advance his own political career. As long as Hylan served as
Hearst's alter ego, their conflict with the governor exemplified the traditional competition between the rulers of the
state and its metropolis. Deprived of his foothold—or

stranglehold—at City Hall, Hearst carried out his implicit
threat and backed Republicans against Smith: Ogden Mills for
governor and Herbert Hoover for president.   The pattern repeated itself when Hearst supported FDR for president in 1932
and Alfred Landon four years later, but by then the behavior
was no longer functional, for age and Al Smith had eliminated
the journalist as a serious contender for office.

It is somewhat easier to specify Hearst's areas of disagreement with President Roosevelt than with Governor Smith,
but what they signify is equally controversial.   Historians
have variously viewed Hearst as a social progressive whose
ideas anticipated the New Deal and as an old progressive who
remained consistent in opposing it.[76]   Of the Smith programs
that the publisher chose to attack, reorganization was congenial
to the old progressives with their zeal for rationality in
government; his fiscal policy was closer in spirit to the New
Deal with its tendency to value humanitarian concerns over
economic orthodoxy.   Hearst and Smith both professed a commitment to municipal ownership of transit, but the publisher accused the politician of hypocrisy for his failure to achieve it.
Here, the newspaperman conveniently overlooked the realities in
the situation of a Democratic executive with a Republican legislature, which exercised a veto over his initiatives.   As
the self-proclaimed champion of the poor, Hearst failed to give
the governor credit for labor legislation and housing policies
designed to relieve their distress.   The sensational stories
of milk scandals left Hearst in the position of the legendary
boy who cried wolf.   In finding rationalizations for his condemnation of Smith, the journalist was pursuing, not policy,
but power.

Governor Smith's counterattack was one of the most popular, if least edifying, episodes in his career.   It promoted
his presidential prospects, since every victory over Hearst was
a source of nationwide publicity and of support from the many
who shared his detestation of the newspaperman.   In eliminating
Hearst as a rival in New York, Smith demonstrated a mastery of

practical politics that enabled him to gain the nomination—
but not the presidency.

CHAPTER 9

SOCIALISM AND SEX—CIVIL LIBERTIES UNDER SMITH

The reconciliation of liberty and authority poses a problem, not only in political theory, but also in practical politics, as Al Smith instinctively understood. During his administration, reorganization transformed the state government into
an instrument, capable of being used to promote the general
welfare through housing subsidies, labor legislation, and public power. In answer to the objection that economic regulation
and public enterprise interfered with property rights, Smith
recognized that government intervention enhanced the liberty of
more people than it inhibited, for it freed the less affluent
from material constraints that confined them as surely as any
exercise of public authority. At the 1915 convention, he had
dismissed the substantive interpretation of due process with
its emphasis on liberty of contract as a misreading of the
constitution. Where his opponents made a fetish of free enterprise, he viewed freedom as intellectual and political—not
merely economic. As governor, he defended civil liberties
against the abuse of power by those who would employ the state
for the suppression of dissent.

In his understanding of civil liberty, Smith came remark-
ably close to the intellectuals of the American Civil Liberties
Union whom Paul L. Murphy has described as the "activist-
libertarians" of the years between World War I and the New Deal.
According to Murphy, they perceived free expression, not only
as an essential attribute of a democratic polity, but also as
a means of promoting social justice and economic equality.
They did not equate government intervention in the economy with
a threat to liberty. Occupying the other end of the spectrum,
the right wing defined freedom largely in economic terms in the
name of which it justified the suppression of labor unions,
radicals, and others who were challenging the status quo.[1]
Smith was neither as radical in his economics, nor as consistent in his devotion to civil liberties as the ACLU leadership

studied by Murphy, but the governor showed little sympathy for
the repressive inclinations of businessmen or professional pa-
triots. He himself experienced the frustration of having his
programs for housing subsidies and public power discussed, not
on their merits, but dismissed cavalierly by being labelled
socialist. Since he appreciated the right to argue for change
as a sine qua non of democracy, he did not acquiesce in the
abuses of the Red Scare in New York. On the question of freedom in the dramatic and literary arts, he was more ambivalent.
Like many civil libertarians, he resented Prohibition as an
abuse of power and a governmental intrusion into the private
lives of its citizens.

In the Smith administration, the fight for civil liberties was waged on two fronts: political and aesthetic. Radicals in politics found their rights violated by those who confused socialism with subversion. Writers and artists who, in
the spirit of naturalism, abandoned the genteel tradition had
their works censored by those who equated sex with pornography.
A threat emerged to freedom of expression, whether it was a
matter of socialism or sex, the civil liberties issues of the
era in New York.

Progressivism offered Smith less guidance on the subject
of individual rights than on the structure of government and
the solution of economic problems. The civil liberties movement did not originate until the end of the progressive era
when the first World War provided an excuse to curtail the
freedom of unpopular minorities. Murphy concluded that "freedom of expression did not rank high in the hierarchy of values"
of the progressives who, in any case, exhibited a wide divergence in their approach to dissent and deviance. Old progressives, he reported, were more likely to oppose the excesses of
the Red Scare than the more subtle pressures for conformity in
the twenties. A history of the American Civil Liberties Union,
on the other hand, suggests that it "borrowed much of its
spirit and its outlook from the Progressives." Other studies
have uncovered a commitment to civil liberties among urban pro-

gressives in general, and settlement workers, in particular.
Nowhere is the variety of attitudes illustrated more dramatically than in California, where the labor leaders accused in
the Preparedness Day bombing and members of the International
Workers of the World found both defenders and oppressors in the
progressive camp. If progressives divided over the proper
limits of political discourse, as moralists they condemned
obscenity as an evil of the cities; as reformers, they proposed
to eradicate it by censorship.[2]

Like many progressives, Smith reacted ambivalently to the
zeal for suppression. His own canon of morality moved him sometimes—but not always—to take repressive action against what offended his sense of decency by violating the genteel tradition.
Toward political deviation, he was more openminded, but not as
constant in his devotion to civil liberties as, for example,
Roger Baldwin. Compared with contemporary politicians on the
other hand, he behaved in a principled and courageous manner
in defending civil liberties against what he acknowledged as
oppressive.

His stand as governor reflected attitudes formed earlier
in his life: by the church that had instructed him in faith
and morals; by the Lower East Side that had exposed him to the
diversity of the American population; and by the elective offices that had enlarged his understanding of democratic government. He was a legislator when the Socialist party elected its
first member to the assembly. In one of Smith's favorite anec-
dotes, he reminisced about his advice to the leadership to give
the newcomer desirable committee assignments in order to famil-
iarize him with the democratic process; the story ended with the
punch line, "he went down to the Hotel Ten Eyck and got a
hair-cut, and you couldn't tell him from a Democrat or a Republican." Smith had told the tale to an appreciative audience
at the constitutional convention when he was scoring a point
against a proposal to make literacy in English a qualification
for voting. The speaker reasoned that disfranchisement would
justify the radicalism of the immigrants whom it deprived of

their rightful voice in public affairs. He generated further
merriment with his reference to the literacy of "a lot of good
readers and writers residing down in Mr. Osborne's Riverside
neighborhood that can not only write their own names but somebody else's as well."[3]

Smith practiced his principles on the Board of Aldermen
when he assumed its presidency at the same time that seven
Socialists joined its ranks. At his very first meeting, he
talked pointedly about the rights of minorities in a representative assembly. In accord with the views he had expressed as
a legislator, if not due to his direct influence, the board
placed a Socialist on every one of its committees. Although
Smith was not present several weeks later when an altercation
followed the unanimous vote of the Socialist delegates against
a measure for the sale of war stamps, the next day he intervened against a move for their expulsion. At the same time he
acceded to the presence of a stenographer to record the deliberations, with the implication that a transcript might provide evidence of disloyalty as grounds for a future ouster. If
Smith generally respected minorities on the left, he was not
immune to the wartime patriotic fervor that contributed to the
onset of the Red Scare.[4]

Smith's first term as governor coincided with the Red
Scare, which confronted the new chief executive with a need to
take a stand on civil liberties.[5] Repression, directed first
against those who harbored antiwar sentiments, spread to include Socialists whose organization condemned American intervention, and ultimately engulfed even moderate reformers and
labor leaders who aimed to improve the lot of the lower classes.
In this phase, public opinion was consciously manipulated to
silence critics of the regnant business ideology and to discredit the proponents of change.

A look at the techniques of repression used elsewhere will
put the Red Scare in New York in perspective. On a national
level, the Overman committee of the United States Senate inves-

tigated the dangers of bolshevism, while the Department of
Justice engaged in questionable searches and seizures, the
wholesale detention of leftists, and the deportation of immigrants. Twice the House of Representatives refused to seat the
Milwaukee Socialist, Victor Berger. As a result of its probe,
the Senate committee recommended a peacetime sedition act to
supplement wartime legislation that inhibited freedom of expression to a degree unequalled since the administration of
John Adams. Many states adopted criminal anarchy statutes,
which generally deviated from the basic assumptions of Anglo-
Saxon justice by penalizing thought rather than deed, association rather than individual guilt. The Federal Bureau of Investigation emerged out of the suspicions of a day when officials were instituting prosecution for the persecution of
holders of unpopular beliefs. Educational institutions came
under fire, and educators were fired for political and economic
heresy. In this atmosphere, vigilantism increased, and patriotic organizations proliferated, for example, the National
Security League with headquarters in New York City.

Since the Red Scare was of greater intensity and duration
in the Empire State than elsewhere, it is a measure of Smith's
stature that he generally resisted its excesses. A number of
factors account for the susceptibility of New York to the mass
hysteria. Immigrants, many of Russian extraction, comprised a
significant proportion of its population. Radicals concentrated in the metropolis with its attraction for the intelligent-
sia. The Socialist party was making inroads at the polls. The
suspect elements attained a level of visibility that frightened
the traditional hinterland and reinforced inclinations to
bigotry.

When witnesses before the Overman committee identified
New York as the focal point of subversion, the congressional
investigation provoked an inquiry by the state legislature.
Alluding to the Senate hearings, the measure to establish the
notorious Lusk committee operated on the assumption of "public
knowledge that there is a large number of persons within the

State of New York engaged in circulating propaganda . . . to
overthrow the Government of this State and the United States."
To combat the putative evil, the lawmakers moved to set up a
joint legislative committee "to investigate the scope, tendencies, and ramifications of such seditious activities." The
state senate adopted the resolution unanimously. In the assembly, the two socialists who debated against the motion lacked
the votes to defeat it. Observing that the best way to prevent
radicalism was to remove the causes of discontent, one of them
voiced a thought that frequently occurred to Governor Smith
when Republicans rejected his proposals for welfare legislation. Assemblyman Charles Solomon also predicted the passage
of the resolution "because there aren't enough men and women
in this chamber who have the courage of their convictions."
There was, however, sufficient disaffection within Democratic
ranks to necessitate the exertion of party discipline to keep
more than eight members from joining the Socialists in voting
against the proposed investigation. In March, 1919, New York
set up a Joint Legislative Committee Investigating Seditious
Activities, with Senator Clayton R. Lusk as chairman and the
attorney general for counsel.[6]

Referring to the new committee, Smith remarked during the
course of a Jefferson Day celebration, "What I am afraid of is
that by the action of the Assembly the Government may be creating something for it to investigate." He condemned the lower
house where labor, health insurance, and public power bills
were languishing in committee after having received senate
approval. The speaker drew a connection between such "senseless opposition to progressive legislation" and radicalism,
which thrived on the social injustice that the measures were
designed to rectify.[7]

Despite the governor's reservations on a policy of suppressing the symptoms without eliminating the causes of unrest,
New York was one of twenty-six states that in 1919 adopted a
red flag law, banning the display of that symbol of the political left. Not only did Smith approve the bill, but he even

reenacted the signing for a film to be used in an Americanism campaign.[8]

The chief executive, who saw no harm in a red flag statute, initially failed to perceive the oppressive potentialities of the Lusk committee. His secretary assured its ranking Democrat of Smith's intention "to co-operate in every way with the work of the Committee." Upon the application of its members, the governor readily authorized a special term of the supreme court to sift the evidence of criminal anarchy that the investigators had unearthed.[9] This led to the runaway grand jury, diverted by the New York City transit situation into probing the administration of Hylan and the influence of Hearst.

Like congressional committees of more recent vintage, the Joint Committee Investigating Seditious Activities confused the legislative purpose of investigation with the executive and judicial role in law enforcement, thereby subjecting innocent persons to the injustice of trial by publicity. In a series of spectacular raids, the committee seized property and detained persons, with utter contempt for constitutional and legal safeguards. In sensational hearings, it victimized industrial unionists, liberal professors, and others whose ideas were distasteful to the members. The inquiry began, in a spirit of zenophobia, in the foreign language press and continued in the New York Public Library where the investigators discovered— the writings of Bakunin. As objects of the raids, the Russian Soviet Bureau, a quasi-diplomatic organization, the Socialist party, and the Rand School suffered various indignities. Since the investigative procedure was better calculated to pursue publicity than truth, it appears that the Lusk committee drew its conclusions before—not from—its research.[10]

Its flagrant abuse of power disillusioned Governor Smith, who had originally been in sympathy with the aims of the committee. Two prominent Democrats served as counsel to defendants in actions brought on the initiative of the joint committee: George Gordon Battle, commissioner in a Moreland Act in-

vestigation of the Department of Farms and Markets, represented
the Russian Soviet Bureau; Samuel Untermyer, adviser to the
administration in water power litigation, defended the Rand
School in court. In July, the chief executive read a telegram
from Untermyer, who denounced the star chamber proceedings of
the legislators and insisted, "They are simply persecuting law-
fully inclined people from whose political views I radically
differ." In response to a complaint about the legislative
committee, the governor's staff disclaimed all responsibility
on the part of the executive.[11]

His first year in office distinguished Smith, on the one
hand, from opportunitists like Lusk who capitalized on the Red
Scare, and on the other, from civil libertarians like Baldwin
who resisted its every manifestation. Unlike the legislative
committee, the chief executive respected lawful dissent, but
he drew the line at lawless action, for he appreciated the
paradox that liberty can prevail only as long as freely elected
government exercises its own claim to self-preservation. In
response to constituents who were calling for the suppression
of bolshevik meetings, he explained, "It is, of course, difficult in each case to determine whether or not the right to
freedom of speech . . . is over-reached and the meeting becomes
seditious and, therefore, criminal." It was preposterous, the
governor understood, to expect the discontented to work legitimately within the system, if they were denied access to the
polls. Shortly before election day therefore, he followed up
a request from the Socialist party to use his authority to
prevent its candidates from being counted out by electoral
fraud. At the end of the year, when the *New York Herald* solicited his opinion, he made a distinction between freedom of
expression and incitement to violence at the same time that he
stated his approval of additional legislation to curb the
latter.[12]

Smith started the New Year as he had ended the old, a
moderate on civil liberties. Condemning revolutionaries out-
of-hand in the 1920 annual message, he wryly noted that they

"are at present receiving an unnecessary amount of advertising, on which they thrive"—an obvious dig at the Lusk committee. The governor did not see any contradiction between deploring nativism and supporting Americanization. He emphasized first amendment freedoms, "for without them government by enlightened will of the majority is not possible." To combat radicalism, he therefore recommended, not repression, but reform, a position taken the preceding year by a Socialist speaking against the formation of the committee on seditious activities.[13]

As a result of his reelection, Charles Solomon was one of five Socialists sent to the assembly in 1920 and expelled in a move for which Congress had set a precedent in the case of Victor Berger.[14] They participated in the organization of the legislature and listened to the message in which the governor declared freedom of expression to be vital to majority rule. Without warning, the Speaker theatrically summoned them to the rostrum where he berated them in these words: "You are seeking seats in this body—you who have been elected on a platform that is absolutely inimical to the best interests of the State of New York and of the United States." In a concerted action, the majority leader introduced a resolution to suspend the five, pending an investigation into their eligibility. The motion passed over the negative votes of four of the Socialists and two Democrats from the Bronx. The resolution and the harangue, which preceded its introduction, contained the questionable assumptions upon which the entire proceedings rested. It would be hard to find a more egregious example of guilt by association, for the accusers held the five men responsible for socialist pronouncements, whether or not they had personally subscribed to them. The two Republicans took offense equally at socialist statements calling for the overthrow of the United States government, supporting the Communist Revolution in Russia, and objecting to American involvement in the First World War. From the party's procedure for the discipline of its members, its accusers inferred that Socialists could not take the oath of office, without committing perjury. Showing

little regard for the constitution that he, too, had sworn to
uphold, the attorney general, who had drafted the assembly resolution, explained that it applied to the five legislators,
not "in their individual capacity, but in their capacity as
members of the Socialist Party of America." Appalled at the
dubious logic and uninformed rhetoric, Louis Waldman, one of
the ousted representatives, would reminisce, "As we stood
facing Sweet, we smiled bitterly, for our party had been split
twice on this very issue and now responsibility for these violent doctrines, which we had rejected, was being laid upon our
shoulders."[15]

Governor Smith criticized the suspension of the assemblymen for reasons that suggest that he, not only adhered to the
rule of law more faithfully than the state's highest legal
officer, but also understood the nature of representative
government better than the lower house of the legislature.
"Although I am unalterably opposed to the fundamental principles of the Socialist Party," the chief executive asserted, "it
is inconceivable that a minority party . . . should be deprived of its right to expression . . . unless the chosen representatives are unfit as individuals." As for the five,
"presumably innocent, until proven guilty, they should have been
allowed to retain their seats." Defining democracy in terms,
not only of ends, but also of a scrupulous regard for means, he
explained, "They are the safeguards against revolution. To
discard the methods of representative government leads to the
misdeeds of the very extremists we denounce—and serves to increase the number of the enemies of orderly free government."[16]

What prompted Smith to make a public declaration on the
rights of the assemblymen is not quite clear. He reported in
his autobiography, "The day after the Socialists were expelled
and after a conference with the leaders of my party, I decided
to issue a statement." The meeting, he recalled, enabled him
to persuade the Democratic legislative leaders so that "they
were entirely in accord with the action which I took." His memory
deceived him on several points. When he wrote expulsion, he

meant suspension. The suspension occurred on January 7; the statement appeared on January 10. He evidently issued it in response to a telegram of the same date in which the *New York American* requested his views for publication.[17] The acquiescence of his legislative leadership seems unlikely in view of the eventual division of Democratic votes on the question of expulsion. One can only conclude that when queried on the sorry affair, he took a principled stand for civil liberties, regardless of the consequences. In his own legislative career, he had displayed a tolerance for dissent, and now, in the presence in the assembly of five Socialists, he saw no conflict between the rights of a minority and a peril to the state, which was illusory to all except the paranoid or opportunist. In contrast to less forthright politicians in the fifties, he neither evaded the issue by availing himself of the excuse that it was a legislative rather than an executive concern, nor was he content to follow where he should have led.

Although Smith dared to do the unpopular thing by speaking out in behalf of the Socialists, his incoming mail ran heavily in favor of his stand. One would like to think that the advantages of education were exhibited in the skeptical reaction to the Red Scare in an articulate sector of the community. Be that as it may, a registered Republican lamented, "When the time has ceased when one can express himself through the ballot, then representative government no longer exists"; another writer told Smith, "it would be a sorry day for you and I if the majority of the voters should become Socialists and as such exclude *all* Democrats & Republicans." A former attorney general denounced the suspension of the Socialists as "tyrannical, intolerant, unnecessary and distinctly un-American" and dismissed the appeal to precedent with the observation that "There is a precedent also for witchburning." For one trade union, the episode simply confirmed the Marxist theory of the futility of political action in a capitalist economy.[18] As Smith had acknowledged, disfranchisement would only stimulate the radicalism it was intended to quell.

Looking beyond the contents of the governor's mailbox, one finds public opinion deeply divided on the ouster of the Socialists. With the notable exception of the *Times*, the press in New York City tended to be critical of the assembly, which found editorial rooms upstate friendlier. Contrary to a common stereotype, the Roman Catholic Church, as reflected in its publications, was far from unanimous in leaning towards repression. Even while justifying the assembly proceedings, the Jesuit weekly, *America*, deemed it "better far to remove the evils of which men can justly complain than to suppress fanatics who may complain unwisely." In Baltimore, the *Catholic Review* reminded its readers that "Socialists Have Rights."[19] In Governor Smith's own archdiocese of New York, the *Catholic News*, without making specific mention of the action against the assemblymen, expressed skepticism of the "Red Menace." Among the clergy, Father John A. Ryan was in a small minority in deploring the unseating of elected representatives, but ironically he approved of legislation to bar Socialists from seeking office.[20]

The governor was less complex in his thought processes and more consistent in his devotion to civil liberties than the priest-professor. During the time that the Assembly Judiciary Committee was conducting its investigation of the Socialists, Smith took every opportunity to affirm his faith in freedom. Speaking in Albany and in Buffalo, he complained that the Republicans, by declining to consider social legislation, were contributing to the radicalism that they then proposed to restrain by unwise measures. In New York City, at the Free Synagogue, he upheld the rights of those who would alter the form of government, so long as they used the techniques of persuasion and the ballot box; at the Fifth Avenue Baptist Church, he recited the anecdote of the legislature's first Socialist and his haircut. Alluding to the session in progress, the chief executive told a group of Democratic women, "You cannot stop disorder and discontent, you cannot stop the man from shouting for the overthrow of the government on the street corner by defeating legislation in an indirect way and by throwing four or five men out of the Assembly."[21]

The attempt to throw five men out of the assembly interfered with the normal conduct of legislative business, as lawmakers interrupted their routine in order to attend the daily
hearings of the Judiciary Committee. The men who led the New
York City and State Bar Associations in protesting against the
proceedings of the committee included Republicans like Stimson
and Hughes, with whom Smith enjoyed good relations, and Democrats like Joseph M. Proskauer, who served as his adviser.
Once the committee overruled their objections, "The conduct of
the investigation was thoroughly in harmony with its illegal-
ity," in the words of Professor Zechariah Chafee of Harvard Law
School.[22]

Although a majority of its members recommended the expulsion of all of the Socialists, the Judiciary Committee divided sharply along ideological and geographical lines. Of
the seven-man majority, only the Democrat, Louis Cuvillier,
came from New York City; the six Republicans represented other
areas of the state. In their report, they elaborated on the
allegations in the resolution that authorized the inquiry. The
majority assumed that the Socialist party was subversive, that
association with it entailed disloyalty to the United States,
that loyalty was a qualification of assembly membership subject to the judgment of the house, and that the Socialists had
perjured themselves in taking the oath of office; therefore,
the report concluded that they should be deprived of their
seats. Rejecting the implications of guilt by association, an
upstate Republican, James Lown, filed a memorandum in which he
advocated the seating of the revisionists, Samuel Orr and
Samuel DeWitt, and the ouster of Louis Waldman, August
Claessens, and Charles Solomon for antiwar or revolutionary
proclivities. The minority that objected to any action against
the Socialists consisted of three Republicans and two Democrats
and, except for a member from Schenectady, represented districts in New York City. As if to illustrate their commitment
to political diversity, the dissenters submitted four different

opinions, but they all agreed in condemning the excommunication
of a party as contrary to the spirit of democratic government
and the letter of the constitution. One of the Democrats in
the minority warned his colleagues, "Since we stand for the
maintenance of constitutional government and demand that the
Socialists respect constitutional authority, we must first our-
selves respect that self-same authority. . . ." The other
feared that the removal of the elected officials "would be in
violation of our own oath of office and jeopardize the principle of constitutional government and civil liberty."[23]

Despite the closeness of the vote in the Judiciary Committee, the assembly overwhelmingly adopted the majority recommendation to expel the five Socialists. The count was 116 to
28 on Waldman, Claessens, and Solomon; 104 to 40 on Orr and
DeWitt. The discrepancy suggests the Lown's distinction between individual and collective responsibility and between
evolutionary and revolutionary socialism made an impression on
some of his colleagues. Republicans tended to favor expulsion
by a wider margin than Democrats, but the division between city
and country outranked party as a determinant, for most of the
negative votes were cast by representatives from New York City,
regardless of affiliation.[24]

During the debate preceding the tally, Waldman recalled,
"While speeches were being made denouncing the Socialist Assemblymen as violators of the law, their accusers were out in the
lobby liquidating the Eighteenth Amendment." They needed stimulation during the marathon session, which continued without
interruption from the afternoon of March 31 to the forenoon of
April 1. Since the law did not provide for the filling of
vacancies arising on or after April 1 except for a special
session, the assemblymen, by delaying their action, spared the
governor the embarrassment of a decision on calling special
elections.[25]

Smith however, could not evade indefinitely the predicament of the densely populated constituencies without representation. The Socialist party petitioned him for a special

election on the technicality that the vacancies had occurred on
the legislative day of March 31, since the deliberations continued without interruption. If Smith rebuffed this suggestion, even its proponent tacitly acknowledged the weakness of
his logic. The Socialist chairman alternately proposed a
special session for which the validity of a new election was
beyond contention. To the chief executive, it seemed inappropriate to contemplate the recall of the legislature while it
was still sitting. When it adjourned without taking effective
action on administrative reform, welfare, or housing, civic
groups joined the Socialists in advocating a special session on
the governor's program for solving these problems. Although
Belle Moskowitz urged Smith to fill the vacant assembly seats
in conjunction with an extra session, other advisers counseled
against the recall of the legislature, in order to avoid the
issue of the Socialists. What moved the governor to reconvene
the lawmakers in September, 1920 was a housing crisis of particular severity in the crowded districts of the ousted assemblymen. At the same time that he announced the extraordinary
session, the chief executive provided for an election to give
these areas the representation to which they were entitled.[26]

All five Socialists won reelection, despite the fact that
the major parties combined to enter a single fusion candidate
in each district. New York City thus demonstrated its disapproval of the expulsion in the same way as Middlesex when it
returned John Wilkes to Parliament and Milwaukee when it sent
Victor Berger back to Congress. After diverting an entire day
of the special session to the issue, the assembly adopted
Lown's formula by excluding Waldman, Claessens, and Solomon,
but not Orr and DeWitt. Smith found no more justification for
the unseating of the three than the earlier exclusion of the
five.[27]

Running for reelection himself about a month after the
extraordinary session, Governor Smith deplored the ejection of
the Socialists, with a perceptive commentary on the proceedings.

In the year 1920 the Assembly spent three and a
half months trying five men duly and properly elected.
. . . They declared them guilty, then tried them and
bounced them. If they had put one-half of the energy,
one-quarter of the thought into a consideration of the
constructive suggestions that were placed before them
the State today would be infinitely better off.28

The legislature that underscored its failure to address
social problems by ousting members with radical solutions
adopted a number of repressive measures in consequence of the
investigation into the qualifications of the Socialists. Although it is customary to attribute all of the 1920 bills en-
dangering civil liberties to the Lusk committee, three of them
originated as a consequence of the work, not of the joint committee, but of the Assembly Judiciary Committee. It recommended legislation to disqualify any party in which noncitizens
played a role. The bills that were introduced however, were so
extreme that only two members of the committee supported them,
and they passed over the opposition of the leadership of both
major parties. Taken together, the three proposals would have
effectively outlawed the Socialist organization: first, by removing from the ballot any party judicially determined to be a
threat to constitutional government; second, by denying its
members the right to hold elective or appointive office; and
third, by authorizing the two houses to withhold the oath of
office from any candidate whose qualifications were under
scrutiny.29 The last represented an obvious move to legitimate
the expulsion of the assemblymen earlier in the session.

Although the Lusk committee began its preliminary report
to the 1920 session by disclaiming any intent to engage in repression, three of its proposals could hardly be construed as
anything else. With the FBI in mind, the joint committee advocated the creation of a new state agency for the prosecution of
criminal anarchy and related offenses. Apprehensive lest
education spread the contagion of revolution, the committee
offered two bills to prevent subversive instruction from infec-
ting the unwitting student: one, for the certification of
teachers on the basis of morality and patriotism; and another,

for the licensing of private schools on the grounds of public interest. The second measure was designed to accomplish by legislation what the committee had been unable to effect by litigation: the closing of the socialist Rand School. Together the provisions would give tyrannical control over the ideological content of instruction to officials with discretion to withhold certificates from teachers and licenses from schools.[30] How the legislators intended the authority to be used can be inferred from the Lusk committee's *Report on Revolutionary Radicalism*, a forty-five hundred page document that indiscriminately condemned as subversive a variety of ideas ranging from anarchism to pacifism, of institutions from the International Ladies' Garment Workers' Union to the American Civil Liberties Union, and of individuals from Jane Addams to David Starr Jordan.[31]

To counteract revolutionary radicalism, the committee also supported a program of Americanization aimed at factory operatives and immigrants, the segments of the population considered most receptive to left-wing propaganda. The committee therefore, sponsored one bill to make adult education more available to these groups and another to train teachers to conduct classes for them. Although the measures grew out of a nativism that Smith often deplored, he willingly signed them into the only laws introduced by the Joint Committee Investigating Seditious Activities to receive his approval.[32]

Before taking action on the more controversial items on the legislative agenda of Lusk's joint committee and the Assembly Judiciary Committee, the governor held a public hearing in the executive chamber. Speakers who objected to the denial of civil liberties collided head-on with the mentality of the Red Scare. One lawmaker dismissed the concern for democratic procedures and free speech as "cheap constitutional law." Turning the pervasive nativism against its spokesmen, Louis Marshall criticized their bills for "Russianizing and Prussianizing" the Empire State. In similar vein, Algernon Lee, director of the Rand School, retitled the measures "acts to render impossible the lawful and orderly solution of social and economic problems and to incite . . . lawless violence."[33]

A sensational episode, involving the socialist academy, diverted the hearing from politics to pornography. Henry Wise Wood, a self-professed superpatriot, read aloud from what he described as a Rand School textbook and then proceeded to denounce all associated with the school as "moral perverts and social defectives." The passage, with its explicit references to the physiology of sex, shocked the audience, while a horrified Smith demanded, "Why don't you send that book to the District Attorney?" The chief executive, who insisted, "There are laws enough to suppress that," refrained from concluding, as the speaker had intended, that the offensive reading matter justified, if it did not necessitate, the licensing bill that had been drafted to close the institution where the volume was circulating.[34]

In his initial reaction to the episode, the director of the Rand School did not differ markedly from the governor. Lee appreciated the fact that Smith did not confuse the issue of obscenity with that of political liberty, which was endangered by the bills under consideration. The recitation shocked the socialist intellectual no less than the devout Catholic. That very evening upon his return from Albany, Lee wrote to the governor an explanatory note in which he acquiesced in the banning of the book. In language that conveys the propriety of the respectable socialist, he could only accuse his traducers of "'lying low' till they could make a sensation by reading out those obscene passages in your presence and in the presence of a large number of refined women and young girls." He confessed a total ignorance of the contents of the volume from which they came. On reading *Married Love*, the educator changed his mind—but not the governor's—about the work, which was on sale, not only at the Rand School Bookstore, but also at such irreproachable emporiums as Macy's and Brentano's. His adversaries, by wrenching certain passages out of context in a way that "even the Bible could be made to appear as a very improper book," had exploited the situation "with the obvious aim of creating a prejudice against the Rand School and in the hope of putting you in a false position before the public if you should thereafter refuse to approve the bills for which they appeared." In his second statement to the governor in two days, Lee described the early marriage manual as "a frank scientific discussion of facts of sex," and expressed the conviction that "no candid reader will find the book lewd in tone or immoral in aim." Smith disagreed. He replied, "I read the book and the facts are not as you state." Part of it, he declared to be "to my mind and way of thinking, obscene and indecent"; therefore, he had encouraged legal action against it. When Wood followed up his performance at the hearing by pressing for the revocation of the Rand School's charter, the chief executive repeated his determination to suppress the volume but remained significantly silent on the school.[35]

Liberal opinion rallied against the legislation for which Wood lobbied so sensationally. His tactics nevertheless, impressed Smith's coreligionist who implored the governor to sign the measures "in the Holy Name of our Saviour, whom the Socialists blaspheme." On a different intellectual plane, the Jesuit weekly, *America*, was less disturbed by the socialist threat to the faith than by the legislative threat to freedom. Unable to attend the governor's hearing on the bills in question, Lillian Wald expressed to him her confidence that "your understanding and your statesmanship will protect this commonwealth from the injury to our democracy" by the exercise of the veto.[36]

The social worker had not misplaced her trust, for Smith did veto the six measures designed to curb radicalism. He explained his disapproval in a series of memorandums, containing not only an eloquent defense of civil liberties, but also a thoughtful exposition on representative government, which requires for its existence the freedom of expression that the bills would jeopardize.

In killing the three bills that, in effect, would have outlawed the Socialist party, the governor argued for freedom of speech, without which elections become meaningless routines. To him, it was axiomatic that in a democracy "no majority should have the right to exclude any minority from its just participation in the functions of government." It was precisely such an abuse of power that he thwarted by withholding approval from legislation to keep a party off the ballot and its adherents out of office. He drew inspiration from the Declaration of Independence which he understood to mean:

> No matter to what extent we may disagree with our neighbor, he is entitled to his own opinion, and, until the time arrives when he seeks by violation of law to urge his opinion upon his neighbor, he must be left free, not only to have it but to express it. . . . Law, in a democracy, means the protection of the rights and liberties of the minority. . . . It is a confession of the weakness of our own faith in the righteousness of our cause, when we attempt to suppress by law those who do not agree with us.[37]

The governor also detected a threat to freedom in the bill recommended by the Joint Legislative Committee Investigating Seditious Activities to create an agency for the prosecution of such activities. He found no reason to deviate from normal law enforcement procedures in these cases. In the words of his veto memorandum, "in a democracy there can be no justification for expanding and increasing the powers of such a secret police bureau in times of peace."[38]

Smith was likewise critical of the Lusk committee's proposals to amend the Education Law. They were detrimental to democracy as well as education, for they would confer autocratic power to suppress ideas objectionable to the authorities. He condemned the loyalty test imposed in the teacher certification bill for denying political freedom to members of the profession and confining public school appointments "to those only who lack the courage or the mind to exercise their legal right to just criticism of existing institutions." He noted the irony of a school licensing bill that would protect America from subversion by provisions that were destructive

of the liberty that the nation was founded to secure. In
vetoing them, he again called upon the Founding Fathers for
justification.

> I might rest upon the saying of Benjamin Franklin
> that, "They that can give up essential liberty to
> obtain a little temporary safety deserve neither
> liberty nor safety." But I go further—the safety
> of this government and its institutions rests upon
> the reasoned and devoted loyalty of its people. It
> does not need for its defense a system of intellec-
> tual tyranny which, in the endeavor to choke error
> by force, must of necessity crush truth as well.39

When Joseph Proskauer was drafting the veto memorandums,
he inserted citations, not only from Franklin and Jefferson,
but also from Alexis de Tocqueville. The chief executive, who
excised the passage from *Democracy in America*, explained to a
mutual friend, "Tell Joe I'm supposed to know Benjamin
Franklin. I'm supposed to know Thomas Jefferson. But if I
had ever used that quotation from that French -- --, everyone
would know that Al Smith never wrote that message."[40]

The common sense that Smith displayed in editing the
memorandum and disapproving repressive legislation was not always exercised by his successor. When the 1921 legislature
reenacted, in slightly altered form, the Lusk committee's bills
for teacher certification and school licensing, Nathan Miller
affixed his signature with a patriotic flourish.[41]

Smith made an issue of the Lusk Laws when the two campaigned against each other a second time. The Democratic
platform advocated their repeal, while the candidate prided
himself on the contrast in the record of the two administrations on the Red Scare. He ridiculed those who succumbed to it
as men who "saw red every place they looked, every countenance
that flashed before them seemed to speak of anarchy, and Bolshevism." As for the notorious statutes that they had enacted,
he told an audience in Buffalo, "If I go back to Albany I will
promise you that nobody around that Capitol will be able to
live with me until they do something about that."[42]

Governor Smith began his second term by urging the legislature to repeal the Lusk Laws. The senate approved the appro-

priate bills quite early in the session when one Republican, a
college professor in private life, joined the Democratic majority in voting for repeal. It faced rougher going in the assembly but eventually succeeded there with the assistance of Republicans from the New York metropolitan area and Schenectady.
The Women's City Club of New York gratefully acknowledged the
role of the chief executive in getting the legislature to reverse itself, while a labor leader happily predicted that
"history wll record its fitting tribute to the man who signed
the bills which repealed the Lusk Laws."[43]

Smith's intervention did not meet with universal approbation although the Red Scare was over, for its ambience
lingered on. "The only charitable view to take," commented
Senator Lusk, "is that the Governor is not thinking clearly on
these subjects." The recent election enabled Smith to retort,
"I will leave it to the people to judge between myself and Lusk
as to who is the better exponent of Democratic government."
Those paragons of patriotism, Henry Wise Wood, Dwight Braman
of the Allied Patriotic Societies, and S. Stanwood Menken of
the National Security League, alike deplored the chief executive's naive indifference to the security of the state. He,
in turn, resented the aspersions that they cast on the patriotism of immigrants and disputed their contention that socialism was incompatible with loyalty to America. The governor
admonished his critics to respect the rights of dissenters and
expressed the view that the determination of truth and the
march of progress both depended upon the clash of ideas.
"There is nothing," he told Menken, ". . . in your suggestion
that the repeal of the Lusk Laws would be regarded as a victory by 'Reds' and 'Parlor Pinks,' which in the slightest
leads me to change my view that the so-called Lusk Laws are
subversive of the fundamental principles of American democracy
and freedom." The exchange earned Smith the admiration of the
editor of the *Nation*, who perceived an irony in the behavior of
the chauvinists who "preach Americanism to others and have not
the faintest conception of what the real fundamentals of Ameri-

can polity are." To a friend who favored the Lusk Laws, Smith explained that they were "undemocratic and un-American" in a letter that reveals the consistency between his stand in public and in private.[44]

Despite Smith's pronounced antipathy to the Lusk Laws, their proponents requested a hearing. If they could not realistically expect to change the governor's mind, perhaps they hoped to rouse public opinion against repeal. It was a futile endeavor with a politician like Smith, adept in the art of appealing to the people. When a defender of the Lusk Laws declared, "I am opposed to this dangerous radical propaganda," Smith replied, "So am I, but I think the way to combat it is by appeal to the common sense of our people." He ridiculed prophecies of the disaster to follow repeal. When one witness predicted an American counterpart to the Russian Revolution, the governor assured him, "Oh, you are afraid of something that is not going to happen."[45] He was impressed less by the analogy between the Bolshevik Revolution and domestic unrest than by that between the liquidation of the opposition in the Soviet Union and the suppression of dissent during the Red Scare.

The hearing dispelled any illusions that the governor could be dissuaded from completing the process that he himself had set in motion to repeal the Lusk Laws. His signature effected the reversal of a policy of the interregnum. The change meant a victory for civil liberties, in general, and for the Rand School, in particular. That embattled institution had been defending itself in a legal action, begun in the Miller administration, to close it down for lack of the license that it would no longer require. The end of litigation, following repeal of the licensing statute, led one observer to conclude that "The cause of liberal education was won, not in the courts but at the polls" by the reelection of Smith.[46]

In his second term, Governor Smith undid much of the damage that the Lusk committee had accomplished, not only by legislation, but also by criminal prosecution. He extended clemency to the men and women convicted of criminal anarchy as a result of the committee's efforts.[47]   Prosecuted under a statute enacted after the assassination of McKinley, a dozen were found guilty of conspiring to overthrow the government, largely on evidence of their connection with the Left-Wing Manifesto, an exercise in Marxist analysis, on which Zechariah Chafee has commented, "Any agitator who read these thirty-four pages to a mob would not stir them to violence, except possibly against himself." The last to be freed was Benjamin Gitlow, whose release was delayed until 1925 by his appeal to the United States Supreme Court, which upheld his conviction, significantly with Holmes and Brandeis dissenting. As Smith began his second administration, he came under fire from Senator Lusk both for his message urging repeal of the teacher certification and school licensing laws and for the first of the pardons in these cases. "If the Governor believes that men should be pardoned because convicted of the crime of 'advocating criminal anarchy,'" Lusk suggested, "he should send in a message asking for repeal of the law."[48]

The senator was taking exception to the first in a series of pardons, that of James Joseph Larkin, left-wing socialist and trade unionist, nationalist in Ireland and pacifist in America, member of the Communist Labor party and communicant of the Roman Catholic Church. In pleading Larkin's case, a spokesman referred to the passage on civil liberties in the governor's annual message, in justification of an immediate release. In extending clemency, the chief executive made a statement that ranks with the original Lusk bill vetoes in its comprehension of the principles of free government. He was liberating Larkin, Smith explained, "not because of agreement with his views, but despite my disagreement with them." The governor averred that Larkin's imprisonment resulted from "a political case where a man has been punished for the statement of his beliefs" and warned lest such proceedings "tend to deter . . . that full and free discussion of political issues which is a fundamental of democracy."[49]

As revealed by the pardon of James Larkin, Smith's understanding of the relationship between civil liberties and political democracy so impressed the editor of the *Century Magazine*
that he held up the New Yorker as "an example which should be
followed by every governor in the United States and by the
President." Questioned on the case of Sacco and Vanzetti, the
anarchists convicted of the murder of a South Braintree pay-
master, Smith observed, "If I were the Governor of Massachusetts, and two men were condemned to death for a crime about
which there is so much doubt that I have to call in a college
president and two judges to tell me what to do, I'd commute
their sentence."[50] Although he never accepted Lusk's challenge
to advocate repeal of the criminal anarchy statute under which
the prisoners in New York were convicted, Smith did not condone
the abuse of power whereby prosecution turned into persecution
for political beliefs. He drew a distinction between word and
deed. As long as they resorted only to persuasion and the
ballot box, he respected the rights of minorities to change
the existing order. In contrast to more reactionary politicians, he recognized the legitimacy of dissent and scrupulously
observed the rights of socialists and labor leaders, groups
particularly vulnerable to oppression in the decade of his
administration.

There was one noteworthy, if understandable, exception to
Smith's tolerance of political minorities: the Ku Klux Klan.
The 1923 session enacted a measure to require organizations
that were defined in such a way as presumably to affect the
Klan alone, to file lists of members and officers with state
authorities. A sponsor of the bill acknowledged the intention
of using the threat of public exposure to discourage people
from joining the KKK, but observers speculated that officials
might apply it to other groups of which they disapproved, for
example the Anti-Saloon League. A Kleagle denounced the
statute as unconstitutional for singling out his association
"and not making its provisions applicable to the Knights of
Columbus" and threatened Smith with political retaliation for

signing the bill into law. In view of its legislative history,
the governor did not display his customary candor at the time
of approval when he stated, "No harm can come to any such membership corporation if its intentions and purposes are honest."[51]

The libertarian principles that governed Smith's response
to the Left failed him in this case of the Right. In dealing
with the Red Scare, he recognized that procedures count, that
to be equitable, they must be neutral and universally applicable, and that officials should take punitive action only
against lawless deeds, not mere association or the expression
of ideas, however distasteful. It is not necessary to hold any
brief for the KKK to suggest that the 1923 law that the governor signed violated most, if not all, of these criteria. The
revival of the Klan arose out of the same ugly emotions in
American life that generated the Red Scare and threatened Smith
directly by its surprising numerical strength in the New York
City suburbs and upstate, by its nativist and anti-Catholic
prejudices, and by its opposition to his presidential aspirations.[52] That Smith could not deal evenhandedly with the group
is comprehensible in the light of the ambivalence of the American Civil Liberties Union, which on at least one occasion, protested only halfheartedly against harrassment of the Klan.
Nothing illustrates the dangerous potentialities of New York's
anti-Klan law better than the fact that its provisions later
served as a model to states adopting legislation to intimidate
black civil rights groups. Although the United States Supreme
Court had upheld the 1923 statute, it overturned the southern
enactments by distinguishing between the viciousness of the KKK
and the virtue of the NAACP. This is no cause for complacency,
if one imagines a hypothetical court reversing the value judgment. As one legal scholar wrote in a commentary on the
earlier decision, the judges skirted the issue "that exposure
is repressive and that this was the purpose of the statute."[53]
The executive and the judiciary both provide evidence for that
law of human nature that the rationalization of repression

varies inversely with the attractiveness of its victims.

The same law of human behavior makes culture even more
vulnerable than politics to the oppressor who justifies censorship in the name of morality. In the twenties, the limitations on individual liberty, whether in the guise of the Red
Scare, Comstockery, or Prohibition, blended into a single crusade against evils that its spokesmen visualized as contamina-
ting American life. The three repressive movements gained
impetus from the wartime tensions and interacted with one
another. Such a relationship is apparent in the dramatic
hearing on the Lusk Laws where the superpatriots stigmatized
instruction at the Rand School as both revolutionary and obscene. Efforts at censorship in the cultural sphere intensified in this era for a number of reasons: a growing candor
on sex in the literary and graphic arts, the rise of little
magazines and innovative publishing houses that ignored conventional taboos, and the growth of the movie industry with its
exploitation of romantic love. If Governor Smith often failed
to discern the implications for civil liberties in the vexa-
tious issue of pornography, even the ACLU shied away from
these cases during much of the decade.[54] Although he did not
consistently defend cultural freedom, he did not go to the
other extreme of acceding to every outcry for suppression. In
their demand for action, the guardians of morality compelled
the governor to take a stand on state regulation of films,
books, and stage plays.

When Smith returned to office in 1923, he found in force,
not only the loyalty test for teachers and the school licensing
measure that he had vetoed, but also motion picture censorship.
The sponsorship by Senator Lusk and the signature by Governor
Miller of all three bills illustrate again the fusion of the
forces of political and cultural repression. The 1921 law
required a license for the exhibition of any film, established
a commission to administer its provisions, and set criteria of
judgment, which the courts today would reject as unconstitu-

tionally vague. At the time, Belle Moskowitz raised objections
that obviously persuaded Smith, when she condemned the bill for
violating alike the principles of civil liberties and the
science of public administration.[55]

The governor's annual message of 1923 contained a moving
passage on civil liberties, which recommended the repeal of
Lusk's measures on teachers, schools, and films. "Censorship
is not in keeping with our ideas of liberty and of freedom of
worship or freedom of speech," Smith insisted. His position on
motion picture censorship revealed both his liberalism and its
limitations. He recognized the film as an instrument of communciation, which was entitled to the protection of the Bill of
Rights. He opposed prior restraint on any form of expression.
While the law should not ban the release of information, he
believed that it could define obscenity and punish those who
distributed it. To him, censorship meant prior restraint, but
after publication, material legitimately came under the provisions of the penal law. Subsequent messages objected to the
arrangements for licensing movies, not only on the grounds of
censorship, but also because the agency involved violated the
canons of administrative reform, which was one of his major
policies. Like so many of his proposals in 1923, this one for
abolition of the motion picture commission received the assent
of the Democratic senate but not of the Republican assembly.[56]

Contemporaries attributed the inaction of the lower house
to the influence of the Roman Catholic Church. Speaking for
the archdiocese of New York, *Catholic News* editorialized
against repeal and denied that state action "to keep indecency
off the screen" interfered with legitimate free expression.[57]
The governor, who had argued the contrary, persisted throughout
his administration in urging the end of motion picture censorship.

His church could neither overcome Smith's antipathy to
motion picture censorship, nor enlist him in a campaign for the
so-called clean books bill, despite the almost universal
backing of the Catholic press. *Catholic News* described the

measure as "a sincere effort to prevent the dissemination of
literature that is calculated to corrupt the morals of the
youth," and summoned the faithful to support the proposal for
the censorship of books. The New York court that refused to
ban the *Satyricon* aroused the ire of the Paulist Fathers who,
in their monthly, *Catholic World*, preached that "obscenity
which is artistic is more dangerous than obscenity which is
crude," and complained that "The only sin known to the critics
is the sin of dullness. The value of Christian modesty and
purity are not merely discounted, but ignored." Not to be out-
done, the Jesuits informed the readers of *America* that "No one
who has dealt with actual conditions in New York can accept the
contention . . . that the present practise of the courts is
sufficient to check the harmful effects of bad books and
plays."[58]

The clean books bill under consideration in 1923 was
drafted to circumvent judicial decisions that had interfered
with the suppression of publications on grounds of obscenity.
To facilitate prosecution, the sponsors proposed to amend the
law in the following ways: to define obscenity, not in a
technical sense, but by common usage; to judge a work, not on
its totality, but on the basis of any objectionable part; to
make obscenity a matter of fact to be tried by a jury, not law
to be determined by a judge; to bar the testimony of experts in
the determination of that fact; and to base the verdict on the
language itself, not its effect upon the reader. On books as
on films, the lower house was the less liberal, for it voted
to amend the criminal law on publications, only to have the
measure fail in the senate. In debating against it, James
Walker quipped, "No woman was ever ruined by a book." *Catholic
News* deplored the role of communicants of the church in defeating the bill, which it so strongly advocated.[59]

The governor encountered pressure from a variety of
sources, not all of them religious, to favor the clean books
bill. It had originated with the New York Society for the Suppression of Vice, which found a ready ally in the Catholic

hierarchy. The crusade gathered momentum during the 1923 session through the efforts of John Ford, a Democratic judge who
was scandalized to discover his unmarried daughter reading
D. H. Lawrence's *Women in Love*. After the legislative setback,
the jurist appealed to Smith to support the measure during his
third term and implored, "Why should you not be with us?" The
chief executive responded, "I cannot say that I am not with you
nor can you say it. I certainly believe in clean literature.
The question in my mind is how to bring it about." The governor was not the only one to be skeptical of the vice society's
program, for the legislature refrained from any action on it
after 1923. Dismayed by the failure of his efforts to censor
others, Ford wrote a book on *Criminal Obscenity* and sent a
copy to Smith who promised to read it "at the first opportunity."[60]

As the prospects dimmed for legislation on obscene books,
the crusaders turned their attention to indecent plays. In
the name of morality, the Catholic press escalated a campaign
to purify the theater. In the summer of 1926, *Catholic World*
declared that "the stage here was never so filthy"; the following winter, *Commonweal* described the playhouses as "badly
in need of moral criticism" and reflected that "often in history theatres have been closed tight for offenses no more
serious than those now visible on Broadway." Simultaneously,
the New York Society for the Suppression of Vice intensified
its efforts against objectionable dramas. The renewed activity
came in part as a response to the character of the season's
productions, which ranged from Eduard Bourdet's sensitive treatment of lesbianism in *The Captive*, which received wide critical
acclaim, to melodramas of little literary but substantial mone-
tary value, which can only be described as sexploitation.[61]
They created enough of a sensation to attract unfavorable attention and critical comment in the governor's circle. History
does not record that Justice Ford's unmarried daughter attended
any of these performances, but Governor Smith inadvertently
did—with serious consequences for theatrical freedom.[62]

The governor reacted to the state of the theater in ways that were consistent both with his moral training as a Roman Catholic and with his understanding that the exercise of free speech required the absence of prior restraint but did not exempt people from punishment for issuing material subsequently adjudged in violation of the law. He expected the city authorities to take legal action to close the offensive plays, a remedy of which he said, "I think it is a great deal better than censorship . . ." before opening night. While he was commended for his involvement by William McAdoo, the judge who presided over the criminal anarchy trials with scant respect for the rights of the defendants, Smith rejoiced that "the boys have started putting the cleaning machine on the whole drama situation." They succeeded in removing *The Captive* from the boards, despite the intervention of Horace Liveright, the publisher primarily responsible for the defeat of the clean books bill.[63]

As in the case of the Red Scare, the lawmakers in Albany were only too eager to legislate against the evils of the metropolis, and they carefully devised a bill to circumvent Smith's reservations and avoid a veto. The enactment, which the legislature adopted and the executive signed in 1927, made it a misdemeanor for any person to be associated with a production that, as a whole or in part, "would tend to the corruption of the morals of youth or others" or that dealt with "the subject of sex degeneracy, or sex perversion." Besides the usual penalty of a fine or imprisonment, the statute provided for a year's revocation of the license of the premises where the offense occurred. For this reason, it was known as the Theater Padlock Law. In order to overcome Smith's objections to censorship, the measure made no provision for prior restraint but imposed punishment after an offending performance. The district attorney of New York County explained to Smith that the proposal's sponsors had included the ban on homosexuality in order to prevent a revival of *The Captive*. Joab Banton also pointed out the advantages of the bill in condemning a work as obscene on the basis of a single passage rather than the totality and in penalizing the owner or lessee of a theater where it played, regardless of any intention to violate the law, a state of mind that was hard to prove. The prosecutor commended the bill to the governor as an effective means of eliminating indecency from the theater.[64]

The impropriety of the bill outweighed that on the stage, according to the Citizens' Union and the American Civil Liberties Union, both of which argued for a veto. The padlock provisions were not comparable to those for the enforcement of Prohibition, for the presence of alcohol is a matter of fact while the presence of pornography is a matter of opinion. "There is no standard by which to measure obscenity . . ." the Citizens' Union declared, for attitudes change so that "Many things that were rejected in 1880 are generally accepted now, whereas many things that were admitted in 1780 are now generally rejected." When the definition of crime is imprecise, the law is conducive to tyranny, explained Arthur Garfield Hays, national director of the ACLU. Indefinite law encourages selective prosecution with the danger that officials may abuse their discretionary authority to harrass those in disfavor. The effect of the measure on the landlord is unfair—if not unconstitutional—for it leaves him unable to predict a violation at the same time that he can be penalized without having any part in the production or the trial by which it is adjudged obscene. Hays denounced as "far worse than censorship" a procedure that might intimidate the theatrical world into avoiding anything offensive to the authorities. He appealed to the governor to live up to his reputation on civil liberties.[65]

The theater padlock measure was an exception to Smith's liberalism. He did agree to defer approval of the bill in order to allow the entertainment industry to present its objections. However, he proceeded with such deliberate haste as to create the impression that he was trying to silence the critics and avoid publicity. The wires, requesting the hearing, reached him on the afternoon of April 5, and he scheduled it

for 1 P.M. on April 6. Despite the general opposition in the
theatrical world, only Lee Shubert's attorney was prepared in
time to contest the proposal. When the lawyer reasoned that it
would deprive a theater owner of property without due process
of law and render him culpable for performances with which he
had nothing to do, Smith rejoined, "you can't convict any man
unless he has guilty knowledge. I do not believe any licensing commissioner would padlock a theatre for something he
couldn't prove the owner . . . knew anything about." The remark was disingenuous, for Banton had explained to the chief
executive the benefit to the prosecution of being able to shut
down a house for exhibiting obscenity, without having to establish the landlord's complicity. As on similar occasions, the
governor made no pretense of neutrality at the hearing. Immediately following its conclusion, he signed the bill.[66]

If *Catholic News* credited Governor Smith with improving
the morality of the stage, the civic organizations questioned
the legitimacy of the means used to achieve this end. Although
he shared the religious editor's values, in other circumstances
he was less cavalier in his treatment of civil liberties. In
this situation, however, it was easy to dismiss the protest
from show business as self-serving. Smith was normally more
receptive to the views of the nonpartisan groups that opposed
the Theater Padlock Law. They were more forceful in defense
of political than cultural freedom, for they were not immune
to the prudery that generated literary repression. It was only
in the late twenties, when Morris Ernst joined the staff, that
the ACLU "learned the facts of life" and actively opposed
literary censorship. Ernst himself later described the theater
statute that Smith approved as "a weapon of intimidation" and
its padlock penalty as "censorship at its worst."[67]

Nevertheless, Zechariah Chafee counted Smith among the
executives who, in the twenties, defended civil liberties
against the repressiveness of the legislative, and the relative
indifference of the judicial, branch. In the finest hours of

his administration, he upheld the rights of Socialists to representation, vetoed the Lusk Laws, and insisted upon their
repeal. If he was less consistent in devotion to cultural than
to political freedom, perhaps it required the development of
totalitarianism to demonstrate the relationship between political tyranny and cultural conformity. Although he approved
restrictions on the theater, he opposed motion picture censorship and refused to yield to the clamor for the clean books
bill. Even when he contributed to suppression on the stage,
he did not abandon the standard of free expression, as he understood it, for the new law did not entail censorship in advance. As Chafee pointed out, the doctrine of no prior restraint has enjoyed a long and honorable history as a criterion
for the development of free institutions, but it is not a sufficient safeguard.[68]

Civil libertarians like Professor Chafee found Smith's
record more impressive than his lapses. The governor, who respected the rights of socialists, shared the inhibitions common
in his own generation on sex, a subject unmentionable in many
respectable circles—at least in mixed company. If he was
blind to the threat that the theater padlock bill posed to
free expression, his attitude on obscenity was undoubtedly
molded by the religious teachings of his church. However, it
is necessary to note that he did not hesitate to act contrary
to the wishes of its leadership, not only on prior restraint
of films and books, but also on the federal child labor amendment. To admit the influence of religion on his thinking, is
not to say, as his more bigoted opponents did in 1928, that
in his official capacity, he submitted to the dictates of the
Roman Catholic hierarchy.

In granting pardon to those convicted of criminal anarchy,
Governor Smith was more magnanimous than the Republican presidents of the 1920s and closer in outlook to the Democratic
chief executive of the 1930s. Many victims of the war and
postwar hysteria languished in federal prisons until FDR's
Christmas amnesty.[69] With the inauguration of President

Roosevelt, a New Deal on civil liberties emerged in Washington, for the administration was more respectful of dissenters among immigrants and trade unionists than its predecessors. In Frank Murphy, Roosevelt had an attorney general who was more sensitive to civil liberties than possibly any other man who has held that post.[70] Neither Smith nor Roosevelt was inclined to repression, but both men fell somewhat short of the standards of the most rigorous civil libertarians. In this respect, the two executives were more alike than is commonly recognized.

WET AND DRY: THE POLITICIAN AND PROHIBITION

Al Smith criticized Prohibition as a violation of civil
liberties. In the case of sumptuary legislation, government
interferes inevitably with the private lives and liberties of
individuals. If opponents like Smith detected a threat to
civil liberties in the noble experiment, its defenders often
justified Prohibition in terms that encouraged political or
cultural repression. Politicians who associated alcohol with
radicalism indulged in an effort to eradicate both. Equating
the evils of obscenity and liquor, vice societies joined the
campaign to ban the second as well as the first. Reflecting
the mood of those who believed in legislating morality by limiting choice, the *Christian Century* declared, "Prohibition is
the censorship of beverages, and censorship is the prohibition
of harmful literature and spectacles." The banning of books
and the outlawing of drinks were equally offensive to libertarians like H. L. Mencken who derided the drys by insisting,
"The Anti-Saloon League is quite as criminal as the boot-
leggers; it devotes itself professionally to violating the Bill
of Rights."[1]

At first, scholars tended to interpret Prohibition in the
same way as Mencken: an abomination inflicted upon the American people by a bigoted, if politically astute, minority. In
time, social scientists learned to take the liquor issue more
seriously as an indication of a profound cleavage between the
predominantly native, Protestant countryside, which exerted
its authority by imposing Prohibition, and the burgeoning
cities, populated by large numbers of immigrants and Roman
Catholics, who formed subcultures in which sociability included
the drinking of wine or beer. In addition, drys generally belonged to the middle class; wets, to the upper or lower. According to a sociologist however, the corelation between social
strata and attitudes toward alcohol reflected, not a class conflict involving economic interests, but a cultural struggle in

which what was at stake was prestige and self-esteem. Older
Americans, sensing a decline in status, compensated by imposing
their value system on the threatening hordes of newcomers.[2]
Even without the handicap of his pronounced antipathy to Prohibition, Al Smith, with his recent immigrant ancestry,
working-class origins, Catholic faith, and urban base, personi-
fied the very forces in American life that the temperance crusaders were striving to suppress.

   Governor Smith, whose administration entitles him to be
acknowledged as a reformer, would have been astounded to learn
that Prohibition, within half a century of its ignominious de-
mise, was being heralded by historians as a significant reform.
For example, Norman H. Clark has interpreted the noble experiment, not as a ludicrous accident, but as a genuine reform with
widespread support among thoughtful Americans who viewed
drinking as a cause of poverty and political corruption and
favored the proscription of alcohol as a reasonable remedy for
such ills. Contrary to the popular stereotype, Prohibition
was at least partially successful, he contended, in reducing
the consumption of alcohol and raising the standard of living.[3]

   In a book that treated Prohibition as a product of the
progressive movement for reform, James H. Timberlake also
proved more sympathetic to the cause than earlier scholars.
Because of a corrupting influence on politics and monopolistic
tendencies, the liquor business became a tempting target of the
drive toward economic regulation and the moralism inherent in
progressivism. Social progressives might favor Prohibition to
relieve poverty. Within the progressive movement, Timberlake
acknowledged, the temperance issue was a divisive force, sepa-
rating those who upheld the middle-class norm from others who
generated urban liberalism and resisted a reform that appeared
repressive to workers and immigrants in the industrial cities.
Research on states as diverse as Washington, Tennessee, and
California has confirmed the impression that many progressive
politicians supported Prohibition, but the Golden State particularly furnishes an example of dissension within the ranks,

between dry Los Angelenos and moister San Franciscans, a division that corelates closely with sentiments against and for
organized labor.[4]

New York State offers an exception to the rule that progressives enlisted in the cause of Prohibition. It attracted
few adherents among either Republican followers of Governor
Hughes, urban liberals in the Democratic organization, or members of the state's Progressive party. The coercive spirit of
Prohibition was implicit in the ideology of the so-called temperance movement from the beginning, when the Empire State
stood in the forefront of the dry crusade. After a prolonged
decline in New York, the temperance drive regained momentum
around the turn of the century, following the active acceptance
of women workers and the rise of the Anti-Saloon League. The
rejuvenated movement posed a sticky problem for a GOP organization that labored to retain its dry constituency upstate without antagonizing its wet contingent in the metropolis. Acting
inconsistently on the liquor issue, the Republicans appeared
hypocritical; in contrast, the party of Al Smith unequivocally
opposed Prohibition.[5]

There is truth in the observation that "Al Smith's political career began in Tom Foley's saloon . . ." for the
taverns, which the drys abhorred, served the cities as centers
of working-class communal life and meeting places for ward
politicians. As a Democratic assemblyman, the future governor
voted against all measures that the drys sponsored, whether
for local option or statewide prohibition. Writing in retirement on *The Citizen and His Government*, Smith condemned the
Eighteenth Amendment as a violation of civil liberties and a
futile effort "to legislate morality into a people from without, when morality . . . must obviously come from within and
be the result of self-restraint, education, and training." The
author insisted, "You cannot make Mr. A believe in prohibition
by shooting Mr. B in an attempt to stop him from making home
brew. . . ."[6]

The New Yorker served as governor of his state at a time
when the nation was engaged in the quixotic endeavor to force
Mr. A to abstain by shooting Mr. B. Smith entered office while
ratification of the Eighteenth Amendment was still pending,
after Congress had enacted wartime prohibition, and shortly before the Volstead Act defined intoxicating beverages as those
containing .5 percent alcohol, in order to prohibit wine and
beer along with hard liquor. His first term coincided with the
onset of Prohibition. If progressivism influenced its adoption,
many progressives, the governor among them, opposed from the
start a policy that ultimately contributed to the dashing of
his presidential hopes.

Prohibition added to Smith's prominence and detracted
from his achievements between his victory in 1918 and his defeat in 1928. The sensational issue affected the outcome of
elections and diverted attention from the economic problems
that the depression would expose.

Ambivalence toward alcohol plagued the GOP as it prepared
for the election of 1918, which would place Smith in the executive chamber. In a conflict over the platform, the wets devised the strategy of a plank pledging the legislators to refrain from ratifying the Prohibition amendment before providing
for an expression of the will of the people in a referendum.
Fearing such a test of strength yet confident of their ability
to control the malapportioned legislature, the drys opted for
the platform to remain silent on the question. In deference to
the prohibitionists, Governor Charles Seymour Whitman exerted
his influence to dissuade the Republican state convention from
inserting a plank on the subject. As a result of the platform
fight, he faced a representative of the disgruntled wets in the
same primary in which Smith received a challenge from an anti-
Tammany Democrat. The organization candidates won their respective contests, the Republican with the backing of the Anti-
Saloon League.[7]

Having risen to a position of dominance in the temperance
movement, the Anti-Saloon League led the drive that culminated
in Prohibition and thereafter assumed direction of the elements
monitoring its enforcement.[8] Eschewing third party politics as
an exercise in futility, the league failed to support the Prohibition party but operated instead by backing Republicans or
Democrats who agreed to do its bidding. Such realism brought
a degree of success that had eluded idealistic reformers for
nearly a century. By promising—or threatening—to deliver
enough votes to affect the balance of power between the major
parties, the organization induced politicians to ban intoxicating beverages. Whether or not the league actually controlled a crucial bloc of votes, candidates and officeholders,
fearful of its power, submitted to a kind of blackmail. The
Anti-Saloon League endorsed candidates solely on the basis of
their voting record on the one issue of alcohol and without any
reference to their personal habits. Consequently, politics
created strange bedfellows of sanctimonious drys and variegated
political hacks, some with a notorious capacity for indulgence.
The self-proclaimed moral forces professed idealism and practiced expediency. Funds for lobbying and for electioneering
came primarily from the membership of the evangelical Protestant churches whose vote loomed so large on election day. A
grass roots constituency and clever tactics made the Anti-
Saloon League one of the most effective pressure groups ever
to operate on the American political scene. With its sectarian
identity, moralism, and modus operandi, the league bears a
striking resemblance to such phenomena of the eighties as the
Moral Majority and the single issue politics of the anti-
abortion crusaders. Witnessing the influence of the Anti-
Saloon League on his contemporaries, Al Smith deplored the
power of such groups to intimidate politicians.[9]

Smith himself never stooped to curry favor with the
league, which opposed him in every race for governor, beginning
in 1918. That year, in an effort the defeat him, the organization distributed a flier publicizing his outspoken stand

against prohibition as an assemblyman. The New York edition of
the *American Issue*, official organ of the Anti-Saloon League,
charged Smith with voting for "liquor, gambling and vice, the
trinity of Hell," and warned that to elevate him to the
governorship would "jeopardize everything in the way of moral
legislation . . . secured by years of ceaseless struggle."
Although the drys had earlier championed the cause of direct
democracy, they now denounced as hypocrisy the candidate's proposal for a referendum on the Prohibition amendment.[10]

The Democratic party, in convention assembled, adopted
the plank for a referendum prior to ratification that the GOP
eliminated from its platform, under the influence of the Anti-
Saloon League. Although Smith believed that the legislature
should defer action on the Eighteenth Amendment until it consulted the people, he supported ratification of the Nineteenth
on the grounds that New Yorkers had already approved woman
suffrage by amending their own state constitution. He agreed
to abide by the results of an advisory referendum on the Prohibition amendment and, in case of an affirmative vote, promised
to "give its passage more sincere aid than the present Governor
did at the last legislative session."[11]

The inconsistency that Smith detected in his rival's
position allowed the Anti-Saloon League to contemplate with
equanimity the prospect of Whitman's defeat, since "it will not
be because of his Prohibition advocacy, but it will be because
of failing to utilize it to its full extent." According to
the *American Issue*, a Republican victory, on the other hand,
would signify "that Prohibition sentiment is vastly stronger
in New York than the election returns will indicate, because
. . . he will have won with the aid of not more than half of
the 'plus' votes that might have been gotten on this moral
issue." In this species of electoral analysis, prohibition
never fails, for it converts defeat into victory. If the dry
candidate wins, the moral is clear. If he loses, he was not
firm enough in the faith. In contrast to the professional dry,
the professional politician attributed his poor showing to the

defection of the wets who were more numerous in the GOP than
the Anti-Saloon League implied. Its superintendent, William
H. Anderson, blamed the outcome, not only on Whitman, but also
on the New York Catholic hierarchy, in language so immoderate
that its archbishop accused him of bigotry.[12] The association
of Prohibition and religion in the gubernatorial fight of 1918
foreshadowed the presidential contest a decade later.

Ratification of the Eighteenth Amendment occupied a
prominent place on the agenda of Governor Smith's first legislative session. Consistent with the position that he had
taken during the campaign, he called upon the state's lawmakers to be guided in their decision by a popular referendum
and expressed his own doubts that the people were ready to
accept such "a rigid restriction upon their personal liberty"
as Prohibition. In denouncing the governor's plan, Anderson
revealed his nativism with a derogatory reference to "the
alien-slum elements of our big cities," who would participate
in such a poll. The Anti-Saloon League took the offensive by
proposing Senator George F. Thompson, a dry Republican, for
president pro tem. The maneuver was successful, not in electing
Thompson, but in extracting from his victorious opponent the
promise of a GOP caucus on ratification. By limiting Republican
defections, the caucus secured the necessary votes for ratification, but not until January 29, at which time the question
was purely academic as New York became the forty-fourth state
to approve the Prohibition article.[13]

Belated ratification signified reluctance on the part of
the lawmakers, who almost immediately appeared to harbor second
thoughts on Prohibition. Two proposals to require a referendum
before legislative action on amendments to the United States
Constitution made their way into the hopper in 1919, and one of
them progressed as far as to receive approval in the lower
house. Like the referendum measure, one of the many Prohibition enforcement bills that was introduced passed the assembly,
but not the senate. The Anti-Saloon League, which was drafting
its own version of a state dry law, asked Smith to specify what

provisions he would be willing to sign, but the governor refused to cooperate.   In view of the dilatory ratification and
the failure of enforcement legislation, the *Times* accused the
legislature of "running with the hare and hunting with the
hounds" in an effort "to please both the liquor interests and
the Anti-Saloon League."[14]

The failure of the league to retire targeted assemblymen
in the November election undermined the credibility of its
claim to deliver a bloc of votes and weakened its influence on
the 1920 legislature; moreover, the chief executive remained
an unreconstructed wet.   In his annual message, he cited
authorities to the effect that the Eighteenth Amendment had
probably not been duly ratified and, if not, states might still
rescind their ratification.   Under these circumstances, Smith
advised the New York legislature to revoke its resolution and
to hold a referendum before taking up the question of Prohibition again.[15]   The state superintendent of the Anti-Saloon
League oppugned the veracity of the message and charged its
author with "servile allegiance to the saloon and the brewery."
"What Anderson said about me," the governor rejoined, "I leave
to his conscience, if he has any. . . ."   A month later,
Smith described the noble experiment as inflicting upon the
American people "a restriction to their personal liberty which
Russia in her palmiest days never dreamt of."[16]

Brief as it was, the Prohibition amendment contained
language that was subject to varying interpretations and
generated controversy, particularly in New York.   What was the
extent of the jurisdiction conferred upon the states by the
concurrent power clause?   What was prohibited in the phrase,
intoxicating liquors?   When Congress submitted an amendment
banning intoxicating rather than alcoholic beverages, many
people operated on the assumption that it applied only to dis-
tilled, not to fermented, drinks.   How much alcohol was intoxicating, and what role might the states play in making the
decision?   A combination of wishful thinking and states' rights
allowed some individuals to conclude that the states could

define intoxicants. If the Constitution was deliberately
ambiguous on the question of alcoholic content, Congress moved
quickly to answer it in the Volstead Act, which prohibited anything with more than .5 percent alcohol. Many politicians,
Governor Smith and a majority of New York's legislators among
them, contested the validity of the congressional definition.[17]

Wets and drys disagreed on the constitutional issues as
the 1920 session grappled with the problem of state enforcement
that its predecessor had evaded. The prohibitionists also
divided among themselves with the result that they introduced
two bills, both incorporating the Volstead Act's definition of
intoxicating liquors but differing from each other by the absence, from the Anti-Saloon League version, of provision for
taxes and officials to enforce the law. The league justified
its preference for the apparently weaker measure on the grounds
that it would furnish Smith with no excuse for a veto because
of expense or patronage. The drys however no longer controlled
the legislature, which considered bills to allow a commerce in
beer and wine, with an alcoholic content ranging as high as 4
and 12 percent respectively, by the simple expedient of declaring them nonintoxicating. Anderson demanded a caucus to
keep the GOP in line behind the Volstead Act definition of
intoxicants, but the November election had deprived the league
of the clout to duplicate the maneuver that had resulted in
ratification the year before. In the end, urban Republicans
united with Democrats to send the governor the Walker-Gillett
bill permitting beverages with as much as 2.75 percent
alcohol.[18]

At the hearing, customary before action on controversial
legislation, Smith made no pretense of suspending judgment on
the measure before him. He served as its advocate in opposition to the drys, who were urging a veto. The subject of contention was whether jurisdiction over the definition of an intoxicating beverage lay with the state legislatures or with
Congress, as the prohibitionists asserted. Correctly relying
on the supremacy of the federal government, they argued that

New York could not constitutionally permit what Congress had
prohibited. The state executive, on the other hand, interpreted the concurrent power clause as conferring some discretion on the states. "I don't believe there is concurrence
where a man acts first and then compels another to act his
way," declared Smith. "If another Congress says that 2 or 3
per cent. alcohol is not intoxicating, and still later another
Congress says 5 per cent. is not intoxicating, have the States
got to abide by that . . . ?" the governor asked counsel for
the Anti-Saloon League. "Congress has not the right to define
an intoxicant," responded the obviously rattled lawyer. A
representative of the Women's Christian Temperance Union held
up to Smith the example of Governor Calvin Coolidge, who had
just vetoed in Massachusetts a statute similar to that before
the New York executive. Less than a week after he had disapproved the Lusk bills, which placed civil liberty in jeopardy,
and a day after a hearing as controversial but not as sensational as that on the antiradical measures generated by the Red
Scare, Smith signed the Walker-Gillett bill for Prohibition enforcement. In a memorandum, which was written with tongue in
cheek or, in imagination, sipping near beer, the governor deferred to the legislature on the definition of the intoxicating
beverages to be prohibited.[19]

     Two weeks after the governor signed the Prohibition en-
forcement bill into law, a decision of the United States
Supreme Court rendered it inoperative. Although it had not
been in effect long enough for New York to be a party to the
litigation, the state enactment was clearly unconstitutional
in the light of the *National Prohibition Cases*. In a majority
opinion, which touched upon the aspects of Prohibition that had
engendered controversy in the legislative session, the Court
ruled: that the Eighteenth Amendment had been duly ratified;
that it conferred upon Congress authority to define intoxicating beverages; that the Volstead Act represented a legitimate exercise of such authority; and that the concurrent power
clause did not give the states the right to act contrary to

congressional legislation. With the invalidation of the New
York statute, William H. Anderson importuned the governor to
put the question of a replacement on the agenda of the special
session of the legislature, convening to consider the housing
shortage. A failure to do so suggested to the Anti-Saloon
League superintendent that Smith was soliciting "wet campaign
funds to re-elect yourself and elect Governor Cox, the Tammany
candidate for President."[20]

Because the party's presidential and gubernatorial candidates were both wet, a prominent upstate Democrat urged Smith
to conciliate the drys in his choice of a running mate and in
the state platform. The organization ignored the advice of
George Foster Peabody when it wrote a plank favoring modification of the Volstead Act along the lines of the defunct Walker-
Gillett measure. On the campaign trail, Smith repeatedly advocated congressional revision of the National Prohibition Act
at the same time that he dutifully acknowledged the obligation
to obey as long as it remained in force. On the other hand,
he held the federal government responsible for its enforcement
and argued against the enactment of a new state statute. Refusing to trim on the subject of alcohol, the governor explained, "I cannot be wet in a wet territory and a dry in a dry
territory." For his candor, the Anti-Saloon League denounced
him for being "as bad on the Prohibition question as the devil
and the brewers want a public official to be."[21]

The league, which so contemptuously dismissed the Democratic nominee, very shrewdly manipulated his Republican opponent. It intervened in the GOP primary to back George F.
Thompson for governor against Nathan L. Miller, and WCTU president, Ella A. Boole, for the United States Senate against the
incumbent, James W. Wadsworth. Unwilling to accept the verdict
of the Republican voters in favor of the organization candidates, the Anti-Saloon League intimated that, in the general
election, it would support the defeated drys on the Prohibition
ticket. By threatening to divert enough votes to a third party
to deprive the Republicans of victory in November, it tipped

the GOP balance towards Prohibition. The *American Issue* warned
Miller that he had "everything to gain and nothing to lose" by
complying with its demands. As he began to make concessions,
Superintendent Anderson announced that his group "refuses to
throw away its club until after it is certain beyond the possibility of question that it will have further use for it."
Succumbing to the pressure, Miller committed himself, not only
to uphold existing law, but also to support a new state
enforcement statute, the organization of the legislature in
such a way as to assure its passage, and the retention of the
Volstead Act.[22]

     With Miller safely in the dry camp, Anderson's club be-
came a boomerang. If Thompson enjoyed no realistic prospect of
election, the more successful his campaign, the more likely it
would be to encompass Miller's defeat. To avert this possibility, the self-proclaimed moral forces were compromised by
the need to abandon a sincere prohibitionist. They engaged in
double-talk that could hardly conceal the reality of their double-
dealing. Without formally endorsing Miller, the *American Issue*
implied its preference for the regular Republican as it editorialized, "we do not think it will help Senator Thompson or the
cause of Prohibition enforcement . . . to have Al. Smith
elected governor, and that it is Smith's friends who are now
most anxious to have the Senator continue to insist that Judge
Miller's statements are not satisfactory on Prohibition."[23]

     If the election returns, in which Thompson ran far be-
hind Boole, confirm the impact of the *American Issue* on its
own readership, they also demonstrate that the Anti-Saloon
League did not determine the outcome of the 1920 race in New
York. The Republican landslide, which temporarily retired
Smith from office, sent the dripping wet Wadsworth back to the
Senate with a much wider margin of victory than that with which
the temporizing Miller entered the executive chamber. In the
contest for governor, the Socialist polled $4\frac{1}{2}$ times as many
votes as the Prohibition candidate and more than twice the
plurality by which the Republican defeated the Democrat. It

was not the drys, but the Socialists, who held the balance of
power and diverted votes from Smith, who had so courageously
defended their right to political participation.[24] The election demonstrates that the league used, against the GOP, tactics very similar to those with which William Randolph Hearst
tried to control the Democratic party: in both cases, the
organization was expected to submit rather than face the threat
of an independent ticket with an attraction for its normal constituency. In the candidacy of Boole, the dry slate of 1920
exemplifies the affinity between the movements for temperance
and women's rights.

Although Nathan Miller did not owe his election to the
drys, he had made them campaign promises on which he had to
deliver. Consequently, the Republican governor proposed and
his first legislative session adopted an enforcement measure
that conformed to the requirements of the Anti-Saloon League.
The Mullan-Gage Act defined intoxicating beverages in the
language of the Volstead Act, levied stiff penalties for violation, and relied on local authorities to enforce the law.
Under the GOP administration, New York joined an array of
states that maintained Prohibition with rigorous legislation,
inadequate appropriations, and lax enforcement.[25]

Prohibition figured prominently in the 1922 election in
New York, but the Mullan-Gage Act, despite its subsequent political significance, received scant attention in the course of
the campaign. Having satisfied the drys by its passage, the
Republicans omitted all reference to Prohibition from their
platform, in an effort to placate the wets. As they had two
years earlier, the Democrats favored revision of the Volstead
Act to permit the traffic in beer and wine. In both campaigns,
Smith stood openly for modification; nevertheless, some party
functionaries believed that he had tried to suppress the plank,
which might embarrass him in his quest for national office, but
a participant in the convention confirmed the role of the
governor in drafting the paragraph, which was fully consonant
with his public statements.[26]

From the Democratic proposal to petition Congress to
liberalize the Volstead Act, Miller inferred an intention to
deceive the voters into believing that the victory of his rival
would render beer and wine available. Smith charged his opponent with distorting the Democratic position in order to evade
an unequivocal stand. The Republican's views however were
clear enough for the Anti-Saloon League to endorse him. Drys
who were contemplating a vote for Smith were admonished by the
American Issue, "See how it looks when you try to pray about
it, and act accordingly." The editor was a man of little
faith, for he armed himself with a convenient rationalization
in the event of a GOP defeat. According to him, wet Republicans were conspiring to sabotage Miller's campaign, blame his
loss on the drys, and wrest control of the organization from
the moral forces.[27] However farfetched this explanation,
Smith's victory did strengthen the wets in the GOP and paved
the way for the surprising session of 1923.

By enhancing his presidential prospects, reelection inevitably posed the question of the impact of Prohibition on
Smith's political future. The *New York Times* speculated on the
intention of Republican lawmakers to repeal the Mullan-Gage
Act and to place him in the unenviable position of antagonizing
either New York wets by a veto or southern Democrats by a
signature. As a member of the Democratic National Committee,
Norman Mack, publisher of the *Buffalo Times*, calculated that
the southerners would not desert the party over Prohibition,
as long as they could preserve states' rights on the Negro
question. In contrast to Mack, who supported repeal, Louis M.
Antisdale of the *Rochester Herald* advised the governor to call
for minor revisions in the state enforcement statute, a petition to Congress for modification of the national law, and a
statewide referendum, which would confirm popular discontent
with the Volstead Act.[28]
When the legislature convened, Smith recommended precisely what his party's platform had advocated: a memorial

asking Congress to change the Volstead Act to legalize wine and
beer. As the joint resolution for this purpose was progressing
through the legislature, the assembly amended the text to require the governor to transmit the petition to the members of
Congress. Because of the obvious design to embarrass Smith
with the unprecedented executive involvement in a legislative
resolution, a democratic member of the lower house accused the
majority of "playing cheap politics." In the course of debate,
Senator Lusk remarked that the change was slight, to which
Senator Walker rejoined, "but the slight was meant for the
Governor." While the matter was under consideration, Smith declared, "if the Republicans haven't nerve enough to go through
with this themselves, and . . . want to shift responsibility to
me, I'll sign it for them. . . . I never yet recommended anything that I was not willing to go through with." To a minister
who objected to the pending resolution, Smith explained, "The
present condition is intolerable. Prohibition seems to have
been impossible of enforcement. Light wines and beer would be
the solution. . . ."[29]

     The proposal to modify the Volstead Act attracted a great
deal of attention, not all of it favorable. Asked to comment
on a New Jersey senator's effort to implement the resolution,
Smith responded offhandedly, "I will be glad to go down and
help him put over his bill if that will get us somewhere where
we can put a foot on the rail again and blow off the froth."
The governor drew a rebuke from both Ohio senators, one of whom
admonished New York "to obey the law and the Constitution
rather than by subterfuge to break down the one and nullify
the other just for the ephemeral, evanescent pleasure of 'putting its foot on the rail and blowing off the foam.'" His
assertion that "As a matter of fact, beer and wine are intoxicating . . ." underlay the dry contention that the desired
change in the National Prohibition Act was tantamount to nullification and that the only way to legalize beer and wine was to
repeal the Eighteenth Amendment. Smith vehemently denied that

he was advocating evasion of either the law or the Constitution,
which banned, not alcoholic, but *intoxicating* drinks, a distinction that justified the resolution he had forwarded to Congress.
"We ask for a reasonable congressional interpretation of what
constitutes an intoxicating beverage," he maintained. As for
his well-publicized nostalgia for the barroom, he could not
claim to be misquoted, but he dismissed it as a jest, mis-
construed by a journalist without a sense of humor.[30] When a
representative from the Buckeye State took up the cry that
modification of the Volstead Act was unconstitutional, the
governor's secretary retorted in exasperation, "you have never
read, and so do not understand the wording of the Eighteenth
Amendment." Amidst the barrage of congressional criticism,
Smith received many expressions of support from, for example,
Representatives John C. Schafer of Wisconsin, C. A. Newton of
Missouri, Frank J. McNulty of New Jersey, and Senator Thomas F.
Bayard of Delaware. From the New York delegation, Congressman
Emanuel Celler wrote Smith to "congratulate you upon your
courage," James Mead expressed a "desire to compliment the
Governor . . . for securing the adoption of the above mentioned
resolutions," and Sol Bloom offered to sponsor them in the
House of Representatives.[31]

     If New York's Democratic congressmen were receptive to
the governor's proposal, her Republican legislators perceived
an advantage in concentrating on state action. In the words of
a GOP assemblyman, "instead of asking Congress to do something
let's set a good example . . . and do away with our present
State enforcement law." The Republican lawmakers echoed their
defeated gubernatorial candidate in interpreting Smith's stand
for modification of the Volstead Act as an implied promise to
give the people wine and beer and, therefore, to repeal the
Mullan-Gage Act. As one of them explained, "if the Governor
did not say it in so many words, he permitted the voters to
infer that he favored the repeal of the Mullan-Gage Act." It
was precisely because the state lacked jurisdiction and only
the national government could legalize wine and beer, that

Smith advocated petitioning Congress to alter the statutory
definition of intoxicating beverages. The governor's office
made a point of reminding correspondents that the Democratic
platform "did not declare in favor of the repeal of the Mullan-
Gage Act. It did declare in the liberalization of the Volstead
Act. . . ."[32]

"Despite what Governor Smith said in his message that the
only relief from the prohibition law was through the National
Congress," Assemblyman Louis Cuvillier insisted on introducing
a bill for repeal of the Mullan-Gage Act, in the belief that
his constituents desired it. Democrats sponsored repeal in
both chambers, but they needed Republican votes for passage in
the lower house. The Anti-Saloon League was no more successful in getting the GOP to caucus to compel its members to block
the Cuvillier bill than it had been in stopping the joint
resolution for modification of the Volstead Act. Republicans
representing the cities combined with Democrats to revoke the
Prohibition enforcement statute, and just before adjournment,
the legislature placed the controversial matter in the lap of
the chief executive.[33]

It is not clear how vigorously Smith intervened to avert
this outcome, which was a source of embarrassment to him.
After the introduction of the Cuvillier bill, the governor "had
quietly done what he could to prevent its passage" by pressing
lawmakers from dry areas upstate to vote against it, according
to Edward J. Flynn. But James A. Farley, who was one of them,
has given conflicting testimony on a conference at which Smith
"talked freely" but did not either give the legislators advice
on how to vote "or disclose what course he himself intended to
pursue." He would not have been displeased by the defeat of
repeal, the future postmaster general inferred, "thus saving
him from the necessity of taking action."[34]

Conflicting goals rendered the necessity unpleasant. The
governor's sympathies lay with the wets from whom he derived
his basic support, both in the electorate at large and in the
Democratic party of his own state. The recent election however

had encouraged presidential ambitions for which he needed the
vote of a Solid South that was predominately dry. A friendly
correspondent perceptively analyzed his dilemma:

> If you have in mind . . . political preferment
> of the highest offices—Governor, the United States
> Senate or any other at the disposal of the people
> of New York State—your approval will go a long ways
> toward continuing your present phenomenal strength.
> If on the other hand you are amenable to the wishes
> of your friends who regard you as preeminently fit-
> ted for the nation's consideration when the 1924
> ticket is to be made up, then a veto would be for-
> tunate.

Because of the political implications, the bill in question
probably generated more mail than any other in Smith's career.
There was no way to give consideration to all of the letters—
except on scales—suggested one wit. "But don't say too much
about that," Smith rejoined, "for they might write them on
heavier paper."[35]

Considerable publicity attended the communications of
Dr. Wesley Wait, who wrote both to Governor Smith and to President Harding to denounce the Cuvillier bill as a violation of
federal authority. The Newburgh dentist likened repeal of the
Mullan-Gage Act to nullification, secession, and treason. To
his amusement, Smith read that other residents of the city on
the Hudson considered his correspondent something of a crank.
The president however took the occasion of his reply to Wait
to exert pressure for a veto. Harding professed himself "fully
in accord" with many of the dentist's observations and alluded
to the inevitable difficulties "if any of the States shall decline to assume their part of the responsibility of maintaining
the Constitution and the laws enacted in pursuance of it."
Despite the implications of the president's remarks, the concurrent power clause of the Eighteenth Amendment did not mandate state enforcement legislation, Smith was assured by a
group of legal authorities, who found ample justification for
repeal of the New York law.[36]

The advice that Smith received in this predicament is
more interesting for what it reveals of the authors than for

any calculable way it influenced his decision. Like many
others who favored a veto of the bill for repeal of the Mullan-
Gage Act, Franklin Delano Roosevelt fully appreciated the
governor's problem. "I am mighty sorry for the extremely difficult position in which you have been placed over this darned
old liquor question," the future president commiserated. But
he added:

> Frankly, it is going to hurt you nationally a
> whole lot to sign the Repealer Bill. This information
> comes from people who like you a lot and admire you a
> lot. . . . Incidentally, they are quite powerful in
> national affairs. On the other hand I well realize
> that the vote in all the cities of this state will
> shriek to heaven if you veto the Bill.

Charles E. Treman, a New Yorker prominent in Democratic affairs,
agreed with FDR that the measure in question would encourage
defiance of the law of the land and feared that it would jeopardize the party's success upstate. Frank E. Gannett, who
published a chain of newspapers in the area, advised Smith to
exercise his veto and threatened, "If he should sign this bill
I don't see how it would be possible for us to lend him any
support in the future." A reporter, who accepted the chief
executive's invitation to state his views, pronounced the
legislative action "a fake remedy for a real demand." Irving
Fisher, the Yale economist who announced in 1929 that the stock
market had attained a permanently high plateau, in 1923 instructed Smith "that Prohibition does represent the view of
the great majority." At Harvard Law School, Felix Frankfurter
observed, "Undoubtedly Smith is 'damned if he does and damned
if he doesn't.' But I venture to say that if he vetoes the
repeal, he will be damned for a comparatively brief time but
if he signs it, he is damned for good." A professional
authority on salvation, Father George Zurcher, warned Smith
that his signature would provide justification for the derogatory slogan, "Rum, Romanism, and Rebellion." Opponents of the
bill appealed to Smith's ambition, when they argued that it
would cost him presidential votes, and to his sense of justice,

when they insisted that it would condone violations of Prohibition.[37]

     In contrast to the supporters of the Mullan-Gage Act,
those who wanted Smith to approve its repeal tended to be less
abstemious in their personal habits, more urban in orientation,
and, if New Yorkers, more likely to be involved in New York
City than upstate politics. They argued that the states were
bound, neither morally nor legally, to supplement federal enforcement and that disrespect for the law was attributable to,
not the absence of state, but the absurdity of national, legislation. As for Prohibition, "its handservants are bribery,
chicanery, and deceit," charged Congressman Celler, who informed Smith that Georgia was enforcing the Fourteenth and
Fifteenth Amendments no better than New York, the Eighteenth.
Jim Farley reminded the executive staff that "The real fellows
who vote our ticket and work for it want the Governor to sign
the bill." According to George Olvany, resistance to Prohibition was a source of strength for the Democratic party in New
York and enabled it to make inroads among wet Republicans. One
of them confirmed Smith's popularity in the unlikely precincts
of the Union League Club and reflected on the inconsistency of
the president who insisted on enforcing the Eighteenth, but
not the Fifteenth Amendment. Warren Worth Bailey, a former
representative from Pennsylvania, and William Cabell Bruce,
senator from Maryland, both denounced the federal government
for attempting to shift to the states the responsibility for
enforcement of its own ill-conceived statute. Sending regrets
that he could not attend the governor's hearing on repeal of
the Mullan-Gage Act, Samuel Gompers expressed the hope of
workingmen that repeal of the state law would lead to modification of the federal, so that they could drink "a glass of
wholesome beer with their meals" and enjoy it "without being
law violators."[38]

     Never in his political career had Smith appeared so in-
decisive and irritable as in the interval between adjournment
and the public hearing. He was noncommittal when he left the

city for a fortnight's holiday and equally so when he returned
in a week, thereby giving rise to speculation on the reasons
for curtailing his vacation. The Coney Island Board of Trade
presented him with a set of golf clubs and the wish that he
hit the ball as hard as the Mullan-Gage Act; he expressed his
thanks in a speech in which he hedged, ". . . I will do the
best I can to sustain and uphold the Constitution of the United
States and the law of this country." His trial balloon, if
such it was, provoked one Tammany chieftain to threaten, "Let
him depend upon William H. Anderson . . . in his Presidential
campaign." Whatever his decision, another affirmed that "it
will make no difference in his relations with Tammany Hall."[39]

When he was conducting the scheduled hearing however, the
governor was reminded, "you are asked to veto that bill by
people who never gave you their support and never will." The
spokesmen for repeal concentrated their attention on the ramifications for civil liberties and on the problem of double
jeopardy, which arose when the same offense was punishable
under both state and federal law. The organized support for
repeal came to a considerable extent from the trade unions.
In addition to such obvious elements as the Anti-Saloon League,
the leading proponents of a veto included federal officials and
representatives of the League of Women Voters and the Women's
City Club. They argued primarily on the grounds of law and
order. One speaker presented the alternatives as a choice
between the Constitution and a cocktail, "The Star Spangled
Banner" and "The Sidewalks of New York." The hearing on repeal
of the Mullan-Gage Act was atypical because of the numbers in
attendance, the high proportion of women among them, and the
silence of Smith who, on this occasion, gave no indication of
his intentions.[40]

Competing claims temporarily immobilized the governor,
for a signature that accorded well with his own inclinations
and the will of his Tammany supporters would antagonize the
party's dry wing, without whose help he could not hope to gain
the presidency. Contemporaries gave conflicting accounts of

the effect of the mutually inconsistent pressures on the
decision-making process. Edward Flynn recollected a conference
at which Boss Murphy threatened to abandon his protégé in the
event of a veto. George Foster Peabody however believed a veto
to be contrary to Smith's own convictions and declined to
recommend one, because "I could not in conscience myself ask
him to do anything which, if he did, I would feel bound to have
less respect for him." Although she herself favored Prohibition, Eleanor Roosevelt assured the governor "that I know
whichever way you decide you will do so because to you it seems
the right thing to do" and confided, "It is rather wonderful to
feel about anyone . . . whatever they do will be according to
honest conviction, unbiased by political pressure or motives
of expediency." From his old friend and political opponent,
Senator Brackett, Smith received the advice, "don't worry now.
You decide as you think is right. . . ." After giving his
approval to the repealer, the chief executive affirmed, "I am
satisfied it was the right thing."[41]

It was a visible relief to the governor to sign the bill
after four weeks of vacillation and a sleepless night following
the hearing. The outcome elicited from Will Rogers the observation, "He didn't have to get all those people up there to
make up his mind for him. We will see now whether he lands in
the White House or the Ash heap. Sentiment in this Country is
overwhelmingly wet. But the Votes in this Country are overwhelmingly Dry."[42]

The memorandum of approval was initially drafted before
the May 31 hearing, which resulted in some changes. Aided by
his secretary, his counsel, and Belle Moskowitz, the governor
worked on the document into the wee hours of the morning on
two consecutive days. Smith dictated the first draft on the
afternoon of Memorial Day and, in consultation with the others,
spent the night revising it. After the governor had presided
over the five-hour hearing, they gathered for a second all-
night session to produce the final version. In composing the
document, Smith consulted a brief by Proskauer, and both of

them used the arguments of the members of bar and bench who had
challenged Harding on the obligations of states under the
Eighteenth Amendment.[43]

His reliance on lawyers accounts for the legalistic
quality of what was probably the longest memorandum that the
governor filed on any bill. In it, he denied that the Constitution imposed upon the states the necessity of adopting enforcement legislation to supplement the Volstead Act or any
other federal statute. A failure to do so however should not
be construed as encouragement to defy the federal law that remained in full force. Smith reminded New Yorkers that repeal
of the Mullan-Gage Act "will not make legal a single act which
was illegal" or "bring back light wines and beer." For this
purpose, he continued to advocate modification of the Volstead
Act. If rescinding the state enforcement law did not relieve
its citizens of obedience to Prohibition, it did eliminate the
danger of double jeopardy for acts of disobedience. Although
his memorandum dealt primarily with the legal and constitutional implications of his action, the governor could not overlook the speculation on its political consequences. With
reference to them, he observed, "I have no political future
that I am willing to attain by the sacrifice of any principle
or . . . what in my mind is for the welfare and the benefit of
this State and Nation."[44]

In reaction to Smith's decision as well as in anticipation of it, political calculation was inevitable. For example,
James Roosevelt Roosevelt wrote the governor "to take my hat
off to you for signing that Mullan Gage repeal," counted him
among the few politicians "who will stand up to their convictions, and the wishes of the people, regardless of the consequences," and acknowledged, "As to those consequences Frank and
I have had some hot arguments. . . . there is not one per
cent of that d - - lot of fanatics and hypocrites . . . who
would vote for you anyway." In contrast, William Jennings
Bryan asserted, "Governor Smith has heard from those who love
to lean on the bar and blow the foam off, the 'boys' who long

for the beer mugs as the children of Israel longed for the
fleshpots of Egypt, but he has not yet heard from the women
whose husbands wasted at the saloon the money that belonged to
the family." Smith, in turn, compared his own election with
the other's perennial candidacy and retorted, "a wise and discriminating electorate usually takes care to see that Mr. Bryan
stays at home."[45]

No single action of Governor Smith aroused as much speculation on his presidential prospects as the signing of the
Cuvillier bill. No other action of the chief executive who reformed the state administration, advanced welfare legislation,
and defended civil liberties was at once so widely publicized
and essentially trivial. Given the facts of constitutional
Prohibition and congressional legislation, repeal of the Mullan-
Gage Act had largely symbolic value. Smith saw no good reason
to veto a measure that coincided with his views on states'
rights, his respect for civil liberties, and his distaste for
Prohibition. One must agree with his admirers who attributed
to conviction rather than expediency the decision to sign the
repealer, for he rarely hesitated to take an unpopular stand,
for example in his defiance of the Red Scare. On the Cuvillier
bill furthermore political considerations cut both ways,
affording certain disadvantages no matter what he did. Meanwhile, New Yorkers violated Prohibition with more or less im-
punity, with and without a state enforcement law, and under
Republican and Democratic administrations alike.

The politics of Prohibition reached a climax in New York
with repeal of the Mullan-Gage Act; thereafter, the question
assumed diminishing importance with the passage of time. Still,
enforcement remained an issue.

In the fall of 1923, Smith attended a governors' conference on Prohibition enforcement held in Washington, D.C.
under the auspices of the federal government. There, he heard
President Calvin Coolidge allude to the Mullan-Gage Act when he
remarked, with reference to the states, that "there is still on

them a joint responsibility to enact and execute enforcement
laws." In contrast, Governor Smith attributed the difficulties
with enforcement, not to the lack of state legislation, but to
the unrealistic definition of intoxicants and to the laxity of
federal authorities. Those present at the gathering agreed on
a recommendation for similar meetings at the state and local
level to deal with the problem.[46]

Consequently, Smith presided over a conference on Prohibition enforcement, held in Albany early in 1924. Palmer
Canfield, federal Prohibition director for New York, took the
initiative in proposing and arranging for the meeting, for
which he secured the governor's cooperation. While they were
laying their plans, the federal official assured the state
executive "that no mention is made of a State Prohibition law
because in the interest of co-operation it would seem desirable
to avoid anything of a political or partisan nature." In his
own address, Canfield abided by his conciliatory policy; but
the United States district attorney complained that repeal of
the Mullan-Gage Act struck "the hardest blow" that the Eighteenth Amendment had sustained, demanded the restoration of the
repealed statute, and protested that "it is idle to talk of
real enforcement without a State law." The governor resented
the insinuation that he was to blame for the widespread evasion
of the law. In his closing remarks, he emphasized the obligation of citizens to obey, and of officials to enforce, the
law and placed responsibility primarily on local and national
administrations, both of which were only too reluctant to
appropriate sufficient funds for this purpose. He could not
conceal his skepticism of Canfield's program for effective
enforcement—"without expense to the State." On the subject of
money, he observed, "Our great weakness is that we have got so
many people . . . who talk dry, but who don't act that way."[47]

Both contemporary and later analyses have tended to confirm Smith's conclusion that Americans got as much Prohibition
as they wanted and were willing to pay for. In 1931, the
National Commission on Law Observance and Enforcement, generally

known as the Wickersham commission, reported that the cooperation recieved by federal authorities "depends largely upon
public sentiment in the particular community" and that New York,
which was located in the nation's "wettest section socially and
politically, and the most difficult from the standpoint of prohibition law enforcement," exhibited a great deal of regional
variation. Historians have shown that neither the dry communities nor "The Amphibious Congress" spent much money on enforcement. If local option still prevailed, a recent study has suggested that Prohibition did reduce the amount of drinking and
raise the standard of living in the workingclass.[48]

The Albany conference, which Smith expected to improve
his image on Prohibition enforcement, encouraged his Republican
opponents to propose a new state law. It suffered the fate of
many bills in his second administration when each party controlled one house of the legislature. In 1924, a Prohibition
measure passed the assembly but not the senate.[49] The Anti-
Saloon League lost influence during the governor's second term
as one legislative session repealed the Mullan-Gage Act and
another declined to replace it.

The group's precipitate fall from grace resulted from
legal action against both the New York Anti-Saloon League and
its superintendent. Although the case against the league for
violating its charter by engaging in politics did not hold up
in court, a jury convicted William H. Anderson of forgery in
handling the association's financial records. Whether sympathetic or hostile to him, students of the sensational trial
believe that it ended in a miscarriage of justice, but convey
the impression that the defendant told something less than the
whole truth on the witness stand. They do suggest that his
uninhibited attacks on the Democratic organization, the
Catholic Church, and New York City had created many enemies
who were ready to believe the worst and therefore eager to
prosecute. During the pretrial investigation, he had alternately charged the district attorney, the governor, and
various legislators with conspiring to persecute him for poli-

tical advantage. Since Anderson had engineered much of the
league's success in the Empire State, his downfall contributed
to its growing impotence. After his release from Sing Sing,
he worked for the American Protestant Protective Alliance,
which mingled nativism with the cause of Prohibition.[50]

In its prejudice against Catholics and its antipathy to
drinking, the alliance symbolized the forces that denied the
Democratic presidential nomination to Smith in 1924. James A.
Farley did not exhibit his famed political acumen after the
signing of the Cuvillier bill when he predicted that Smith
would gain the designation and go on to win the election. Donn
Neal has demonstrated that the governor entered the race, less
with the hope of getting on the ticket that year than of
keeping William Gibbs McAdoo off. President Wilson's son-in-
law was persona non grata to the city machines because of his
support for Prohibition and his endorsement by the Klan. Although religion and alcohol both weighed against Smith at the
convention in Madison Square Garden, Robert K. Murray believed
that Prohibition was the more important of the two and an issue
that historians have often underestimated. The governor owed
his defeat to qualities that "may have put Smith in tune with
the sidewalks of New York," but "jarred on Main Street," and
exacerbated the cultural divisions in the Democratic organization. According to David Burner, urban working-class voters,
who defected from the GOP in the twenties, shifted their
allegiance to the Progressive party in 1924 before giving it
to the Democrats in later years.[51] The cities did posses
sufficient strength however to deprive McAdoo of the nomination
and to reelect Governor Smith.

In the state contest, Smith ran on a platform that
promised "a continuance of the policy of enforcement of every
law" at the same time that it exhorted Congress to modify the
Volstead Act. This would mean, he told an audience in Elmira,
"that Kansas can be as dry as Sahara . . . and New York can
have light wines and beer of a non-intoxicating character."
Speaking in the same community, Theodore Roosevelt, Jr.

affirmed his willingness to sign a new enforcement statute. Even this address did not satisfy the Anti-Saloon League, which deplored his legislative record and suspected him of equivocation. Only when he committed himself to the precise measure sponsored by the dry group, did it offer him its belated endorsement. Despite the intervention of the Anti-Saloon League, the Republican lost by a narrow margin, which led H. L. Mencken to observe, "this grossly corrupt and evil organization came very near getting control of the State of New York . . . . It was defeated only by the great popularity of the Hon. Al Smith. That is to say, it was defeated only by the votes of Jews and Catholics, neither of whom, by the current dogma, ought to be allowed to vote at all."[52]

The election put the GOP in control of both houses and therefore in a position to confront the governor with a new enforcement bill. But the Republican leadership resisted the pressure from the drys for the necessary caucus at the same time that the chief executive repulsed any suggestion that he reverse himself. To one advocate, he digressed on the hypocrisy of the moral forces as he commented, "I hope you will note that the so-called 'righteous gentlemen' who propose a new state enforcement law do not provide for the appropriation of a single dollar to make it effective." Even without any provision for expenditures, the Wales-Jenks bill failed in the senate after passing in the assembly in both sessions of Smith's third term.[53]

It is indicative of the growing ascendancy of wets within the GOP that by 1926 they commanded the votes, not only to block enforcement legislation, but also to adopt a proposal for a referendum. If the governor signed the Karle-Phelps bill, the November ballot would include a proposition, asking the voters whether or not to petition Congress to exempt from Prohibition fermented drinks, "which are not in fact intoxicating as determined in accordance with the laws of the respective states." In short, did they favor the modification of the Volstead Act, which Smith had long been advocating and which

many New York representatives in Washington were now sponsoring?[54]

The fact that the governor's attitude on the subject was
well known did not deter partisans on both sides from offering
him advice. Louis Marshall, who gave invaluable service in the
fight for public power, took fifteen pages to explain why the
referendum and what it proposed were unconstitutional. Another
lawyer reassured the chief executive on the constitutionality
of the measure; an assemblyman, who supported it, divided New
Yorkers into two categories: "those who have a little still
and those who still have a little."[55]

Desirous of playing for a veto against all odds, the New
York State Civic League took the initiative in requesting a
hearing. Inevitably, the governor's hearing on the Karle-
Phelps bill invoked comparison with the one three years earlier
on the Cuvillier bill. In contrast to the previous occasion,
the participants contended with civility, the wets outnumbered
the drys, and the former enjoyed the benefits of organization
in the Moderation League and the Association Opposed to the
Prohibition Amendment. Smith himself appeared at ease and
communicative as he engaged the prohibitionists in spirited
repartée over the alcoholic content of intoxicating liquor and
the potability of 2.75 beer. The referendum procedure appealed
to him on democratic principles, particularly in a situation
where inequitable apportionment gave the drys an unfair advantage in the legislature. He even suggested resort to the convention method for repeal of the Eighteenth Amendment, if
Congress defied the popular will on wine and beer. Recognizing
that their presence might be counterproductive, Anti-Saloon
League officials did not even attend the governor's hearing to
protest the bill. His signature, upon adjournment, was a foregone conclusion.[56]

With the Prohibition question before the electorate, the
Republicans urged the people to vote in the referendum and the
Democrats urged them to vote yes. Because the GOP platform
hedged on the referendum and promised to uphold "the cause of

law and order," the *Times* summarized the party's convention as
running a wet ticket on a dry platform. But the reporter did
not measure humidity with the same instrument as the Anti-
Saloon League whose counsel, Wayne B. Wheeler, condemned the
Prohibition plank as evidence of the "depravity to which political leaders in a State like New York will bend for the booze
vote."[57]

The candidates for governor could not evade the issue
raised by the proposition on the ballot. Ogden L. Mills defended the referendum against the objections of the Anti-Saloon
League and accepted its outcome as a mandate, either to reenact
a state enforcement statute, or to press for revision of the
federal statute. Smith embarrassed his opponent by exposing
the split in Republican ranks that accounted for the party's
inconsistency on Prohibition, which he dramatized in a scenario
entitled "The Hypocrisy, Double-Dealing and Double-Crossing of
the Republican State Machine." The governor, who was committed
to an affirmative position, inquired, "how does Congressman
Mills advise his followers to vote on this Referendum?"[58] He
responded, ". . . I would not even advise my wife," but acknowledged that he intended to vote yes. As if to compensate, he
launched into strictures on law enforcement with the implication that the incumbent was responsible for the notorious violation of the liquor law.[59]

Despite his promise to improve enforcement, Ogden
Livingston Mills was the only one of Smith's challengers who
failed to adjust his stand on Prohibition in order to curry
favor with the Anti-Saloon League. The beverage that figured
in the congressman's campaign was not alcoholic—but bovine,
as he revived the milk issue, apparently under the impression
that the Hearst press influenced more votes than the *American
Issue*. The dry journal detected no difference on Prohibition
between Smith and Mills. When an independent dry candidate
withdrew from the race, the Anti-Saloon League declined to
support the Prohibition party nominee for governor.[60] Realistically anticipating a Smith victory that it was powerless

to avert, the pressure group maneuvered to avoid the appearance of defeat.

In its effort to rule or ruin the GOP, the league concentrated on depriving James W. Wadsworth of his seat in the United States Senate even though his Democratic rival, Robert F. Wagner, was equally unsatisfactory on the "moral issue." For this purpose, the dry organization backed Franklin W. Cristman on the Independent Republican line. The regular Republican, whose ancestors settled New England and fought in the American Revolution, had befriended Smith when the city man was an obscure assemblyman and the upstate landholder, Speaker of the lower house. Mutual respect and friendship did not prevent the two from differing in politics, for Wadsworth was a conservative Republican who opposed woman suffrage, the child labor amendment, and progressive taxation. Their relation nevertheless sparked rumors of a deal in which they would undermine their respective running mates. Still professing his personal admiration, Smith called for the senator's retirement, "because he does not fairly represent in my opinion, the progressive thought of the state." Although this statement squelched much of the talk, the *American Issue* continued to harp on the story of an unholy coalition, not only in the prose of its editorial pages, but also in doggerel:

> Hello old top! I'm Jimmie,
> The friend of your friend Al.
> Although he's not a gentleman
> He is a useful Pal.
> Who runs against the one of us
> The other'll make run slowly,
> Ogden will follow Theodore
> And hunt the "ovis poli."[61]

With some justification, the drys could claim credit for the defeat of Wadsworth—but not of Mills. Smith polled a clear majority of the votes cast while his running mate won only by a plurality far smaller than the total received by Cristman. Nevertheless, the *American Issue* attributed Smith's success to the Republican failure to satisfy the dry constituency "when Governor Whitman faltered . . . , when Governor

Miller failed to maintain a fortright [sic] attitude on the
subject of prohibition, when Theodore Roosevelt, Jr., trimmed
. . . and made a plea for wet votes in New York city and dry
votes up-state."[62]

The Anti-Saloon League perceived a victory for Prohibition, not only in Republican defeats, but also in the referendum—which recorded 1,763,070 ballots for modification of the
Volstead Act, 598,484 against, and 546,236 blank or void! With
some temperance groups boycotting the referendum, the drys had
acted in advance to discredit it and discount its results.
With a remarkable capacity for self-deception, they subsequently
tabulated in their putative dry majority, not only those who
voted no, but also those who refrained from balloting on the
proposition, the registered voters who did not go to the polls,
and the eligible voters who had failed to register. Referenda
in eight states disclosed five, among them New York, with public opinion in favor of modification. To Smith, unlike the
Anti-Saloon League, these elections demonstrated that if the
will of the people were to prevail, "we should see the end of
prohibition."[63]

Encouraged by the referendum, the governor appealed to
the legislature to renew its petition to Congress to amend the
National Prohibition Act. In 1927, the lawmakers complied
without the political posturing that had accompanied a similar
resolution four years earlier. Furthermore, state enforcement
legislation, which was introduced in Smith's final term, made
no headway in the legislature. The wets had gained enough
ground in the GOP to avert the passage of such a measure, which
shortly before his presidential campaign, would have confronted
Smith with a decision as distasteful as that on repeal of the
Mullan-Gage Act.[64] Because he had approved that bill, his
opponents continued to blame him for the endemic lawlessness.
But it is fair to conclude that the degree of compliance with
Prohibition was a cause—not an effect—of legislation in New
York.

In the Smith administration, Prohibition proved to be a distraction that affected politics more than government and national more than state politics. Smith agonized over the Mullan-Gage bill because of the impact of his decision, not on the life of the people of New York, but on his presidential prospects. Prohibition was an element in the complex of cultural values dividing the Democrats in their marathon convention of 1924 where Smith wrestled McAdoo to a deadlock. At a reunion of delegates to the 1915 constitutional convention, the master of ceremonies introduced the governor with the remark that unless the Democratic organization "wishes to go down to deserved defeat as the party of sumptuary law and religious intolerance, he will soon be nominated for President of the United States."[65]

Regardless of the politics of Prohibition, Smith perceived it as a genuine civil liberties issue. Few in the metropolitan, working-class, ethnic milieu that nurtured him considered drinking sinful in an age when devout Catholics like the governor took sin as seriously as the evangelical Protestants who led the dry crusade. Under Prohibition, government interfered with the personal behavior of citizens who accepted drinking as a normal part of private life, and many showed their resentment by defiance of the law.

Was Al Smith one of them? Probably, although on the matter of his personal habits, it is hard to distinguish fact from rumor. FDR was presumably knowledgeable when he reported that Smith, like his peers, was accustomed to drinking beer, that he experimented with whiskey during Prohibition, but that it was groundless to fear that "he has ever been or would ever be a drunkard." In his administration, the Executive Mansion "was never exactly arid," according to Ed Flynn, who told an anecdote about being assigned to detain the visiting Josephus Daniels, a prominent dry, until the evidence of conviviality could be cleared away. The editor of the *Nation* professed admiration of Smith for refusing to be a hypocrite like the myriads of politicians who voted dry and drank.[66]

Because Smith was an outspoken wet, historians must cal-
culate the politics of Prohibition in explaining his failure to
be elected president. It is possible to maintain, as some
scholars have done, that Prohibition was largely irrelevant,
that the GOP took credit for prosperity, and that no Democrat
would have won in 1928. One can discount the liquor issue also
by suggesting that it served many drys as a smoke screen to conceal the religious prejudice behind their opposition to Smith.
Still another view recognizes the genuine convictions that motivated prohibitionists to oppose a prominent wet. It is also
reasonable to identify Prohibition as a symbol of the differences between competing subcultures that were fractionating the
Democratic party and the electorate in 1928. On the eve of
the election, H. L. Mencken had the last word:

> If Al wins tomorrow, it will be because the American
> people have decided at last to vote as they drink,
> and because a majority of them believe that the
> Methodist bishops are worse than the Pope. If he
> loses, it will be because those who fear the Pope
> outnumber those who are tired of the Anti-Saloon
> League.
> . . . .
>   There remain only Prohibition and religion, or
> more accurately, only religion, for Prohibition, in
> the dry areas, has long ceased to be a question of
> government or even of ethics, and has become purely
> theological.[67]

If the drys enjoyed a triumph in 1928, it was a pyrrhic
victory and the beginning of the end of Prohibition. Although
FDR had advised Smith to moderate his views and cultivate the
drys, the new governor differed from his predecessor less in
substance than in tact. If Governor Roosevelt preached law
enforcement, he made no move to revive a state Prohibition
statute. As the presidency came within his grasp, he favored
repeal of the Eighteenth Amendment and states' rights, which he
took care to explain would accommodate the feelings of dry
constituencies as well as wet. One historian has added repeal
to relief, recovery, and reform as categories of New Deal
action and goals of liberalism in the thirties.[68] After

Roosevelt's inauguration in Washington, modification of the
Volstead Act and repeal of the Prohibition amendment followed
in quick succession. Here as elsewhere, the breach between
Smith and Roosevelt has tended to obscure the continuities between the respective administrations.

CHAPTER 11

SUMMONS TO THE WIDER FIELD OF ACTION

On August 22, 1928 at the Capitol, where he had first been inaugurated as governor of New York State nearly ten years before, Alfred Emanuel Smith formally accepted the Democratic nomination for president of the United States. The record of the intervening decade had earned him the designation and compelled the party to break with precedent by naming a Roman Catholic as its standard-bearer. Voicing genuine conviction, he affirmed, "with humble reliance upon the aid of Divine Providence, I accept your summons to the wider field of action."[1]

In his address of acceptance, the New Yorker applied to the nation at large the principles of public administration and institutional economics that had guided him in his stewardship of his native state. If his reservations about Prohibition commanded more attention than his pronouncements on important questions of domestic and foreign policy, a similar disproportion had characterized the publicity on his governorship. In the course of his remarks, the Democrat made it clear that he did not share Republican complacency in the prosperity of the twenties. Having condemned the GOP for ignoring the plight of agriculture, labor, and small business, Smith expressed an uneasiness over the growing concentration of wealth. As he surveyed the economy, he identified what would be later recognized as symptoms of the oncoming depression. In contrast to his political opponents, Smith called for government that was popular, not elitist; "constructive, not destructive; progressive, not reactionary." Endowing his generalizations with meaning, he averred support specifically for public power, the vetoed farm bills, and "progressive legislation for the protection and advancement of working men and women." Unconscious of inconsistency, the speaker ascribed his political faith to "the idealism of the party of Jefferson, Cleveland, and Wilson," for in Smith's mind, the presidents symbolized democracy—with a small *d* as well as a large.[2]

Not long after the New Yorker's first inauguration,
President Wilson had confided to an anti-Tammany Democrat, "I
hope and believe that you will not be disappointed in Governor
Smith" and characterized the new executive as someone who "feels
in an unusual degree the impulses and compulsions of the changed
order of the nation's and the world's affairs."[3] Smith fulfilled the president's expectation by the way he handled the
immediate problem of postwar reconstruction. Instead of defining reconstruction narrowly in the sense of favors to returning veterans, the governor accepted it as a challenge to
modernize the administration and render it more effective in
assisting all citizens to cope with change. However interpreted,
progressivism and the New Deal both constituted movements to
make government relevant to the realities of life in twentieth
century America. The 1928 candidate demonstrated his capacity
to govern through an administration influenced by progressivism
and anticipating the New Deal, despite his ambivalence toward
the one and his rejection of the other. His career in Albany
places Smith in a reform tradition that extends from progressivism to the New Deal.

Reviewing Smith's legislative career in a 1928 campaign
biography, Franklin Delano Roosevelt found his subject adopting
"what Woodrow Wilson would have called 'liberal thought'" and
emerging "on the side of the progressives."[4] Yet the assemblyman had been ambivalent to Senator Roosevelt and Governor
Hughes and downright antagonistic to the publisher, William
Randolph Hearst, despite the fact that all three men possessed
progressive credentials. These relationships afford insight
into the nature and limitations of Smith's progressivism.

Smith was selective, accepting those elements of progressivism that appealed to him on rational, humanitarian, or expedient (they won votes) grounds and rejecting those that
appeared detrimental to the party to which he owed an intense
loyalty. Hearst's infidelity would have made him anathema even
if he had not been competing with Smith for political prefer-

ment. Given the antiorganization bias of many reformers, Smith
could not be expected to go along with their proposals to undermine the machines in the name of good government and direct
democracy. On the other hand, he approved of home rule as a
distinct benefit to his native city and the referendum as a
technique that he often used to advantage. As chief executive,
he achieved spectacular success in reconstructing the state
government in keeping with the efficiency economy movement,
through changes recommended by Governor Hughes and advanced by
the constitutional convention of 1915.

Smith showed mixed feelings, not only on the governmental,
but also on the economic, programs of the progressive reformers.
If the governor did not share the enthusiasm for trust-busting,
it can be argued that by the twenties economic concentration was
a national problem that defied solution at other levels of administration. Even where monopoly fell within state jurisdiction however, as in the case of the dairy and construction industries, he was unwilling to lose votes by proposing regulation.
On the other hand, for certain natural monopolies, utilities
such as hydroelectricity and city transit, he favored public
ownership. From the Factory Investigating Commission to his
retirement from office, he championed the labor and welfare
legislation that was a hallmark of what scholars have variously
termed social progressivism or urban liberalism. As early as
the constitutional convention, he defended such measures with
a pragmatic rationale that repudiated laissez-faire economics,
conservative Darwinism, and the mechanical jurisprudence.

Students of intellectual history have analyzed a progressive climate of opinion that is recognizable in Smith's attitudes, not only at the constitutional convention, but also
throughout his gubernatorial career. Addressing the New York
State Federation of Labor, the governor argued, "the Due Process of the Law clause in the Constitution was never intended
to prevent the State from enacting legislation to safeguard the
health and welfare of the people." His views on this occasion
reflected the pragmatic "attack on formalism or abstractionism,"

which challenged the validity of absolute truths, whether meta-
physical, economic, or legal, and undermined faith in laissez-
faire, the Protestant ethic, and the substantive interpretation
of due process. In their stead, progressive thinkers offered
what one scholar has identified as "the ideological means to
dissolve away conservatism's steel chain of ideas"; another,
"new ways of thinking about reality, ways which would permit
action to take place with regard to that reality"; and a third,
"the rival philosophy of the general-welfare state." These
studies suggest that pragmatism, institutional economics, legal
realism, and social Christianity furnished the progressive era
with a foundation for reform on which the New Deal subsequently
built.[5] The intellectuals who sparked the earlier reform movement became in time "the *philosophes,* the encyclopedists of the
Roosevelt 'revolution.'"[6] Their ideas permeated the consciousness of Alfred E. Smith, a practical politician without intellectual pretensions, but with a very good mind.

The pragmatic frame of reference enabled Smith to justify
a program of reform recognized as progressive as far back as
Benjamin Parke De Witt's pioneering work on the movement. A
progressive himself, the author characterized the reformers'
goals in democratic and humanitarian terms involving governmental action, particularly on the part of the states, to improve
the lot of the people through such expedients as labor legislation and social insurance. Appearing in 1915, his book did
not anticipate a substantial contribution from the conservative
Democratic party, but a recent synthesis has shown that the
years in which De Witt was writing witnessed a transformation
that left the GOP less, and its opponents more inclined to
liberal reform. The last impression gains credence from John D.
Buenker's study of the progressivism of new stock Democrats in
the industrial states of the Northeast and Midwest, politicians
like Al Smith who favored labor legislation, trade unionism,
utilities regulation, and progressive taxes. In addition, a
succession of monographs on social work, voluntary organizations, and settlement houses has confirmed a continuity between

progressivism and the New Deal in the pursuit of social justice.[7]

Ample documentation exists to illustrate the salience of
social justice, the city, and the Democratic machine in progressivism in New York State during the politically formative
years of Al Smith. A generation ago, in their narrative of progressivism, the authors of *A Short History of New York* paid considerable attention to labor laws, Boss Murphy, and the legislative leaders from New York City. Without ignoring the differences between trade unionists and progressives, Irwin
Yellowitz concluded that the two cooperated to promote certain
significant laws, partly because the New York State Federation
of Labor was more sympathetic to legislative solutions than its
national counterpart. The leading authority on Governor Hughes
perceived in his administration a social consciousness that set
a precedent for Governor Smith. J. Joseph Huthmacher insisted
on the importance of Tammany Hall and welfare legislation in
the Empire State's progressivism, a relationship examined further in his study of Robert Wagner and in George Martin's biography of Frances Perkins. That landmark of social progressivism, the New York State Factory Investigating Commission,
has received careful analysis, albeit by a scholar who, in contrast to the above biographers, emphasized the disjunction between the progressive movement and the New Deal.[8]

Whether progressivism engendered conflict or represented
consensus in American life, historians have failed to reach consensus on the nature and consequences of the movement. As one
of them who did assume a basic continuity between the economic
intervention of the New Deal and the experience of the earlier
decades explained, "In the reaction of the 1920's and the disillusionment of the great depression, it was easy to view the
reform efforts of the previous years with pessimism and cyni-
cism."[9] In the reaction of the 1950s and the disillusionment
of the New Left, there recurred just such a tendency to under-
estimate the reforms of the first half of the century and even
to hold the reformers responsible for whatever the observer

considered distasteful in contemporary American life. Two
decades of scholarly reconsideration exposed the progressives
as self-seeking and status conscious, technocratic and bureau-
cratic, and basically conservative, with a program of reform
designed to deflect the threat of radical change in the interest
of the lower classes. In this perspective, progressivism was
neither democratic nor humanitarian, and it did little to promote government, either by the people, or for the people.[10]

Smith's progressivism was not of this variety. George E.
Mowry's progressive profile did not delineate the features of
Al Smith; he had little in common with Richard Hofstadter's
status-seekers; the New Yorker was the very antithesis of Otis
L. Graham's old progressives, although like them he disdained
the New Deal. Hofstadter detected a paradox in the two personas
of the governor: machine politician from Tammany Hall and progressive reformer. A subsequent scholar resolved the progressive paradox by ascribing to progressivism the neutrality of
a technique, which "lent itself equally to social control and
to social release."[11] Smith adapted progressive means to the
end of social release, but the revisionists have tended to
identify the reform movement with social control. Impressed by
the expert advice to the factory commission and by the constitutional convention's paradigm for efficient and economical
administration, Smith utilized the first to fashion labor legislation and the second to reconstruct the state government into
a more effective tool to serve the common man.

Governor Smith was the product of a progressive era subject to such divergent interpretations that by 1970 one scholar
insisted that the progressive movement "did not exist in historical reality, only in historians' minds."   Less troubled
by the logical inconsistences in a nomenclature that applies to
liberal and reactionary forces alike, another suggested that
"contemporary journalists, not blessed with the analytical and
taxonomical skills of college professors, perceived the common
elements in the uproar around them, and they were right to
speak of a progressive movement." The contradictions in the

movement expressed the perplexities of real people who desired
to improve the lot of their fellow citizens at the same time
that they feared the consequences of reform, according to a
later article. Attempting a synthesis after a decade of argument, a recent book accepts the term *progressivism*, despite
its ambiguities, as "a useful catch-all," a classification
that enhances understanding of twentieth century America.[12]
The progressivism that made so profound an impression on
Assemblyman Smith is central to any evaluation of the distinction with which he subsequently served as governor.

    To recognize Smith as a progressive reformer is not to
ignore his role as a professional politician, but rather to
concur with Otis Pease that the virtue of our political life
rests in the combination of the idealism of the one with the
skills of the other. Smith exemplified the politician as reformer, but the campaign of 1928 obscured the achievements of
the governor in the image of a provincial machine politician.[13]
The stereotype distorted the reality from which it derived.
The Democratic organization did give Smith his chance in politics, he rose to power as its representative, and based his
career on loyalty to the party, which repaid him in kind. In
a revealing episode, the new chief executive persuaded the
independent, Frances Perkins, to register as a Democrat.
Throughout his eight years in office, he rarely lost control of
his fellow Democrats in the legislature. The notable exception
occurred in 1923 when the Democratic senate voted to repeal the
Mullan-Gage Act and to adopt the Ferris amendment; however, in
the second instance, the governor mobilized his forces to bring
about the measure's defeat in a referendum. In general, the
organization deferred to him, not only in the matter of policy,
but also of appointments, for Charles Francis Murphy placed
the governor's success above considerations of patronage.
When the boss died, Smith assumed his mantle of leadership,
which was confirmed by the deposition of Hylan and the defeat
of Hearst. As William Allen White observed, "Smith took

orders from Tammany until he was able to give orders."[14]
The Democratic party in New York City provided Al Smith with
his political identity and a primary source of supporters.

Despite his allegiance to an organization that made a
fine art of the distribution of patronage, the governor earned
the approbation of civil service reformers whose attitude toward
machine politicians generally varied from contempt to condescen-
sion. When the Civil Service Reform Association met at about
the midpoint of his tenure as chief executive, those present
concurred in the judgment that he had surpassed even Governor
Theodore Roosevelt in his adherence to the merit system. Smith
began his first term by appointing to the sensitive position of
superintendent of public works an apolitical colonel who had
just returned from designing roads in France, "because I want
to get the Highway Dept. out of politics." In an amusing incident, a congressman protested, "I have a very high ideal of
righteousness, honor and integrity in public service, but . . .
I have not reached your altitude," to Smith's son-in-law, the
Republican superintendent of the state police, who had just
rejected the legislator's overtures on behalf of job applicants.[15]

The record of his incumbency enabled Smith to work
effectively with such groups as the Civil Service Reform Association, which took a nonpartisan approach to government, based
their recommendations on the assumptions of the developing
social sciences, and valued the advice of well-trained professionals. These organizations and the experts who staffed them
were a source of strength and inspiration to Governor Smith.
In reconstructing the state government, he carried out a plan
originating in the New York Bureau of Municipal Research and
backed by the City Club, the Citizens' Union, and the New York
State Association, which also authored his state park plan.
The governor's Reconstruction Commission, which proposed vari-
ations on the bureau's theme of administrative reform and initiated the association's study of parks, outlined many of the
policies to which the Smith administration owed its good repute.

In affirmation of the progressive faith in experts, the commission functioned as a veritable brain trust, employing among
others, the political scientist, Robert Moses, the social
worker, Belle Moskowitz, and the architect, Clarence S. Stein,
all of whom continued to be identified with achievements of the
Smith regime. The chief executive deferred to an internation-
ally known authority, Dr. Hermann Biggs, for initiatives in
public health; in school finance and prison reform, Smith relied on the wisdom of professional educators and criminologists
respectively.

By following the advice of experts, the Democratic politician gained favor, not only with progressives, who defined
reform in terms of nonpartisan administration, but also with
some influential Republicans. If Robert Moses was a maverick
within the GOP when Smith named him secretary of state in the
reformed government, reorganization would have been inconceivable under a Democratic executive without the cooperation of
such highly placed Republicans as Henry L. Stimson and Charles
Evans Hughes, who overcame the opposition of the old guard
within the majority party. In bringing the efficiency economy
movement to a successful culmination in New York, Smith capitalized on the respect that he had earned from prominent Republicans at the constitutional convention. Their esteem was
apparent when he visited Washington where Hughes "rushed out
to the reception room to greet him and ushered the Governor
into the inner office with a friendly arm around his shoulder,"
in a display of affection unusual for the reserved secretary of
state.[16] The same progressive Republicans were in accord with
Smith in resisting the oppression of the Red Scare. The partisanship of the 1928 campaign obscures the popularity that
Governor Smith enjoyed among independents and among New York
Republicans with minimal ties to the state machine.

New York social workers, many of whom had campaigned for
Theodore Roosevelt in 1912, numbered among Governor Smith's
supporters and intimates. Belle Moskowitz, "the Colonel House
of the Smith Administration," had worked at the Educational

Alliance and awakened to political consciousness in the Progressive crusade. As a young widow, Belle Israels had discovered much in common with Henry Moskowitz, including their professional interest in social work and their political interest in the Progressive party. After their marriage, Henry showed his enthusiasm for Governor Smith by writing one campaign biography in 1924 and coauthoring a second a few years later.[17] Settlement house workers who made their mark in the Smith administration included Frances Perkins and Clarence S. Stein; from her House on Henry Street, Lillian Wald offered encouragement to the governor. He was understandably popular with the members of a profession that had generated labor and welfare legislation during the progressive era, was striving to preserve the spirit of reform in the twenties, and would flock to the New Deal. Smith also provided opportunity for public-interest lawyers like Julius Henry Cohen to experiment with the instrument of the public corporation, which FDR later used to advantage.[18] Liberal lawyers and social workers formed an important part of Smith's constituency.

If labor leaders maintained cordial but less intimate relations with Smith, he enjoyed popularity in trade union circles, particularly in his native state. In the first half of this century, reformers tended to be paternalistic in their attitudes towards labor, but Governor Smith and Senator Wagner, both of whom began by representing working-class districts in the legislature, stood out as exceptions, in their sympathy for unions. Unlike many of his progressive friends, Smith did not distrust organization, whether in the form of a labor union or a political party. Not only did his administration recognize the right of labor to organize and to bargain collectively, but it proposed an anti-injunction measure to protect the right to strike. When the chief executive did intervene in stoppages, he showed a concern for the workers and a respect for their organizations that endeared him to the labor movement. Its leaders in New York appreciated the effectiveness of the Labor Department under Smith and favored the social legislation that

he sponsored. Consequently, the New York State Federation of
Labor backed him at the polls, and successive presidents of the
AFL, Samuel Gompers and William Green, spoke generous words of
praise. The formal neutrality of the national organization did
not prevent many union officials from campaigning for Smith in
1928.

Although Smith enjoyed a higher level of support from
organized labor than from the black community, its members were
beginning to waver in their traditional Republican allegiance
during his years in office. Not-so-benign neglect by the GOP
had prompted the formation of the United Colored Democracy at
the time of New York City's consolidation. Tammany Hall under
Murphy's leadership courted the black vote in a variety of ways,
including the distribution of patronage, but the insensitivity
of his successor dissipated some of the goodwill that the boss
had so carefully cultivated in Harlem. Throughout the twenties,
New York Negroes continued to favor the GOP in national elections, while voting Democratic frequently in city contests and
occasionally in statewide polls. Each time he ran for governor,
Smith campaigned in Harlem.[19]

Consequently, Smith made inroads in the normally Republican, black electorate of New York City. In 1918, the NAACP's
Crisis carried a two-page advertisement that appealed to Negro
voters by citing Tammany Hall's sympathy with their aspirations
and Smith's legislative record on welfare and civil rights.
Even the *New York Amsterdam News*, a black paper that never supported Smith, found words of praise for his first administration; in gaining a second term, he compiled a sizable majority
in Harlem. Two years later, the socialist *Messenger* refrained
editorially from choosing between Smith and Norman Thomas, but
Chandler Owen advised the journal's readers to cast their
ballots for the Democrat.[20] Although estimates vary on the
magnitude of the Smith vote among Harlem blacks in 1924 and
1926, it is safe to say that the governor did better there than
previous Democrats but not so well as in 1922.[21] Backing Mills
in 1926, the *Amsterdam News* derided Smith's performance as

governor and described him as "a cool, calculating politician
who will let nothing stand between him and his desire to be
named by his party for the Presidency."[22]

It comes as no surprise that the Harlem newspaper opposed
Smith in 1928. The *Amsterdam News* remained Republican during
this era, not merely through inertia, but from a conviction
that any Democrat, no matter how fair to blacks in the state,
would cater to southern prejudice once he aspired to national
office. Even at the beginning of the decade, the editorial
pages expressed reservations about Smith on that score, and the
passing years confirmed the editor's distrust of the governor
and his party. Perpetuating the negative stereotype of Tammany
Hall, the columns charged the county organization and the United
Colored Democracy with protecting crime and vice in Harlem.
Smith's veto of a bill to provide additional judges in the municipal courts appeared to the editor of the *News* as a device to
prevent the elevation of blacks to the bench. If the paper
lacked perspective on this issue, because the governor consistently disapproved on principle comparable measures with
which the state legislature tried to intervene in city affairs,
the editor was on firmer ground in condemning the administration
for its failure to appoint blacks to positions of power and
prestige.[23]

With less justification, the *Amsterdam News* held Smith
responsible for the fact that the black contender, Harry Wills,
was unable to challenge Jack Dempsey for the heavyweight title.
The paper implied that the governor, with his eye on the White
House, had exerted his influence to prevent the interracial
bout, in order to avoid offending the South. Anticipating a
proposal for the match, D. Walker Wear, a member of the License
Committee of the State Athletic Commission sought guidance,
only to be reminded by the governor that the decision rested
with the commissioners. In his response to Wear, however,
Smith did affirm, "I can only say to you that I have a great
faith in the document known as the 'Declaration of Independence' and one passage of it which reads, 'All men are created

equal.'" Agitation for a Dempsey-Wills fight continued from
1922 to 1926 when the combination of Dempsey's loss to Gene
Tunney and of Wills's to Jack Sharkey rendered the question
academic. Several of the officials involved, including a Miller
appointee, reversed themselves over the years, but in the end
the New York authorities ruled in favor of Wills and were out-
manuevered by the promotion of a Dempsey-Tunney contest in
Pennsylvania.[24]

In its editorials on the campaign of 1928, the *Amsterdam
News* repeated and supplemented its objections to Smith, but the
black press no longer exhibited the nearly unanimous Republi-
canism of an earlier generation. If the paper reflected the
prevalent Protestant moralism in its criticism of the governor's
stand on Prohibition, as a black publication it detected a particular danger in his desire to leave the definition of intoxicating beverages to the states: states' rights was often a
code word for allowing the former Confederacy to trample on
civil rights. The *News* perceived racism in the remarks of
Democratic spokesmen who tried to distance their candidate from
the minority, in response to rumors of blacks in his entourage.
Reviewing the Negro experience with the Wilson administration,
the editor concluded that the GOP "is still the only ship in
sight." Writing in the *Crisis*, W. E. B. DuBois found little
to choose between the major parties and their candidates, both
of whom "stand for exactly the same thing: oligarchy in the
South; color caste in national office holding; and recognition
of the rule of organized wealth." The Harvard-educated social
scientist therefore recommended a vote for Norman Thomas.
Hardly oblivious to Smith's shortcomings with regard to black
people, the *Messenger* preferred him because of his record on
social legislation and suggested that "it would be striking a
severe blow at intolerance, prejudice and bigotry if Negroes
should help send this Catholic gentleman to the White House."[25]

Blacks who favored Smith often proceeded on the assumption that the enemy of their enemy constituted a friend. A
common foe was the Ku Klux Klan, which antagonized Smith more

by religious, than by racial, prejudice, as it blocked his political advancement. His concern for the rights of minorities focused on European ethnics of Catholic and Jewish faith and on socialists. The governor who resisted the Red Scare and the dry crusade resented the nativism in both: the anti-Semitism of the first and the anti-Catholicism of the second. He prided himself on the religious diversity of subordinates selected, in his words, "without regard to politics, religion or any other consideration except the ability, the integrity and the fitness of the appointee." Only the black press took cognizance of the absence of dark skins from official circles. Despite the growth in their numbers in the Empire State, blacks left little trace in the voluminous records of the governor; they were indeed the invisible men and women of the Smith administration. If he thought about them at all, he must have been unconscious of their grievances and convinced of his own rectitude. On the occasion of his second election as governor, his friend, the performer Eddie Dowling, encouraged him to "go up to Albany and say Hullo. And hustle right on to Washington. The Catholic, the Jew, and the Negro need you Al, very badly."[26]

Enough Negroes concurred so that two important studies of black history could designate 1928 as a turning point in the electoral politics of the race. Even the limited attraction of Smith combined with growing disillusionment at the lily-white policy of the GOP to accelerate the shift of blacks from the Republican to the Democratic party, which culminated under the influence of the New Deal. In the estimate of a contemporary politician, "Hoover carried the white South, but Smith the Negro."[27]

In his magisterial, but incomplete, study of *The Age of Roosevelt*, Arthur M. Schlesinger, Jr. observes: "If a somewhat reluctant Al Smith had pioneered the way for Negroes in politics, he had done the same—and with the same reluctance—for women." Indeed, the Smith administration in New York drew support from the ranks of labor, blacks, women, and intellectuals whom Schlesinger identifies as members of the Roosevelt coalition.[28]

Having just obtained the vote in New York State, women were active in Smith's campaigns for governor as far back as 1918. In the assembly, he gained their favor by reversing himself to support a suffrage amendment to the state constitution, which he had initially opposed. With an eye on the newly enfranchised voters, his nonpartisan campaign committee included a women's division. Belle Moskowitz, who made arrangements for him to address the Women's University Club in 1918, has been credited with conceiving, not only the Reconstruction Commission of his first term, but also the campaign strategy of mobilizing supporters outside the ranks of Democratic regulars. Consequently women played an important part in his campaigns and subsequently in his administration. His very first year in office, Smith convened a special session of the legislature to ratify the Nineteenth Amendment to the United States Constitution. Many of the women who contributed to its success helped to elect Smith by using the skills they had mastered in the suffrage movement.[29]

Al Smith, the compleat politician, rewarded their efforts by according women an unaccustomed measure of recognition in his administration. If it was his own idea to appoint a woman to a high level post, because "women have got the vote," he chose Frances Perkins for the Industrial Commission out of respect for the competence that the social worker had demonstrated in lobbying for labor laws. In addition, the governor, who departed from convention in public but not in private life, accepted her decision to use her maiden name so that today few people recall that she was Mrs. Paul C. Wilson. When Governor Roosevelt was preening himself on promoting Perkins to head the Labor Department, she had the grace—and temerity—to suggest that "it was more of a victory for Al to bring himself to appoint a woman . . ." in defiance of precedent.[30] While elevating Perkins, FDR rejected his predecessor's recommendation to employ Belle Moskowitz as the governor's secretary.

Although she had not served in an official capacity, from her office at Democratic party headquarters, Moskowitz exercised greater influence on the Smith administration than any other adviser, according to such diverse contemporary observers as Frances Perkins, Ed Flynn, and the journalist, Henry F. Pringle.[31]

Although Smith prided himself on the number of well-qualified women whom he had placed in administrative positions, among feminists, policy rather than patronage determined reactions to the governor. The legislative programs that attracted the social feminists often antagonized their more radical sisters who combined a commitment to total gender equality with a belief in classical economics. Not only did the laws that protected working women discriminate against them by depriving them of the income available to men from hazardous occupations and long hours, but such statutes clearly violated the spirit of free enterprise. The National Woman's party, which had lobbied against the forty-eight hour law, preferred Hoover in 1928, but social feminists numbered among the governor's most effective campaigners. He appreciated their contribution to reform at the same time that he acknowledged, "but I am unable to subscribe to the theory of absolute equality between men and women," a stand unacceptable to the proponents of ERA then as now. The election of 1928 exposed many fault lines in American life, one of which separated radical feminists from social feminists who tended to favor Smith. If J. Stanley Lemons is correct in contending "that the social feminists constituted an important link in the chain from the progressive era to the New Deal," it is not surprising to find them supporting Governor Smith, for whom this study makes a comparable claim.[32]

Social feminists formed one of many blocs, persuaded by Smith's policies to cast the votes that four times elected him governor. In New York's black electorate, his administration made inroads that would culminate in a massive shift to the Democratic party during the thirties. Labor leaders and social workers, who formed a prominent part of the New Deal coalition, gave their support to President Roosevelt and Governor Smith for similar reasons. Activists in the various nonpartisan organizations inspired by progressivism perceived in the governor a statesman who would fulfill their desires for reform, whether by labor legislation, adherence to the merit system in civil service, or efficient and economical government. Reorganization and the executive budget gained him a following among progressive Republicans. He transcended his Tammany origins to become a politician with appeal to independents and certain elements in the GOP and a factor in the transformation of his own Democratic party into a vehicle for urban liberalism. It is now time to accept his oft-repeated invitation to look at the record to understand why he was able to combine such divergent forces into the electoral coalition that repeatedly returned him to the Executive Mansion. Al Smith, the politician, succeeded as a votegetter in unlikely precincts because of the substantial achievements of Governor Smith, the reformer.

Inspired by the legacy of progressivism and the reports of the Reconstruction Commission, already in his first term, Governor Smith announced almost all the policies that require consideration in a review of the record of his eight years in office. If reconstruction is defined literally in the context of immediate postwar adjustment, rent control was its most conspicuous achievement. The governor, however, gave a much broader mandate to his commission, which produced the plans for administrative reform and health centers that were implemented in later years, proposals on housing that eventuated in the legislative compromise of 1926, and a program of health insurance that did not survive defeat in his initial administration. At this time too, Smith called for legislative action on measures of the urban progressives for forty-eight hours and minimum wages for women and children and public development of water power.

A number of sensational issues distracted the public in the early twenties and made it difficult for the new chief executive to gain a hearing for his constructive policies.

Although he did persuade his first legislature to reform and
extend workmen's compensation, the Republican majority took
advantage of the Red Scare to block additional labor legislation and public power. The most important accomplishment of
Smith's first administration was the essentially negative one
of vetoing the Lusk bills. Meanwhile, Prohibition enforcement
and the feud with Hearst dominated the headlines. By keeping
the publisher off the Democratic ticket, Smith increased his
political capital; by winning reelection in 1922, the governor
managed to eliminate the vestiges of the Red Scare in New York.
But the lawmakers who repealed the Lusk Laws approved by
Governor Miller also voted to rescind the Mullan-Gage Act,
thereby confronting Smith with a politically embarrassing decision. Less newsworthy but more noteworthy were the public
health and child welfare measures that he sponsored successfully
in his second term.

His third term was even more productive. In the elections of 1925, Smith demonstrated his skill as a politician by
repulsing Hylan's bid for a third term as mayor and made his
mark as a reformer by promoting three amendments to the constitution: for reorganization, funding of public works, and grade
crossing elimination. With the triumph of Walker, Smith gained
mastery of his own party; with the success of the referendum,
he routed his Republican opponents. If his efforts to modernize
the administration culminated in the amendment of 1925 and the
State Departments Law the following year, the process of re-
forming the government yielded important by-products: the
compromise on state parks and preventing private enterprise
from capitalizing on hydroelectric resources in the public domain. Although he failed to persuade GOP lawmakers to subsidize residential construction, the legislation of 1926 did make
a modest start toward recognition of governmental responsibility for the provision of affordable housing.

Although, in his last term, Smith failed both to pursue
the idea of a state housing bank and to induce the legislature
to create a power authority, it is misleading to conceive of

his fourth administration as an anticlimax between the remarkable progress of the middle years and the sensational presidential campaign ahead. The process of administrative reform
culminated in the ratification of a constitutional amendment
for an executive budget at the same time that the voters rejected one for a four-year term, which Smith opposed because it
scheduled statewide contests to coincide with presidential elections. Taking full advantage of the provisions already in
force, the governor demonstrated the efficiency and economy of
the reforms to which he had committed his administration. In
the realm of labor legislation, he finally secured passage of
a forty-eight hour law more acceptable than the one that he had
earlier vetoed. Smith ended his last term by reaching many of
the goals on welfare and governmental operations that he had
set in his first. In the process, he rarely departed from
the principled devotion to civil liberties that had characterized his reaction to the Red Scare. It was a goodly heritage
that he bequeathed to his successor, along with potential
conflicts over budgetary procedures and water power, in which
Roosevelt carried on the Smith tradition.

To identify Smith as an important source of the New Deal
is to imply a basic continuity between the administrations of
Governor Roosevelt and his predecessor. Her official experience in New York prompted Frances Perkins to reflect, "I can't
separate in my memory what was accomplished in the Smith
regime . . . and in the Roosevelt regime. They are not
separable in the labor field, or . . . in any other field."
Before accepting appointment from FDR, she ascertained his
willingness to persist with Smith's policies on labor. Having
served Smith in the inconspicuous, but influential, position of
bill drafting commissioner, Samuel I. Rosenman hesitated to
become counsel to Governor Roosevelt out of concern that the
new chief executive would be less liberal than the old. The
lawyer enabled FDR to perpetuate Smith's programs without
relying on personnel whose primary loyalty was to the ex-

governor. As a result, comprehensive studies of Roosevelt's
governorship begin by estimating his debt to Smith. Bernard
Bellush assumed that "the foundations for Roosevelt's four
years as Governor were well laid by the Happy Warrior"; Frank
Freidel described Smith's policies as "the foundation but not
the structure" of the Roosevelt administration, which placed
increasing emphasis on farm problems in an endeavor to attract
the rural as well as the urban vote. In a more recent effort
to put New York's chief executives in historical perspective,
Smith and Roosevelt are both classified among the greats in a
tradition of "positive liberalism," which made government an
instrument of social justice. Given a decade of their leadership, "Many New Deal programs did not seem so new to New
Yorkers . . ." according to the historians of the Empire
State.[33]

Many knowledgeable observers, including FDR himself,
recognized the extent to which the New Deal derived from the
Smith administration. The idea was a commonplace to the New
Yorkers in the president's cabinet, Farley and Perkins. To
the secretary of labor, the New Deal of President Roosevelt was
inconceivable without the example of Governor Smith. In her
unfinished manuscript on "The Al Smith I Knew," she insisted
that "he should be remembered as a great governor, the forerunner of the New Deal, and as a man who was honest, openminded, devoted to his party, and loyal to his friends." She
was convinced that her book on Smith would be important because
he prepared the way for the New Deal. Using the Perkins papers
for their study of Smith, the Josephsons agreed that he had
fathered the welfare state so commonly associated with the
Roosevelt presidency. Smith's governorship offered "a detailed
preview of the New Deal" to another biographer who concluded
that "It was the first hurrah . . . of the new politics" and a
precursor, not only of the New Deal, but also of the Fair Deal,
the New Frontier, and the Great Society.[34]

After taking into account the difference in context between a state in a decade of prosperity and the nation in a

time of depression, one can find New Deal analogies for Governor Smith's major policy initiatives. The failed drive for
federal administrative reorganization grew out of the same
efficiency economy movement that spawned consolidation and the
executive budget in New York. The increase in magnitude and
the change in purpose of the state debt demonstrated that Smith
placed humanitarian considerations above fiscal orthodoxy in a
hierarchy of values that would permit Roosevelt to condone deficit finance. If FDR literally inherited his commitment to
conservation, it gained reinforcement from his experience with
the Empire State's park plan. Smith set legislative precedents
for provisions in such trademarks of the New Deal as the
National Housing, Fair Labor Standards, and Social Security
Acts. It is hard to imagine the creation of the Tennessee
Valley Authority without a decade of devotion to public power
by the governors of New York as well as the senator from
Nebraska.

     The continuity of policy rested on a common conceptual
framework within which Smith and Roosevelt both operated, despite the vast discrepancy in their educational attainments.
Neither man was doctrinaire; neither one held sacrosanct the
abstractions of due process and laissez-faire that had long
interfered with legislative solutions to the economic problems
of the unprivileged. Both assumed governmental responsibility
for the welfare of the people, and both were innovative in
meeting it. Both were pragmatic, as the term is used in common
parlance, if not in philosophical discourse. A study of FDR's
economic thought shows that he did not enter the White House in
ignorance of the discipline but "had a well-developed economic
philosophy—largely derived from Progressivism," a description
that also fits Al Smith. The author, who does recognize the
role of Smith in the development of Roosevelt's ideas, fails to
identify the school of institutional economics whose analysis
permeated what FDR learned from his university professors; and
Al Smith, from the more scholarly of his political confreres.[35]
Not only the programs, but also the climate of opinion of

Washington in the thirties, resembled that of Albany in the
twenties.

Any attempt to identify Smith as a source of the New Deal
is complicated by the diversity of scholarly opinion on the
Roosevelt years. Historians have disagreed, not only on the
substantive quality of the New Deal, but also on its relationship to progressivism. Recent work, much of it quantitative,
on the history of electoral politics arrives at contradictory
conclusions about the Roosevelt constituency and when and how
it coalesced. What follows is a brief survey of the historiographic trends that are significant for an assessment of the
affinities between the Smith governorship and the Roosevelt
presidency.

My claim that Smith represents a transitional stage between progressivism and the New Deal rests on an assumption of
basic continuity between the two reform movements. The impact
of the first upon the second is confirmed, not only in many of
the studies of progressivism discussed above, but also in the
comprehensive treatments of FDR by Arthur Schlesinger, Jr. and,
to a lesser extent, by Frank Freidel.[36]

Perhaps the most influential challenge to the thesis of
continuity came from Richard Hofstadter who suggested that, unlike progressivism, the New Deal involved "not so much moral
reformation as economic experimentation." Consequently, Otis
L. Graham, Jr. found that a majority of the old progressives in
his sample rejected the New Deal; he explained their opposition
to FDR by the conservative nature of progressive reform and the
consistency with which the middle class reformers adhered to
their original ideals despite—or perhaps because of—the
changing times.[37] In the light of his behavior during the
thirties, Smith's career appears to substantiate this hypothesis. But in the first third of the century, neither by precept
nor example, did he conform to the stereotype of the old progressives. Furthermore, his working-class background and
machine affiliation set him apart from them. On the other
hand, when Graham identified the minority of old progressives

who did favor the New Deal as predominently social workers in
the big cities, particularly New York, he was describing the
kind of people who exerted influence on the Smith administration.
Furthermore, Richard George Frederick, in his work on the old
progressives in the twenties, discovered that the 1928 election
accelerated their movement from the Republican to the Democratic party, a development that culminated in the following
decade[38] and would imply continuity between Smith and FDR.

The continuity becomes apparent when scholars extend their
investigation of progressive origins beyond the middle class
and small towns to the immigrant population of the cities, as
in the work of J. Joseph Huthmacher and John D. Buenker. The
latter resolved the paradox of progressivism by explaining how
the coalition disintegrated in the twenties into its separate
socioeconomic components with mutually inconsistent goals; in
the thirties, urban liberals surfaced in the New Deal ranks and
middle class natives in the opposition.[39]

In their reactions to the New Deal, historians have divided along much the same lines—but not in the same proportions—as the old progressives: liberals wrote approvingly;
conversatives denounced the deviation from tradition; and radicals lamented that FDR "did enough to save the system, but not
enough to redeem it." The traits that liberal scholars like
Schlesinger, Freidel, and William E. Leuchtenburg found praiseworthy in FDR, a flexibility that enabled him to deal with
economic problems without the inhibitions imposed by dogma, a
compassion exhibited by government intervention in the economy
on behalf of the common man, and a capacity for leadership that
increased the effectiveness of the executive branch, all these
had contributed to the success of Governor Smith. The percep-
tions with which James MacGregor Burns improved our understanding of the president incidentally offer insight into the
governor. *Roosevelt: The Lion and the Fox* is hard to classify,
standing as it does somewhere between the laudatory work of the
liberals and the iconoclasm of the Left. On its pages, admiration of the chief executive contrasts oddly with the scathing

criticism: "He could not reshape his party, reorient foreign
policy attitudes, reorganize Congress and the bureaucracy, or
solve the economic problem largely because he lacked the necessary intellectual commitment to the right union of ends and
means." What is important to the argument of my book is Burns's
identification of Roosevelt with a conservative tradition that
includes respect for religion, responsibility for the poor,
and amenability to reform—but not idolization of laissez-
faire.[40] Except for the differences attributable to social
class, the observations on Roosevelt's conservatism can be
applied equally well to Governor Smith.

Radical historians attacked FDR for his conservatism;
conservatives, for his radicalism. Paul K. Conkin, Barton J.
Bernstein, and Ellis W. Hawley went farther than Burns in their
analyses of Roosevelt's intellectual limitations and the New
Deal's failures to achieve social justice and to dislodge
vested interests, in other words, the chief executive's unwillingness to effect a radical transformation in our national
life. From the opposite end of the political spectrum, Edgar
Eugene Robinson and John T. Flynn objected to the radicalism
of the president whom they criticized for breaking with American tradition. They interpreted the New Deal as autocratic,
fiscally irresponsible, and socialistic.[41] If the charges
from the Right sound familiar, they were also leveled against
Governor Smith for his policies on administrative reform,
public works bonds, and housing, labor, and water power, respectively. The Smith and Roosevelt administrations encountered
opposition on similar grounds because the governor and the
president pursued comparable policies.

Another way to probe the continuities in government is
through the examination of voting patterns or the history of
electoral politics. Stability and change in the alignment of
voters imply continuity and discontinuity in the policies of
the officials they elect. No contest has engendered more controversy in the scholarly literature than 1928, a condition

that complicates efforts at interpreting the career of the
Democratic presidential candidate.

Samuel Lubell laid down the lines for subsequent inquiry
in 1952 in *The Future of American Politics* where he asserted,
"the Republican hold on the cities was broken not by Roosevelt
but by Alfred E. Smith. Before the Roosevelt Revolution there
was an Al Smith Revolution." The journalist rested his case on
demographic trends: urbanization and the coming-of-age of the
new immigrants' children, who registered their approval of the
welfare state in the voting booths. Lubell's interpretation
appealed to Lawrence H. Fuchs who contributed the chapter on
1928 to the detailed *History of American Presidential Elections*
published in 1971.[42]

Between the appearance of the two works and continuing
on to this day, a self-conscious methodology was being used to
test Lubell's hypothesis and to formulate alternatives. What
may be called the quantitative study of electoral politics bases
its argument on sophisticated statistical manipulation, applies
social science theory, and/or is practiced more frequently by
political scientists than historians. What follows is a survey
of the trends in this literature as it bears on the question of
continuity between Smith and Roosevelt.

The starting point in academic discourse on the subject
is a 1955 article in the *Journal of Politics* where V. O. Key,
Jr. concluded that for New England but not necessarily for the
rest of the nation, "the Roosevelt revolution of 1932 was in
large measure an Al Smith revolution of 1928. . . ." Key's
paper not only pinpointed 1928 as a critical election or turning
point, from the Republican majorities normal since 1896 to the
Democratic majorities of the thirties and forties, but also
posited a theory of critical elections and used statistical
evidence to identify crucial contests. Walter Dean Burnham's
comprehensive monograph refined critical election theory by
introducing the concept of an almost cyclical process of partisan alignment and by assigning realignment, not just to individual elections and voter behavior, but to longer time periods

and new directions in policy that would reinforce voting pref-
erences. A realigning era occurred, he asserted, between 1927
and 1931; the election of 1928 did anticipate the Democratic
majorities that found satisfaction in the New Deal. Although
the historian, Carl N. Degler, was not deliberately testing
the political scientists' hypothesis, he did use statistical
analysis to measure partisan realignment in selected cities in
1928. Consequently, he maintained that "the forces which would
consummate the Roosevelt revolution were already in motion in
1928 in behalf of Alfred E. Smith." The governor's working-
class, ethnic, and religious origins appealed to urbanites of
comparable background, many of whom had not previously voted,
but would subsequently persist in their loyalty to the Democratic party. In a recent monograph based on statistics and
survey research, Kristi Andersen, like Degler, attributed realignment primarily to mobilization of new voters rather than
to the conversion of those who switch their party affiliation.
Avoiding the question of critical election theory, she explained
realignment between 1928 and 1936 in terms of the increasing
participation of urban lower classes, which counted on Democrats
like Smith and FDR to serve interests long overlooked in the
political process.[43]

    Several students of electoral politics expressed reserva-
tions about the above work with its implication that Al Smith
activated the so-called New Deal coalition. "Perhaps . . .
that is what should have happened. That it did happen can be
established only through detailed analysis of the actual voting
record," concluded a 1969 article by Jerome M. Clubb and Howard
W. Allen. They speculated that 1928 may have been a deviating
rather than a critical election and that only the Great Depression confirmed the majority of voters in an allegiance to the
Democratic party. When, in collaboration with others, Clubb
provided the detailed analysis, it vindicated his initial
skepticism. *Partisan Realignment* identified 1928 as a stage
in the disintegration of an earlier party system and 1932 as
the critical election for the formation of a Democratic

majority, despite the fact that in certain regions of the country Smith and Roosevelt did receive comparable voter support.
The authors also explained that, in realignment, voter affiliation and government policy reinforce each other as in the case
of the welfare legislation of the New Deal. Writing in *Social
Science History,* David F. Prindle, like Andersen, insisted on
the importance of voter turnout and mobilization in partisan
realignment but found existing scholarship inadequate to determine which election between 1920 and 1940 was critical for the
rise of a Democratic majority. With regard to the disagreement
over the significance of 1928, he acknowledged "elements of
truth" in each of the varying interpretations.[44]

In contrast to Prindle and others who expressed some
reservations, two historians have completely denied the validity
of using the study of electoral politics to trace the origins
of the New Deal back to Governor Smith. Writing in the *Journal
of Interdisciplinary History,* Bernard Sternsher took his
colleagues to task in 1975 for ignoring a generation of research
that cast doubts on Lubell's conclusions. For Sternsher, the
critical election occurred in 1936, for "without the depression
and the New Deal there would have been no . . . acquisition by
the Democrats of normal majority status to point back to while
designating the election of 1928 as the initiator of that process." In 1976 in the *American Historical Review*, Allan J.
Lichtman also rejected 1928 as a turning point in political
alignment, but he went further by discrediting the critical
election theory on which such designations are based. Following
up in a book that is notable for its mastery of both literary
and statistical sources, he identified religion as the most
important determinant of the 1928 vote. Consequently, he emphasized the discontinuity between the twenties and thirties:
"Rather than forging durable new alignments . . . Smith's candidacy generated an intense conflict between Catholics and Protestants that only marginally affected subsequent patterns of
politics." Lichtman did however discover that the Smith tally
increased as the economic status of the voters declined! Still

he maintained that 1928 witnessed neither a "revolt of the
cities," nor an "Al Smith revolution."[45]

A study of electoral behavior in New York State failed to
identify 1928 as a critical election but did produce evidence
that would suggest substantial continuity between the twenties
and thirties. Lee Benson and his colleagues found that the era
of Republican primacy ended with the initial election of
Governor Smith and that the new alignment, with its Democratic
majorities, exhibited marked stability throughout the years
from 1918 to 1940.[46]

What can be said about the vexed issue of continuity between the Smith administration and the New Deal, after examining
the literature on electoral politics? It is inconclusive. Not
only do the various studies arrive at mutually inconsistent
interpretations, but they start from different hypotheses and
utilize different statistical techniques, which in turn rest on
assumptions incapable of being proven—or disproven. Given the
conflicting conclusions and the variety of ways of reaching
them, it is possible to affirm with absolute certainty, neither
that continuity exists, nor that it does not exist. The
research however does present important evidence to suggest
that Lubell was far from mistaken in his intuition on the significance of Al Smith for the New Deal, an interpretation supported in this book by the study of policy.

Eleanor Roosevelt wrote to commend Smith on his speech
accepting the Democratic presidential nomination. Even as she
voiced her disagreement with his stand on Prohibition, she expressed admiration of his courage in being faithful to his own
convictions. In view of the sequel, it is interesting to note
that she singled out for special praise Smith's defense of
public power on the Tennessee and Colorado rivers. When he won
his party's nomination, his archbishop penned a note of con-
gratulation and "offered my Mass for you alone that God might
deign to bless and guide you in a supreme moment of your own
life as well as in a real critical hour for our country and

our church." When Smith lost the election, one of his instruc-
tors at Saint James sent a message of consolation to which the
governor responded, "You taught me to say 'Thy Will be done on
Earth as it is in Heaven,' and I never say it without meaning
it." Conversing with Frances Perkins about the 1928 defeat, he
mused, "Well, the time just hasn't come when a man can say his
beads in the White House."[47]

This feeling of disillusionment embittered Smith's retirement. We are concerned here with the years after 1928 only to
the extent that they enlarge our understanding of what went before, of what his governorship means in the larger perspective
of American history. The outline of his life after defeat is
familiar: how his relations with Governor Roosevelt cooled;
how Smith found employment in the world of business; how he
lent himself to the stop-Roosevelt effort at the 1932 convention;
how he became increasingly critical of the New Deal; how he
played a prominent role in the ultraconservative Liberty League;
and finally, how he decided to "take a walk" out of the Democratic party in 1936.[48] So vehemently did he turn against the
president that an observer remarked that Smith "was presenting
Roosevelt with the sidewalks of New York one brick at a time."[49]

A thorough study of Smith's governorship leads inevitably
to the common sense conclusion that Smith had changed by the
time he assailed FDR. This interpretation has come increasingly
under fire from scholars who assume that the transformation was
more apparent than real, that the times had changed—but not
the man, who seemed liberal in the conservative decade of prosperity and conservative in the more radical decade of depression. To these writers, the attack on the New Deal requires
no explanation, for the attacker was adhering to political
principles from which he had never departed. In the words of
one article, "The Alfred E. Smith who opposed Franklin D.
Roosevelt in 1936 was being agonizingly consistent with the
Alfred E. Smith who opposed Herbert Hoover in 1928."[50] My research shows that Smith was not conservative in the twenties;
therefore, I contend that he was not consistent in the thirties.

It is time to review the reasons why I cannot accept the revisionists' thesis.

They base their case primarily on economics. No change of heart need explain Smith's objections to the New Deal, because he had always favored limited and frugal government. He was a Jeffersonian democrat who believed in laissez-faire and balanced budgets—not a social democrat who harbored schemes for government interference with the sacred law of supply and demand. A man who valued the common interest above special interests, he resented the class conflict generated by FDR's broker state.

The features of the governor are distorted beyond recognition in this sketch of the ex-governor. As early as the constitutional convention, Smith repudiated the economic ideology that stood as a barrier to desirable legislation; he persisted in his attitude throughout his tenure as chief executive. Whether in the form of housing subsidies, rural health centers, mothers' pensions, protective labor legislation, or public power, government intervention in the economy figured prominently in his recommendations to the legislature. When an opponent complained of the housing bank as a violation of Jeffersonian principles, Smith was quick to retort that the shortage of accommodations had not been acute in the age of Jefferson. Nor did Governor Smith take more seriously the accusations of class conflict and socialism being used to discredit his programs for parks, housing, and hydroelectricity. As for fiscal orthodoxy, he departed from tradition by promoting bonds for veterans' pensions, public works, and grade crossing elimination and entertained no scruples on amending the state constitution to facilitate the novel indebtedness. Governor Smith made a fetish, neither of constitutionalism, nor of economic theory.

He did however profess an attachment to states' rights, particularly in the matter of Prohibition. This leads some scholars to attribute the quarrel with the president to Smith's constant devotion to decentralization. Hardly convincing in

the case of a structural reformer whose achievements concentrated authority in New York in the hands of the chief executive! Whatever he said on the subject of states' rights,
Governor Smith (unlike Nathan L. Miller) showed little compunction over accepting congressional grants-in-aid under the
Sheppard-Towner Act and supporting the federal child labor
amendment. It is reasonable to construe the governor's infre-
quent pronouncements on federal-state relations, less as the
reflection of an enduring commitment to states' rights, than as
an example of a well-known law of American political behavior:
a politician's appreciation of the exercise of power varies
directly with his involvement and inversely with his distance
from its locus. In the context of the federal system, the
governor's preference for states' rights does not make his later
opposition to the New Deal predictable.

Those who perceive the actions of the officeholder as an
indicator of the reactions of the defeated candidate argue, not
only from the evidence on states' rights and economic theory,
but also from an analysis of the political spectrum. Even in
the twenties, they contend, Smith represented a conservative
element within his own party in contrast to its more radical
agrarian wing. But the radicalism of the populists has been
exaggerated, and farming regions were among the first to defect
from the New Deal, which retained support in the big cities
that Smith had so neatly symbolized. Some historians classify
the governor as a conservative because he intended to amelio-
rate conditions—not to overthrow the system. The same holds
true for FDR, so this hardly explains the rupture between the
two men.

Why did Smith desert his party and denounce the New Deal?
Not out of a conservatism manifest—but misjudged—prior to
1928! An answer to the question rests on what happened after
1928—not before. All I can do here is outline, without any
claim to originality, those approaches that I find most convincing.

When she dictated her memoirs, Frances Perkins pondered long over the painful estrangement between the two leaders to whom she owed her own political advancement and whom she held in great respect.[51] She has left a poignant account of Smith's pathetic eagerness to influence the administration of his successor in Albany. If it was imperative for the new governor to declare his independence of the old, it was only human for the ex-governor to resent it. The election of one and the defeat of the other inevitably made Roosevelt and Smith competitors for the presidential nomination, no matter how sincere the latter in expressing his intention to retire from public life. Smith attributed his defeat to religious bigotry, not only among the voters, but also among the politicians of his own party who had failed to give his candidacy the support to which he felt entitled. If bitterness fueled rather than quenched Smith's ambition, it also distorted his perception of FDR whom he had always underrated. The very pragmatism that had inspired Governor Smith to experiment with creative solutions to public problems constricted the vision of the businessman striving to preserve his financial security from the ravages of depression. America looked very different from the Empire State Building than from the New York State Capitol or the White House. Perkins deemed all these explanations, however valid, insufficient to explain ultimately why Smith opposed New Deal policies deriving from precedents in his own administration. In the end, she could only speculate on some episode, unknown to her, that so antagonized Smith that he was unable to acknowledge the continuity between his own programs and those of the president.[52]

Smith's place in American history is secured by the deeds of the governor—not the words of the ex-governor. Puzzled by his defection, President Roosevelt reflected, "Practically all the things we've done in the Federal Government are like things Al Smith did as Governor of New York. They're things he would have done if he had been President of the United States."[53]

NOTES TO CHAPTER 1

1. *New York Times,* January 2, 1919; *New York Herald,* January 2, 1919; *New York World,* January 2, 1919; Norman Hapgood and Henry Moskowitz, *Up from the City Streets: Alfred E. Smith* (New York: Harcourt, Brace and Company, 1927).

2. N.Y., *Public Papers of Alfred E. Smith Governor,* 1919:7-8 (hereafter cited as AES, *Public Papers*).

3. Consideration of Smith's education and ethnicity relies heavily on Frances Perkins' contributions: Frances Perkins, "Alfred E. Smith," chaps. 2, 3, Frances Perkins Papers—Susanna W. Coggeshall Collection, Custody of George Martin, New York; Matthew Josephson and Hannah Josephson, *Al Smith: Hero of the Cities: A Political Portrait Drawing on the Papers of Frances Perkins* (Boston: Houghton Mifflin Company, 1969), pp. 8-18, 33-41.

4. Edward M. Levine, *The Irish and Irish Politicians: A Study of Cultural and Social Alienation* (Notre Dame: University of Notre Dame Press, 1966); William V. Shannon, *The American Irish* (New York: Macmillan Company, 1963), chap. 4.

5. William Allen White, *Masks in a Pageant* (New York: Macmillan Company, 1928), pp. 465-79; William H. Allen, *Al Smith's Tammany Hall: Champion Political Vampire* (New York: Institute for Public Service, 1928); Roy V. Peel, *The Political Clubs of New York City* (New York: G. P. Putnam's Sons, 1935); Nancy Joan Weiss, *Charles Francis Murphy, 1858-1924: Respectability and Responsibility in Tammany Politics* (Northampton, Mass.: Smith College, 1968); Thomas M. Henderson, *Tammany Hall and the New Immigrants: The Progressive Years* (New York: Arno Press, 1976).

6. N.Y., Secretary of State, *Manual for the Use of the Legislature of the State of New York,* 1904-14 (hereafter cited as *Legislative Manual*).

7. The most comprehensive accounts of Smith's career in the assembly are: Oscar Handlin, *Al Smith and His America* (Boston: Little, Brown and Company, 1958), pp. 27-60; Louis Daniel Silveri, "The Political Education of Alfred E. Smith: The Assembly Years, 1904-1915" (Ph.D. dissertation, St. John's University, 1964); David Richard Colburn, "Alfred E. Smith: The First Fifty Years, 1873-1924" (Ph.D. dissertation, University of North Carolina, 1971, reproduced by University Microfilms), chaps. 4, 5.

8. Richard L. McCormick, "Prelude to Progressivism: The Transformation of New York State Politics, 1890-1910," *New York History* 59 (1978):253-76; Robert F. Wesser, *Charles Evans Hughes: Politics and Reform in New York 1905-1910* (Ithaca, N.Y.: Cornell University Press, 1967).

9. Silveri, "Political Education of Alfred E. Smith."

10. *Report of the Committee on Legislation of the Citizens' Union*, 1909, 1910, 1911, 1913 (hereafter cited as *CU Report*).

11. Alfred B. Rollins, Jr., *Roosevelt and Howe* (New York: Alfred A. Knopf, 1962), pp. 8-15, 23-37, 48-55, 88-114; Frank Freidel, *Franklin D. Roosevelt,* vol. 1, *The Apprenticeship* (Boston: Little, Brown and Company, 1952), chap. 6; Franklin D. Roosevelt, *The Happy Warrior Alfred E. Smith: A Study of a Public Servant* (Boston: Houghton Mifflin Company, 1928), pp. 3-5.

12. Jacob Alexis Friedman, *The Impeachment of Governor William Sulzer* (New York: Columbia University Press, 1939), passim and pp. 270, 268; Josephson and Josephson, *Al Smith,* pp. 149-51.

13. J. Joseph Huthmacher, "Charles Evans Hughes and Charles Francis Murphy: The Metamorphosis of Progressivism," *New York History* 46 (1965):25-40; idem, *Senator Robert F. Wagner and the Rise of Urban Liberalism* (New York: Atheneum, 1968), chaps. 1, 3; idem, *Massachusetts People and Politics 1919-1933* (Cambridge: Belknap Press of Harvard University Press, 1959), pp. 63-65.

14. Leon Stein, *The Triangle Fire* (Philadelphia: J. B. Lippincott Company, 1962); N.Y., *Senate Documents,* 1912, no. 30; 1913, no. 36; 1915, no. 43; N.Y., *Assembly Documents,* 1914, no. 28; Thomas Jefferson Kerr IV, "New York Factory Investigating Commission and the Progressives" (D.S.S. dissertation, Syracuse University, 1965, reproduced by University Microfilms).

15. Alfred E. Smith, *Up to Now: An Autobiography* (New York: Viking Press, 1929), p. 71; Alden Hatch, *The Wadsworths of the Genesee* (New York: Coward-McCann, 1959), p. 166; *CU Report,* 1908, 1911.

16. N.Y., *Record of the Constitutional Convention 1915,* 4 vols., unrevised, passim and pp. 26, 4394 (hereafter cited as *Record CC 1915*).

17. Ibid., pp. 4394-96, 619; *New York Times,* October 9, 1915; Finla G. Crawford, "Constitutional Developments 1867-1915," in *History of the State of New York,* 10 vols., ed. Alexander C. Flick (New York: New York State Historical Association, 1933-37), 7:233-36.

18. *Record CC 1915,* p. 1091.

19. Ibid., pp. 4327-30, 1589-1612, 3222-37, 3542-47, 4269-74, 2108-2112.

20. Hapgood and Moskowitz, *Up from the City Streets,* p. 102; Henry F. Pringle, *Alfred E. Smith: A Critical Study* (n.p.: Macy-Masius, 1927), p. 186; Root to Alfred Holman, October 1, 1928, Elihu Root Papers, Library of Congress, Washington, D.C.; Alphonso T. Clearwater to AES, March 14, 1927

George B. Graves Papers, Franklin D. Roosevelt Library, Hyde
Park; Henry L. Stimson and McGeorge Bundy, *On Active Service in
Peace and War* (New York: Harper and Brothers, 1948), pp. 67-68.

21.   Joseph C. Beckmann III, "The Tiger's Son, Alfred E.
Smith: An Interpretive Biography" (Senior essay, Columbia
College, 1965), pp. 46-49, 53-55.

22.   *Record CC 1915*, p. 3767; *Citizen's Union Searchlight*,
February 18, 1918; James A. Farley, *Behind the Ballots: The
Personal History of a Politician* (New York: Harcourt, Brace
and Company, 1938), pp. 23-24.

23.   AES, *Up to Now*, pp. 159-60.

24.   *New York Times*, July 9, 10, 14, 15, 1918; [George R.
Van Namee?] to Murphy, June 14, 1918, George R. Van Namee
Papers, Library of the Fresno Diocesan Chancery and Academy of
California Church History, Fresno, Calif.

25.   *New York Times*, July 17, 23, 24, 25, August 6, 7,
September 4, 13, 1918; *New York Evening Journal*, July 23,
August 5, 1918.

26.   Freidel, *Franklin D. Roosevelt: The Apprenticeship*,
pp. 338-43, 370.

27.   Donn Charles Neal, "The World Beyond the Hudson:
Alfred E. Smith and National Politics, 1918-1928" (Ph.D. dis-
sertation, University of Michigan, 1973, reproduced by Univer-
sity Microfilms), pp. 113-14; Pringle, *Alfred E. Smith*, p. 231;
Osborn to Peabody, September 26, 1918; Peabody to J. Augustus
Kellogg, September 20, 1918; Edmund H. Titchener to Peabody,
September 21, 1918; Peabody to Elmer J. West, September 30,
1918, George Foster Peabody Papers, Library of Congress,
Washington, D.C.

28.   AES, *Up to Now*, pp. 162-63, 280-82; Andy Logan,
Against the Evidence: The Becker-Rosenthal Affair (New York:
McCall Publishing Company, 1970); Josephson and Josephson, *Al
Smith*, pp. 191-98; Louis M. Hacker and Mark D. Hirsch,
Proskauer: His Life and Times (University of Alabama Press,
1978), p. 53.

29.   *New York Times*, September 27, October 21, 25, 29,
31, 30, 23, 26, 1918.

30.   *Legislative Manual*, 1919; AES, *Up to Now*, pp. 164-
67; *New York Times*, December 13, 1918.

31.   Elkus to AES, August 19, 1920, Alfred E. Smith
Official Correspondence, New York State Archives, Albany (here-
after cited as AES Official Correspondence); *New York Times*,
July 29, October 1, 5, 8, 12, 16, 17, 21, 22, 26, 31, 1920.

32.   Wald to Proskauer, October 8, 1920, Lillian D. Wald
Papers, New York Public Library, New York; W. A. Swanberg,
Citizen Hearst: A Biography of William Randolph Hearst (New
York: Charles Scribner's Sons, 1961), p. 335; *New York Evening
Journal*, November 1, 1920.

33. *Legislative Manual,* 1921; AES, *Up to Now,* p. 221; *New York Times,* March 18, 1923.

34. Robert Moses, *Working for the People: Promise and Performance in Public Service* (New York: Harper & Brothers, 1956), p. 32.

35. *New York Times,* January 17, February 2, July 8, 1922.

36. AES to FDR, July 24, 1922; FDR to AES, July 28, August 13, 1922; AES to FDR, August 15, 1922; FDR to Julia Sanders, August 22, 1922; FDR to Cox, December 8, 1922, Franklin D. Roosevelt Papers, Franklin D. Roosevelt Library, Hyde Park.

37. *New York Evening Journal,* September 18, 1922; Farley, *Behind the Ballots,* pp. 30-32; *New York Times,* September 12, 20, 1922.

38. *New York Evening Journal,* September 22, 1922; *New York Times,* September 26, 1922; Farley, *Behind the Ballots,* pp. 33-37; Charles Michelson, *The Ghost Talks* (New York: G. P. Putnam's Sons, 1944), p. 224; Swanberg, *Citizen Hearst,* pp. 340, 346; Ferdinand Lundberg, *Imperial Hearst: A Social Biography* (New York: Equinox Cooperative Press, 1936), p. 254; Edward J. Flynn, *You're the Boss* (New York: Viking Press, 1947), p. 36.

39. Herbert C. Pell Reminiscences, pp. 310-12, Oral History Project, Columbia University, New York (hereafter cited as Columbia Oral History); *New York Times,* September 28, 29, 1922.

40. AES, *Up to Now,* pp. 232-34; Pringle, *Alfred E. Smith,* pp. 48-60; Farley, *Behind the Ballots,* pp. 32-37; Flynn, *You're the Boss,* pp. 34-36; *New York Times,* May 21, September 30, 1922.

41. *New York American,* October 1, 6, 1922.

42. AES to Stimson, October 7, 1922; Stimson to AES, October 3, 1922, Henry L. Stimson Papers, Yale University Library, New Haven.

43. Miller's campaign addresses, in the order cited, can be found in the *New York Times,* October 4, 12, 7, 1922; AES, Campaign Addresses, October 21, 17, 30, 19, 1922, Alfred E. Smith Personal Papers, New York State Library, Albany (hereafter cited as AES Papers).

44. *New York Times,* November 3, 1922.

45. FDR to AES, October 25, 1922, FDR Papers; FDR to AES, November 9, 1922, AES Papers; *Legislative Manual,* 1923; John D. Hicks, *Republican Ascendancy 1921-1933* (New York: Harper & Row, 1960), pp. 87-88.

46. AES to FDR, November 15, 1922, FDR Papers; *New York Times,* December 29, 1922, January 2, 1923.

47. Neal, "World beyond the Hudson," pp. 209-19; William H. Harbaugh, *Lawyer's Lawyer: The Life of John W. Davis* (New York: Oxford University Press, 1973), pp. 226, 243-49.

48. W. A. Swanberg, *Norman Thomas: The Last Idealist* (New York: Charles Scribner's Sons, 1976), pp. 90-94; Lawrence H. Madaras, "Theodore Roosevelt, Jr. versus Al Smith: The New York Gubernatorial Election of 1924" *New York History* 47 (1966):372-90; Eleanor Roosevelt, *This I Remember* (New York: Harper & Brothers, 1949), pp. 31-32; AES, *Public Papers,* 1924: 700.

49. Eleanor Alexander Roosevelt, *Day Before Yesterday: The Reminiscences of Mrs. Theodore Roosevelt, Jr.* (Garden City, N.Y.: Doubleday & Company, 1959), p. 161; Norman Thomas, p. 40, Columbia Oral History; *Legislative Manual,* 1925; *New York Times,* March 29, 1925.

50. *New York Times,* January 2, 1925.

51. See chap. 3 below.

52. Mills to Henry L. Stoddard, October 2, 1926, Ogden L. Mills Papers, Library of Congress, Washington, D.C.; Mills's campaign addresses, October 13, 14, 15, 1926, AES Papers; AES's campaign addresses, AES, *Public Papers,* 1926:798-808, 842-44, 872-73, quotations on 807-8, 842.

53. *New York Times,* March 13, 4, 1927; *Legislative Manual,* 1927.

54. *New York Times,* November 6, 1926, January 1, 1927, November 8, 11, 1922, November 6, 1924, October 1, 1926; AES, *Public Papers,* 1927:10.

55. David H. Beetle, *The New York Citizen: The Guide to Active Citizenship in the Empire State* (Houston, N.Y.: Elsevier Press, 1955), p. 94.

56. Frank Freidel, *Franklin D. Roosevelt,* vol. 2, *The Ordeal* (Boston: Little, Brown and Company, 1954), pp. 249-55 and passim.

57. Frank Freidel, *Franklin D. Roosevelt,* vol. 3, *The Triumph* (Boston: Little, Brown and Company, 1956), p. 1; FDR, *Happy Warrior;* Eleanor Roosevelt, *This I Remember,* p. 50; Frances Perkins, *The Roosevelt I Knew* (New York: Viking Press, 1946), p. 35.

58. Warren Moscow, *Politics in the Empire State* (New York: Alfred A. Knopf, 1948), p. 11; Robert H. Connery and Gerald Benjamin, *Rockefeller of New York: Executive Power in the Statehouse* (Ithaca, N.Y.: Cornell University Press, 1979), p. 438.

59. Arthur S. Link, "What Happened to the Progressive Movement in the 1920's?", *American Historical Review* 64 (1959): 850; Oswald Garrison Villard, *Prophets True and False* (New York: Alfred A. Knopf, 1928), pp. 9, 17.

1. AES, *Up to Now;* idem, *The Citizen and His Government* (New York: Harper and Brothers, 1935).

2. The ensuing discussion of progressive reforms in the structure and function of government relies upon the following: Benjamin Parke De Witt, *The Progressive Movement: A Non-Partisan, Comprehensive Discussion of Current Tendencies in American Politics* (New York: Macmillan Company, 1915), chaps. 10, 11, 13; A. E. Buck, *The Reorganization of State Governments in the United States* (New York: Columbia University Press, 1938), pp. 6-27; Leslie Lipson, *The American Governor from Figurehead to Leader* (Chicago: University of Chicago Press, 1939), pp. 31-99; Samuel Haber, *Efficiency and Uplift: Scientific Management in the Progressive Era 1890-1920* (Chicago: University of Chicago Press, 1964), intro., chap. 6; Martin J. Schiesl, *The Politics of Efficiency: Municipal Administration and Reform in America 1880-1920* (Berkeley: University of California Press, 1977).

3. Haber, *Efficiency and Uplift,* p. xii; De Witt, *Progressive Movement,* p. 208; Richard S. Childs, *Civic Victories: The Story of an Unfinished Revolution* (New York: Harper & Brothers, 1952), pt. 1.

4. Jane S. Dahlberg, *The New York Bureau of Municipal Research: Pioneer in Government Administration* (New York: New York University Press, 1966); Schiesl, *Politics of Efficiency;* John D. Buenker, *Urban Liberalism and Progressive Reform* (New York: Charles Scribner's Sons, 1973), chap. 4.

5. Merlo J. Pusey, *Charles Evans Hughes* (New York: Macmillan Company, 1951), chap. 26; Stimson and Bundy, *On Active Service,* chap. 3; Gerald D. McKnight, "The Perils of Reform Politics: The Abortive New York State Constitutional Reform Movement of 1915," *New York Historical Society Quarterly* 63 (1979):202-27.

6. Thomas Schick, "The New York State Constitutional Convention of 1915 and the Modern State Governor" (Ph.D. dissertation, New York University, 1976, reproduced by University Microfilms), chaps. 2, 3; McKnight, "Perils of Reform Politics."

7. *Record CC 1915,* pp. 3222-37, quotations on pp. 3222, 3237, 2342, 2331-32.

8. Ibid., pp. 3955, 2319, 3228-37, 4328-30, 1589-1612, quotation on pp. 1608-9; Schick, "N.Y. Constitutional Convention of 1915," p. 165.

9. Schick, "N.Y. Constitutional Convention of 1915," chap. 4; McKnight, "Perils of Reform Politics," pp. 217-27.

10. *Record CC 1915,* pp. 972-73, 1136-50, 3204-22, 3353-55, 4428-31.

11. Perkins, *Roosevelt I Knew,* pp. 50-51; Frances Perkins, 2:215, Columbia Oral History.

12. AES, *Public Papers,* 1919:30-31, 48-53, quotation on 31; 1920:570.

13. *New York Times,* February 5, 10, March 19, 1919; AES, *Public Papers,* 1919:51, 670-71.

14. AES, *Public Papers,* 1919:48-51, 586-676; 1920:207-51, 569-79; *New York Times,* January 25, 1919.

15. N.Y., *Report of Reconstruction Commission to Governor Alfred E. Smith on Retrenchment and Reorganization in the State Government,* October 10, 1919; AES, *Public Papers,* 1919: 585-614 prints pt. 1 of the text of the report.

16. Robert Caro, *The Power Broker: Robert Moses and the Fall of New York* (New York: Alfred A. Knopf, 1974), chap. 6, quotation on p. 98.

17. AES, *Public Papers,* 1919:591.

18. Ibid., 593, 585.

19. Ibid., 1920:116-18; Stimson to William A. Prendergast, November 26, 1919, Stimson Papers.

20. *New York Times,* February 11, April 5, 7, 20, 25, 26, 1920; *New York State Legislative Record and Index* (Albany: Legislative Index Publishing Company, 1902-), 1920 (hereafter cited as *Legislative Index*); *CU Report,* 1920; Moses, Memorandum on Action of 1920 Legislature with Reference to the Reorganization of the State Government, May 10, 1920, AES Official Correspondence.

21. Moses to Peabody, December 20, 1919; Wickersham et al. to Peabody, February 3, 1920, Peabody Papers.

22. "Speeches of Hon. Alfred E. Smith and Hon. Charles E. Hughes at the City Club of New York, December 8, 1919," AES Papers; AES, *Public Papers,* 1919:790-96; 1920:628-39.

23. *New York Times,* March 13, 1920; Martin Saxe, p. 31, Columbia Oral History; AES, *Public Papers,* 1920:653-56, quotation on 653.

24. *New York Times,* April 21, 1920; *New York World,* April 21, 1920.

25. Moses to AES, May 26, 1920; Walter T. Arndt to AES, May 25, 1920; Raymond V. Ingersoll to AES, April 27, 1920, AES Official Correspondence; Stimson to Moses, May 1, 1920, Stimson Papers.

26. [AES] to Raymond V. Ingersoll, May 4, 1920; [AES] to Richard S. Newcomber, May 20, 1920; Moskowitz to AES, June 1, 1920; Moses, "Suggested Statement by the Governor Regarding Results of 1920 Legislative Session and Need of a Special Session," May 28, 1920, AES Official Correspondence.

27. *New York Times,* August 5, September 25, October 8, November 1, 1920.

28. Ibid., September 23, July 29, 1920; Stimson to Miller, August 3, 1920; Miller to Stimson, August 12, September 1, 1920; Stimson to Root, October 11, 1920, Stimson Papers.

29. N.Y., *Public Papers of Nathan L. Miller Governor,* 1921:48-53; *Laws of the State of New York Passed at the 1921 Session of the Legislature,* chaps. 50, 90, 336, 475 (hereafter cited as *Laws of N.Y.*); *CU Report,* 1921.

30. *New York Times,* March 9, 31, 1921; *State Bulletin of the New York State Association,* 1 (January 1, 1921):passim and 15; Alfred E. Smith, "How We Ruin Our Governors," *National Municipal Review* 10 (1921):277-80.

31. *New York Times,* October 5, 11, 12, 15, November 5, 2, 1922.

32. Moses to AES, December 7, 1922, and enclosed Memoranda, AES Official Correspondence; AES, *Public Papers,* 1923:51-52.

33. *Legislative Index,* 1923; *New York Times,* March 21, 22, 1923; AES, *Public Papers,* 1923:538-39, 155-60.

34. *New York Times,* March 23, 24, 26, 29, 1923; *New York World,* March 26, 1923; [AES] to Elkus, March 30, 1923, George B. Graves Papers.

35. Stimson to AES, March 31, 1923 ; Walter T. Arndt to AES, April 5, 1923, AES Official Correspondence; *New York Times,* April 5, 1923.

36. AES, *Public Papers,* 1923:573-83, quotations on 574, 576; *New York Times,* March 23, 25, April 4, 11, 1923.

37. AES, Address to Syracuse Chamber of Commerce, April 3, 1923, AES Papers; *New York Times,* April 19, 20, 29, 1923.

38. *Legislative Index,* 1923; AES, *Public Papers,* 1923: 545-47.

39. *New York Herald,* October 8, 1923; *New York Times,* October 11, 18, November 6, 1923; *Legislative Manual,* 1923, 1924.

40. AES, *Public Papers,* 1924:43-46, 522-23; *New York Times,* February 8, 29, 1924; *Legislative Index,* 1924.

41. *New York Times,* March 27, 31, 28, 1924; Clippings from *Black River Democrat,* April 3, 1924; *Troy Observer,* March 30, 1924; *Larchmont Times,* April 3, 1924, AES Official Correspondence.

42. AES to Stimson, April 1, 1924, AES Official Correspondence; *New York Times,* April 8, 1924; *Legislative Index,* 1924.

43. *New York Times,* April 9, 1924; AES, *Public Papers,* 1924:539-42; Diary of Henry L. Stimson, June 10, 1924, Yale University Library, New Haven.

44. AES, *Public Papers,* 1924:644-53, 721-26, 655, 684, 687-88, 692, 713-14.

45. Peabody to AES, September 8, 1924, Peabody Papers;
AES, *Public Papers,* 1924:627.

46. *New York Times,* September 26, October 15, 1924;
Stimson to Trubee Davison, October 16, 1924, Stimson Papers.

47. *New York Times,* January 7, February 8, March 8, 18,
1925; *Legislative Index,* 1925.

48. Stimson to AES, March 2, 1925; [George B. Graves?]
to Stimson, March 4, 1925, AES Official Correspondence; "Notes
on Meeting of Group of Citizens at Luncheon at the Bankers Club
at 12:30 P.M. Thursday, March 5, 1925 To Consider an Executive
Budget System for the State," AES Papers; *New York Times,* March
12, 1925; Stimson to Charles J. Hewitt, March 26, 1925; Stimson
to George K. Morris, March 10, 1925, Stimson Papers.

49. AES, *Public Papers,* 1925:75-76.

50. *New York Times,* March 12, 8, 1925.

51. AES, *Public Papers,* 1925:343-46.

52. Ibid., 74-75; *New York Times,* February 8, 13, 14,
1925.

53. *New York Times,* November 30, December 3, 6, 1924.

54. Ibid., January 7, March 17, March 20, 1925.

55. Ibid., February 2, 13, October 24, 26, 29, 30, 1925;
James W. Wadsworth, Jr. to Root, August 30, 1925, Root Papers.

56. [AES] to State Committeemen and County Chairmen,
October 26, 1925; "Statement of Governor Alfred E. Smith with
Reference to the Constitutional Amendments to be Voted on at the
Coming Election" [Autumn, 1925]; AES to Walter T. Arndt, Octo-
ber 19, 1925, AES Official Correspondence; *New York Times,*
October 18, 27, 31, 28, 30, 1925.

57. *Legislative Manual,* 1926; Lippman to AES, November
6, 1925, AES Official Correspondence; *New York Times,* November
5, 1925.

58. AES, *Public Papers,* 1925:239-40; Walter T. Arndt to
AES, June 19, 1925, AES Official Correspondence.

59. *New York Times,* June 21, 23, 1925; Childs to Hughes,
July 1, 1925; [AES] to McGinnies, July 14, August 10, 1925, AES
Official Correspondence; Root to James Wadsworth, Jr., August
28, 1925, Root Papers; AES, *Public Papers,* 1926:598; AES, *Up to
Now,* pp. 255-56; Hapgood and Moskowitz, *Up from the City Streets,*
pp. 229-30. In his autobiography, Smith wrote that the leaders
accepted Moses but turned down Ingersoll and Moskowitz. He must
be mistaken with regard to the first. Moses was on the governor's list of nominees, but did not serve. It is highly unlikely that he declined. Hapgood and Moskowitz state that McGinnies
rejected "the three men and one woman most actively identified
with the whole movement." This refers to Mrs. Moskowitz,
Ingersoll, and undoubtedly Moses. I cannot identify the fourth

person that these authors had in mind. Moses did serve as the governor's appointee on a Reorganization Commission which succeeded the original one. Perhaps this explains the confusion.

60. Childs to Hughes, July 1, 1925; Childs to AES, July 16, 1925, AES Official Correspondence; Childs to Stimson, November 11, 1925, Stimson Papers; *New York Times,* June 23, November 15, 20, 21, 1925.

61. Frankfurter to Stimson, November 27, 1925, Stimson Papers.

62. Stimson to AES, November 30, December 3, 1925 and enclosed Memorandum, AES Official Correspondence.

63. [AES] to Stimson, December 7, 1925; Stimson to AES, December 9, 1925, AES Official Correspondence.

64. [AES] to Wagner, December 7, 1925, AES Official Correspondence.

65. Stimson, Memorandum on State Reconstruction, November 19, 1925-January 4, 1926; idem, Memorandum on State Reconstruction Commission [December, 1925 or January, 1926], Stimson Papers.

66. Stimson, Memorandum on State Reconstruction, November 19, 1925-January 4, 1926; Machold and Stimson, Report as to the Constitutional Budget, January 14, 1926; Stimson to Root, February 3, 1926, Stimson Papers.

67. Stimson to Parton Swift, December 30, 1925; Stimson to Alfred E. Marling, Swift, and Wagner, January 15, 1926; Stimson to Root, February 3, 1926, Stimson Papers.

68. Moses to AES, February 2, 1926 and enclosed Childs Memorandum on the Machold-Stimson Constitutional Budget, AES Official Correspondence.

69. Stimson, Memorandum, February 9, 1926, Stimson Papers; [AES] to Proskauer, February 8, 1926, George B. Graves Papers.

70. AES, *Public Papers,* 1926:601-5, 644-45, quotation on 603.

71. Stimson, Memorandum, December 3, 1925, AES Official Correspondence; AES, *Public Papers,* 1926:601.

72. Stimson, Memorandum, December 3, 1925, AES Official Correspondence; *New York Times,* December 30, 1925; AES, *Public Papers,* 1926:599.

73. AES, *Public Papers,* 1926:599-643.

74. Ibid.; Stimson to AES, November 30, 1925; idem, Memorandum, December 3, 1925, AES Official Correspondence; Stimson, Memorandum on State Reconstruction, January 6, 1926, Stimson Papers; [George B. Graves?] to Norman Mack, January 9, 1926, AES Official Correspondence; *New York Times,* January 20, 1926. For the Department of Agriculture and Markets, see below, chap. 8.

75. *New York Times,* February 24, March 2, 1926.

76. Stimson, Memorandum, February 9, 1926, Stimson Papers; *New York Times,* February 11, 16, March 10, 1926.

77. *Legislative Index,* 1926; *Laws of N.Y.,* 1926, chaps. 343, 347, 348, 349, 350, 352, 353, 354, 427, 437, 544, 546, 553, 584, 606, 614, 619, 646, 651. The complete text of the State Departments Law can also be found in N.Y., Executive Chamber, *The Reorganized State Government,* 1926, pp. 27-96.

78. *New York World,* March 17, 1926; William L. Russell to AES, March 24, 1926, Laws of 1926, chap. 584, Bill Jacket Collection, New York State Archives, Albany (hereafter cited as Bill Jackets); AES, *Public Papers,* 1928:626-27.

79. Finla G. Crawford, "Administrative Reorganization in New York State," *American Political Science Review* 21 (1927): 358; N.Y., Constitutional Convention Committee 1938, *Reports and Studies,* 8:300 (hereafter cited as *Reports and Studies*).

80. AES, *Public Papers,* 1926:600; AES, *Up to Now,* pp. 256-57; *New York Times,* March 3, 1926.

81. *New York Times,* May 22, 23, 1926.

82. Ibid., October 3, 1926; Mills, Campaign Addresses, October 14, November 1, 1926, AES Papers.

83. *New York Times,* October 27, 1926.

84. AES, *Public Papers,* 1926:866-67, 799-800, 826-27; *New York Times,* October 9, 1926; Stimson to AES, November 11, 1926, Stimson Papers.

85. Joseph McGoldrick, "Governor Smith Introduces the Cabinet in New York State," *National Municipal Review* 16 (1927): 226.

86. Hapgood and Moskowitz, *Up from the City Streets,* pp. 234-39; AES, *Public Papers,* 1927:313-14, 316-17, 319-20; N.Y., Governor's Cabinet, Minutes of Meetings, February 23, March 8, June 2, August 24, October 11, 1927, April 4, 1928, New York State Archives, Albany (hereafter cited as Cabinet Minutes); Caro, *Power Broker,* pp. 262-63.

87. Cabinet Minutes, February 23, 1927:17.

88. Lynton K. Caldwell, *The Government and Administration of New York* (New York: Thomas Y. Crowell Company, 1954), pp. 86-91.

89. *New York Times,* March 2, September 28, 1926; AES, *Public Papers,* 1926:810.

90. *Laws of N.Y.,* 1926, chap. 546, concurrent resolutions; Arndt to Stimson, April 26, 1926; Stimson to Arndt, April 27, 1926, Stimson Papers.

91. *New York Times,* March 29, 1927.

92. Ibid., March 30, 31, April 1, 1927; Stimson to AES, March 29, 1927, AES Official Correspondence.

93. AES, *Public Papers,* 1927:462-63; *New York Times,* October 1, 1927; *Legislative Manual,* 1928.

94. Cabinet Minutes, August 24, 1927:82-88, 93-95; October 11, 1927:45-97, quotation on 53.

95. Ibid., August 24, 1927:95; October 11, 1927:56, 55.

96. Ibid., October 11, 1927:54.

97. *New York Times,* March 27, April 2, 1924.

98. AES, *Public Papers,* 1926:714-15.

99. Cabinet Minutes, February 23, 1927:3-9, quotation on 6-7; AES, *Public Papers,* 1928:194-96.

100. On workmen's compensation, see below, chap. 6; on state parks, chap. 4.

101. *New York Times,* June 27, 1928.

102. Bernard Bellush, *Franklin D. Roosevelt as Governor of New York* (New York: Columbia University Press, 1955), chap. 2.

103. AES, *Public Papers,* 1926:601, 66; *New York Times,* February 24, 1926; *Legislative Index,* 1926.

104. AES, *Public Papers,* 1927:35; *Legislative Index,* 1927.

105. Mills to George K. Morris, September 22, 1927; Knight to Mills, September 24, 1927; Mills to Knight, September 26, 1927, Mills Papers; *New York Times,* September 21, October 1, 1927.

106. AES, *Public Papers,* 1927:469-82, quotations on 476, 478, 482; *New York Times,* October 29, 1927.

107. *New York Times,* November 3, 4, 5, 6, December 13, 1927.

108. Ibid., November 9, 10, 11, 12, 1927.

109. Ibid., January 4, February 23, 1928; AES, *Public Papers,* 1928:18-19.

110. *New York Times,* February 26, 1928; AES, *Public Papers,* 1928:731-33, 737-50.

111. *New York Times,* March 18, 19, 20, 22, 23, 1928; Wickersham to Knight and McGinnies, March 20, 1928 in Press Release, March 21, 1928, AES Official Correspondence; *Legislative Index,* 1928.

112. AES, *Public Papers,* 1919:33, 35, 40-41; 1920:32-33, 50-51; 1923:52, 57-59; 1924:67-68; 1925:58, 78-81; 1926:68-70; 1927:65-66; 1928:95-98; *New York Times,* March 14, 19, April 18, May 5, 1923; *CU Report,* 1923.

113. Dahlberg, *New York Bureau of Municipal Research,* pp. 241-42; FDR's remark is cited in both major studies of New Deal reorganization: Barry Dean Karl, *Executive Reorganization and*

Reform in the New Deal: The Genesis of Administrative Management, 1900-1939 (Cambridge: Harvard University Press, 1963), p. 28; Richard Polenberg, *Reorganizing Roosevelt's Government: The Controversy over Executive Reorganization 1936-1939* (Cambridge: Harvard University Press, 1966), p. 8.

NOTES TO CHAPTER 3

1. Otis L. Graham, Jr., *The Great Campaigns: Reform and War in America, 1900-1928* (Englewood Cliffs, N.J.: Prentice-Hall, 1971), pp. 4, 29, 133; Buenker, *Urban Liberalism and Progressive Reform,* pp. 118-33; Melvin G. Holli, *Reform in Detroit: Hazen S. Pingree and Urban Politics* (New York: Oxford University Press, 1969), chap. 8.

2. Schiesl, *Politics of Efficiency,* chap. 5 and pp. 95, 110; Dahlberg, *New York Bureau of Municipal Research,* chap. 2 and p. 43.

3. James T. Crown, "The Development of Democratic Government in the State of New York through the Growth of the Power of the Executive since 1920" (Ph.D. dissertation, New York University, 1956), pp. 135-36; AES, *Public Papers,* 1927:29; AES, *Up to Now,* p. 352.

4. Pusey, *Charles Evans Hughes,* p. 213; Wesser, *Charles Evans Hughes,* pp. 345-46.

5. *Reports and Studies,* 10:85-87.

6. *Record CC 1915,* pp. 1288-91.

7. AES, *Public Papers,* 1920:417-18; *Laws of N.Y.,* 1920, chap. 872; *Legislative Manual,* 1921; *New York Times,* September 1, 1921.

8. AES, *Public Papers,* 1923:73; *Laws of N.Y.,* 1923, Concurrent Resolutions; *Legislative Manual,* 1924; *New York Times,* October 21, 28, 1923.

9. *New York Times,* January 25, 1919.

10. C. Floyd Haviland to AES, February 8, 1923 and enclosed Statement regarding State Hospital Construction; William L. Russell to AES, February 1, 19, 1923, AES Official Correspondence; *New York Times,* February 19, 20, 1923.

11. AES, *Public Papers,* 1923:95-100; Marshall to AES, March 3, 1923, AES Official Correspondence; *Laws of N.Y.,* 1923, chap. 591.

12. C. Floyd Haviland and Sullivan W. Jones to AES, April 24, 1923; [AES] to Homer Folks, July 7, 1923; Citizens' Committee on the Protection of the State's Unfortunates, *Protection of the State's Unfortunates: A Booklet of Information for Voters concerning the Development, Work and Needs of the State Hospitals*

and State Charitable Institutions, with Special Reference to the Proposed Bond Issue, September, 1923; Folks to AES, April 20, 1926; AES to Frank Hedley, October 18, 1923; Haviland to George R. Van Namee, November 5, 1923, AES Official Correspondence; AES, *Public Papers,* 1923:642, 648-57; *Legislative Manual,* 1924.

13. Wickersham to AES, March 4, 1924, AES Official Correspondence; AES, *Public Papers,* 1927:323-24; 1928:56-57.

14. New York State Association Committee on State Park Plan, *A State Park Plan for New York with a Proposal for the New Park Bond Issue,* December, 1922; Moses to AES, December 7, 1922, AES Official Correspondence; *Legislative Index,* 1923.

15. AES, *Public Papers,* 1923:183; George Foster Peabody to Moses, March 3, April 19, 1923, Peabody Papers; Cleveland Rodgers, *Robert Moses: Builder for Democracy* (New York: Henry Holt and Company, 1952), pp. 33-34.

16. AES, *Public Papers,* 1924:189-93, 366-68; *Legislative Index,* 1924; *New York Times,* December 1, 1924.

17. AES, *Public Papers,* 1919:104-42, 203-43, 716-22; 1920: 301-12, 370-400, 587-92, quotation on 592.

18. *New York Times,* September 29, October 4, 5, 12, 17, 24, 1922.

19. Ibid., October 11, September 30, 1922; Henry Moskowitz, *Alfred E. Smith: An American Career* (New York: Thomas Seltzer, 1924), pp. 90-98, quotations on pp. 94-95; AES, Campaign Address, October 24, 1922, AES Papers.

20. AES, *Public Papers,* 1923:616-26, quotations on 616-17, 625.

21. *New York Times,* October 2, 26, 1924; AES, *Public Papers,* 1924:674-82, 694-96.

22. *New York Times,* October 4, 24, 1922.

23. C. K. Yearley, *The Money Machines: The Breakdown and Reform of Governmental and Party Finance in the North, 1860-1920* (Albany: State University of New York Press, 1970).

24. Ibid., pp. 241-50; National Industrial Conference Board, *State Income Taxes,* vol. 1, *Historical Development* (New York, 1930), pp. 66-78; N.Y., *Legislative Documents,* 1919, no. 115, pp. 67-69; *New York Times,* February 13, April 9, 18, 1919; *Legislative Index,* 1919; *Laws of N.Y.,* 1919, chap. 627.

25. AES, *Public Papers,* 1919:774-75.

26. *Laws of N.Y.,* 1923, chap. 547.

27. AES, *Public Papers,* 1924:35-36, 305; AES, *Up to Now,* p. 339; Morgenthau to AES, February 28, 1924, AES Official Correspondence; *New York Times,* January 15, February 6, 8, 1924; *Laws of N.Y.,* 1924, chaps. 27, 310.

28. AES, *Public Papers,* 1924:681-82.

29. Moses to AES, February 20, 1924; John A. Wilbur to AES, January 19, 1924, AES Official Correspondence; AES, *Public Papers,* 1924:242-48; *Legislative Index,* 1924.

30. *Legislative Index,* 1924; AES, *Public Papers,* 1925:742.

31. AES, *Public Papers,* 1925:32-35, 41-42, 67-72.

32. *New York Times,* February 27, 28, March 6, 10, 1925; AES, *Public Papers,* 1925:729-32.

33. *New York Times,* March 17, 18, 19, 21, 14, 5, 6, 1925.

34. AES, *Public Papers,* 1925:469-91.

35. *New York Times,* March 15, 25, 26, 1925; AES, *Public Papers,* 1925:273-92, 299, 300, 302, 319, 333-42; *Laws of N.Y.,* 1925, chaps. 196, 237.

36. *New York Times,* March 13, 21, 1925.

37. Ibid., January 30, February 12, 19, March 13, 24, 27, 1925; AES, *Public Papers,* 1925:175-77; *Legislative Index,* 1925.

38. *New York Times,* April 8, 1925.

39. AES, *Public Papers,* 1925:734-54, quotations on 734, 741.

40. Ibid., 543-56; *New York Times,* June 2, 1925; Wickersham to Stimson, June 2, 1925, Stimson Papers; Adelbert Moot to AES, June 1, 1925, AES Official Correspondence.

41. *New York Times,* June 3, 4, 1925; Stimson to AES, June 8, 1925, Stimson Papers; Tumulty to AES, June 4, 1925, George B. Graves Papers; Celler to AES, June 8, 1925, and enclosure; [AES] to J. DuPratt White, June 18, 1925, AES Official Correspondence.

42. AES, *Public Papers,* 1925:512-19, 556-76, quotations on 516, 557.

43. [Mark Graves?], Suggestions or Arguments Which May Be Used in the Debate between Governor Smith and Judge Miller with respect to the Proposed Constitutional Amendment [between June 26 and July 9, 1925], Mark Graves Papers, New York State Archives, Albany.

44. *New York Times,* July 10, 1925; AES, *Public Papers,* 1925:576-601, quotations on 576, 594; [AES] to Proskauer, July 14, 1925, George B. Graves Papers.

45. *New York Times,* August 31, 1925; Mills to Adelbert Moot, September 28, 1925; Davis to Mills, September 21, 1925, Mills Papers.

46. Copy of Richard S. Childs to Charles Evans Hughes, July 1, 1925, AES Official Correspondence.

47. AES, *Public Papers,* 1925:609-17, 676-77; Citizens' Committee on Bond Issue Amendment, Press Releases, October 19-22, 26, 28-30, November 1, 2, 1925; idem, *The Origin of the Proposed*

Bond Issue Amendment, Purposes for Which Bond Issue Is Needed, The Origin of the Proposed Bond Issue Amendment and What the Money Is Needed for, The Use of Money Costs Money—But It Is *Worth It, On the Inside Looking Out, How About the "Blank Check" Idea?, If You Were Building a House, But Why Not Submit Each Project to Popular Vote* [October-November, 1925]; Citizens' Committee to Support the Amendment, *Plain Facts about the Permanent Public Works Constitutional Amendment* [October, 1925], AES Official Correspondence. The text of the last item, without Smith's introductory statement, appears in AES, *Public Papers,* 1925:660-77.

48. Sullivan W. Jones, Memorandum, April 10, 1924, AES Official Correspondence; AES, *Public Papers,* 1925:549-52, 619-32.

49. Walter Tallmadge Arndt to AES, October 13, 1925, AES Official Correspondence; "Constitutional Amendments to Be Voted on November 3," *State Bulletin of the New York State Association,* Reprint, AES Papers.

50. AES, *Public Papers,* 1925:635-59.

51. N.Y., Legislature, Special Joint Committee on Taxation and Retrenchment, *The Debt of the State of New York: With Special Reference to the Proposed Bond Issues for Improvements and Grade Crossing Elimination,* October 24, 1925; *New York Times,* October 27, 28, 1925.

52. AES, *Public Papers,* 1925:602-9; *New York Times,* October 18, 25, 28, 29, 6, November 2, 1925; Colvin to George B. Graves, October 21, 1925, and enclosure, AES Official Correspondence.

53. [AES] to Adolph S. Ochs, September 25, 1925, George B. Graves Papers; *New York Times,* November 1, 1925.

54. Miller to Root, October 16, 1925, Root Papers; *New York Times,* November 2, 1925; *Legislative Manual,* 1926; AES, *Public Papers,* 1925:687.

55. Mills to John Knight, November 10, 1925, Mills Papers.

56. Alfred E. Smith, *Progress of Public Improvements: A Second Report to the People of the State of New York,* October, 1928; Cabinet Minutes, March 9, 1927:22-28; June 2, 1927:16-20; August 24, 1927:67-69.

57. Cabinet Minutes, February 23, 1927:28-70; March 9, 1927:22-28; June 2, 1927:16-72; August 24, 1927:2-82, 96-110, quotation on 99; October 11, 1927:3-43, 67-89; April 4, 1928: 19-43.

58. David J. Rothman, *Conscience and Convenience: The Asylum and its Alternatives in Progressive America* (Boston: Little, Brown and Company, 1980), passim and p. 6.

59. David R. Colburn, "Governor Alfred E. Smith and Penal Reform," *Political Science Quarterly* 91 (1976):315-27.

60.   Adolph Lewisohn to AES, April 8, 1920 and Summary
Report of Prison Survey Committee; Lewisohn to AES, October 4,
1920, AES Official Correspondence; N.Y., *Report of the Prison
Survey Committee,* 1920.

61.   AES, *Public Papers,* 1923:69; 1924:155-89; *Laws of
N.Y.,* 1924, chap. 601.

62.   James L. Long to Terrence Farley, April 30, 1924;
E. R. Cass to AES, April 24, 1924 and enclosures, Laws of 1924,
chap. 601, Bill Jackets; AES, *Public Papers,* 1924:365-66.

63.   AES, *Public Papers,* 1926:59-60, 635-39.

64.   Edwin H. Sutherland and C. E. Gehlke, "Crime and
Punishment," President's Research Committee on Social Trends,
Recent Social Trends in the United States (New York: McGraw
Hill, 1933), pp. 1123-46, 1155-65; Rothman, *Conscience and Con-
venience,* passim and chap. 5.

65.   John Alan Hamilton to AES, January 29, 1926; [AES] to
Hamilton, February 26, 1926, AES Official Correspondence; AES,
Public Papers, 1926:195-96; N.Y., *Legislative Documents,* 1926,
no. 84; 1927, no. 94; *Laws of N.Y.,* 1926, chaps. 416, 418, 419,
421, 436, 445, 457, 461, 464, 465, 475, 478, 702, 705, 737; 1927,
chaps. 265, 266, 327, 337, 338, 342, 355, 356, 548.

66.   AES, *Public Papers,* 1926:247-49.

67.   J. Ellswerth Missall, *The Moreland Act: Executive
Inquiry in the State of New York* (New York: King's Crown Press,
1946), pp. 4-21; AES, *Public Papers,* 1926:513-64; 1927:315-16,
412; Osborne to AES, July 24, 1923 and enclosed Memorandum on
the Prison Situation in New York State, AES Official Correspondence.

68.   Lawrence Veiller, "Turning the Criminals Loose,"
World's Work 53 (1927):546-55; AES, *Public Papers,* 1927:332-36,
quotation on 334; [AES] to Veiller, March 11, 1927; William M.
Ross to AES, March 23, 1927; George Gordon Battle to AES, March
19, 26, 1927, AES Official Correspondence.

69.   New York State Crime Commission, Minutes, December 7,
1927:3128-200; Barnes to AES, December 16, 1927; Glueck to AES,
December 8, 1927; Menninger to AES, December 15, 1927; Davis to
AES, December 22, 1927, AES Official Correspondence.

70.   New York State Crime Commission, Minutes, December 7,
1927:3158; AES, *Public Papers,* 1923:69-70; 1919:32; *New York
Times,* June 1, 1920.

71.   Frances Doherty, "Participation of the Executive in
Educational Legislation in the State of New York 1777-1938"
(Ph.D. dissertation, New York University School of Education,
1947), pp. 139-52, 164-80, 192-95; AES, *Public Papers,* 1919:
32, 286-88; 1925:360-65; 1926:412-15; Cabinet Minutes, March 9,
1927:97.

72. Wayne W. Soper, "Development of State Support of Education," *Bulletin of the University of the State of New York* number 1019 (1933):42-43, 51-55.

73. Edward Paul DeAntoni, "Coming-of-Age in the Industrial State—The Ideology and Implementation of Rural School Reform, 1893-1925: New York as a Case Study" (Ph.D. dissertation, Cornell University, 1971, reproduced by University Microfilms).

74. Soper, "Development of State Support of Education," pp. 43-46; Carl George Benenati, "The State Politics of Educational Decision Making for K-12 Public Education in New York State, 1920-1970" (Ph.D. dissertation, Syracuse University, 1971, reproduced by University Microfilms), pp. 55-56, 70-80, 95-96.

75. Soper, "Development of State Support of Education," pp. 46-55; DeAntoni, "Coming-of-Age in the Industrial State," pp. 204-26; Benenati, "State Politics of Educational Decision Making in N.Y.," pp. 80-98; Doherty, "Participation of the Executive in Educational Legislation," pp. 156-64.

76. AES, *Public Papers*, 1924:52-53, 277-82; Mark Graves to George B. Graves, May 23, 1924; Frederick M. Davenport to AES, April 30, 1924, AES Official Correspondence; N.Y., *Legislative Documents*, 1925, no. 97, passim and pp. 15-16; *Laws of N.Y.*, 1925, chaps. 673, 674, 675.

77. Adelbert Moot to AES, December 17, 1923; [AES] to Moot, December 27, 1923, AES Official Correspondence; Moot to AES, September 15, 1924, George B. Graves Papers; Moot to AES, April 15, 1925, Laws of 1925, chap. 673; C. P. Wells to AES, April 7, 1925; A. J. Merrill to AES, April 7, 1925; Frank R. Wassung to AES, April 7, 1925, Laws of 1925, chap. 675, Bill Jackets; Frank Pierrepont Graves to AES, August 8, 1927, AES Official Correspondence.

78. *New York Times*, November 7, 1925; AES, *Public Papers*, 1926:58-59, 250-351, quotation on 264; 1927:62, 78-106, 173-74, 339; *Laws of N.Y.*, 1927, chap. 572.

79. Benenati, "State Politics of Educational Decision Making in N.Y.," p. 98; AES, *Public Papers*, 1928:46; W. C. Bagley, "Alfred E. Smith's Record in the Promotion of Public Education," *School and Society* 60 (1944):243.

80. Edmund A. Moore, *A Catholic Runs for President: The Campaign of 1928* (New York: Ronald Press, 1956), p. 91; Copy of Graves to Edward T. Reilly, November 10, 1924; [AES] to Earnest Hamlin Abbott, March 19, 1923, AES Official Correspondence; AES, *Public Papers*, 1927:356, italics added.

81. *Reports and Studies*, 4:490-97; 10:45-47.

82. Perkins, 2:265-68, Columbia Oral History.

83. *New York Times*, May 19, 1927.

84. Connery and Benjamin, *Rockefeller of New York*, chap. 6; *Reports and Studies*, 4:531-40; Daniel R. Fusfeld, *The Eco-*

nomic Thought of Franklin D. Roosevelt and the Origins of the New Deal (New York: Columbia University Press, 1956), p. 93.

85.   Lewis H. Kimmel, *Federal Budget and Fiscal Policy 1789-1958* (Washington, D.C.:   Brookings Institution, 1959), pp. 175-228; Robert Lekachman, *The Age of Keynes* (New York: Random House, 1966), chap. 5.

NOTES TO CHAPTER 4

1.   *New York Times,* May 19, 1927.

2.   Frank Graham, Jr., *Man's Dominion: The Story of Conservation in America* (New York: M. Evans and Company, 1971); William Henry Harbaugh, *The Life and Times of Theodore Roosevelt,* new rev. ed. (New York: Collier Books, 1963), pp. 314-15; John Ise, *Our National Park Policy: A Critical History* (Baltimore: Johns Hopkins Press, 1961).

3.   Ise, *Our National Park Policy,* pp. 294-95; Freeman Tilden, *The State Parks: Their Meaning in American Life* (New York: Alfred A. Knopf, 1962), pp. 3-12.

4.   Eugene James O'Neill, "Parks and Forest Conservation in New York 1850-1920" (Ed.D. project, Columbia University, 1963, reproduced by University Microfilms).

5.   AES, *Public Papers,* 1919:599-600; N.Y.S.A., *State Park Plan,* p. 2.

6.   Caro, *Power Broker,* pp. 129-42, 166.

7.   N.Y.S.A., *State Park Plan,* passim and p. 5; Moses to AES, December 7, 1922, and enclosed Memorandum on Proposed Statutory Reorganization, AES Official Correspondence.

8.   AES, *Public Papers,* 1923:109-11, 181-88.

9.   John Barton Payne to AES, January 18, 1924, AES Official Correspondence; New York State Association Committee on State Park Plan, *The State Park Plan for New York: Revised to Show Progress to Date with the Proposal for the New Park Bond Issue,* 2nd ed., January, 1924, passim and p. 7, annotated copy in AES Official Correspondence; AES, *Public Papers,* 1924: 189-93; *Laws of N.Y.,* 1924, chaps. 189, 112, 88, 603, 602.

10.   Caro, *Power Broker,* pp. 157-63, 169-71; N.Y., *Legislative Documents,* 1926, no. 37, passim and p. 22.

11.   Moses to AES, May 21, 1925, AES Official Correspondence; De Forest to Stimson, November 17, 1924, Stimson Papers.

12.   Chester R. Blakelock, *History of the Long Island State Parks* (Long Island: Long Island Forum, 1949), pp. 11-12; Rodgers, *Robert Moses,* p. 42.

13. Julius L. Sackman and Russel D. Van Brunt, eds.,
Nichols' The Law of Eminent Domain, 3rd ed. (Albany: Matthew
Bender and Company, 1950-53), 6:9, 11-17; *Laws of N.Y.*, 1916,
chap. 451.

14. Each of the four detailed narratives of the conflict
over the Taylor Estate takes a partisan stand regarding the
conduct of the park commission: the first three, pro; the last
one, con. Moses presented the case for the defense during the
special session of the legislature in June, 1925 in a paper to
be found in AES, *Public Papers*, 1925:530-35 under the title,
"The President of the Long Island State Park Commission Sub-
mits . . . History of the Taylor Estate Controversy." Blakelock, executive secretary of the commission, in his *History of
the Long Island State Parks*, pp. 21-30, and Rodgers, in his
authorized biography, *Robert Moses*, pp. 44-48, relied heavily
on the official account, although both carried the story to its
conclusion several years later. On the other hand, Caro, in
Power Broker, chaps. 11, 12, criticized Moses for arbitrary
and unscrupulous action in violation of the rights of the land-
owners in this and other cases. See also Scudder to Moses,
July 25, 1924; Beekman Winthrop to Moses, September 23, 1924,
Pauchogue Land Corporation v. Long Island State Park Commission,
248 N.Y. 635 (1928), Papers on Appeal.

15. Transcript of Jury Trial, *Pauchogue Land Corporation
v. Long Island State Park Commission*, 248 N.Y. 635 (1928),
Papers on Appeal; Harry T. Peters to AES, October 8, 1924;
Moses to AES, October 10, 1924, AES Official Correspondence.

16. Minutes of Deer Range Corporation, October 28, 1924,
Pauchogue Land Corporation v. Long Island State Park Commission,
248 N.Y. 635 (1928), Papers on Appeal.

17. Transcript of Jury Trial; Resolution Adopted by the
Long Island State Park Commission, November 26, 1924, *Pauchogue
Land Corporation v. Long Island State Park Commission*, 248 N.Y.
635 (1928), Papers on Appeal.

18. Transcript of Jury Trial; Resolution Adopted by the
Long Island State Park Commission, November 26, 1924; AES,
Approval of Resolution, December 3, 1924, *Pauchogue Land Corporation v. Long Island State Park Commission*, 248 N.Y. 635
(1928), Papers on Appeal. Caro, in *Power Broker*, pp. 187-88,
in a graphic account of the public hearing, had Havemeyer refer to the prospective users of the park as rabble and Smith,
in righteous indignation, grab a pen and sign the form then and
there. However dramatic this scenario, it is not altogether
accurate, for the documents in Papers on Appeal show that he
did not take action until December 3.

19. Transcript of Jury Trial, *Pauchogue Land Corporation v. Long Island State Park Commission*, 248 N.Y. 635 (1928),
Papers on Appeal.

20. Moses to Pauchogue Land Corporation, December 4, 1924, *Pauchogue Land Corporation v. Long Island State Park Commission*, 248 N.Y. 635 (1928), Papers on Appeal; Goldsmith, Memorandum on Appropriation of Lands for Long Island Park, December 4, 1924, AES Official Correspondence.

21. Statement under Rule 234, *Pauchogue Land Corporation v. Long Island State Park Commission*, 248 N.Y. 635 (1928), Papers on Appeal; Arthur W. Page to Stimson, December 2, 1924, Stimson Papers.

22. AES, *Public Papers*, 1925:62-64, 88-95.

23. *Dubuque Herald*, February 4, 1925, Clipping, AES Official Correspondence; *New York Herald Tribune*, February 26, 1925; Charles Downing Lay, *A Park System for Long Island*, February 1925; Jerome V. Jerome, Richard Melville, and Charles Suydam, Jr., *State Parks* [March, 1925], AES Official Correspondence; Wald to Eberly Hutchinson, March 26, 1925, Wald Papers.

24. *New York Times*, February 12, 13, 27, March 6, 1925.

25. AES, *Public Papers*, 1925:236-39. In *Power Broker*, chap. 10, Caro charged Moses, "the best bill drafter in Albany," and Smith's choice for chairman of the State Council of Parks and of the Long Island State Park Commission, with duplicity in framing the park measures of 1924 by inserting provisions to magnify his own power. On pp. 174-75 and pp. 185-86, Caro used entry and appropriation, which the legislature was eliminating in the Thayer bill of 1925, as an example of the deviousness of Moses. As explained above, however, administrative procedure in eminent domain was not uncommon and had applied to parks at least as far back as 1916.

26. *New York Times*, March 27, 1925; *Legislative Index*, 1925.

27. AES, *Public Papers*, 1925:295-99; *New York Times*, April 3, 1925; *New York Herald Tribune*, April 3, 1925.

28. Amended Complaint, April 30, 1925, *Pauchogue Land Corporation v. Long Island State Park Commission*, 248 N.Y. 635 (1928), Papers on Appeal.

29. *New York Times*, May 17, 1925; AES to Arthur W. Page, April 23, 1925; Stimson to Page, April 29, 1925; Stimson to Charles E. Shepard, May 25, 1925, Stimson Papers; Stimson to AES, May 18, 1925; [AES] to Stimson, May 20, 1925, AES Official Correspondence.

30. Stimson to AES, June 8, 1925, Stimson Papers; [AES] to Moses, May 20, 1925; Moses to AES, May 21, 1925, AES Official Correspondence.

31. *New York Times*, March 27, April 10, 1925.

32. AES to FDR, May 21, 1925, FDR Papers; Minutes of the State Council of Parks, May 14, 1925; Gannett to AES, May 28, 1925, AES Official Correspondence; *New York Times*, May 27, 28, 1925.

33. AES, *Public Papers,* 1925:17-18, 758-65; *New York Times,* June 13, 1925.

34. [AES] to J. DuPratt White, June 18, 1925; Clearwater to AES, June 20, 1925, AES Official Correspondence; Stimson to Clearwater, June 15, 1925, Stimson Papers; FDR to the Editor, June 15, 1925; FDR to James W. Wadsworth, June 18, 1925, FDR Papers.

35. [AES] to George Gordon Battle, June 8, 1925; Battle to AES, June 12, 19, 1925, and enclosures, AES Official Correspondence; Hylan to AES, June 12, 1925, George B. Graves Papers.

36. *New York Times,* June 22, 1925.

37. Ibid., June 23, 1925; AES, *Public Papers,* 1925:249-68; Rose A. Pedrick to AES, June 16, 1925, AES Official Correspondence.

38. AES, *Public Papers,* 1925:522-23; Copy of Moses to William Delavan Baldwin, June 2, 1925; [AES] to Walter T. Arndt, June 24, 1925; AES to Nelson S. Spencer, June 24, 1925, AES Official Correspondence.

39. *New York Times,* June 24, 25, 1925; AES, *Public Papers,* 1925:524-29.

40. *New York Times,* June 24, 25, 26, 1925. In his account of the special session in *Power Broker,* pp. 199-202, Caro alleged that Smith tried to blackmail the Westchester delegation into supporting him by threatening to veto a bill for a new county charter that was then on his desk. The official record in the governor's *Public Papers,* 1925:376-78, however, shows that he signed the bill on April 9, shortly after the regular session adjourned.

41. *New York Times,* June 27, 1925.

42. AES, *Public Papers,* 1925:358-60.

43. *New York Times,* June 26, 27, 1925; Stimson to John H. Finley, June 15, 1925, Stimson Papers; *New York Herald Tribune,* June 11, 27, 1925; Caro, *Power Broker,* chap. 11.

44. *New York Times,* September 11, 1925; Macy to AES, September 11, 1925; Macy to Heckscher, September 11, 1925, *Pauchogue Land Corporation v. Long Island State Park Commission,* 248 N.Y. 635 (1928), Papers on Appeal.

45. H. F. Whitney to Long Island State Park Commission, September 23, 1925; Resolution of Long Island State Park Commission, September 23, 1925; Transcript of Jury Trial; AES, Approval of Entry and Appropriation, September 23, 1925; Moses to Pauchogue Land Corporation, September 24, 1925, *Pauchogue Land Corporation v. Long Island State Park Commission,* 248 N.Y. 635 (1928), Papers on Appeal; *New York Times,* September 25, 1925.

46. Joseph S. Auerbach to Macy, October 5, 1925, Mills Papers; Suffolk County Taxpayers' Association, *Park Memorandum,* August 24, 1925; Copy of Suffolk County Park Committee, Report to the Board of Supervisors, November 10, 1925, Stimson Papers; Copy of Charles B. Davey to Edward Floyd-Jones, February 19, 1926, Assembly, 1926, int. 1665, print 2317, Veto Jacket Collection, New York State Archives, Albany (hereafter cited as Veto Jackets).

47. Shiebler to Stimson, December 3, 11, 1925, March 12, 1926; Stimson to Shiebler, December 9, 1925, April 9, 16, 1926, Stimson Papers.

48. Shiebler to Stimson, December 8, 1925, ibid.; AES, *Public Papers,* 1926:361-63, 369-70, 386-90.

49. AES, *Public Papers,* 1926:359, 375-77; [AES] to Joseph M. Proskauer, April 2, 1926; Proskauer to AES, March 29, 1926, George B. Graves Papers.

50. AES, *Public Papers,* 1926:623-26; *Laws of N.Y.,* 1926, chap. 619.

51. AES, *Public Papers,* 1923:541-43; Carl Sherman to AES, January 15, 1923; Francis X. Disney to AES, January 2, 29, 1925; Disney to George B. Graves, February 8, 1926; Disney to AES, December 9, 1926, AES Official Correspondence; *New York v. Santa Clara Lumber Company,* 215 App. Div. 47-48 (1926); 225 App. Div. 716 (1928).

52. Stimson, Memorandum, December 2, 1925, AES Official Correspondence; AES, *Public Papers,* 1926:617-18; *Laws of N.Y.,* 1926, chap. 437.

53. AES, *Public Papers,* 1926:55; *New York Times,* January 26, February 25, 1925; Caro, *Power Broker,* pp. 207-11; Copy of Shiebler to George K. Morris, March 10, 1926; Copy of Shiebler to Charles D. Hilles, April 4, 1926; Copy of Shiebler to Charles J. Hewitt, March 10, 1926; Copy of Shiebler to Eberly Hutchinson, March 10, 1926, Stimson Papers.

54. *Laws of N.Y.,* 1926, chap. 16.

55. Minutes of the Second Hearing on the Estimates and Maps Submitted by the State Council of Parks, March 16, 1926, AES Official Correspondence.

56. Shiebler to Hewitt and Hutchinson, March 19, 1926; Stimson to Hewitt, March 18, 1926; Hewitt to Stimson, March 22, 1926; Hutchinson to Stimson, March 20, 1926; De Forest to Stimson, May 6, 1926; Stimson to Hutchinson, March 23, 1926, Stimson Papers.

57. [AES] to De Forest, April 22, 1926; [AES] to Stimson, April 22, 1926; De Forest to AES, April 27, 1926; [AES] to Stimson, May 8, 1926; Stimson to AES, May 11, 1926, AES Official Correspondence; Stimson, Memorandum on Long Island Parkways, May 20, 1926; Stimson to Scudder, June 15, 1926, Stimson Papers.

58. Moses to AES, June 26, 1926; Frederick Stuart Greene to AES, August 7, 1928, AES Official Correspondence; AES, *Public Papers,* 1928:702-9, 720; *New York Times,* August 17, 18, 1928.

59. Rodgers, *Robert Moses,* chap. 4; Caro, *Power Broker,* pp. 276-80, 299-304.

60. *Pauchogue Land Corporation v. Long Island State Park Commission,* 243 N.Y. 15-28 (1926).

61. Ibid.

62. Transcript of Trial, June 3, 4, 7, 1926; Selah B. Strong, Judgment, June 7, 1926; Walter H. Pollak, Affidavits, June 8, 15, 1926; George D. Carrington, Brief for Defendants-Appellants [between July and October, 1926], *Pauchogue Land Corporation v. Long Island State Park Commission,* 218 App. Div. 785 (1926), Papers on Appeal; *Pauchogue Land Corporation v. Long Island State Park Commission,* 218 App. Div. 785 (1926).

63. Transcript of Trial, December 13-30, 1926, *Pauchogue Land Corporation v. Long Island State Park Commission,* 248 N.Y. 635 (1928), Papers on Appeal.

64. Ibid.

65. Ibid.

66. *Pauchogue Land Corporation v. Long Island State Park Commission,* 248 N.Y. 635-36 (1928); [AES] to George Foster Peabody, July 21, 1928; George B. Graves, Press Release, July 19, 1928, AES Official Correspondence; *Pauchogue Land Corporation v. Long Island State Park Commission,* 278 U.S. 657 (1929); *New York Times,* December 22, 1929.

67. *Flagg v. Moses,* 132 Misc. 494-97 (1928).

68. Moses to AES, December 17, 1924; Clearwater to Moses, December 12, 1924, AES Official Correspondence; *New York Times,* February 27, June 25, 1925.

69. Moses to AES, May 28, 1926, and enclosure; [AES] to Moses, June 3, 1926; Report of a Special Committee of the State Council of Parks, July 23, 1926; Ansley Wilcox to Moses, July 2, 1926, and enclosed Resolutions; Alexander Macdonald and Moses to AES, May 25, 1927; [AES] to De Forest, May 25, 1927, AES Official Correspondence; AES, *Public Papers,* 1928:170-72.

70. Wilcox to AES, June 22, 1926; Wilcox to Moses, August 5, 1926; Copy of Clearwater to De Forest, March 28, 1927; De Forest to AES, April 1, 1927; Clearwater to AES, June 29, 1927; Moses to AES, July 15, 1927; [AES] to Clearwater, July 22, 1927; Clearwater to AES, July 2, 1928; Moses, Memorandum, July 11, 1928, AES Official Correspondence; Caro, *Power Broker,* chap. 14 and p. 253.

71. Edgar B. Nixon, ed., *Franklin D. Roosevelt and Conservation 1911-1945* (Washington, D.C.: United States Government Printing Office, 1957), 1:52, 57-58; Rodgers, *Robert Moses*, p. 39; Caro, *Power Broker,* pp. 291-98.

72. FDR to George B. Graves [November, 1926], and enclosure; Joseph H. Wilson to Graves, November 24, 1926; [Graves] to FDR, November 30, 1926, AES Official Correspondence; Freidel, *Franklin D. Roosevelt: The Ordeal,* pp. 219-21; Caro, *Power Broker,* pp. 287-91.

73. FDR to AES, December 3, 1926; Moses to AES, December 23, 1926; [AES] to FDR, January 10, 1927, AES Official Correspondence.

74. FDR to AES, December 14, 1927; [AES] to FDR, January 23, 1928; FDR to AES, January 30, 1928; [AES] to FDR, February 3, 1928, AES Official Correspondence.

75. Caro, *Power Broker,* chaps. 12-16 and p. 241.

76. AES, *Public Papers,* 1926:54.

77. *New York Times,* June 14, 1925; AES, *Public Papers,* 1927:72.

78. Nixon, *Franklin D. Roosevelt and Conservation,* 1: 86-89; Bellush, *Franklin D. Roosevelt as Governor,* pp. 94-98; Freidel, *Franklin D. Roosevelt: The Triumph,* chap. 16 and p. 232.

79. Donald C. Swain, *Federal Conservation Policy 1921-1933* (Berkeley: University of California Press, 1963); Ise, *Our National Park Policy.*

80. *New York Times,* May 19, 1927, March 9, 1928.

NOTES TO CHAPTER 5

1. The housing question is surveyed from different perspectives in the following: James Ford, *Slums and Housing: With Special Reference to New York City* (Cambridge: Harvard University Press, 1936); Roy Lubove, *The Progressives and the Slums: Tenement House Reform in New York City 1890-1917* (Pittsburgh: University of Pittsburgh Press, 1962); Anthony Jackson, *A Place Called Home: A History of Low-Cost Housing in Manhattan* (Cambridge, Mass.: MIT Press, 1976).

2. Lubove, *Progressives and the Slums,* p. 251; Edith Elmer Wood, *Recent Trends in American Housing* (New York: Macmillan Company, 1931), passim and p. 8; Robert Moore Fisher, *Twenty Years of Public Housing: Economic Aspects of the Federal Program* (New York: Harper & Brothers, 1959), pp. 73-79.

3. Edith Berger Drellich and Andrée Emery, *Rent Control in War and Peace: A Study Prepared for the Laws and Administration Committee of the Citizens' Housing Council of New York* (New York: National Municipal League, 1939), pp. 10-32; "Housing after World War I: Will History Repeat Itself," *National Housing Bulletin of the National Housing Agency* no. 4 (1945).

4. AES, *Public Papers,* 1919:50, 671-73.

5. Ibid., 753-56; *New York Times,* May 17, 1919.

6. *New York Times,* May 18, April 13, 1919.

7. [AES] to Lockwood, May 16, 1919; Copy of Lockwood to Abram I. Elkus, May 17, 1919, AES Official Correspondence; *New York Times,* May 11, June 11, 1919.

8. *New York Times,* May 1, 7, 9, June 15, 1919.

9. AES, *Public Papers,* 1919:674-76; [AES] to James P. Maher, June 12, 1919, AES Official Correspondence.

10. AES, *Public Papers,* 1919:86-88, 676-79.

11. *Laws of N.Y.,* 1919, chaps. 647-50; *New York Times,* June 17, 18, August 5, 1919.

12. AES, *Public Papers,* 1920:203-7.

13. Ibid., 207-51; Moskowitz to AES, April 14, 1920, AES Official Correspondence.

14. N.Y., *Legislative Documents,* 1920, no. 14; *New York Times,* April 1, March 30, 23, 1920; Minutes of Joint Hearing by the Senate and Assembly Committees on Cities, March 23, 1920, AES Official Correspondence.

15. *Laws of N.Y.,* 1920, chaps. 130-39, 209-10; *New York Times,* April 1, 1920. For a thorough analysis of the emergency rent laws, see Drellich and Emery, *Rent Control.*

16. Walter T. Arndt to AES, May 27, 1920; Raymond V. Ingersoll to AES, April 27, 1920; Moskowitz to AES, June 1, 1920; Moskowitz to AES [May, 1920], and enclosed Memorandum on Housing; [AES] to Moskowitz, May 11, 1920, AES Official Correspondence.

17. [AES] to W. A. Morrison, June 4, 1920, AES Official Correspondence; AES, *Up to Now,* pp. 269-70. For the Red Scare, see below, chap. 9.

18. AES to James C. Sheldon, August 10, 1920, AES Official Correspondence; *New York Times,* August 7, 14, 26, September 3, 14, 1920.

19. *New York Times,* August 17, 1920; Digest of Recommendations on Housing [September, 1920]; Benjamin C. Marsh to AES, August 31, 1920; P. R. Moses to AES, September 3, 1920; Copeland to AES, September 10, 1920; Levy to AES, July 23, 1920;

Osborn to AES, September 17, 1920; Real Estate Board of New
York, *Recommendations on Legislation to Relieve the Housing
Shortage* [September, 1920]; Stewart Browne to AES, September
16, 1920; S. Fullerton Weaver to AES, September 16, 1920, and
enclosed Memorandum; George Gordon Battle to James A. Parsons,
September 22, 1920, and enclosed Plan for Relieving the Short-
age of Homes; [AES] to Battle, September 23, 1920, AES Official
Correspondence.

20.   AES, *Public Papers,* 1920:273-79.

21.   N.Y., *Legislative Documents,* 1920 (Extraordinary
Session), no. 11.

22.   The following analysis of the emergency rent laws
depends heavily on two legal references: Roy T. Ambert, ed.,
*McAdam's Rights, Duties, Remedies, and Incidents Belonging to
and Growing out of the Relation of Landlord and Tenant,* 5th ed.
(New York: Baker, Voorhis & Co., 1934), 1:102-3, 113-14, 124-
25, 155; 2:1132-36; Joseph Rasch, *The New York Law of Landlord
and Tenant and Summary Proceedings* (New York: Baker, Voorhis
& Co., 1950), 1:8-9, 125-26, 145-50; 2:795-809.

23.   *Laws of N.Y.,* 1920, chaps. 942-45, 947-48, 950-53.

24.   Untermyer to AES, August 14, 1920; AES to Untermyer,
September 11, 1920; Untermyer to AES, September 12, 1920, AES
Official Correspondence; *New York Times,* October 14, 1920;
Henry F. Pringle, *Big Frogs* (New York: Macy-Masius, 1928), pp.
139-52; *Legislative Index,* 1920.

25.   N.Y., *Legislative Documents,* 1920 (Extraordinary
Session), no. 11, p. 20; AES, *Public Papers,* 1920:276-78; De
Forest to AES, September 23, 1920; Lawson Purdy to AES, Septem-
ber 20, 1920; Charles Loring Brace to AES, September 21, 1920;
[AES] to Brace, September 23, 1920; John J. Murphy to AES,
September 25, 1920, AES Official Correspondence.

26.   [Jeremiah F. Connor] to Graves, August 17, 1920;
Graves to Connor, August 25, 1920; Robert Murray Haig, "The
Exemption of Mortgage Interest as a Solution of the Housing
Problem," n.d.; Walter H. Knapp, Memorandum in Opposition to
Senate Bill No. 1, Int. No. 1, September 23, 1920, AES Official
Correspondence; AES, *Public Papers,* 1920:276; N.Y., *Legislative
Documents,* 1920 (Extraordinary Session), no. 11, pp. 17, 20;
Legislative Index, 1920; *Laws of N.Y.,* 1920, chap. 949.

27.   Samuel McCune Lindsay, *Economic Aspects of the So-
Called Emergency Housing Legislation of 1920 in New York State
and the Alleged Housing Shortage in New York City,* n.d.; [AES]
to Raymond V. Ingersoll, September 30, 1920, AES Official Correspondence; *New York Times,* September 28, November 1, 1920.

28.   [Jeremiah F. Connor?] to Moskowitz, November 11,
1920, AES Official Correspondence; AES, *Public Papers,* 1920:
676-84.

29. AES to Charles D. Newton, October 14, 1920, AES Official Correspondence; Franklin A. Smith, *Judicial Review of Legislation in New York 1906-1938* (New York: Columbia University Press, 1952), p. 171; Drellich and Emery, *Rent Control,* pp. 33-35, 113; N.Y., *Legislative Documents,* 1922, no. 60, pp. 19-35, 247; *Laws of N.Y.,* 1922, chaps. 663, 664.

30. Lockwood to AES, January 29 [1923]; Untermyer to AES, January 30, March 5, 1923; [AES] to [Lockwood and/or Untermyer], [January or February, 1923], AES Official Correspondence; *Legislative Index,* 1923; AES, *Public Papers,* 1923: 196-201; *Laws of N.Y.,* 1923, chap. 694.

31. AES, *Public Papers,* 1923:257; Felix Weill to AES, August 12, 1923; Joseph A. Gavagan to George R. Van Namee, October 17, 1923; [AES] to Weill, August 16, 1923, AES Official Correspondence.

32. *Laws of N.Y.,* 1923, chaps. 278, 874, 892; Jabez E. Cunningham to AES, May 21, 1923, Laws of N.Y., 1923, chap. 892, Bill Jackets; Samuel B. Hand, *Counsel and Advise: A Political Biography of Samuel I. Rosenman* (New York: Garland Publishing, 1979), pp. 9-13; *New York Times,* May 23, 1923.

33. AES, *Public Papers,* 1924:77-149, 49; *New York Times,* February 7, 12, 1924; *Laws of N.Y.,* 1924, chap. 6.

34. *Laws of N.Y.,* 1924, chap. 629; Clarence M. Lewis to AES, April 30, 1924; Cohen to Terence Farley, April 21, 1924; Seabury C. Mastick to Farley, April 21, 1924; Chauncey B. Griffen to AES, April 18, 1924, Laws of N.Y., 1924, chap. 629, Bill Jackets.

35. N.Y., *Legislative Documents,* 1926, no. 40; 1927, no. 85; *Laws of N.Y.,* 1926, chap. 6; 1927, chap. 568.

36. N.Y., *Legislative Documents,* 1928, no. 85; *New York Times,* March 19, 1928; *Laws of N.Y.,* 1928, chap. 826; Frank W. Demuth to AES, March 29, 1928, Laws of N.Y., 1928, chap. 826, Bill Jackets.

37. N.Y., *Legislative Documents,* 1922, no. 60; 1923, no. 48.

38. Lockwood to AES, January 29 [1923]; Untermyer to AES, January 30, 1923, AES Official Correspondence; *New York Times,* January 17, 1923; *Legislative Index,* 1923.

39. [George R. Van Namee] to Gilbert H. Montague, January 10, 1923, AES Official Correspondence; *Legislative Index,* 1923; *New York Times,* January 25, February 1, 1923; Mills to AES, November 3, 1923, Mills Papers.

40. *New York Times,* February 15, 1923.

41. Richard Hofstadter, *The Age of Reform: From Bryan to F.D.R.,* Vintage bks. ed. (New York: Random House, 1955), chaps. 4, 6.

42. AES, *Public Papers*, 1923:196-201; AES to Stein, October 13, 1923, AES Official Correspondence; Roy Lubove, *Community Planning in the 1920's: The Contribution of the Regional Planning Association of America* (Pittsburgh: University of Pittsburgh Press, 1963); Clarke A. Chambers, *Seedtime of Reform: American Social Service and Social Action 1918-1933* (Minneapolis: University of Minnesota Press, 1963), pp. 133-38.

43. AES, *Public Papers*, 1924:77-79, 50, 283-84; *Legislative Index*, 1924, 1925.

44. AES, *Public Papers*, 1925:192-233, quotation on 203.

45. William M. Calder to AES, December 28, 1923; AES to Calder, January 7, 1924, AES Official Correspondence.

46. AES, *Public Papers*, 1926:52-54; 1924:283-95; *Laws of N.Y.*, 1924, chaps. 87, 284.

47. Julius Henry Cohen, *They Builded Better Than They Knew* (New York: Julian Messner, 1946), pp. 119-21; Gerald Fetner, "Public Power and Professional Responsibility: Julius Henry Cohen and the Origins of the Public Authority," *American Journal of Legal History* 21 (1977):15-39; Cohen to AES, January 21, 1926, AES Official Correspondence; AES, *Public Papers*, 1926:146-51.

48. AES, *Public Papers*, 1926:151-93.

49. Alfred E. Smith, "To Stimulate Low-Cost Housing," *American City Magazine* 34 (1926):127-28; Clipping from *Michigan Daily*, March 17, 1926, AES Official Correspondence; *New York Times*, March 15, 1926.

50. Bailey Burritt to AES, March 24, 1926, and enclosures; I. Randolph Jacobs to AES, January 13, 1926; Henry Brady to AES, March 18, 1926, AES Official Correspondence; Arthur Mann, *La Guardia: A Fighter against His Times 1882-1933* (Philadelphia: J. B. Lippincott Company, 1959), p. 256.

51. *Legislative Index*, 1926; Memorandum for Art [between February 22 and March 2, 1926], AES Official Correspondence; *New York Times*, March 11, February 28, March 13, 1926.

52. *New York Times*, February 23, 24, March 12, 22, 27, 31, 1926.

53. Walter Stabler to AES, March 26, 1926, AES Official Correspondence; [AES] to Cohen, March 19, 1926, George B. Graves Papers.

54. AES, *Public Papers*, 1926:232-46; Fetner, "Public Power and Professional Responsibility," pp. 16-18, 27-30.

55. AES, *Public Papers*, 1926:658-59; Hofstadter to AES, April 2, 1926; Cohen to AES, April 5, 1926, and enclosed Suggested Plan of Discussion, Memorandum #2, Supplementary Notes, AES Official Correspondence.

56. Minutes of Hearing on the Downing-Bloch Bill and the Nicoll-Hofstadter Bill, April 7, 1926, AES Official Correspondence; *New York Times,* April 8, 1926.

57. Cohen to AES, April 8, 19, 1926, AES Official Correspondence.

58. Cohen to AES, April 19, 1926; Nicoll to AES, April 20, 1926, AES Official Correspondence.

59. *Laws of N.Y.,* 1926, chap. 823.

60. Cohen, *They Builded Better Than They Knew,* p. 123; Cohen to AES, May 3, 1926, Laws of N.Y., 1926, chap. 823, Bill Jackets; AES, *Public Papers,* 1926:427-29.

61. Darwin James to AES, December 1, 1926, AES Official Correspondence; *New York Times,* December 16, 1926; June 8, 1927.

62. Louis H. Pink, *The New Day in Housing* (New York: John Day Company, 1928), pp. 118-24; *New York Times,* November 7, 1927.

63. [AES] to Edward W. Murphy, February 5, 1926, AES Official Correspondence; *New York Times,* December 16, 1926; AES, *Public Papers,* 1928:612-14.

64. Ford, *Slums and Housing,* 2:693-95; Wood, *Recent Trends in American Housing,* chap. 14; Pink, *New Day in Housing,* passim and pp. 187, ix.

65. AES, *Public Papers,* 1923:258; 1925:350; 1927:156; AES to Darwin R. James, February 10, 1927, AES Official Correspondence.

66. AES, *Public Papers,* 1924:610-13; Mel Scott, *American City Planning since 1890* (Berkeley: University of California Press, 1969).

67. Scott, *American City Planning,* pp. 255-60.

68. Wood, *Recent Trends in American Housing,* p. 202. Dorothy Shaffter, *State Housing Agencies* (New York: Columbia University Press, 1942).

69. Fisher, *Twenty Years of Public Housing,* pp. 81-125; Timothy L. McDonnell, *The Wagner Housing Act: A Case Study of the Legislative Process* (Chicago: Loyola University Press, 1957), pp. 54-56, 88-89; Fetner, "Public Power and Professional Responsibility," p. 17.

1. Pink, *New Day in Housing*, p. x.

2. De Witt, *Progressive Movement*, chaps. 1, 12, and p. 24; Russell B. Nye, *Midwestern Progressive Politics: A Historical Study of Its Origins and Development 1870-1958* (East Lansing: Michigan State University Press, 1959), pp. 181-90; Buenker, *Urban Liberalism and Progressive Reform*, passim and p. viii; Robert Bremner, *From the Depths: The Discovery of Poverty in the United States* (New York: New York University Press, 1956), chap. 8 and p. 138; Allen F. Davis, *Spearheads for Reform: The Social Settlements and the Progressive Movement 1890-1914* (New York: Oxford University Press, 1967), passim and p. xiii.

3. Hofstadter, *Age of Reform*; George E. Mowry, *The Era of Theodore Roosevelt and the Birth of Modern America 1900-1912* (New York: Harper & Row, 1958); Gabriel Kolko, *The Triumph of Conservatism: A Reinterpretation of American History, 1900-1916* (Chicago: Quadrangle Books, 1967); Robert H. Wiebe, *The Search for Order 1877-1920* (New York: Hill and Wang, 1967); Otis L. Graham, Jr., *An Encore for Reform: The Old Progressives and the New Deal* (New York: Oxford University Press, 1967); James Weinstein, *The Corporate Ideal in the Liberal State: 1900-1918* (Boston: Beacon Press, 1968).

4. Elizabeth Faulkner Baker, *Protective Labor Legislation: With Special Reference to Women in the State of New York* (New York: Columbia University Press, 1925), pp. 24-102; John R. Commons et al., *History of Labor in the United States,* 4 vols. (New York: Macmillan Company, 1918-35), 3:660-85; Judith A. Baer, *The Chains of Protection: The Judicial Response to Women's Labor Legislation* (Westport, Conn.: Greenwood Press, 1978).

5. Commons, *History of Labor,* 3:399-697; Walter I. Trattner, *Crusade for the Children: A History of the National Child Labor Committee and Child Labor Reform in America* (Chicago: Quadrangle Books, 1970); Roy Lubove, *The Struggle for Social Security 1900-1935* (Cambridge: Harvard University Press, 1968); Hace Sorel Tishler, *Self-Reliance and Social Security 1870-1917* (Port Washington, N.Y.: Kennikat Press, 1971); Clara M. Beyer, *History of Labor Legislation for Women in Three States,* U.S. Department of Labor Women's Bureau Bulletin no. 66 (Washington, D.C., 1929), p. 12.

6. George E. Mowry, *The California Progressives* (Berkeley: University of California Press, 1951); Robert S. Maxwell, *La Follette and the Rise of the Progressives in Wisconsin* (Madison: State Historical Society of Wisconsin, 1956), pp. 59, 153-55; Hoyt Landon Warner, *Progressivism in Ohio 1897-1917* (Columbus: Ohio State University Press, 1964), pp. 23, 213-16, 329-30, 334-37; Davis, *Spearheads for Reform,* chap. 6.

7. Irwin Yellowitz, *Labor and the Progressive Movement in New York State, 1897-1916* (Ithaca: Cornell University Press, 1965); Wesser, *Charles Evans Hughes,* pp. 307-22; Pusey, *Charles Evans Hughes,* p. 212.

8. Kerr, "New York Factory Investigating Commission"; AES, *Up to Now,* chaps. 6-8, and p. 96.

9. George Martin, *Madam Secretary: Frances Perkins* (Boston: Houghton Mifflin Company, 1976), pts. 2, 3; Perkins, "Al Smith as I Knew Him" [November 22, 1957], pp. 17-22, Frances Perkins Papers, Labor-Management Documentation Center, M. P. Catherwood Library, Cornell University, Ithaca, N.Y.; Perkins, 1:162, Columbia Oral History.

10. N.Y., *Senate Documents,* 1913, no. 36, pp. 215, 286; 1915, no. 43, passim and p. 73; 1912, no. 30, p. 110.

11. *Record CC 1915,* pp. 1802-60, 2082-2121.

12. Ibid., pp. 2111, 2110.

13. Ibid., pp. 2108, 4127.

14. *New York Times,* October 30, 1918.

15. AES, *Public Papers,* 1919:35-38.

16. *New York Times,* October 30, 1918; AES, *Public Papers,* 1919:350-51; Connor to George R. Van Namee, March 18, 1919, AES Official Correspondence.

17. AES, *Public Papers,* 1919:351-56, 66-67; [AES] to John Mitchell, June 27, 1919; Mitchell to AES, July 14, 1919, AES Official Correspondence; *Laws of N.Y.,* 1919, chap. 629.

18. [AES] to John Haag, July 1, 1919; Haag to AES, July 8, 1919; Jonah J. Goldstein to AES, April 3, 1919, AES Official Correspondence; AES, *Public Papers,* 1919:356-64.

19. Dawson to AES, June 2, August 12, 1919; Connor to AES, August 22, 1919, AES Official Correspondence.

20. AES, *Public Papers,* 1919:364-409.

21. Ibid.; N.Y., State Industrial Commission, *Answer of State Industrial Commission to the Report of Jeremiah F. Connor Moreland Act Commissioner on State Insurance Fund,* 1919; Missal, *Moreland Act,* pp. 82-84.

22. [James A. Parsons?] to Connor, December 3, 1919, AES Official Correspondence; AES, *Public Papers,* 1920:68-73, 403; *Laws of N.Y.,* 1920, chaps. 527, 529, 530, 532, 539.

23. AES, *Public Papers,* 1920:34-35; *Laws of N.Y.,* 1920, chaps, 538, 760; Martin, *Madam Secretary,* pp. 141-45; Perkins, 2:399-400, Columbia Oral History.

24. AES, *Public Papers*, 1920:71; Bernard Shientag to George R. Van Namee, February 20, 1920; [Van Namee] to Edward Warner, March 5, 1920, AES Official Correspondence; *Legislative Index*, 1924-28; *New York Times*, March 24, 1927.

25. AES, *Public Papers*, 1919:64-66, 616-26, 636-43; Belle Moskowitz to George Foster Peabody, March 24, 1919, Peabody Papers; *New York Times*, April 9, May 14, 1919.

26. *Proceedings of the New York State Federation of Labor*, 1917:72-78; AES, *Public Papers*, 1919:42; [George R. Van Namee] to Claude C. Granger, May 24, 1919; Benjamin B. Lawrence to AES, January 9, 1919; [AES] to Lawrence, January 14, 1919, AES Official Correspondence; George F. Chandler, pp. 70-72, Columbia Oral History; AES, *Up to Now*, pp. 179-81; Josephson and Josephson, *Al Smith*, pp. 347-49.

27. Chandler, p. 77, Columbia Oral History.

28. Edward J. Davis to AES, March 5, 1919; Chandler to George R. Van Namee, March 7, 1919; [Van Namee] to Davis, March 8, 1919, AES Official Correspondence.

29. H. T. Sherman to AES, June 7, 1919; Frank Morrison to AES, June 20, 1919; George R. Van Namee to Morrison, June 23, 1919, AES Official Correspondence.

30. Martin, *Madam Secretary*, chap. 13; Chandler, pp. 72-75, Columbia Oral History; *New York Times*, July 15, 1919; Press Release, July 19, 1919; William J. Gillen to AES, September 2, 1919; [AES] to Gillen, September 5, 1919, AES Official Correspondence.

31. AES to Foster Studholme, August 19, 1919; George P. Dutton to AES, August 20, 23, 25, 1919, AES Official Correspondence.

32. Edgar T. Brackett to AES, September 4, 1919; [George R. Van Namee?] to Brackett, September 8, 1919, AES Official Correspondence.

33. Samuel Beskin to AES, September 18, 1919; George P. Dutton to George R. Van Namee, September 18, 25, 1919; [AES] to Beskin, September 26, 1919, AES Official Correspondence.

34. Chandler to AES, September 22, 1919; George P. Dutton to AES, September 24, 1919; William Pfaff to AES, September 25, 1919; [AES] to Pfaff, September 26, 1919; William J. Griffiths to George R. Van Namee, November 25, 1919; Dutton to Van Namee, November 8, 1919; [Van Namee] to Griffiths, December 24, 1919; Franklin D. Locke to AES, December 30, 1919; Norman Mack to AES, January 2, 1920; Samuel B. Botsford to AES, January 7, 1920; [Van Namee] to Botsford, January 14, 1920, AES Official Correspondence.

35. Moskowitz to AES, August 27, September 4, 1919, AES Official Correspondence; AES, *Public Papers*, 1919:553-84; 1920:513-16.

36.   AES to Bernard L. Shientag, October 22, 1919; Perkins to AES, October 27, 1919; Bernard Nolan to Perkins, November 8, 1919; Nolan to AES, November 8, 1919, AES Official Correspondence.

37.   Jesse Thomas Carpenter, *Competition and Collective Bargaining in the Needle Trades, 1910-1967* (Ithaca: New York State School of Industrial and Labor Relations, Cornell University, 1972), pp. xix-xx, 1-89; David Gurowsky, "Factional Disputes within the ILGWU, 1919-1928," (Ph.D. dissertation, State University of New York at Binghamton, 1978, reproduced by University Microfilms), pp. 12-26; Transcript of Hearing upon the Matters in Dispute between the Cloak, Suit, and Skirt Manufacturers' Protective Association and the International Ladies' Garment Workers' Union and the Joint Board of the Cloak Makers' Unions, January 5, 1920; Report of the Governor's Special Labor Board for the Settlement of the Controversy in the Cloak, Suit, and Skirt Industry, January 26, 1920; Joseph Barondess to AES, January 6, 27, 1920; Louis Langer to AES, February 9, 1920, AES Official Correspondence.

38.   AES, *Public Papers*, 1924:579-83; Louis Levine, *The Women's Garment Workers: A History of the International Ladies' Garment Workers' Union* (New York: B. W. Huebsch, 1924), chap. 23; Louis H. Solomon to AES, July 9, 1924; Morris Sigman to AES, July 14, 1924; [AES] to Hillquit, July 25, 1924; Hillquit to AES, July 17, 1924, AES Official Correspondence.

39.   Gurowsky, "Factional Disputes within the ILGWU;" Joel Seidman, *The Needle Trades* (New York: Farrar & Rinehart, 1942), pp. 153-69.

40.   AES, *Public Papers*, 1926:680-96; *New York Times*, June 2, July 2, 15, November 13, 14, 1926.

41.   *New York Times*, April 13, 1919; AES, *Public Papers*, 1919:35-38.

42.   Ronald L. Numbers, *Almost Persuaded: American Physicians and Compulsory Health Insurance, 1912-1920* (Baltimore: Johns Hopkins University Press, 1978); *New York Times*, March 6, 17, 1919.

43.   AES, *Public Papers*, 1919:76-82; *New York Times*, March 21, April 13, 15, 16, 17, 18, 1919.

44.   Davenport to AES, June 14, 1919; [AES] to Bloom, September 18, 1919, AES Official Correspondence; AES, *Public Papers*, 1919:668.

45.   AES, *Public Papers*, 1920:33-37; *New York Times*, March 23, January 6, April 24, 1920; *Legislative Index*, 1920; Mary E. Dreier to AES, May 1, 1920, AES Official Correspondence.

46.   *New York Times*, September 25, October 14, 15, 16, 31, 1920; Wald to Joseph M. Proskauer, October 8, 1920, Wald Papers.

47.   Bernard L. Shientag to AES, June 22, 1921; AES, Campaign Addresses, October 27, 28, November 4, 1922, AES Papers.

48.   *New York Times,* October 7, 15, 14, 1922; AES, Campaign Address, October 27, 1922, AES Papers.

49.   *New York Times,* February 3, 1923; AES, *Public Papers,* 1923:64-65, 112-16; 1924:58-60.

50.   AES, *Public Papers,* 1924:433-40; *New York Times,* January 17, 1924; John P. Coughlin to AES, January 18, 1924; Thomas J. Curtis to AES, January 16, 1924; Florence Kelley to AES, January 19, 1924; Perkins to AES, January 19, 1924, AES Official Correspondence.

51.   Minutes of the Hearings in the Matter of the Investigation of Charges Made by Associated Industries against the State Department of Labor, January 22, 23, 1924, AES Official Correspondence.

52.   Owen R. Lovejoy to AES, January 28, 1924, AES Official Correspondence; Martha Bruere to AES, February 12, 1924; Daly to AES, January 24, 1924; [AES] to Daly, January 25, 1924; Daly to AES, January 28, 1924, George B. Graves Papers; Belle Zeller, *Pressure Politics in New York* (New York: Prentice Hall, 1937), pp. 49-55.

53.   *New York Times,* December 16, 25, 1922; December 12, 1923; AES, *Public Papers,* 1923:64-67, 70-72; 1924:51-52, 61-64; Baker, *Protective Labor Legislation,* pp. 168-202.

54.   *Legislative Index,* 1923, 1924; [AES] to Charles E. Donohue, May 4, 1923, George B. Graves Papers; AES, *Public Papers,* 1924:295-97.

55.   George R. Van Namee, Press Release, February 19, 1923; Shientag to AES, April 12, 1923; [AES] to Shientag, April 17, 1923, AES Official Correspondence; Chambers, *Seedtime of Reform,* pp. 70-72; AES, *Public Papers,* 1923:193-96.

56.   John Duffy, "The American Medical Profession and Public Health: From Support to Ambivalence," *Bulletin of the History of Medicine* 53 (1979):1-22; Lloyd C. Taylor, Jr., *The Medical Profession and Social Reform, 1885-1945* (New York: St. Martin's Press, 1974); Walter I. Trattner, *Homer Folks: Pioneer in Social Welfare* (New York: Columbia University Press, 1968), pp. 168-72; C.-E. A. Winslow, *The Life of Hermann M. Biggs: Physician and Statesman of the Public Health* (Philadelphia: Lea and Febiger, 1929), passim and p. 254; *New York Times,* July 14, 1923.

57.   AES, *Public Papers,* 1919:644-70; 1920:35-37; Winslow, *Life of Hermann M. Biggs,* pp. 345-55.

58.   George R. Van Namee, Press Release, February 17, 1923; Memorandum for Governor on Program for Physicians' Conference, February 26, 1923; Fragment of Minutes of Conference on Public Health and Medical Practice, February 26, 1923,

AES Official Correspondence; "Conference on New York State
Medical Problems," *Journal of the American Medical Association*
80 (1923):648; Editorial, *Journal of the AMA* (80):1244-45;
Editorial, *New York State Journal of Medicine* 23 (1923):
168-69.

59. "Report of the Governor's Medical Advisory Committee," *N.Y.S. Journal of Medicine* 23 (1923):220-22; [AES] to
Samuel J. Kopetsky, March 15, 1923; Kopetsky to AES, March 16,
1923, AES Official Correspondence.

60. AES, *Public Papers,* 1923:176-81; *Laws of N.Y.,*
1923, chaps. 662, 638, 637; "House of Delegates," *N.Y.S.
Journal of Medicine* 23 (1923):270; Mathias Nicoll, Jr. to
James A. Parsons, May 18, 1923, Laws of 1923, chap. 662, Bill
Jackets; Winslow, *Life of Hermann M. Biggs,* pp. 367-70.

61. J. Stanley Lemons, *The Woman Citizen: Social
Feminism in the 1920s* (Urbana: University of Illinois Press,
1973), chap. 6 and p. 176; AES, *Public Papers,* 1923:67, 213;
Laws of N.Y., 1923, chap. 843; Narcissa Cox Vanderlip and
Betty W. Mitchell to AES, May 5, 1923, George B. Graves Papers.

62. AES, *Public Papers,* 1923:67; 1925:48; Editorial,
N.Y.S. Journal of Medicine 26 (1926):65; "Governor Smith at the
Annual Meeting," *N.Y.S. Journal of Medicine* 28 (1928):600.

63. Janet Marie Wedel, "The Origins of State Patriarchy
during the Progessive Era: A Sociological Study of the
Mothers' Aid Movement," (Ph.D. dissertation, Washington Univer-
sity, 1975, reproduced by University Microfilms); David M.
Schneider and Albert Deutsch, *The History of Public Welfare in
New York State 1867-1940* (Chicago: University of Chicago
Press, 1941), pp. 180-91; *New York Times,* March 25, 1915; *Laws
of N.Y.,* 1915, chap. 228; Tishler, *Self-Reliance and Social
Security,* p. 142.

64. Schneider and Deutsch, *History of Public Welfare
in New York State 1867-1940,* pp. 237-38; AES, *Public Papers,*
1920:129-30; *Laws of N.Y.,* 1920, chaps. 699, 700.

65. N.Y., *Legislative Documents,* 1922, no. 84; 1923, no.
111; 1924, no. 88; AES, *Public Papers,* 1923:70-72, 202-3; *Laws
of N.Y.,* 1923, chaps. 730, 731, 733; 1924, chap. 458; Mary C.
Tinney to AES, April 18, 1923, AES Official Correspondence;
John Hylan to AES, May 23, 1923, Laws of 1923, chap. 730, Bill
Jackets; Schneider and Deutsch, *History of Public Welfare in
New York State 1867-1940,* pp. 259-60.

66. AES, *Public Papers,* 1923:71; 1924:63-64; 1925:57;
1927:64; 1928:77-78; N.Y., *Legislative Documents,* 1923, no.
111, pp. 13-15.

67. N.Y., *Legislative Documents,* 1925, no. 106, p. 32;
New York Times, September 26, 27, 1924; [AES] to Frederick H.
Allen, December 9, 1924, George B. Graves Papers.

68. AES, *Public Papers*, 1925:57-58; *New York Times*, January 8, 22, 28, 1925; *Legislative Index*, 1925.

69. Jeremy P. Felt, *Hostages of Fortune: Child Labor Reform in New York State* (Syracuse: Syracuse University Press, 1965), chap. 8; Ida Blair to Perkins, May 22, 1925; Perkins to Blair, June 29, 1925, Frances Perkins Papers, Butler Library Special Collections, Columbia University, New York.

70. Morgan J. O'Brien to AES, December 29, 1924; Mary G. Kilbreth to AES, December 13, 1924, AES Official Correspondence.

71. Perkins to Ida Blair, June 29, 1925, Perkins Papers; Perkins, 2:255-63, Columbia Oral History; Martin, *Madam Secretary*, pp. 186-92; Vincent A. McQuade, *The American Catholic Attitude on Child Labor since 1891: A Study of the Formation and Development of a Catholic Attitude on a Specific Social Question* (Washington, D.C.: Catholic University of America, 1938), chaps. 4, 5, 8.

72. *New York Times*, October 2, 4, 29, 1924; AES, *Public Papers*, 1924:628-33, 683-84, 689-90, 702.

73. *New York Times*, September 27, 26, 1924.

74. AES, *Public Papers*, 1925:56, 247-48; N.Y., Legislature, *Legislative Bills*, 1925, Assembly int. no. 1142; *New York Times*, February 26, March 22, 12, 24, 28, 1925; *Legislative Index*, 1925.

75. *New York Times*, April 17, 1925; AES, *Public Papers*, 1925:352-54.

76. AES, *Public Papers*, 1926:51, 211-13; *New York Times*, February 20, 25, March 10, 1926; *Legislative Index*, 1926.

77. AES, *Public Papers*, 1926:49, 629-30; *Laws of N.Y.*, 1926, chap. 427.

78. N.Y., *Legislative Documents*, 1927, no. 69, pp. 16-19; *Laws of N.Y.*, 1927, chap. 453; John M. O'Hanlon to AES, March 28, 1927; Merwin K. Hart to AES, February 2, 1927, and enclosed Annotated Digest of Report of National Industrial Conference Board on the Forty-Eight-Hour Law and New York State Industry; Mrs. Clarence M. Smith, Statement [March, 1927?], Laws of 1927, chap. 453, Bill Jackets; AES, *Public Papers*, 1927:169-70.

79. AES, *Public Papers*, 1925:53-56, 241-42; *New York Times*, January 26, 1925; *Legislative Index*, 1925.

80. N.Y., *Legislative Documents*, 1925, no. 80; AES, *Public Papers*, 1925:379-80, 325-28.

81. *New York Times*, February 26, March 10, 1926; AES, *Public Papers*, 1926:47-50; 1927:54; N.Y., *Legislative Documents*, 1927, no. 69, pp. 23-57; *Laws of N.Y.*, 1927, chaps. 553-58.

82. *New York Times,* January 24, 25, 1928; Perkins to AES, February 17, 1928, AES Official Correspondence.

83. *New York Times,* January 25, 26, 27, 31, February 1, 1928; N.Y., *Legislative Documents,* 1928, no. 87; *Laws of N.Y.,* 1928, chaps, 749, 752, 754, 755.

84. Rogers, p. 82, Columbia Oral History.

85. AES, *Public Papers,* 1928:423-519, quotations on 441, 448; AES to FDR, December 26, 1928, FDR Papers.

86. AES, *Public Papers,* 1928:52-55, 66-78.

87. For a contrary interpretation, which tends to find a disjunction between Smith and the New Deal on labor and welfare, see: Louis Corrado Zuccarello, "The Political Thought of Alfred E. Smith" (Ph.D. dissertation, Fordham University, 1970, reproduced by University Microfilms); Samuel B. Hand, "Al Smith, Franklin D. Roosevelt, and the New Deal: Some Comments on Perspective," *Historian* 27 (1965):366-81; Jordan A. Schwarz, "Al Smith in the Thirties," *New York History* 45 (1964):316-30; David Burner, *The Politics of Provincialism: The Democratic Party in Transition, 1918-1932* (New York: Alfred A. Knopf, 1968), pp. 187-90; Paul A. Carter, *Another Part of the Twenties* (New York: Columbia University Press, 1977), pp. 95-96; Kerr, "New York Factory Investigating Commission," pp. 263-71. In the opinion of the present author, these studies err, either be defining progressivism so narrowly as to exclude the ramifications of social progressivism, or by distorting Smith's career before 1928 to make it more consistent with his position after his defeat.

88. AES, *Public Papers,* 1928:616-25; Frank X. Schwab to AES, February 21, 1928; William J. Dalton to AES, March 9, 1928, AES Official Correspondence.

89. *New York Times,* October 31, 1920, October 4, 1924, October 12, 1926, August 29, 31, 1928; Irving Bernstein, *The Lean Years: A History of the American Worker 1920-1933* (Boston: Houghton Mifflin Company, 1960), p. 104.

90. Bernstein, *Lean Years,* pp. 104, 75-80, 508, 510-11; Vaughn Davis Bornet, *Labor Politics in a Democratic Republic: Moderation, Division, and Disruption in the Presidential Election of 1928* (Washington, D.C.: Spartan Books, 1964), passim and pp. 229-30. For quantitative studies of the election of 1928, see below, chap. 11.

91. John M. O'Hanlon to Michael E. Sherman, March 7, 1927, AES Official Correspondence; Bernstein, *Lean Years,* pp. 394-95; AES, *Public Papers,* 1919:762-68, quotation on 764; 1920: 656-61; 1923:631-40, quotation on 631; 1925:769-74; Arthur Schlesinger, Jr., *The Age of Roosevelt: The Coming of the New Deal* (Cambridge, Mass.: Houghton Mifflin Company, 1959), chap. 24.

92. Martin, *Madam Secretary,* p. ix; Perkins, 5:39-40, Columbia Oral History; Milton Derber and Edwin Young, eds., *Labor and the New Deal* (Madison: University of Wisconsin Press, 1957), pp. 161-62, 178-82, 230-31, 271; Trattner, *Homer Folks,* pp. 114-17.

93. Perkins, "Al Smith as I Knew Him," pp. 7-8, 1-2, Perkins Papers, Cornell.

94. AES, *Citizen and His Government,* p. 146; Chambers, *Seedtime of Reform;* Buenker, *Urban Liberalism and Progressive Reform.*

NOTES TO CHAPTER 7

1. Samuel P. Hays, *Conservation and the Gospel of Efficiency: The Progressive Conservation Movement 1890-1920* (Cambridge: Harvard University Press, 1959), passim and pp. 2, 3; J. Leonard Bates, "Fulfilling American Democracy: The Conservation Movement, 1907 to 1921," *Mississippi Valley Historical Review* 44 (1957):29-57, quotations on 29, 31; Judson King, *The Conservation Fight: From Theodore Roosevelt to the Tennessee Valley Authority* (Washington, D.C.:   Public Affairs Press, 1959), passim and p. xvi.

2. Harbaugh, *Life and Times of Theodore Roosevelt,* chap. 19 and p. 304.

3. George W. Norris, *Fighting Liberal: The Autobiography of George W. Norris* (New York: Macmillan Company, 1945), pp. 160-65; Norman L. Zucker, *George W. Norris: Gentle Knight of American Democracy* (Urbana: University of Illinois Press, 1966), pp. 75-78, 113-16; Richard Lowitt, *George W. Norris: The Persistence of a Progressive 1913-1933* (Urbana: University of Illinois Press, 1971), pp. 20-32; idem, "A Neglected Aspect of the Progressive Movement: George W. Norris and Public Control of Hydro-electric Power, 1913-1919," *Historian* 27 (1965):350-65.

4. Roger C. Thompson, "The Doctrine of Wilderness: A Study of the Policy and Politics of the Adirondack Preserve-Park" (Ph.D. dissertation, State University College of Forestry at Syracuse University, 1962), pp. 180-205; Wesser, *Charles Evans Hughes,* pp. 179-80, 336-38; Pusey, *Charles Evans Hughes,* pp. 213-14; Alfred B. Rollins, Jr., "The Political Education of Franklin Roosevelt: His Career in New York Politics, 1909-1928" (Ph.D. dissertation, Harvard University, 1953), pp. 264-65; A. Blair Knapp, "Water Power in New York State," *National Municipal Review Supplement* 19 (1930):140-41.

5. *Record CC 1915,* pp. 3554-55, 3544-45, 2978-79.

6. AES, *Public Papers,* 1919:34-35; *Legislative Index,* 1919; *New York Times,* April 16, 1919.

7.   AES, *Public Papers,* 1919:175-76.

8.   Ibid., 1920:43-44; *Legislative Index,* 1920.

9.   AES, *Public Papers,* 1920:336-37.

10.   King, *Conservation Fight,* chap. 6; Hays, *Conservation and the Gospel of Efficiency,* pp. 73-81; Swain, *Federal Conservation Policy,* pp. 113-14.

11.   *Laws of N.Y.,* 1921, chap. 579; Miller, *Public Papers,* 1921:87-91; Knapp, "Water Power in NYS," pp. 125-30.

12.   AES, Campaign Address, October 16, 1922, AES Papers; *New York Times,* September 30, 29, October 28, 1922.

13.   AES, *Up to Now,* pp. 247-48; *New York Times,* November 23, 24, 1922; Markham to AES, November 23, 1922, AES Official Correspondence.

14.   Preston J. Hubbard, *Origins of TVA: The Muscle Shoals Controversy, 1920-1932* (Nashville: Vanderbilt University Press, 1961), chaps. 1-5; Lowitt, *George W. Norris 1913-1933,* chap. 14; Frank E. Smith, *The Politics of Conservation* (New York: Random House, 1966), p. 168.

15.   AES, *Public Papers,* 1923:81-82, 138-41; Frank C. Perkins to AES, March 5, 1923; William P. Capes to AES, January 26, 1923, AES Official Correspondence; *Legislative Index,* 1923.

16.   Thompson, "Doctrine of Wilderness;" Frank Graham, Jr., *The Adirondack Park: A Political History* (New York: Alfred A. Knopf, 1978), chaps. 12, 14, 15, 17, 19, 22; Knapp, "Water Power in NYS," pp. 148-49.

17.   *Laws of N.Y.,* 1922, chap. 413; Miller, *Public Papers,* 1921:91; Ellwood M. Rabenold to AES, May 21, 1923, AES Official Correspondence; *New York Times,* September 30, 1922.

18.   Rabenold to AES, May 21, 1923, AES Official Correspondence.

19.   Ibid.

20.   Frank L. Bell to Parsons, April 13, 20, 1923; George E. Van Kennen to Bell, April 10, 1923; Rabenold to AES, May 21, 1923, AES Official Correspondence; David Lewis Nass, "Public Power and Politics in New York State, 1918-1958" (Ph.D. dissertation, Syracuse University, 1970, reproduced by University Microfilms), pp. 9-11.

21.   Marshall to AES, August 14, 1923, AES Official Correspondence; Thompson, "Doctrine of Wilderness," pp. 157-68.

22.   Agar to AES, August 17, 1923; [AES] to Agar, August 20, 1923; Moses to AES, September 5, 1923, AES Official Correspondence; AES, *Public Papers,* 1923:567-68.

23.   Saranac Lake Chamber of Commerce et al. to AES, October 16, 1923; Dwight B. LaDu to AES, October 19, 1923, AES Official Correspondence; AES, *Public Papers,* 1923:647-49.

24. *New York Times,* December 4, 1923; Louis Marshall, *Louis Marshall Champion of Liberty: Selected Papers and Addresses,* ed. Charles Reznikoff (Philadelphia: Jewish Publication Society of America, 1957), p. 1042.

25. Thompson, "Doctrine of Wilderness," pp. 215-39; Marshall to AES, August 14, 1923; Agar to AES, August 17, 1923; Saranac Lake Chamber of Commerce et al. to AES, October 16, 1923; [AES] to Agar, August 20, 1923, AES Official Correspondence; Marshall, *Louis Marshall Champion of Liberty,* pp. 1042-44.

26. Erwin Wilkie Bard, *The Port of New York Authority* (New York: Columbia University Press, 1942); Cohen, *They Builded Better Than They Knew,* pp. 248-50, 261, 289-306; Fetner, "Public Power and Professional Responsibility."

27. Cohen, *They Builded Better Than They Knew,* pp. 330-31; idem, Legal Opinion, December 5, 1923; Minutes of Conference on Water Power Development, December 12, 1923, AES Papers.

28. AES, *Public Papers,* 1924:36-43.

29. *New York Times,* January 3, 25, 1924; Rabenold to AES, January 14, 1924; idem, Memorandum for Water Power Legislation, January 14, 1924, AES Official Correspondence; Copy of Moses to Adelbert Moot, February 14, 1924 and enclosed Act creating the New York State Power Authority, Peabody Papers.

30. *New York Times,* February 27, 1924.

31. *Legislative Index,* 1924; AES, *Public Papers,* 1923: 301-3.

32. *New York Times,* October 24, September 26, 1924.

33. AES, *Public Papers,* 1924:661-68, quotations on 667, 706, 663.

34. AES, *Public Papers,* 1925:36-37, 234-36; *Legislative Index,* 1925; Lowitt, *George W. Norris 1913-1933,* chap. 7.

35. AES, *Public Papers,* 1926:33-34, 141-44.

36. *New York Times,* February 2, 3, 1926; AES, *Public Papers,* 1926:591-93.

37. John A. Dix to AES, March 1, 1926, AES Official Correspondence; *New York Times,* February 12, 1926.

38. Young to AES, February 23, 1923; T. Harvey Ferris to George R. Van Namee, November 13, 1924, AES Official Correspondence.

39. Cohen to AES, January 16, 1926; [AES] to Cohen, January 18, 1926; Cohen to AES, January 21, 1926, AES Official Correspondence; *New York Times,* February 9, 1926; AES, *Public Papers,* 1926:594.

40. Young to AES, February 23, 1926, AES Official Correspondence; *New York Times,* February 24, 1926.

41. AES, *Public Papers*, 1926:648-52, 659-61; *Legislative Index*, 1926.

42. *New York Times*, March 26, 1926.

43. See above, chap. 2. Childs to Stimson, November 11, 1925, Stimson Papers.

44. AES, *Public Papers*, 1926:622-28; *Laws of N.Y.*, 1926, chap. 619.

45. Knapp, "Water Power in NYS," pp. 130-36; *New York Times*, January 27, 1926.

46. *New York Times*, January 27, February 2, 3, 8, 16, 17, 26, 1926; Edward V. Canavan to AES, March 10, 1926, AES Official Correspondence.

47. New York State Association, Memorial to the State Water Power Commission, February 3, 1926; Emergency Water Power Committee, Press Release, February 15, 1926, AES Official Correspondence; AES, *Public Papers*, 1926:645; *New York Times*, February 25, May 7, June 3, 4, 30, September 25, October 26, 1926.

48. Marshall to AES, July 9, August 26, 1926; [AES] to Marshall, August 27, 1926; John G. Agar et al. to AES, October 25, 1926, and enclosed Memorandum; [AES] to Agar, October 27, 1926, AES Official Correspondence; Thompson, "Doctrine of Wilderness," pp. 239-43.

49. AES, *Public Papers*, 1926:836, 819.

50. Ibid., pp. 817-23; Mills, Campaign Addresses, October 30, [October 11], 1926, AES Papers.

51. AES, *Public Papers*, 1926:836-37, 820-23, 847-49; Anon. letters, no addressee, October 18, 20, 1926, AES Papers.

52. Edward V. Canavan to AES, November 13, 1926, AES Official Correspondence.

53. AES, *Public Papers*, 1926:700; Adolph C. Hottenroth to AES, November 4, December 10, 1926, AES Official Correspondence.

54. AES, *Public Papers*, 1926:700-705.

55. Cohalan to AES, December 4, 8, 1926; [AES] to Cohalan, December 7, 1926, AES Official Correspondence.

56. AES, *Public Papers*, 1926:706, 708; *New York Times*, December 5, 8, 9, 1926; Marshall, *Louis Marshall Champion of Liberty*, pp. 1046-47.

57. Edward W. Cady, Jr. to AES, December 3, 1926, AES Official Correspondence; AES, *Public Papers*, 1926:707-8; *New York Times*, December 10, 1926; Marshall, *Louis Marshall Champion of Liberty*, p. 1047.

58. F. W. Moore, to AES, December 9, 1926; Herbert Bayard Swope to AES, December 8, 1926, AES Official Correspondence; *New York Times,* December 12, 1926.

59. Knight to Mills, December 8, 1926, Mills Papers.

60. AES, *Public Papers,* 1927:43-47; Cohen, Material in Support of Governor Smith's Policy for the Development of Hydro-electric Power through a State Water Power Authority, December 22, 1926; idem, Memorandum, December 22, 1926, AES Papers; *New York Times,* January 25, 1927.

61. *Legislative Index,* 1927; *New York Times,* March 12, 15, 16, 22, 1927; AES, *Public Papers,* 1927:110-17, 134.

62. AES, *Public Papers,* 1928:26-29, 100, 146-47; *New York Times,* March 23, 1928.

63. AES, *Public Papers,* 1928:202-3.

64. [AES] to Marshall, March 23, 1928; Jacob Gould Schurman, Jr. to AES, March 28, 1928; Edward Hagaman Hall to AES, March 9, 1928; Willis H. Sargent to AES, April 5, 1928; Louis Marshall to AES, March 22, 23, 24, 1928, Assembly, int. 1648, print 2204, Veto Jackets; idem to AES, March 28, 1928, Assembly, 1928, int. 1645, print 2158, Veto Jackets; AES, *Public Papers,* 1928:202-4.

65. AES, *Public Papers,* 1928:639; Lowitt, *George W. Norris 1913-1933,* chap. 23.

66. Alfred E. Smith, *Campaign Addresses of Governor Alfred E. Smith* (Washington, D.C.: Democratic National Committee, 1929), pp. 61-76.

67. Lowitt, *George W. Norris 1913-1933,* chap. 27 and p. 401; Norris, *Fighting Liberal,* p. 287; King, *Conservation Fight,* chaps. 18, 21.

68. AES, *Campaign Addresses,* pp. 68-72; Zeller, *Pressure Politics in New York,* pp. 63-83, quotation on p. 78.

69. Nixon, *Franklin D. Roosevelt and Conservation,* 1: 65-66; Bellush, *Franklin D. Roosevelt as Governor,* chap. 10 and p. 219.

70. Fetner, "Public Power and Professional Responsibility," pp. 38-39; Nass, "Public Power and Politics in NYS," chap. 3, pp. 22-23, 202-3; Frank E. Smith, *Politics of Conservation,* p. xi.

1.   Frank E. Smith, *Politics of Conservation,* pp. 168-69; Mowry, *California Progressives,* pp. 23-24; Warner, *Progressivism in Ohio,* pp. 24, 72-74; Ransom E. Noble, Jr., *New Jersey Progressivism before Wilson* (Princeton: Princeton University Press, 1946), p. 92.

2.   The following account of Hearst's career up to 1918 relies primarily on: Swanberg, *Citizen Hearst,* bk. 4; James Myatt, "William Randolph Hearst and the Progressive Era, 1900-1912" (Ph.D. dissertation, University of Florida, 1960, reproduced by University Microfilms); Roy Everett Littlefield III, "William Randolph Hearst: His Role in American Progressivism" (Ph.D. dissertation, Catholic University of America, 1979, reproduced by University Microfilms).

3.   Oliver Carlson and Ernest Sutherland Bates, *Hearst: Lord of San Simeon* (New York: Viking Press, 1936), p. 206.

4.   Ibid., p. 165.

5.   Rodney P. Carlisle, *Hearst and the New Deal: The Progressive as Reactionary* (New York: Garland Publishing, 1979), p. 4.

6.   Citizens' Union, *Searchlight,* October 25, 1917; Myatt, "William Randolph Hearst and the Progressive Era," p. 159.

7.   See above, chap. 1; *New York Evening Journal,* August 5, 1918; *New York American,* November 5, 1918; *New York Times,* October 21, 29, November 2, 1918.

8.   AES, *Public Papers,* 1919:33-34; *New York Times,* January 1, 1919.

9.   The following account of public transportation in New York City at the time that Smith became governor of the state is based on a variety of older and recent works: James Blaine Walker, *Fifty Years of Rapid Transit 1864 to 1917* (New York: Law Printing Company, 1918); Harry James Carman, *The Street Surface Railway Franchises of New York City* (New York: Longmans, Green and Company, 1919); *Reports and Studies,* 5:108-41; James Joseph McGinley, *Labor Relations in the New York Rapid Transit Systems 1904-1944* (New York: King's Crown Press, 1944), chaps. 2, 3; Joel Fischer, "Urban Transportation: Home Rule and the Independent Subway System in New York City, 1917-1925" (Ph.D. dissertation, St. John's University, 1978, reproduced by University Microfilms), chap. 1; Charles W. Cheape, *Moving the Masses: Urban Public Transit in New York, Boston, and Philadelphia 1880-1912* (Cambridge: Harvard University Press, 1980), introd., pt. 1.

10.   *New York American,* January 4, 11, 1919; *New York Times,* January 11, 25, 26, 31, 1919.

11.   *Legislative Index,* 1919; Copy of George Foster Peabody to Edward Berwind, March 17, 1919; H. B. Weatherwax to Peabody, March 22, 1919, AES Official Correspondence; *New York Times,* April 3, 4, 1919.

12. McGinley, *Labor Relations in the New York Rapid Transit Systems*, pp. 72-74; Martin Landau, "The New York Public Service Commission, 1907-1930: A Study of Regulation in Its Political Environment" (Ph.D. dissertation, New York University, 1952, reproduced by University Microfilms), pp. 1-83; AES, *Public Papers*, 1919:32-33; *New York Times*, March 14, 1919; *Laws of N.Y.*, 1919, chaps. 263, 520.

13. AES, *Public Papers*, 1919:36-37.

14. *New York Times*, January 4, 9, 18, 19, 1919; John J. Dillon, *Seven Decades of Milk: A History of New York's Dairy Industry* (New York: Orange Judd Publishing Company, 1941), chap. 19.

15. Swann to AES, January 3, 1919; F. W. Applegate to AES, January 7, 1919; William Budd to AES, January 7, 1919; H. L. Hyde to AES [January, 1919]; Special Message to the Legislature, January, 1919; [George R. Van Namme] to A. Berg, August 2, 1919, AES Official Correspondence.

16. Swann to AES, January 3, 1919, and enclosed Memorandum; Elon R. Brown to AES, December 23, 1918, AES Official Correspondence; AES, *Public Papers*, 1919:67-69.

17. *New York American*, April 25, May 12, 10, 20, 1919.

18. Hylan to AES, July 7, 1919; Terence Farley to George R. Van Namee, July 15, 1919, and enclosed Memorandum for Commissioner Nixon, AES Official Correspondence; *New York Times*, July 17, 1919.

19. [AES] to M. F. McDonogh, August 22, 1919; Terence Farley to AES, July 16, 1919, and enclosed Statement, AES Official Correspondence; *New York American*, July 23, 1919.

20. *New York Evening Journal*, July 11, 30, 1919.

21. *New York American*, July 30, August 5, July 26, August 12, 1919.

22. *New York Evening Journal*, July 22, 24, 23, 26, 28, 1919.

23. Ibid., August 8, 1919; AES, *Public Papers*, 1919: 453-61; Minutes of Hearing on High Cost of Living, September 17, 1919, AES Official Correspondence.

24. *New York Evening Journal*, September 6, 1919; AES, *Public Papers*, 1919:539-52, quotation on 540.

25. *New York Times*, August 21, 1919; AES, *Public Papers*, 1919:328-33, quotation on 328; 1920:479-92; Joseph M. Proskauer, *A Segment of My Times* (New York: Farrar, Straus and Company, 1950), pp. 171-72.

26. *New York Times*, February 19, 1920; *New York American*, October 25, 1919.

27. *New York Times,* July 29, 1919; *New York Evening Journal,* August 29, 1919; *New York American,* October 8, 16, 14, 1919; William J. Gillen to AES, September 2, 1919, AES Official Correspondence.

28. *New York Times,* October 19, 1919; AES to Hylan, October 22, 1919, AES Official Correspondence.

29. *New York Times,* October 28, 1919.

30. AES, *Public Papers,* 1919:776-84; Anon., Untitled Manuscript containing a digest of Hearst press from January 1 to October 7, 1919 [October, 1919], AES Papers.

31. *New York Times,* November 2, 6, 1919.

32. *New York American,* January 4, 1920; *New York Times,* January 7, 8, 1920.

33. [AES] to George W. Perkins, November 11, 1919, AES Official Correspondence; AES, *Public Papers,* 1920:73-74, 585-86.

34. Reconstruction Commission to AES, November 17, 1919, AES Official Correspondence; AES, *Public Papers,* 1919:458-60, 505-16; 1920:73-94, 167-72, quotation on 92.

35. AES, *Public Papers,* 1919:466-549; 1920:125-28; [AES] to John Jerome Rooney, September 7, 1920, AES Official Correspondence.

36. On Smith, see for example: Pringle, *Alfred E. Smith,* pp. 21-32; Hapgood and Moskowitz, *Up from the City Streets,* pp. 210-13; Josephson and Josephson, *Al Smith,* chap. 11; on Hearst: Carlson and Bates, *Hearst,* pp. 206-9; Swanberg, *Citizen Hearst,* bk. 4.

37. *New York American,* January 5, 1920; *New York Times,* October 26, 28, 1920; *New York Evening Journal,* October 30, 1920.

38. Pringle, *Alfred E. Smith,* pp. 33-39; See above, chap. 1.

39. *Laws of N.Y.,* 1921, chaps. 134, 335; McGinley, *Labor Relations in the New York Rapid Transit Systems,* pp. 74-76; Fischer, "Urban Transportation," pp. 122-53; Landau, "New York Public Service Commission," pp. 84-89, 145-337, 379-97.

40. AES, Campaign Addresses, October 26, November 2, 1922, AES Papers; *New York Times,* October 6, November 4, 1922.

41. *New York Times,* October 10, 1923; *New York American,* October 12, 1923.

42. Nancy Joan Weiss, *Charles Francis Murphy, 1858-1924: Respectability and Responsibility in Tammany Politics* (Northampton: Smith College, 1968), pp. 62-63; Swanberg, *Citizen Hearst,* pp. 368-74; Nat Ferber, *I Found Out: A Confidential Chronicle of the Twenties* (New York: Dial Press, 1939), chaps 12-16, 19; *New York American,* October 22, 23, 1923.

43. *New York Times,* October 31, November 4, 7, 8, 1923.

44. Ibid., May 5, 11, 15, 16, 23, July 15, 1924.

45. Weiss, *Charles Francis Murphy.*

46. Swanberg, *Citizen Hearst,* pp. 370-71; *New York American,* July 20, 29, 1924; *New York Times,* July 25, 26, 1924.

47. *New York American,* October 27, 1926; October 6, 30, 1924.

48. Landau, "New York Public Service Commission," pp. 95-98; AES, *Public Papers,* 1923:53-57, 209-12.

49. *Laws of N.Y.,* 1923, chap. 891; *New York Times,* April 20, 23, 27, May 3, 1923; Fischer, "Urban Transportation," pp. 161-231; AES to Joseph M. Price, May 4, 1923, AES Official Correspondence.

50. *New York Times,* April 27, 1923; *New York American,* April 26, 1923.

51. *New York Times,* April 11, 1924; Hylan to AES, April 26, 1924, Laws of 1924, chap. 573, Bill Jackets; *Laws of N.Y.,* 1924, chap. 573; McGinley, *Labor Relations in the New York Rapid Transit Systems,* pp. 77-79; AES, *Public Papers,* 1924:46-49, 298-300.

52. Fischer, "Urban Transportation," chaps. 4, 5; AES, *Public Papers,* 1925:158-69; *New York Times,* January 6, 1925; *New York American,* October 30, 1924.

53. Clarence J. Shearn to AES, November 24, 1924; [AES] to Shearn, November 25, 1924; AES, Statement, November 30, 1924, AES Official Correspondence; AES, *Public Papers,* 1924:590-94; *New York Times,* December 2, 1924.

54. *New York Times,* January 4, 1925; AES, *Public Papers,* 1925:135-58.

55. *Laws of N.Y.,* 1925, chap. 641; AES, *Public Papers,* 1925:129-34.

56. *New York American,* February 9, 17, March 30, 1925; *New York Times,* February 10, 1925; Grenville Howard to AES, February 17, 1925, AES Official Correspondence.

57. *New York American,* May 24, 1925.

58. Bard, *Port of New York Authority;* Cohen, *They Builded Better Than They Knew,* pp. 291-97; [AES] to Mills, January 31, 1925; Mills to AES, February 2, 1925; Cohen to AES, February 3, 1925, AES Official Correspondence.

59. Edward J. Flynn, *You're the Boss,* pp. 46-52; *New York Times,* June 18, July 9, 22, 29, 1925; *New York American,* July 26, 1925.

60. [Walter T. Arndt] to William Jay Schieffelin, July 13, 1925, Citizens' Union Collection, Columbia University Library, New York; *New York Times,* August 5, 1925.

61. Edward J. Flynn, *You're the Boss,* pp. 50-53; Gene Fowler, *Beau James: The Life and Times of Jimmy Walker* (New York: Viking Press, 1949); George Walsh, *Gentleman Jimmy Walker: Mayor of the Jazz Age* (New York: Praeger Publishers, 1974); Perkins, 2:345-49; 3:407-11, Columbia Oral History.

62. *New York Evening Journal,* August 12, 11, 1925; *New York American,* August 19, 1925.

63. AES, *Public Papers,* 1925:774-79; *New York Times,* August 29, 1925.

64. *New York Times,* August 29, September 1, 10, 1925.

65. Ibid., August 30, September 5, 6, 12, 1925.

66. *New York American,* August 30, September 3, 4, 1925.

67. *New York Times,* September 16, 17, 1925.

68. Ibid., September 18, 1925; *New York American,* September 18, 1925; Mann, *La Guardia: A Fighter against His Times,* p. 265.

69. *New York American,* October 30, 31, 1925; *New York Times,* November 5, 1925.

70. Herbert Mitgang, *The Man Who Rode the Tiger: The Life and Times of Judge Samuel Seabury* (Philadelphia: J. B. Lippincott Company, 1963), p. 169; Swanberg, *Citizen Hearst,* pp. 337-38; *New York Times,* May 17, 1925.

71. Ferdinand Pecora, pp. 410-20, 429-34, Columbia Oral History; Copy of Louis I. Harris to Ogden Mills, October 8, 1926, AES Papers; R. E. McGahen to AES, June 29, 1926, AES Official Correspondence; AES, *Public Papers,* 1926:672-74.

72. William Jay Schieffelin to AES, October 21, 1926; [AES] to Schieffelin, October 23, 1926, AES Official Correspondence.

73. *New York American,* October 5, 13, 19, 1926; Mills, Campaign Address, October 15, 1926, AES Papers; *New York Times,* October 16, 1926.

74. AES, *Public Papers,* 1926:807-10, 842-44, 863-65, 867-73, quotation on 872-73.

75. Ibid., 1927:308-12; Ferdinand Pecora, pp. 431-34, Columbia Oral History; John W. Hahner to William Allen, March 2, 1927, AES Official Correspondence.

76. Myatt, "William Randolph Hearst and the Progressive Era," chap. 9; Carlisle, *Hearst and the New Deal.*

1. Paul L. Murphy, *The Meaning of Freedom of Speech: First Amendment Freedoms from Wilson to FDR* (Westport, Conn.: Greenwood Publishing Company, 1972).

2. Ibid., p. 18, chaps, 6, 7; Donald Johnson, *The Challenge to American Freedoms: World War I and the Rise of the American Civil Liberties Union* (n.p.: University of Kentucky Press, 1963), chap. 8 and p. 198; John P. Roche, *The Quest for the Dream: The Development of Civil Rights and Human Relations in Modern America* (New York: Macmillan Company, 1963), pp. 22-23; Davis, *Spearheads for Reform*, p. 229; Mowry, *California Progressives*, pp. 200, 293-94; Paul S. Boyer, *Purity in Print: The Vice-Society Movement and Book Censorship in America* (New York: Charles Scribner's Sons, 1968), chap. 2.

3. *New York Times*, February 24, 1920; *Record CC 1915*, pp. 2946-47.

4. AES, *Up to Now*, p. 157; *New York Times*, January 10, February 27, 28, 1918.

5. For an overview of the Red Scare in the nation and New York, see Zechariah Chafee, Jr., *Free Speech in the United States* (Cambridge: Harvard University Press, 1941); Robert K. Murray, *Red Scare: A Study in National Hysteria 1919-1920* (Minneapolis: University of Minnesota Press, 1955); Murphy, *Meaning of Freedom of Speech*; Julian F. Jaffe, *Crusade against Radicalism: New York during the Red Scare, 1914-1924* (Port Washington, N.Y.: Kennikat Press, 1972).

6. Patricia Wesson Wingo, "Clayton R. Lusk: A Study of Patriotism in New York Politics, 1919-1923" (Ph.D. dissertation, University of Georgia, 1966, reproduced by University Microfilms), pp. 6-22; *Legislative Index*, 1919; *New York Times*, March 21, 27, 1919.

7. AES, *Public Papers*, 1919:749-53.

8. Walter Gellhorn, ed., *The States and Subversion* (Ithaca: Cornell University Press, 1952), p. 360; *New York Times*, May 8, 18, 1919.

9. [George R. Van Namee] to John J. Boylan, May 13, 1919; Edward Swann to AES, July 8, 1919, AES Official Correspondence; AES, *Public Papers*, 1919:327.

10. Lawrence H. Chamberlain, *Loyalty and Legislative Action: A Survey of Activity by the New York State Legislature 1919-1949* (Ithaca: Cornell University Press, 1951), chap. 1; Wingo, "Clayton R. Lusk," chaps. 2, 3; Jaffe, *Crusade against Radicalism*, chap. 5.

11. Untermyer to AES, July 23, 1919; James Myers to AES, July 10, 1919; [George R. Van Namee?] to Myers, July 21, 1919, AES Official Correspondence.

12. AES, *Public Papers,* 1919:722-23; [Julius Gerber] to AES, October 24, 1919; [AES] to Henry Stanley Renaud, October 31, 1919; R. E. Enright to AES, October 28, 1919; News Editor of the *New York Herald* to AES, December 2, 1919; AES, Statement [December, 1919], AES Official Correspondence.

13. AES, *Public Papers,* 1920:30-31.

14. For a detailed account of the episode, see Louis Waldman, *Albany: The Crisis in Government: The History of the Suspension, Trial and Expulsion from the New York State Legislature in 1920 of the Five Socialist Assemblymen by Their Political Opponents* (New York: Boni & Liveright, 1920); Chafee, *Free Speech in the United States,* pp. 269-82; Jaffe, *Crusade against Radicalism,* chap. 6; Wingo, "Clayton R. Lusk," chap. 4.

15. *New York Times,* January 8, 9, 1920; Louis Waldman, *Labor Lawyer* (New York: E. P. Dutton and Company, 1944), p. 91.

16. AES, *Public Papers,* 1920:581.

17. AES, *Up to Now,* p. 201; *New York Times,* January 11, 1920; City Editor of the *New York American* to AES, January 10, 1920, AES Official Correspondence.

18. William Lundgren to AES, January 11, 1920; F. W. White to AES, January 21, 1920; William Schuyler Jackson to AES, January 21, 1920; Central Labor Union of Amsterdam, New York, Resolution [January, 1920], AES Official Correspondence.

19. Jaffe, *Crusade against Radicalism,* pp. 149-50; *America,* January 31, 1920, p. 327; April 17, 1920, pp. 596-97; Francis L. Broderick, *Right Reverend New Dealer: John A. Ryan* (New York: Macmillan Company, 1963), p. 114.

20. *Catholic News,* January 17, 1920; Broderick, *Right Reverend New Dealer,* pp. 113-15, 140-53; John A. Ryan, *Social Doctrine in Action: A Personal History* (New York: Harper & Brothers, 1941), pp. 162-66.

21. AES, *Public Papers,* 1920:640, 649, 651-53; *New York Times,* February 24, March 27, 1920.

22. *New York Times,* February 9, January 14, 1920; Felix Frankfurter to Stimson, January 12, 1920, Stimson Papers; Chafee, *Free Speech in the United States,* p. 276.

23. N.Y., *Legislative Documents,* 1920, no. 35, pp. 2673-2802, quotations on pp. 2772, 2802.

24. *New York Times,* April 2, 1920.

25. Waldman, *Labor Lawyer,* p. 108; *New York Times,* April 1, 1920.

26. S. John Block to AES, April 7, 1920; AES to Block, April 10, 1920; Raymond V. Ingersoll to AES, April 27, 1920; Walter T. Arndt to AES, May 27, 1920; Belle Moskowitz to AES, July 30, 1920, AES Official Correspondence; AES, *Up to Now*, pp. 269-70; AES, *Public Papers*, 1920:14-18, 582.

27. *New York Times*, September 17, 22, 1920; Theodorus Bailey to AES, September 27, 1920; [AES] to Bailey, September 30, 1920, AES Official Correspondence.

28. *New York Times*, October 31, 1920.

29. N.Y., *Legislative Documents*, 1920, no. 35, p. 2715; *New York Times*, April 21, 24, 1920; *Legislative Index*, 1920.

30. N.Y., *Legislative Documents*, 1920, no. 52; *Legislative Index*, 1920; Chafee, *Free Speech in the United States*, pp. 306-17.

31. N.Y., *Legislative Documents*, 1921, no. 50; Chamberlain, *Loyalty and Legislative Action*, pp. 34-40; Wingo, "Clayton R. Lusk," chap. 8.

32. N.Y., *Legislative Documents*, 1920, no. 52, pp. 5-7; AES, *Public Papers*, 1920:414-15; *Laws of N.Y.*, 1920, chaps. 851, 852.

33. *New York Times*, May 15, 1920.

34. Ibid.

35. Algernon Lee to AES, May 14, 1920; idem, Memorandum to the Governor, May 15, 1920; [AES] to Lee, May 18, 1920; Henry Wise Wood to AES, May 19, 1920; [AES] to Wood, May 20, 1920, AES Official Correspondence.

36. *New York Times*, May 4, 1920; Mabel T. R. Washburn to AES, May 15, 1920, AES Official Correspondence; *America*, April 24, 1920, p. 17; Wald to AES, May 13, 1920, Wald Papers.

37. AES, *Public Papers*, 1920:330-33.

38. Ibid., pp. 367-68.

39. Ibid., pp. 368-70.

40. In *A Segment of My Times*, p. 46, where he told the anecdote, Proskauer mistakenly associated it with the events of 1923 when the Lusk Laws of the Miller administration were repealed. An examination of the documents reveals that the tale must refer to the veto memorandums cited above.

41. *Laws of N.Y.*, 1921, chaps. 666, 667; Miller, *Public Papers*, 1921:161-65.

42. *New York Times*, September 30, 1922; AES, Campaign Addresses, November 4, October 28, 1922, AES Papers.

43. AES, *Public Papers*, 1923:61-62; *New York Times*, February 28, April 25, 1923; Martha L. Draper to AES, April 28, 1923; Abraham Lefkowitz to AES, April 27, 1923, Laws of 1923, chap. 799, Bill Jackets.

44. *New York Times,* January 19, 21, 1923; Braman to AES, April 9, 1923, Laws of 1923, chap. 798; Menken to AES, March 15, 1923, Laws of 1923, chap. 799, Bill Jackets; AES, *Public Papers,* 1923:540-41; Oswald Garrison Villard to AES, March 31, 1923; [AES] to Edward G. Riggs, March 1, 1923, AES Official Correspondence.

45. Stewart Browne to AES, May 16, 1923, Laws of 1923, chap. 798, Bill Jackets; *New York Times,* May 23, 1923.

46. AES, *Public Papers,* 1923:292-93; *Laws of N.Y.,* 1923, chaps. 798, 799; Chafee, *Free Speech in the United States,* pp. 311-17.

47. AES, *Public Papers,* 1923:483-86; 1924:469; 1925: 446-47. For a detailed account of the criminal anarchy cases, see: Jaffe, *Crusade against Radicalism,* chap. 8; Harold Josephson, "The Dynamics of Repression: New York during the Red Scare," *Mid-America* 59 (1977):131-46.

48. Chafee, *Free Speech in the United States,* p. 319; *New York Times,* January 19, 1923.

49. Emmet Larkin, *James Larkin: Irish Labour Leader 1876-1947* (Cambridge: M.I.T. Press, 1965); *New York Times,* January 10, 1923; AES, *Public Papers,* 1923:483-85.

50. Glenn Frank, "Al Smith Pardons Jim Larkin," *Century Magazine* 105 (1923):797-800; Proskauer, *A Segment of My Times,* p. 45.

51. *Laws of N.Y.,* 1923, chap. 664; *New York Times,* January 17, February 23, May 28, 1923; AES, *Public Papers,* 1923:291-92.

52. For perspective on the Ku Klux Klan in the first half of this century, see Arnold Rice, *The Ku Klux Klan in American Politics* (Washington, D.C.: Public Affairs Press, 1962); David M. Chalmers, *Hooded Americanism: The First Century of the Ku Klux Klan 1865-1965* (Garden City, N.Y.: Doubleday & Company, 1965); Kenneth T. Jackson, *The Ku Klux Klan in the City 1915-1930* (New York: Oxford University Press, 1967).

53. Murphy, *Meaning of Freedom of Speech,* p. 164; David Fellman, *The Constitutional Right of Association* (Chicago: University of Chicago Press, 1963), pp. 62-73.

54. Boyer, *Purity in Print,* chaps. 3, 4.

55. *Laws of N.Y.,* 1921, chap. 715; Wingo, "Clayton R. Lusk," pp. 136-49; Moskowitz to George Foster Peabody, March 31, 1921, Peabody Papers.

56. AES, *Public Papers,* 1923:59-62; 1924:66; 1925:73-74; 1926:64-65; 1927:63; 1928:92-93; *New York Times,* March 21, May 4, 1923.

57. *New York Times,* February 15, 1923; *Catholic News,* March 17, 1923.

58. *Catholic News*, April 28, 1923; "Editorial Comment," *Catholic World* 116 (1922):392-99; *America*, May 12, 1923, pp. 86-87.

59. N.Y., Legislature, *Legislative Bills*, 1923, Senate int. no. 1701; Walker Gilmer, *Horace Liveright: Publisher of the Twenties* (New York: David Lewis, 1970), pp. 60-80, quotation on p. 79; *Catholic News*, May 12, 1923.

60. Boyer, *Purity in Print*, chaps. 4, 5; Ford to AES, December 5, 1924; [AES] to Ford, December 10, 1924, AES Official Correspondence; Ford to AES, December 8, 1926; [AES] to Ford, December 20, 1926, George B. Graves Papers.

61. "Editorial Comment," *Catholic World* 123 (1926): 545-47; *Commonweal*, January 12, 1927, p. 259; Boyer, *Purity in Print*, pp. 129, 161-64; Arthur Garfield Hays, *Let Freedom Ring* (New York: Liveright Publishing Company, 1937), pp. 237-45.

62. Rose A. Pedrick to AES, February 9, 1927; William Church Osborn to AES, February 4, 1927, George B. Graves Papers; *New York Times*, April 7, 1927.

63. [AES] to McAdoo, February 9, 1927; McAdoo to AES, February 10, 1927, AES Official Correspondence; [AES] to Rose A. Pedrick, February 10, 1927, George B. Graves Papers; Arthur Garfield Hays, *Let Freedom Ring*, pp. 245-66.

64. *New York Times*, February 4, March 18, 1927; *Laws of N.Y.*, 1927, chap. 690; Banton to AES, April 5, 1927, Laws of 1927, chap. 690, Bill Jackets.

65. R. E. McGahen to AES, April 5, 1927; Hays, Memorandum of Law Re: Senate Bill No. 1769 [April, 1927], Laws of 1927, chap. 690, Bill Jackets.

66. *New York Times*, April 6, 7, 1927; AES, *Public Papers*, 1927:176-77.

67. *Catholic News*, April 16, 1927; Charles Lam Markmann, *The Noblest Cry: A History of the American Civil Liberties Union* (New York: St. Martin's Press, 1965), pp. 300-302; Morris L. Ernst and Alexander Lindey, *The Censor Marches On: Recent Milestones in the Administration of the Obscenity Law in the United States* (New York: Doubleday, Doran & Company, 1940), p. 64.

68. Chafee, *Free Speech in the United States*, pp. 354, 9-22.

69. William Preston, Jr., *Aliens and Dissenters: Federal Suppression of Radicals 1903-1933* (Cambridge: Harvard University Press, 1963), pp. 239-41, 259-72.

70. For civil liberties under the New Deal, see Murphy, *Meaning of Freedom of Speech*, chap. 14; Roche, *Quest for the Dream*, chaps, 6, 7; Jerold S. Auerbach, "The Depression Decade," in *The Pulse of Freedom: American Liberties 1920-1970s*, ed. Alan Reitman (New York: W. W. Norton & Company, 1975), pp. 65-104.

1. Andrew Sinclair, *Prohibition: The Era of Excess* (Boston: Little, Brown and Company, 1962), pp. 126-27; Boyer, *Purity in Print,* pp. 151-54; H. L. Mencken, *A Carnival of Buncombe,* ed. Malcolm Moos (Baltimore: Johns Hopkins Press, 1956), p. 122.

2. With some overlap, the successive stages in the study of Prohibition are represented by Charles Merz, *The Dry Decade* (Garden City, N.Y.: Doubleday, Doran & Company, 1930); Sinclair, *Prohibition;* Joseph R. Gusfield, *Symbolic Crusade: Status Politics and the American Temperance Movement* (Urbana: University of Illinois Press, 1963).

3. Norman H. Clark, *Deliver Us from Evil: An Interpretation of American Prohibition* (New York: W. W. Norton & Company, 1976).

4. James H. Timberlake, *Prohibition and the Progressive Movement 1900-1920* (Cambridge: Harvard University Press, 1963); Norman H. Clark, *The Dry Years: Prohibition and Social Change in Washington* (Seattle: University of Washington Press, 1965); Paul E. Isaac, *Prohibition and Politics: Turbulent Decades in Tennessee 1885-1920* (Knoxville: University of Tennessee Press, 1965); Gilman M. Ostrander, *The Prohibition Movement in California, 1848-1933* (Berkeley: University of California Press, 1957).

5. William John Jackson, "Prohibition as an Issue in New York State Politics, 1836-1933" (Ed.D. dissertation, Teachers College, Columbia University, 1974, reproduced by University Microfilms), pp. 51-59; John Joseph Coffey, "A Political History of the Temperance Movement in New York State, 1808-1920" (Ph.D. dissertation, Pennsylvania State University, 1976, reproduced by University Microfilms).

6. Sinclair, *Prohibition,* chap. 4 and p. 76; *American Issue,* New York ed., October 12, 1918; AES, *Citizen and His Government,* pp. 190-91.

7. *New York Times,* July 5, 20, 26, August 11, 14, 1918; *Legislative Manual,* 1919.

8. A general survey of the Anti-Saloon League can be found in: Peter H. Odegard, *Pressure Politics: The Story of the Anti-Saloon League* (New York: Columbia University Press, 1928); Timberlake, *Prohibition and the Progressive Movement,* chap. 5. The league's operation in New York is covered in: Zeller, *Pressure Politics in New York,* pp. 222-28; Coffey, "Political History of the Temperance Movement in New York State," chap. 8.

9. AES, *Up to Now,* p. 114.

10. *American Issue,* N.Y. ed., October 26, November 2, 1918.

11. *New York Times,* July 24, September 27, 1918.

12. *American Issue,* N.Y. ed., November 9, 1918; *New York Times,* November 7, 1918; Odegard, *Pressure Politics,* pp. 24-27.

13. William John Jackson, "Prohibition as an Issue in New York State Politics," pp. 142-47; AES, *Public Papers,* 1919: 33; *American Issue,* N.Y. ed., January 11, 1919; *New York Times,* January 24, 28, 30, 1919.

14. *Legislative Index,* 1919; *New York Times,* February 15, April 21, 1919.

15. *New York Times,* January 7, 1920; AES, *Public Papers,* 1920:32-33.

16. *New York Times,* January 8, 9, February 6, 1920.

17. Clark, *Deliver Us from Evil,* pp. 8-9, 130-34; William John Jackson, "Prohibition as an Issue in New York State Politics," pp. 154-55.

18. N.Y., Legislature, *Legislative Bills,* 1920, Senate int. nos. 58, 829; *American Issue,* N.Y. ed., February 7, 1920; *Legislative Index,* 1920; *New York Times,* March 19, April 25, 1920; *Laws of N.Y.,* 1920, chap. 911.

19. *New York Times,* May 21, 1920; AES, *Public Papers,* 1920:418-19.

20. *National Prohibition Cases,* 253 U.S. 350 (1920); Anderson to AES, September 21, 1920, AES Official Correspondence.

21. Peabody to AES, July 31 [1920], Peabody Papers; *New York Times,* August 5, October 5, 22, 1920; *American Issue,* N.Y. ed., October 2, 1920.

22. *New York Times,* September 7, 15, 1920; *American Issue,* N.Y. ed., October 2, 9, 23, 1920.

23. *American Issue,* N.Y. ed., October 23, 30, 1920.

24. *Legislative Manual,* 1921.

25. Miller, *Public Papers,* 1921:67-70; *Laws of N.Y.,* 1921, chaps. 155, 156; Merz, *Dry Decade,* pp. 201-7.

26. *New York Times,* September 29, 30, October 26, 1922; Pell, pp. 312-13; Edward J. Flynn, pp. 3-4, Columbia Oral History; William Church Osborn to AES, May 9, 1923, AES Official Correspondence.

27. *New York Times,* October 31, November 1, 1922; *American Issue,* N.Y. ed., October 28, 1922.

28. *New York Times,* November 25, 1922; Mack to AES, December 23, 1922, AES Official Correspondence; Antisdale to George R. Van Namee, December 11, 1922, George B. Graves Papers.

29. AES, *Public Papers,* 1923:62–63; *New York Times,* February 20–22, 1923; [AES] to Melville Terwilliger, February 15, 1923, AES Official Correspondence.

30. *New York Times,* March 9, 1923; Frank B. Willis to George R. Van Namee, March 29, 1923, AES Official Correspondence; AES, *Public Papers,* 1923:531–37.

31. John G. Cooper to George R. Van Namee, March 12, 1923; [Van Namee] to Cooper, March 15, 1923; Schafer to Van Namee, March 13, 1923; Newton to Van Namee, March 8, 1923; McNulty to Van Namee, March 22, 1923; Bayard to Van Namee, March 9, 1923; Celler to AES, March 12, 1923; Mead to Van Namee, March 13, 1923; Bloom to Van Namee, March 8, 1923, AES Official Correspondence.

32. *New York Times,* January 9, 29, 1923; [Governor's Aide] to Howard D. Smith, February 15, 1923, AES Official Correspondence.

33. William John Jackson, "Prohibition as an Issue in New York State Politics," pp. 169–77; *New York Times,* January 10, 17, February 14, March 28, May 4, 5, 1923.

34. Edward J. Flynn, *You're the Boss,* pp. 40–41; Farley, *Behind the Ballots,* pp. 40–41.

35. B. F. Yoakum to AES, May 21, 1923, AES Official Correspondence; *New York World,* May 22, 1923.

36. Wait to AES, May 8, 1923; Copy of Wait to Warren G. Harding, May 8, 1923; Albert G. Dunkell to AES, May 20, 1923; Clipping from *New York Times,* May 17, 1923; E. Henry Lacombe et al. to AES, May 19, 1923, AES Official Correspondence.

37. FDR to AES, May 21, 1923; Treman to George R. Van Namee, May 10, 1923; Gannett to AES, May 14, 1923; Gannett to George R. Lunn, May 9, 1923; Frank L. Hopkins to AES, May 29, 1923; Fisher to AES, May 12, 1923, AES Official Correspondence; [Frankfurter] to Henry Moskowitz, May 22, 1923, AES Papers; Odegard, *Pressure Politics,* p. 27.

38. Emanuel Celler to AES, May 8, 1923; Farley to James A. Parsons, May 12, 1923; Olvany to AES, May 23, 1923; Webster C. Estes to AES, May 24, 1923; Bailey to AES, May 7, [1923]; Bruce to AES, May 15, 1923, AES Official Correspondence; Gompers to AES, May 29, 1923, Laws of 1923, chap. 871, Bill Jackets.

39. *New York Times,* May 8, 15, 20, 21, 23, 25, 1923.

40. Ibid., June 1, 1923.

41. Edward J. Flynn, *You're the Boss,* pp. 39–41; Peabody to Robert H. Treman, May 15, 1923, Peabody Papers; Eleanor Roosevelt to AES, June 1, [1923]; Edgar Truman Brackett to AES, May 31, 1923; [AES] to Roosevelt, June 6, 1923, George B. Graves Papers.

42. *Laws of N.Y.*, 1923, chap. 871; *New York Times*, June 2, 17, 1923.

43. George R. Van Namee, Memorandum, June 2, 1923, Van Namee Papers; Austen G. Fox to Joseph Proskauer, May 12, 1923, with enclosures; Fox to Proskauer, May 26, 1923; Copy of E. Henry Lacombe et al. to AES, May 19, 1923, AES Papers; [AES] to Lacombe, June 6, 1923, AES Official Correspondence.

44. AES, *Public Papers*, 1923:293-303.

45. James Roosevelt Roosevelt to AES, June 2, 1923, AES Official Correspondence; *New York Times*, June 10, 1923; AES, *Public Papers*, 1923:555.

46. *New York Times*, October 21, 1923.

47. Canfield to AES, November 15, December 31, 1923; [AES] to Canfield, November 23, 1923; [George R. Van Namee?] to Canfield, February 6, 12, 1924; Canfield, Address, Press Release, February 21, 1924; William Hayward, Address, February 20, 1924, AES Official Correspondence; AES, *Public Papers*, 1924: 514-19.

48. U.S., Congress, Senate, *Enforcement of the Prohibition Laws*, 71st Cong., 3d sess., 1931, document no. 307, 1:40; 4:passim and 679; Sinclair, *Prohibition*, chap. 14, pp. 192-97; Merz, *Dry Decade*, chap. 5, pp. 201-7; Clark, *Deliver Us from Evil*, pp. 145-65.

49. *New York Times*, February 27, 1924; *Legislative Index*, 1924.

50. William John Jackson, "Prohibition as an Issue in New York State Politics," pp. 177-81; Odegard, *Pressure Politics*, pp. 215-18, 228-40; Pringle, *Big Frogs*, pp. 174-91; Anderson to AES, July 16, August 20, 22, 1923, AES Official Correspondence.

51. Farley to AES, June 20, 1923, George B. Graves Papers; Neal, "World beyond the Hudson," chap. 4; Robert K. Murray, *The 103rd Ballot: Democrats and the Disaster in Madison Square Garden* (New York: Harper & Row, 1976), passim and p. 63; Burner, *Politics of Provincialism*, chap. 4.

52. *New York Times*, September 27, October 17, 18, 1924; *American Issue*, N.Y. ed., October 18, 25, November 1, 1924; Mencken, *Carnival of Buncombe*, pp. 122-23.

53. *New York Times*, January 15, 1925; Robert H. Treman to AES, November 17, 1924; [AES] to Treman, November 25, 1924; Mrs. Frankie Griffin Merson to AES, March 1, 1926; [AES] to Merson, March 5, 1926, AES Official Correspondence; *Legislative Index*, 1925, 1926.

54. *Laws of N.Y.*, 1926, chap. 850; *New York Times*, March 28, April 16, 17, 20, 1926.

55. Marshall to AES, May 18, 1926; Louis O. Van Doren to AES, April 21, 1926; Julius S. Berg to AES, May 11, 1926, Laws of 1926, chap. 850, Bill Jackets.

56. *New York Times,* April 22, May 19, 1926; *American Issue,* N.Y. ed., May 29, 1926; AES, *Public Papers,* 1926:438-39.

57. *New York Times,* September 28, 29, 1926.

58. Ibid., September 28, 1926; AES, *Public Papers,* 1926: 813-17.

59. *New York Times,* October 18, 1926.

60. *American Issue,* N.Y. ed., October 16, 30, 1926.

61. Martin L. Fausold, *James W. Wadsworth, Jr.: The Gentleman from New York* (Syracuse: Syracuse University Press, 1975), chaps. 1-7 and p. 194; *American Issue,* N.Y. ed., October 2, 16, 1926.

62. *Legislative Manual,* 1927; *American Issue,* N.Y. ed., November 13, 1926.

63. *Legislative Manual,* 1927; *American Issue,* N.Y. ed., October 30, November 27, 1926; *New York Times,* November 7, 1926.

64. AES, *Public Papers,* 1927:66-67; *Legislative Index,* 1927, 1928; *New York Times,* January 3, 1928.

65. Transcript of Re-Union of Ex-Members of New York State Constitutional Convention of 1916 [*sic*], December 17, 1926, Stimson Papers.

66. Freidel, *Franklin D. Roosevelt: The Ordeal,* p. 167; Edward J. Flynn, *You're the Boss,* p. 66; Villard, *Prophets True and False,* pp. 7-8.

67. Roy V. Peel and Thomas C. Donnelly, *The 1928 Campaign: An Analysis* (New York: Richard R. Smith, 1931), p. 71; Ruth C. Silva, *Rum, Religion, and Votes: 1928 Re-Examined* (University Park: Pennsylvania State University Press, 1962), p. 5; Sinclair, *Prohibition,* chap. 15; Robert Moats Miller, *American Protestantism and Social Issues 1919-1939* (Chapel Hill: University of North Carolina Press, 1958), chap. 4; Murray, *The 103rd Ballot,* pp. 273-82; Mencken, *Carnival of Buncombe,* pp. 205-6.

68. Clark, *Deliver Us from Evil,* pp. 203-5.

1. AES, *Campaign Addresses,* p. 1.

2. Ibid., pp. 1-26.

3. Woodrow Wilson quoted in Ellen Shaw Barlow to AES, August 9, 1920, AES Official Correspondence.

4. FDR, *Happy Warrior Alfred E. Smith,* p. 7.

5. AES, *Public Papers,* 1919:764; Morton White, *Social Thought in America: The Revolt Against Formalism* (Boston: Beacon Press, 1957), passim and p. 12; Eric F. Goldman, *Rendezvous with Destiny: A History of Modern American Reform,* rev. ed. (New York: Random House, 1956), passim and pp. 123-24; Walter T. K. Nugent, *From Centennial to World War: American Society 1876-1917* (Indianapolis: Bobbs-Merrill Company, 1977), chap. 5 and p. 137; Sidney Fine, *Laissez Faire and the General-Welfare State: A Study of Conflict in American Thought 1865-1901* (Ann Arbor: University of Michigan Press, Ann Arbor Paperbacks, 1964), passim and p. 167.

6. Morton White, *Revolt Against Formalism,* p. 238.

7. De Witt, *Progressive Movement;* Lewis L. Gould, *Reform and Regulation: American Politics, 1900-1916* (New York: John Wiley & Sons, 1978); Buenker, *Urban Liberalism and Progressive Reform;* Bremner, *From the Depths;* Chambers, *Seedtime of Reform;* Davis, *Spearheads for Reform.*

8. David M. Ellis et al., *A Short History of New York State* (Ithaca: Cornell University Press, 1957), chap. 29; Yellowitz, *Labor and the Progressive Movement in N.Y.;* Robert F. Wesser, "Charles Evans Hughes and the Urban Sources of Political Progressivism," *New York Historical Society Quarterly* 50 (1966):365-400; Huthmacher, "Charles Evans Hughes and Charles Francis Murphy;" idem, *Senator Robert F. Wagner,* chaps. 1-3; Martin, *Madam Secretary,* chaps. 8-10; Kerr, "New York Factory Investigating Commission."

9. Harold U. Faulkner, *The Decline of Laissez Faire 1897-1917* (New York: Harper & Row, Harper Torchbooks, 1968), passim and p. 382.

10. Hofstadter, *Age of Reform;* Mowry, *Era of Theodore Roosevelt;* Haber, *Efficiency and Uplift;* Kolko, *Triumph of Conservatism;* Wiebe, *Search for Order;* Otis L. Graham, Jr., *Encore for Reform;* Weinstein, *Corporate Ideal in the Liberal State.*

11. Hofstadter, *Age of Reform,* p. 298; Wiebe, *Search for Order,* p. 223.

12. Peter G. Filene, "An Obituary for 'The Progressive Movement,'" *American Quarterly* 22 (1970):32; Otis L. Graham, Jr., *Great Campaigns,* p. 154; Don S. Kirschner, "The Ambiguous Legacy: Social Justice and Social Control in the Progressive Era," *Historical Reflections* 2 (1975):69-88; Nugent, *From Centennial to World War,* p. 117.

13. Otis A. Pease, "The Reformer and the Politician," *Key Reporter* 34 (1969):2-4; Burner, *Politics of Provincialism,* chap. 7.

14. Perkins, 2:36-48, Columbia Oral History; AES, *Up to Now,* pp. 216, 219; Edward J. Flynn, *You're the Boss,* pp. 38-39; Proskauer, *Segment of My Times,* pp. 42-43; William Allen White, *Masks in a Pageant,* p. 477.

15. Elbridge L. Adams to AES [1924], George B. Graves Papers; Notes from Mrs. Frederick Stuart Greene, n.d., Perkins Papers; Copy of Clarence MacGregor to John A. Warner, July 8, 1926, AES Official Correspondence.

16. Pusey, *Charles Evans Hughes,* p. 604.

17. Pringle, *Alfred E. Smith,* pp. 61-73; Moskowitz, *Alfred E. Smith;* Hapgood and Moskowitz, *Up from the City Streets.*

18. Davis, *Spearheads for Reform;* Chambers, *Seedtime of Reform;* Fetner, "Public Power and Professional Responsibility," pp. 15-18, 38-39.

19. Elbert Lee Tatum, *The Changed Political Thought of the Negro 1915-1940* (New York: Exposition Press, 1951), pp. 64-103; Edwin R. Lewinson, *Black Politics in New York City* (New York: Twayne Publishers, 1974), pp. 17-18, 42-47, 59-63; Gilbert Osofsky, *Harlem: The Making of a Ghetto: Negro New York, 1890-1930,* 2d Harper Torchbook ed. (New York: Harper and Row, 1971), pp. 169-70.

20. *Crisis* 17 (November, 1918):44-45; *New York Amsterdam News,* January 3, 1923; Osofsky, *Harlem: The Making of a Ghetto,* pp. 169, 257; "Editorials," *Messenger* 6 (1924):339; Chandler Owen, "How the Negro Should Vote in the Campaign," ibid., pp. 290-99.

21. W. E. B. DuBois, in his editorial column, "Opinion," in the *Crisis* 29 (December, 1924):55, credited Smith with a majority of Harlem's black vote in 1924; Tatum, in *Changed Political Thought of the Negro,* p. 103, claimed a plurality for the governor throughout the area both in 1924 and 1926; but Osofsky, in *Harlem: The Making of a Ghetto,* tabulated a majority there for the Republican contenders in both elections.

22. *New York Amsterdam News,* October 20, 1926.

23. Ibid., December 6, 1922; July 25, 1923; April 29, 1925; May 11, 1927.

24. Ibid., August 22, 1923; April 29, 1925; Wear to AES, June 8, 1923, George B. Graves Papers; Randy Roberts, *Jack Dempsey: The Manassa Mauler* (Baton Rouge: Louisiana State University Press, 1979), pp. 141-48, 212-19.

25. *New York Amsterdam News,* October 3, August 29,
September 19, October 31, 1928; W. E. B. DuBois, "Postscript,"
Crisis 35 (November, 1928):381; ibid. (October, 1928), p. 346;
ibid. (September, 1928), p. 312; "Editorials," *Messinger* 10
(1928):109.

26. AES, *Campaign Addresses,* pp. 48, 51-54; Dowling to
AES, November 21, 1922, George B. Graves Papers.

27. John Hope Franklin, *From Slavery to Freedom: A
History of Negro Americans,* 3d ed. (New York: Alfred A. Knopf,
1967), pp. 524-29; Tatum, *Changed Political Thought of the
Negro,* pp. 99-160, quotation on p. 108.

28. Arthur M. Schlesinger, Jr., *The Age of Roosevelt:
The Politics of Upheaval* (Boston: Houghton Mifflin Company,
1960), chap. 23 and p. 438.

29. AES, *Up to Now,* p. 126; Josephson and Josephson,
Al Smith, pp. 191-95; Perkins, 2:521-22, 3:277-78, Columbia
Oral History.

30. Perkins, 1:431-44, passim and 440, Columbia Oral
History; Martin, *Madam Secretary,* pp. 141-45; Perkins,
Roosevelt I Knew, p. 55.

31. Freidel, *Franklin D. Roosevelt: The Triumph,* pp.
17-19; Perkins, 3:14-23; Edward J. Flynn, pp. 8-9, Columbia
Oral History; Pringle, *Alfred E. Smith,* pp. 61-73.

32. William Henry Chafe, *The American Woman: Her
Changing Social, Economic, and Political Roles, 1920-1970*
(New York: Oxford University Press, 1972), chap. 5; William
L. O'Neill, *Everyone Was Brave: A History of Feminism in
America* (Chicago: Quadrangle Books, 1971), p. 292; AES, *Up to
Now,* pp. 191-95; Lemons, *Woman Citizen,* chap. 5 and pp. viii-ix.

33. Perkins, 2:469-70, Columbia Oral History; Hand,
Counsel and Advise, pp. 18-19, 24-26; Bellush, *Franklin D.
Roosevelt as Governor,* passim and p. 33; Freidel, *Franklin D.
Roosevelt: The Triumph,* passim and p. 12; Donald M. Roper,
"The Governorship in History," *Proceedings of the Academy of
Political Science* 31 (May, 1974):16-30; Ellis et al., *Short
History of New York,* pp. 418-19.

34. Perkins, *Roosevelt I Knew,* p. 157; Farley, *Behind
the Ballots,* p. 216; Perkins, "Al Smith as I Knew Him," pp.
7-8, Perkins Papers, Cornell; idem, "The Al Smith I Knew,"
Frances Perkins Papers—Coggeshall Collection, Butler Library
Special Collections, Columbia University, New York; Josephson
and Josephson, *Al Smith,* pp. xi-xii; Richard O'Connor, *The
First Hurrah: A Biography of Alfred E. Smith* (New York: G. P.
Putnam's Sons, 1970), p. 137.

35. Fusfeld, *Economic Thought of Franklin D. Roosevelt,*
p. 5 and passim.

36. See above, n. 7; Schlesinger, *Age of Roosevelt: The Politics of Upheaval*, chaps. 13, 21; Frank Freidel, *Franklin D. Roosevelt*, vol. 4, *Launching the New Deal* (Boston: Little, Brown and Company, 1973), pp. 64-66, 304-5, 340.

37. Hofstadter, *Age of Reform*, pp. 316-17; Graham, *Encore for Reform*. Graham's bibliographic essay (pp. 219-34), although inevitably somewhat dated, offers an unsurpassed review of the literature on the relationship between progressivism and the New Deal.

38. Richard George Frederick, "Old Visions and New Dreams: The Old Progressives in the 1920's" (Ph.D. dissertation, Pennsylvania State University, 1979), pp. 194-98.

39. J. Joseph Huthmacher, "Urban Liberalism and the Age of Reform," *Mississippi Valley Historical Review* 49 (1962): 231-41; idem, "Charles Evans Hughes and Charles Francis Murphy"; Buenker, *Urban Liberalism and Progressive Reform*, chap. 6.

40. Albert U. Romasco, "Hoover-Roosevelt and the Great Depression: A Historiographic Inquiry into a Perennial Comparison," in *The New Deal*, vol. 1, *The National Level*, eds. John Braeman et al. (Columbus: Ohio State University Press, 1975), pp. 3-25, quotation on p. 21; Schlesinger, *Age of Roosevelt: The Coming of the New Deal*; idem, *Age of Roosevelt: The Politics of Upheaval*; Freidel, *Franklin D. Roosevelt: Launching the New Deal*; William E. Leuchtenburg, *Franklin D. Roosevelt and the New Deal 1932-1940* (New York: Harper & Row, 1963); James MacGregor Burns, *Roosevelt: The Lion and the Fox* (New York: Harcourt, Brace and Company, 1956), passim and pp. 403, 234-41.

41. Paul K. Conkin, *The New Deal* (New York: Thomas Y. Crowell Company, 1967); Barton J. Bernstein, "The New Deal: The Conservative Achievements of Liberal Reform," in *Towards a New Past: Dissenting Essays in American History*, Vintage bks. ed., ed. Barton J. Bernstein (New York: Random House, 1969), pp. 263-88; Ellis W. Hawley, *The New Deal and the Problem of Monopoly: A Study in Economic Ambivalence* (Princeton: Princeton University Press, 1966); Edgar Eugene Robinson, *The Roosevelt Leadership 1933-1945* (Philadelphia: J. B. Lippincott Company, 1955); John T. Flynn, *The Roosevelt Myth*, rev. ed. (New York: Devin-Adair Company, 1956).

42. Samuel Lubell, *The Future of American Politics* (New York: Harper & Brothers, 1952), chap. 3 and p. 35; Lawrence H. Fuchs, "Election of 1928," in *History of American Presidential Elections 1789-1968*, ed. Arthur M. Schlesinger, Jr., 4 vols. (New York: Chelsea House Publishers, 1971), pp. 2585-2609.

43. V. O. Key, Jr., "A Theory of Critical Elections,"
Journal of Politics 17 (1955):3-18, quotation on 4; Walter
Dean Burnham, *Critical Elections and the Mainsprings of American Politics* (New York: W. W. Norton & Company, 1970), chaps.
1-3; Carl N. Degler, "American Political Parties and the Rise
of the City: An Interpretation," *Journal of American History*
51 (1964):41-59, quotation on 51; Kristi Andersen, *The Creation
of a Democratic Majority 1928-1936* (Chicago: University of
Chicago Press, 1979).

44. Jerome M. Clubb and Howard W. Allen, "The Cities
and the Election of 1928: Partisan Realignment?" *American
Historical Review* 74 (1969):1205-20, quotation on 1220; Jerome
M. Clubb, William H. Flanigan, and Nancy H. Zingale, *Partisan
Realignment: Voters, Parties, and Government in American His-
tory* (Beverly Hills, Calif.: Sage Publications, 1980); David
F. Prindle, "Voter Turnout, Critical Elections, and the New Deal
Realignment," *Social Science History* 3 (1979):144-70, quotation
on 154. The content of *Partisan Realignment* was anticipated in
the earlier work of two of its three authors, Jerome M. Clubb
and William H. Flanigan, who collaborated with Walter Dean
Burnham in contributing "Partisan Realignment: A Systemic
Perspective" to *The History of American Electoral Behavior*,
eds. Joel H. Silbey, Allan G. Bogue, and William H. Flanigan
(Princeton: Princeton University Press, 1978), pp. 45-77;
furthermore, this chapter makes extensive reference to the
research of Nancy H. Zingale, the third author of the subse-
sequent volume.

45. Bernard Sternsher, "The Emergence of the New Deal
Party System: A Problem in Historical Analysis of Voter
Behavior," *Journal of Interdisciplinary History* 6 (1979):127-49,
quotation on 142; Allan J. Lichtman, "Critical Election Theory
and the Reality of American Presidential Politics, 1916-1940,"
American Historical Review 81 (1976):317-51; idem, *Prejudice
and the Old Politics: The Presidential Election of 1928*
(Chapel Hill: University of North Carolina Press, 1979), passim
and p. 201. In his book (pp. 180-82), Lichtman exaggerated
Smith's conservatism and commitment to laissez-faire in the
twenties.

46. Lee Benson, Joel H. Silbey, and Phyllis F. Field,
"Toward a Theory of Stability and Change in American Voting
Patterns: New York State, 1792-1970," in *History of American
Electoral Behavior*, ed. Silbey, pp. 78-105.

47. Eleanor Roosevelt to AES, August 28, 1928; Patrick
Cardinal Hayes to AES, June 30, 1928; [AES] to Rev. Brother
Baldwin, December 7, 1928, George B. Graves Papers; Perkins,
Roosevelt I Knew, p. 46.

48. For the fullest accounts of Smith's later years, see:
Josephson and Josephson, *Al Smith*, chaps. 15, 16; Handlin, *Al
Smith*, chaps. 7, 8; Schwarz, "Al Smith in the Thirties"; George
Wolfskill, *The Revolt of the Conservatives: A History of the*

American Liberty League 1934-1940 (Boston: Houghton Mifflin Company, 1962).

    49.   John T. Flynn, *Roosevelt Myth,* p. 85.

    50.   Hand, "Al Smith, Franklin D. Roosevelt, and the New Deal," p. 381. Smith's consistent conservatism is the subject of four studies: two dissertations with the same title, "The Political Thought of Alfred E. Smith," of which the one by Zuccarello, already cited, is more comprehensive and convincing than the other (Ph.D. dissertation, New York University, 1963, reproduced by University Microfilms) by Martin I. Feldman, who hedges on the issue; and two journal articles, Hand's "Al Smith, Franklin D. Roosevelt, and the New Deal," and Schwarz's "Al Smith in the Thirties," which approach the question from different angles.   Zuccarello, who defines his terms explicitly, prefers not to apply the label *conservative* to Smith, but agrees with the others in substance, if not semantics. Works that refer briefly to Smith's consistent conservatism include: Kerr, "New York Factory Investigating Commission," pp. 267-71; Burner, *Politics of Provincialism,* pp. 187-90; Carter, *Another Part of the Twenties,* pp. 95-96, 101-2.

    51.   Perkins, 2:699-700; 3:5-42, 63-80, 328-31, 340-44, Columbia Oral History.

    52.   Martin, *Madam Secretary,* p. 487.

    53.   Perkins, *Roosevelt I Knew,* p. 157.

NOTE ON UNPUBLISHED MANUSCRIPT SOURCES

Albany, New York is the first stop on the itinerary of the scholar interested in Alfred E. Smith. The state capital houses Smith manuscripts in five separate collections, divided between the New York State Archives and the New York State Library. First in size and in importance for the gubernatorial years is the Official Correspondence of Governor Alfred E. Smith in the archives. Although the Alfred E. Smith Papers in the library date primarily from the campaign of 1928 and from the 1930s, on state issues and elections, the contents are distinguishable only in quantity from the Official Correspondence. In both groups of manuscripts, the incoming correspondence is more revealing than the outgoing, which discloses little that was not a matter of public record. Additional letters and memoranda to the governor have found their way into the archives' Bill Jacket Collection and Veto Jacket Collection, both utilized more frequently by practicing attorneys than by historians. In the archives, it is also possible to consult the Minutes of the Meetings of the New York Governor's Cabinet on six occasions during Smith's last term.

Two men who held the position of secretary to Governor Smith have left manuscripts now available to historians. The Franklin D. Roosevelt Library at Hyde Park, New York contains by far the more important of these collections, the George B. Graves Papers, which only the materials in Albany surpass as a source of information on Smith. Indeed, there is no clear rationale to explain why some items ended up in the possession of the secretary rather than his employer. Amidst the clippings and memorabilia that comprise the bulk of the George R. Van Namee Papers in the Library of the Fresno Diocesan Chancery and Academy of California Church History in Fresno, California, the careful searcher can find a few significant documents.

Frances Perkins has provided important data on Smith, not only because she served as a member of the Industrial Commission in his administration, but also because she remained in touch with him to the end of his life and was preparing a biography of him at the time of her death. She deposited her manuscripts in the Special Collections of the Butler Library of Columbia University in New York City. I am indebted to her daughter, Susanna Coggeshall, for permission to use the restricted portion of the Frances Perkins Papers there and also for her willingness to share some recollections of her mother and of Governor Smith. Perkins' biographer, George Martin of New York City, was generous in allowing me access to Frances Perkins Papers of which Ms. Coggeshall had given him temporary custody in order to facilitate his research. These include a draft of Perkins' work on Smith. The texts of lectures that she delivered on Smith survive in the Frances Perkins Papers in the Labor-Management Documentation Center of the M. P. Catherwood Library at Cornell University in Ithaca, New York. The Reminiscences of Frances Perkins, which contain frequent references to Smith, constitute one of the more voluminous memoirs in the Oral History Project of Columbia University.

In manuscript repositories in and near New York, one may consult the papers of other individuals and organizations for the light that they shed on Governor Smith. The Henry L. Stimson Papers in the Yale University Library in New Haven, Connecticut are particularly valuable on reconstruction of the state government and implementation of the state park plan, but Stimson's Diary has only an occasional entry regarding the governor. If the subject of parks also figures in the Franklin D. Roosevelt Papers in the presidential library at Hyde Park, FDR's correspondence deals in addition with state Democratic politics in the Smith years. In the Library of Congress in Washington, D.C., correspondence with and/or about Governor Smith occurs in the Papers of Ogden L. Mills, George Foster Peabody, and Elihu Root. A prominent social worker recorded her impressions of the Smith administration in the Lillian D. Wald Papers in the New York Public Library in New York City. An interoffice communication on public finance is filed in the Mark Graves Papers in the New York State Archives in

Albany. In addition to the Perkins' manuscripts cited above, the Columbia University Library has a few items on Smith in its Citizens' Union Collection.

For more than a generation, the pioneering Oral History Project at Columbia University has served students of American politics; in the last decade, microform has increased its accessibility. In addition to the Frances Perkins memoir discussed above, the Reminiscences of the following individuals are cited in the course of this work on Governor Smith: George F. Chandler, Edward J. Flynn, Ferdinand Pecora, Herbert C. Pell, Lindsay Rogers, Martin Saxe, and Norman Thomas.

Papers on Appeal in the case of *Pauchogue Land Corporation v. Long Island State Park Commission*, 248 N.Y. 635 (1928) proved essential to an understanding of the conflict over Heckscher State Park. This record contains, not only a transcript of the jury trial and lawyers' briefs, but also a wealth of historical documentation submitted in the form of exhibits. New York designates certain courts as repositories for the Papers on Appeal, which I consulted in the Law Library of the New York State Supreme Court for Kings County in Brooklyn, New York.

In the case of a few individuals who were very close to Governor Smith, the search for manuscripts yielded no returns. The Belle Lindner Moskowitz Papers in the Library of Connecticut College for Women in New London provides no record of her association with the chief executive. I was unable to gain access to any papers of Robert Moses or Joseph M. Proskauer.